9AR

A TO Z OF LATINO AMERICANS

LATINOS IN THE ARTS

STEVEN OTFINOSKI

Facts On File
An imprint of Infobase Publishing

Latinos in the Arts

Facts On File, Inc.
An imprint of Infobase Publishing
132 West 31st Street
New York NY 10001

Library of Congress Cataloging-in-Publication Data
Otfinoski, Steven.
Latinos in the arts / by Steven Otfinoski.
p. cm.—(A to Z of Latino Americans)
Includes bibliographical references and index.
ISBN 978-0-8160-6394-9 (alk. paper)
1. Hispanic American arts—United States—21st century. 2. Hispanic Americans—United States. I. Title. II. Series.
NX512.3.H57083 2007
700.89'68073—dc22 2006016900

Facts On File books are available at special discounts when purchased in bulk quantities for businesses, associations, institutions, or sales promotions. Please call our Special Sales Department in New York at (212) 967-8800 or (800) 322-8755.

You can find Facts On File on the World Wide Web at http://www.factsonfile.com

Text design by Annie O'Donnell
Cover design by Salvatore Luongo
Composition by CGI
Cover printed by Yurchak Printing, Landisville, Pa.
Book printed and bound by Yurchak Printing, Landisville, Pa.

Printed in the United States of America

This book is printed on acid-free paper.

Contents

LIST OF ENTRIES

ACKNOWLEDGMENTS

The author would like to especially thank the following people for their invaluable help and support in putting together this book: Yolanda Retter Vargas, from the University of California–Los Angeles (UCLA) Chicano Studies Research Center Library and Archive; Elizabeth Ferrer, independent curator and writer; Kathleen Adrian and Joan Stahl, of the Smithsonian American Art Museum (SAAM); Dustin Belyeu, director of Nedra Matteucci Galleries, Santa Fe, New Mexico; and Dr. Judy Larson, director of the National Museum of Women in the Arts; Washington, D.C.

I would also like to thank the following artists and their representatives for providing photographs and information about themselves: Iris Nelia Aranda; Judy Baca; Carlos Castellanos; Elena Climent; Al Diaz; Maria Emilia; Robert French; Harry Gamboa, Jr.; Guillermo Gómez-Peña; Robert Legorreta; Alma Lopez; Jesús Moroles; Victor Ochoa; Lourdes Portillo; Frank Romero; Jorge Tacla; Irvin L. Trujillo; Consuelo Jiménez Underwood; and Andrew Zermaño.

AUTHOR'S NOTE

In 2003, the U.S. Census Bureau declared Latinos to be the nation's largest minority group, making up 14 percent of the population. Experts have predicted that by the year 2100, one in three U.S. residents will be Latino.

Everywhere you look in the United States today Latinos are exercising their newfound power. Economically, the Latino market is estimated at more than $636 billion annually. In politics, Latino Americans are becoming a powerful voting block. Mexican-American governor Bill Richardson of New Mexico is a leader in the National Democratic Party. In 2004, the first Latino senators in 25 years were elected in Florida and Colorado. In May 2005, Democrat Antonio Villarigosa was elected mayor of the country's second-largest city, Los Angeles (LA), California. He is the first Latino mayor of LA in 133 years. Latino culture, arts, and architecture are a dominant force in the Southwest, southern Florida, and much of California.

Yet, a visit to your local library will reveal surprisingly few books about Latinos. While the section devoted to African-American culture, literature, and issues is a full one, that for Latino Americans is bare in comparison. How can this be for the nation's largest minority?

There are a number of reasons for this neglect. For many North Americans, Latinos are the invisible minority. Socially and culturally, many older Latinos have largely kept to themselves in large cities such as New York and Los Angeles, while many upwardly mobile young Latinos have successfully integrated themselves into U.S. society. Many younger Latinos were raised without a speaking knowledge of Spanish.

Another reason why Latino culture may be overlooked may be the great diversity it encompasses. Unlike many minorities in this country, Latino Americans do not come from one country or region but from 18 different nations and the Commonwealth of Puerto Rico, a part of the United States. While the great majority of Latino Americans trace their roots to Mexico, Puerto Rico, or Cuba, there are significant numbers of them from Central and South America and the Caribbean, especially the Dominican Republic.

Each of these peoples has its own culture and traditions, although they all, with a few exceptions, share a common language, Spanish, brought by the explorers and missionaries of Spain who first "discovered" and colonized these lands. But it is not only a language that they share.

The 178 artists in this book represent both performing artists (actors, musicians, singers, dancers, comedians) and visual artists (painters, sculptors, filmmakers, photographers, and other fine artists). The selection is not exhaustive and is meant to be a cross section of Latino artists, not a definitive list. That would take a much larger book, if not a series of them. The author has tried to highlight artists who have been pioneers or innovators in their field and those who reflect Latino culture and traditions.

While the greatest number of people in this book are Mexican, Cuban, or Puerto Rican in ancestry, Spain is also represented, as is nearly every South American country and several Central American nations. At the same time, the author has confined himself to artists who were born in the United States or who settled here permanently after emigrating from a Latin country. Puerto Rican artists who reside in Puerto Rico and not on the mainland have not been included. Several Brazilian-born artists have been included even though Brazil, settled by the Portuguese, is not a Spanish-speaking Latino country. But Brazilians are in spirit and culture closely connected to their Latin neighbors. Besides, what performer better represented Latin America in the United States in the 1940s than Brazilian movie musical star Carmen Miranda?

A few words need to be said about terminology. Why do we use *Latino* and not *Hispanic* in this book? For many years, *Hispanic* was the preferred term, applied to Americans from Mexico, the Caribbean, and South and Central America. *Hispanic* is derived from *España* (Spain), the country that conquered the indigenous peoples and colonized their lands in the 16th and 17th centuries. For many contemporary people, *Hispanic* smacks of a colonialism that they would rather forget. *Latino* does not apply to Spain but rather to the Latin ancestry of the Spanish language. Of course, there are people, including some of the individuals in this book, who reject the term *Latino* as well. But, in general, it seems to be the more acceptable term in today's world. When speaking specifically of a female artist, the word *Latina* is used, and *Latino* is used for a male artist.

Finally, there is *Chicano.* The word is more than a short form of *Mexican American.* It is also a political and historic term that became popular in the 1960s and 1970s when it was used by United Farm Workers (UFW) leader Cesar Chavez (César Chávez) to identify the underprivileged Mexican Americans whom he represented in California and the Southwest. The Chicano art movement that came about in those years was closely identified with the greater Chicano struggle, and many of the artists who were a part of it still proudly consider themselves Chicanos or Chicanas. For some younger artists and performers, the term is not a part of their experience and has less relevance.

INTRODUCTION

"[W]hat seems to me particularly notable is not the diversity of the Hispanic groups and the differences among them," writes the Mexican writer Octavio Paz, "but rather their extraordinary cohesion, a cohesion not expressed politically but in collective acts and attitudes."

This cohesion is dramatically apparent when considering Latino artists. While these creative men and women are all individuals with their own personal means of expression, for many of them their ethnic roots have played a significant role in their careers. Certain common themes reoccur in their work.

Among these themes, especially for the visual artists, are the traditions and spiritual elements of the Roman Catholic Church, first brought to Latin America in the 16th century by the missionaries who accompanied explorers and conquistadores. This influence can be most clearly seen in the *Santeros* of the Southwest. Their expressive wooden carvings of Jesus, Mary, and the saints, go back to the 18th-century artist Pedro Antonio Fresquís and continues down to such contemporary practitioners as Luis Tapia and Charles M. Carrillo. Religious imagery and symbols can be seen in the more secular art of a wide range of contemporary artists from the dark fatalistic paintings of Cuban-American Carlos Alfonzo to the more celebratory altar arrangements dedicated to famous Latinas of Mexican-American Amalia Mesa-Bains.

Another theme that runs through Latino art is the struggle for social justice. The crusade for Chicano rights that began with Cesar Chavez in the 1960s gave birth to an art movement that included posters, murals, sculptures, and paintings by such socially committed artists as Victor Ochoa, Frank Romero, Patssi Valdez, and Andrew Zermeño. Many of these artists moved on to more personal artistic expression, but many retain their commitment to social change in the United States for Latinos and other minorities.

Filmmakers such as Luis Valdez and Moctesuma Esparza also sprang from the Chicano movement of the 1960s, while many Latino actors have played the role of social activists both on and off the screen. Their number include Raúl Juliá; Ricardo Montalbán, founder of Nosotros, an organization that promotes and encourages Latinos in the entertainment industry; Esai Morales; Edward James Olmos; Martin Sheen; and Jimmy Smits.

Some actors—such as Olmos, Andy Garcia, Salma Hayek, and Jennifer Lopez—have gained the power as directors and producers to initiate their own film projects that focus on Latino history, concerns, and issues. This influence has only recently been earned. Early Latino entertainers, particularly in the film and television industries, were most often trapped in limited stereotypical roles that tended to denigrate their culture and people. These included the Mexican spitfire (Lupe Vélez, Rita Moreno); the exotic female

(Raquel Torres, Dolores del Rio); the lazy, comic Mexican (Leo Carrillo); the zany Latin entertainer (Carmen Miranda, Olga San Juan); and the ever-popular Latin lover (Fernando Lamas, Ricardo Montalbán). That all these performers managed to breathe life and personality into these stereotypes that they were often forced to play speaks volumes about their talent and determination. Some of them, such as Montalbán and Moreno, eventually broke through the stereotype barriers to play a wide range of characters and become stars and role models for a new generation of Latino performers. Other actors achieved stardom by changing their names and not drawing attention to their Latino backgrounds. How many of their fans even today know that Rita Hayworth, Anthony Quinn, Martin Sheen, and Raquel Welch all have Latino roots?

By the same token, a number of Latino singers, including Joan Baez, Vikki Carr, Eydie Gormé, and Linda Ronstadt, rediscovered their roots relatively late in successful careers and found a new audience and market for their music. Other musicians, including Selena, Ricky Martin, and Gloria Estefan, moved effortlessly from Spanish-language music to mainstream American pop.

As one reads about the lives of these Latino American artists, one may be surprised by the range of their talents and achievements, be inspired by their struggle to succeed, and be moved at how many of them have given back to the community that produced them. As Latino Americans take their rightful place in U.S. society, their stories need to be told and serve as models, not just for a new generation of Latinos but for all Americans. Their story is the story of the Americas—North and South.

A

Aguilera, Christina
(Christina Maria Aguilera)
(1980–) *pop singer, songwriter*

One of the most celebrated female pop vocalists of the last decade, Christina Aguilera, with her four-octave range, has a voice and technique that surpasses most of her competitors. She was born Christina Maria Aguilera on Staten Island, a borough of New York City, on December 18, 1980. Her father, Fausto Aguilera, is from Ecuador and immigrated to the United States to serve in the military. Her mother, Shelley Fidler, of Irish descent, is a gifted violinist who played with the Youth Symphony Orchestra in her teens. The family moved frequently from one military post to another as Christina was growing up.

The Aguileras separated in 1986, and Christina's mother took her and a younger sister Rachel to live with her in Wexford, Pennsylvania, a suburb of Pittsburgh, where she remarried. Christina already displayed a beautiful singing voice and from age six competed in local talent shows. In 1988, she appeared as a contestant on the popular television show *Star Search* but did not win. However, she was a star in Pittsburgh, where she frequently sang the national anthem before games of the Pittsburgh Steelers football team and the Pittsburgh Penguins hockey team.

Aguilera auditioned for the *New Mickey Mouse Club* on TV's Disney Channel in 1990, but despite her obvious talent, she was turned down as too young for the program. Two years later, now 12, she was invited to join the show. Among her fellow Mouseketeers were future stars Britney Spears and Justin Timberlake. The show folded two years later, and Aguilera returned to Pittsburgh. Anxious to record, she sent a tape to a singing competition in Japan. The winner would record a duet with Japanese pop star Keizo Nakanishi. Aguilera won the competition and flew to Japan to record the song "All I Wanna Do" with Nakanishi. It became a major hit in Japan, and Aguilera went on tour with the Japanese singer.

On her return to the States, Aguilera was asked to record the ballad "Reflection" from Disney's latest animated feature, the Chinese saga *Mulan* (1998). The song was only a mild success on the adult contemporary charts, but its wide exposure in the movie led RCA Records to sign Aguilera to a recording contract. Her debut album, *Christina Aguilera* (1999), was a smash, immediately taking the #1 spot on the pop charts. One cut from the album, "Genie in a Bottle," went to #1 on the singles' charts and stayed there for five weeks. Two other album cuts, "What a Girl Wants" and "Come on over Baby (All I Want Is You)," both followed it to the top of the charts. The album eventually ended up selling 8 million copies. At the 42nd Grammy Awards, Britney Spears was expected to win in the category of Best New Artist. To the surprise of everyone, including Aguilera, she won the award.

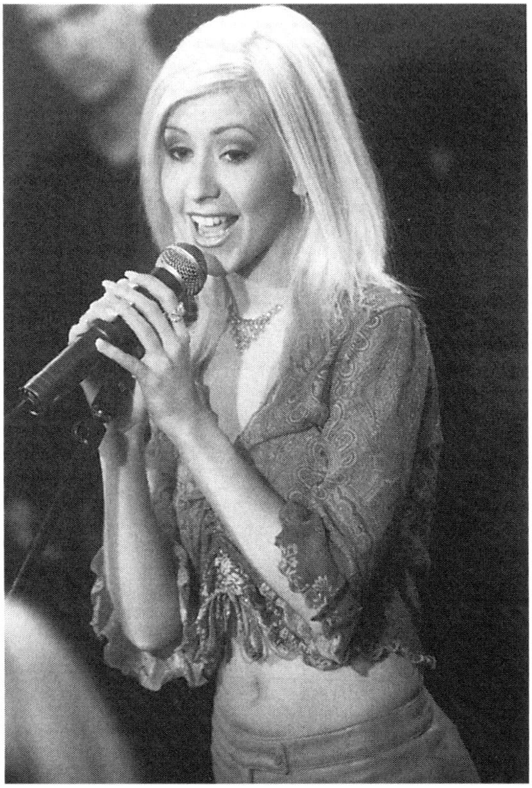

Pop singer Christina Aguilera's career began as a Mouseketeer on the Disney Channel's *The New Mickey Mouse Club. (Photofest)*

Her next album was the Spanish language *Mi Reflejo* (My reflection) (2000). Aguilera was embraced by young Latino listeners and became that rare crossover from the pop to the Latino market, even though she did not speak Spanish and had to learn the lyrics phonetically. The album sold 3 million copies and earned her a second Grammy for Best Latin Artist. To consolidate her affinity for Latino music, she recorded a duet with pop star RICKY MARTIN, "Nobody Wants to Be Lonely," in late 2000. It became a worldwide hit.

Aguilera joined forces with four other female singers—Pink, Lil' Kim, Mya, and Missy Elliott—to record a remake of the 1970s LaBelle hit "Lady Marmalade" for the soundtrack of the movie musical *Moulin Rouge* (2001). It became another huge hit and earned her a third Grammy for Best Pop Collaboration with Vocals.

After releasing a well-received Christmas album, *My Kind of Christmas,* Aguilera recorded *Stripped* (2002), an album that showed a new maturity in her singing and choice of material. She co-wrote six of the songs and produced one. "Getting older, you just don't want to sing fluffy," she has said. "You just have more things to say about real life and real people and the bitterness that you get from people."

In 2003, Aguilera released the music video *Dirrty,* a performance of the hit song from her *Stripped* album. Tattoos, body piercings (most of which she had removed by 2004), and very sexy outfits have not hurt record sales, despite some controversy over her new raunchy image. *Rolling Stone* magazine has declared *Dirrty* the most played music video of all time.

Aguilera is a spokesperson for Coke, Versace, and MAC–cosmetics. She won her fourth Grammy in 2004 for Best Female Pop Vocal Performance for her recording of "Beautiful." She married music executive Jordan Bratman in November 2005. Her latest studio album, *Back to Basics* (2006), a scintillating blend of soul, jazz, and blues, presented a new, sophisticated Aguilera and was well received by the public and critics.

A pop-music megastar around the world, Christina Aguilera believes she has the staying power of such role models as Julie Andrews and Whitney Houston. "I'm in it for the long run," she said in a recent interview.

Further Reading

Dominguez, Pier. *Christina Aguilera: A Star Is Made: The Unauthorized Biography.* Phoenix, Ariz.: Colossus Books, 2003.

Golden, Anna Louise. *Christina Aguilera.* New York: St. Martin's Press, 2000.

Korman, Susan. *Christina Aguilera* (Latinos in the Limelight). New York: Chelsea House, 2001.

Oqunnaike, Lola. "Aguilera, That Dirrty Girl, Cleans Up Real Nice." *New York Times,* July 30, 2006, Arts and Leisure section, pp. 1, 25.

Talmadge, Mary. *Christina Aguilera* (Celebrity Bios). Danbury, Conn.: Children's Press, 2001.

Further Listening

Back to Basics. RCA, double CD, 2006.

Christina Aguilera. BMG, CD, 1999.

Mi Reflejo. Sony International, CD, 2000.

Stripped. RCA, CD, 2002.

Alcaraz, Lalo (Eduardo Lopez)

(1964–) *editorial cartoonist, cartoonist*

One of the few Latino American cartoonists to be nationally syndicated, Lalo Alcaraz uses his biting wit and satire to criticize U.S. policy toward Latinos and other minorities while he defends their rights.

He was born Eduardo Lopez in Tijuana, Mexico, on April 16, 1964, the son of Mexican immigrants. His parents met in an English as a second language (ESL) class. Six weeks after his birth, the family moved to San Diego.

As a child, Lopez drew constantly. He was inspired to draw comics after discovering Gus Arriola's *Gordo* comic strip in the funny pages of the newspaper. By the late 1980s, he was drawing editorial cartoons under the name Lalo Alcaraz for *L.A. Weekly,* a Los Angeles Latino paper. His bold, larger-than-life style with its childlike captions attracted the attention of the Universal Press Syndicate, which picked up his one-panel editorial cartoon feature *La Cucaracha* (Spanish for "cockroach"). It was soon appearing twice weekly in more than 50 newspapers, including the *Los Angeles Times* and the *Boston Globe.*

While his satire made people think about issues affecting Latinos, Alcaraz also wanted to educate. In 1990, he illustrated *Latino USA: A Cartoon History,* written by college professor Ilan Stavan. Although witty and humorous in both artwork and text, the book took a serious look at Latinos in U.S. history. One critic called it "required reading for anyone interested in democratic inclusive history writing."

In 2002, Alcaraz transformed *La Cucaracha* into a daily narrative comic strip with ongoing characters. The central characters are Eddie Lopez, a reporter for bilingual Latino newspaper the *Barrio Bugle,* and radical Internet blogger Cuco Rocha. Like Garry Trudeau, creator of the comic strip *Doonesbury,* Alcaraz is not afraid to satirize American politicians and social issues head-on but does so with plenty of humor.

"Some folks have asked me if I wouldn't be happier in my 'home country,'" he wrote in the introduction of a book collection of his cartoons. "I usually reply, 'Dear moron, the United States is my home country, and yes, I wish I could be happier here.'"

Although he is highly critical of government and its institutions, Alcaraz has a healthy skepticism toward just about everyone and everything—including himself. He has defined a political cartoonist as "an opinionated jerk with a pen."

Lalo Alcaraz has won numerous awards for his work, including four Southern California Journalism Awards for Best Cartoon in Weekly Paper. He is also the recipient of the Los Angeles Hispanic Public Relations Association's Premio Award for Excellence in Communications. He lives and works in Los Angeles.

Further Reading

Alcaraz, Lalo. *La Cucaracha.* Kansas City, Mo.: Andrews McMeel Publishing, 2004.

———. *Migra Mouse: Political Cartoons on Immigration.* New York: RDV Books, 2004.

Beltran, Raymond R. "Up Close and Laughing with Lalo." Calaca Press Web Site. Available online. URL: http://calacapress.com/raymondbeltran/raylalo.html. Downloaded on September 12, 2006.

Jones, Vanessa E. "Drawing on Culture," *Boston Globe,* July 3, 2001, p. E1.

La Cucaracha: The Syndicated Daily Comic Strip by Lalo Alcaraz. Available online. URL: http://www.lacucaracha.com. Downloaded on April 21, 2005.
Stavans, Ilan, and Lalo Alcaraz. *Latino USA: A Cartoon History.* New York: Basic Books, 2000.

Alfonzo, Carlos
(1950–1991) *painter*

Considered one of the most promising American artists of the 1980s for his expressionistic paintings that exorcised his personal demons, Carlos Alfonzo died tragically just as he was on the brink of greater fame. He was born in Havana, Cuba, on September 24, 1950. When dictator Fidel Castro took power in 1959, Alfonzo's parents chose to remain in the new communist state that Castro established. Alfonzo's artistic gifts exhibited themselves early, and in 1969, he entered the San Alejandro School of Fine Arts, Cuba's most celebrated art academy. After graduating in 1973, he taught art briefly at art centers in the Havana region. He then studied art history at the University of Havana, receiving a degree in 1977. During this time, he had his first major solo exhibition at a Havana gallery.

As an artist and a homosexual (a brief marriage ended in divorce), Alfonzo felt that his creativity was severely restricted in Castro's regimented socialist state. In 1980, along with more than 10,000 other Cubans, he fled in a boat from Mariel Harbor, seeking political asylum in the United States. He settled in Miami, Florida, and found adjustment to his exiled state so difficult that he was unable to paint for a year. He eventually found work painting restaurant and hotel murals for an interior designer. He resumed his career as an artist and in 1982 traveled to New York, where he greatly admired the work of such American artists as Jackson Pollack and Mark Rothko. He tried to imitate their abstract expressionistic works but in a few years had developed his own unique figurative style. Alfonzo's work became highly personal and was affected when he tested positive for the human immunodeficiency virus (HIV). The closeness of death thereafter became a major theme in his work. His canvases were filled with symbolic images and figures that reflected his fascination with religions, damnation, and salvation. "My work has been nourished by two currents—one, the Cuban, of drama and chaos; and two, the American, of rationality and structure," he once said. "Between these two currents my work grows."

Alfonzo was fascinated by the two central religions of Cuba—Roman Catholicism and Santeria, an African religion brought to the island by African slaves. His dark, dreamlike canvases were filled with religious imagery, including Catholic crucifixes and martyred saints as well as the axes and skulls imagery of Santeria.

His work began to attract critical attention. He earned a fellowship from the National Endowment for the Arts (NEA) in Painting in 1984. In 1987, Alfonzo's paintings were considered one of the highlights in the traveling exhibition *Hispanic Artists in the United States,* organized by the Corcoran Gallery of Art in Washington, D.C., and the Museum of Fine Arts in Houston, Texas. Wealthy art patron Craig Robin gave Alfonzo a spacious studio in Miami Beach, providing him at last with the economic freedom to devote himself full time to painting.

More exhibitions in both solo and group shows followed. In 1990, Alfonzo was invited to exhibit his work in the prestigious Biennial of American Painting at the Whitney Museum of American Art in New York City. *Artnews* magazine named him one of the 10 artists to watch in the 1990s.

But by then Alfonzo had been diagnosed with the deadly virus acquired immunity deficiency syndrome (AIDS). Facing death, the artist took his art in an entirely new direction. His so-called black or blood paintings were dark, simply composed, and filled with both the specter of death and the hope of an afterlife. His last completed painting, *Blood,* depicted his soul, a brown form, declining into death.

Carlos Alfonzo died on February 19, 1991, in Miami from an AIDS-related cerebral hemorrhage. In 1998, the Hirshhorn Museum and Sculpture Garden opened the first major retrospective of his work, titled *Triumph of the Spirit: Carlos Alfonzo, a Survey, 1975–1991.* "Alfonzo's impassioned canvasses trace the struggle of the human spirit by relating one man's poignant journey," wrote the exhibit's curator Olga M. Viso.

Further Reading

Alfonzo, Carlos. *The Art of Carlos Alfonzo: January 7, 1988 to February 5, 1988.* Miami: Frances Wolfson Art Gallery, Miami-Dade Community College, 1988.

Cockcroft, James D., assisted by Jane Canning. *Latino Visions: Contemporary Chicano, Puerto Rican, and Cuban American Artists.* New York: Franklin Watts, 2000, pp. 42–44.

Viso, Olga M. *Triumph of the Spirit: Carlos Alfonzo, a Survey, 1975–1991.* Seattle: University of Washington Press, 1998.

Almaraz, Carlos

(1941-1989) *painter, muralist, printmaker*

A Chicano (Mexican-American) artist whose work helped bring mainstream recognition to the plight of his people, Carlos Almaraz had a vibrant expressionistic style that exuded life and optimism even when dealing with the grimmest subject matter. He was born in Mexico City, Mexico, on October 5, 1941, and moved to the United States with his family while still a child. The Almarazes settled in Chicago and later moved to East Los Angeles, California. Carlos attended California State College–Los Angeles and the University of California–Los Angeles (UCLA). In 1965, already an aspiring artist, he moved to New York City where he lived for five years. He studied every prevalent art trend of the day, including abstract expressionism and minimalism. The insularity of the New York art world dissatisfied him, and he returned to Los Angeles to create a populist art for the Chicano people.

Almaraz was quickly drawn into social activist Cesar Chavez's United Farm Workers Union (UFW), which sought to reform an unjust system for migrant farm workers through protests and strikes. Almaraz created murals, banners, and other practical artwork for Chavez and also created set designs for El Teatro Campesino, a traveling theater company made up of Chicano farm workers. They performed social plays to raise funds for the UFW and its activities.

Around this time Almaraz joined with fellow Chicano artists Robert de la Rocha, Gilbert "Mager" Lujan, and FRANK ROMERO to form Los Four, a Chicano art collective. Their goal was to get their street art recognized by the established Los Angeles art community.

Traveling to Mexico, Almaraz was inspired by the murals of such masters of the form as Diego Rivera and Jose Clemente Orozco. Through the 1970s, he painted murals celebrating Chicanos and other minority groups throughout the Los Angeles area. In 1974 he earned a master of fine arts (M.F.A.) degree from the Otis Art Institute. In the 1980s, his work began to appear regularly in galleries and museum shows, largely thanks to his acceptance into the Jan Turner Gallery in Los Angeles.

Almaraz's paintings and his other artworks have a restless energy. He brought his figures to life with vibrant lines and bold color schemes. His *Echo Park* painting series, with its vivid scenes of city street life, are among his best-known works.

Almaraz was a harsh critic of U.S. society and its materialism. *Greed,* a symbolic painting of two vicious dogs fighting over a bone, is set against a rust-red lunarlike desert landscape. One of his last paintings before his untimely death from AIDs-related causes is *Death Rides By* (1989), which depicts a ghostly skeletal figure of Death racing across the canvas on a horse. The epitaph on Almaraz's tombstone reads: "Here lies a chap quick as a cat and short one life."

Carlos Almaraz remains a major influence on a new generation of Latino artists. His wife, Elsa Flores Almaraz, is also an artist and frequently collaborated with him.

Further Reading

Almaraz, Carlos. *Moonlight Theater: Prints and Related Works.* Los Angeles: Grunwald Center for the Graphic Arts, 1991.

Nieto, Margarita. "Oral History Interview with Carlos Almaraz." Smithsonian Archives of American Arts. Available online. URL: http://www.aaa.si.edu/oralhist/almara86.htm. Downloaded on August 15, 2005.

Romero, Frank. *Los Four: Almaraz, de la Rocha, Lujan, Romero: Art Gallery, University of California, Irvine, November 10 to December 9, 1973: Los Angeles County Museum.* Irvine: School of Fine Arts, University of California, 1973.

Yorba, Jonathan. *Arte Latino: Treasures from the Smithsonian American Art Museum.* New York: Watson-Guptill Publications, 2001, pp. 10–11.

Almendros, Néstor
(Néster Almendros Cuyas)

(1930–1992) *cinematographer, documentary filmmaker, film producer*

One of Hollywood's most gifted cinematographers, Néstor Almendros created texture and color that heightened the dramatic impact of the work of some of the world's finest filmmakers.

He was born Néster Almendros Cuyas in Barcelona, Spain, on October 30, 1930. At age 14, he moved with his family to Cuba, where his father had been sent into exile for opposing Spanish dictator Francisco Franco. Almendros attended the University of Havana, where he studied philosophy and literature. But it was film that became his strongest passion, and he wrote film reviews for journals and founded a cineclub in Havana where he screened foreign films.

At age 20, Almendros worked on an amateur film with celebrated Cuban filmmaker Tomás Gutiérrez Alea. He went on to study cinematography at the Centro Sperimentale di Cinematografia in Rome, Italy. Back in Cuba, he served as cameraman or director on six short documentaries at the Instituto del Arte and Industria Cinematografica. Two of these films focused on social injustice in Cuba under dictator Fidel Castro, who seized power in 1959. The government banned these films, and Almendros left Cuba to live and work in Paris, France. There he found work as a cameraman in television and soon came to the attention of leading French filmmakers Erich Rohmer and François Truffaut. He worked with both directors on such classic films as Rohmer's *My Night at Maud's* (1969) and *Chloe in the Afternoon* (1972) and Truffaut's *The Wild Child* (1969) and *The Story of Adele H.* (1975). In *The Wild Child,* Almendros's evocative black-and-white photography perfectly captured the film's 19th-century setting.

Almendros's first important Hollywood film was *Days of Heaven* (1978) directed by Terrence Malick. Almendros's glorious sun-lit visuals, most of which was shot during the "golden hours" (the first hour of dawn and the last hour of dusk), of this period drama set in the American Midwest were so stunning that they almost dwarfed the story of a tragic love triangle. For this film, he earned his first and only Academy Award for best cinematography.

Almendros was immediately in demand by some of America's top directors. He worked with Robert Benton on *Kramer vs. Kramer* (1979), *Places in the Heart* (1984), and *Nadine* (1987). He also shot *Sophie's Choice* (1982) for Alan J. Pakula and Martin Scorsese's segment of the anthology film *New York Stories* (1989).

Despite his success as a cinematographer on fictional features, Almendros never lost his love for

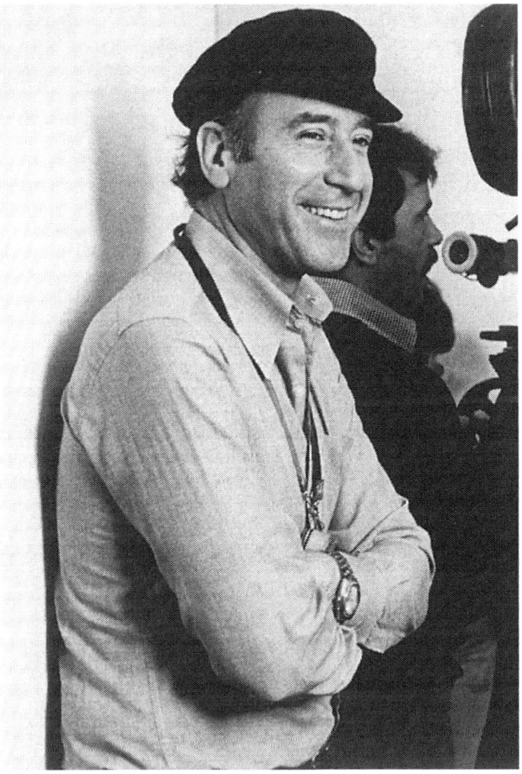

One of Hollywood's finest cinematographers, Néstor Almendros was also a skillful documentary filmmaker. *(Photofest)*

directing documentaries. In 1984, he made *Nobody Listened,* a biting exposure of Castro's Cuba, with codirector Jorge Ulla. The English translation of his professional autobiography *A Man with a Camera,* originally written in French, was published to great acclaim the same year. Néstor Almendros died at age 62 of acquired immune deficiency syndrome (AIDS) disease in New York City on March 4, 1992.

Further Reading

Almendros, Néstor. *A Man with a Camera.* New York: Farrar Straus Giroux, 1986.

Film Reference. "Néstor Almendros," Film Reference.com. Available online. URL: http://www.filmreference.com/Writers-and-Production-Artists-A-Ba/Almendros-Nést or.html. Downloaded on March 31, 2006.

The Internet Movie Database. "Néstor Almendros," The Internet Movie Database. Available online. URL: http://www.imdb.com/name/nm0000743/. Downloaded on September 12, 2005.

Further Viewing

Days of Heaven (1978). Paramount Home Video, VHS/DVD, 1998/2003.

Nobody Listened (1984). Facets Video, DVD, 2005.

Visions of Light: The Art of Cinematography (1998). Image Entertainment, DVD, 2000.

Anthony, Marc
(Marco Antonio Muñiz)

(1969–) *Latin and pop singer, songwriter, actor*

A major Latin singer who has triumphantly made the crossover to the pop market, Marc Anthony's passionate tenor has attracted legions of listeners, whether he is singing fiery Latin funk or middle-of-the-road pop.

He was born Marco Antonio Muñiz in New York City on September 16, 1969, into a large Puerto Rican family with four brothers and three sisters. His father was his first and best teacher, instructing him in composition and music theory. As a child, Marco listened to the music of RUBÉN BLADES, WILLIE COLÓN, and JOSÉ FELICIANO, among other Latino-American singers.

At age 12, his gift for singing was discovered by demo and commercial producer David Harris, who also hired his sister. While gaining experience in the recording studio working for Harris, Anthony also began to write songs. He gave one song to his friend Latina hip-hop singer Safire to record on her debut album. "Boy, I've Been Told" became a top–40 hit on the singles charts.

Anthony sang backup and was a featured vocalist on one cut on Safire's album. He also sang on albums by the Latin Rascals and Menudo. About the same time, he made his film debut, starring and singing in the Latino musical *East Side Story* (1988). The film's score was composed by producer and deejay Little Louie Vega, who was so impressed by Anthony's performance that he offered to work with him on an album. The result, *When the Night Is Over,* was released in 1991 and featured hip-hop Latin music. The album showed that Anthony was part of a greater tradition of Latino music, featuring guest appearances by legendary percussionist TITO PUENTE and bandleader Eddie Palmieri. A single taken from the album, "Ride on the Rhythm," was released and shot to #1 on Billboard's dance music chart. Anthony's place in Latino music was further solidified when he played as the opening act at a celebration of the release of Puente's 100th album at New York's Madison Square Garden.

For his next album, Anthony turned to the popular Latin dance music, salsa, with which he had had little experience. "This gives me the opportunity to establish new goals; it gives me new life," he said at the time. "And that's what keeps a person like me going." The album, *Otra Nota* (1993), became a smash and put Anthony in the forefront of salsa singers. One song on the album he cowrote and sang with his father.

Anthony's film career continued to blossom. He played a Latino disco singer in *Carlito's Way,* (1993), starring Al Pacino, and had small parts in *Hackers* (1995) and *The Substitute* (1996). He was a convincing drug addict in director Martin Scorsese's grim urban drama *Bringing Out the Dead* (1999), starring Nicholas Cage. The same year, Anthony costarred with one of his idols Rubén Blades on Broadway in the short-lived Paul Simon musical, *The Capeman.*

After two more hit salsa albums produced by Sergio George, Anthony made the crossover to the English-language market, signing a $30-million recording contract with Columbia Records. His first album with the label, *Marc Anthony* (1999), soared to #1 on the charts with a blend of Latino funk and smooth adult contemporary music. *Libre* (2001), his next album, was a return to his salsa roots and earned him some of his best reviews to date. The critics were less impressed by *Mended* (2002), complaining that its pop ballads were bland and lacked the passion of Anthony's best music. Yet, his fans did not seem to mind, and the record sold well. He released *Sigo Siendo Yo,* a Spanish-greatest hits album in July 2006.

Marc Anthony divorced his first wife, former Miss Universe Dayanara Torres Delgado, in 2004 and four days later made headlines by marrying singer/actress JENNIFER LOPEZ. The two sing a duet on his 2004 album *Amar sin Mentiras.* Anthony has a daughter Ariana by a previous relationship and two sons, Cristian Anthony and Ryan Anthony, by Torres.

Further Reading

All Music Guide. "Marc Anthony." All Music Guide Web Site. Available online. URL: http://www.allmusic.com/cg/amg.dll?p=amg&sql=11:7krsa9tgh23g~T1. Downloaded on April 28, 2005.

Johns, Michael-Anne. *Marc Anthony.* Kansas City, Mo.: Andrews McMeel Publishing, 2000.

Vaerla, Jose. "Marc Anthony: The Voice of a New Millennium." *Latin Beat Magazine,* 1 May 2000, p. 43.

Further Listening

Desde Un Principo: From the Beginning. Sony International, CD, 1999.

Libre. Sony International, CD, 2001.

Marc Anthony. Sony, CD, 1999.

Further Viewing

Bringing Out the Dead (1999). Paramount Home Video, VHS/DVD, 2000/2003.

Aranda, Iris Nelia (Irisne)

(1967–) *painter, sculptor, muralist, ceramist, interior designer*

Born deaf, Iris Nelia Aranda found a way to communicate with the world through her visionary art.

She was born in Panama on October 14, 1967. She grew up in a hearing family that did not expose her to sign language or any part of deaf culture. Frustrated by her inability to communicate with people, she began to express herself from the age of nine through drawing and painting. Her first subject was the seaside, which she often visited with her family. "As a child I basked in the beauty of the waves and sand . . . ," she remembers. "My parents recall my surprise and inspiration at the salty taste of seawater." She was also inspired to be an artist by visits to the Museo de Arts Contemporaneo in Panama City. "There I found not only a connection between my heart and the visual arts, but support from the professional community," she says.

Her parents encouraged her artistic talent, and she attended the Justo Arosemana Institute, receiving a bachelor of arts (B.A.) in 1984. Aranda continued her studies at the University of Panama in Panama City, where she received technical degrees in applied arts design (1983) and plastic art (1987). She went on to earn a master of arts (M.A.) in applied arts design at the university in 1997.

While attending an international conference on deaf education on the island of Bermuda, Aranda met a woman who would change her life. Alisha Bronk was an advocate for the deaf, having grown up with two deaf brothers in Wisconsin. The two women struck up a friendship, and Bronk invited Aranda to come to the United States where she felt she could better pursue her career as an artist.

She joined Bronk, who became her manager, in Kenosha, Wisconsin, where she lives and works

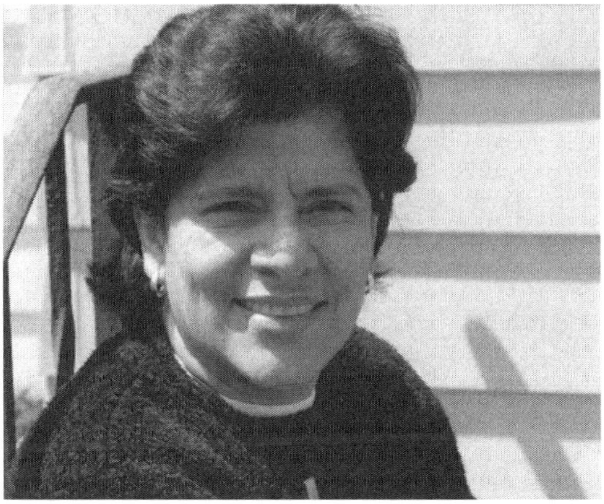

Born and raised in Panama, Iris Nelia Aranda is deaf and has found a powerful means of communication through her art. *(Iris Nelia Aranda)*

today. During the past 15 years, Aranda has sold 40,000 original paintings and prints. She has created art for such major companies as Coca-Cola and Colgate and has sold her work to Very Special Art, an affiliate of the John F. Kennedy Center for the Performing Arts in Washington, D.C. She has also designed corporate and home interiors.

Aranda has held children's art workshops at the Wisconsin School for the Deaf and the Milwaukee Sign Language Immersion School, among others. She has exhibited her work in the United States, Panama, the Dominican Republic, Honduras, Mexico, Chile, France, and Egypt. Her work was represented in the second biennial art exhibition of Panama in 2004–05. She signs her artwork "Irisne."

"All my figures, whether plants, animals, fruits or human forms, reverberate in the depths of my starry, surreal skies," she explains. "My soul is drawn to living lineal figures and natural cylindrical shapes. My colors fuse freshness, harmony and spontaneity—the joy and rush of life in the natural world of animals, water and climate that flows from within my art."

Further Reading

Aranda, Iris Nelia. Personal interview with the author.

Prins, Katie. "Iris Nelia Aranda: The Art of Experience," *CSD Spectrum,* Fall/Winter 2004, p. 11.

Archuleta, Felipe
(Felipe Benito Archuleta)
(1910–1991) *folk carver*

An artist who did not begin to carve wood figures until he was in his mid-50s, Felipe Benito Archuleta almost single-handedly revived the traditional Mexican art form known as *bultos.*

He was born in Santa Cruz, New Mexico, in the Sangre de Cristo Mountains on August 23, 1910. The eldest of six children, Felipe and his family lived in abject poverty. After a minimum of schooling, he went to work as a migrant farmworker in neighboring Colorado. During the Great Depression of the 1930s, he became a stonemason through the federal agency, the Works Progress Administration (WPA).

Archuleta later settled down in Tesuque, New Mexico, in a simple adobe house and worked as a carpenter for more than 30 years. Unemployed in the mid–1960s, he experienced a religious awakening and prayed to God to give him guidance. He claimed that God directed him to carving. He began to carve small animals—sheep, burros, cats—out of cottonwood or elm, which he sold to gift shops and art galleries. Using only a few carpenters' tools, Elmer's glue, and house paint, Archuleta created fantastic creatures with great snouts, enlarged genitals, and wild eyes. Soon, he was fashioning larger, more wild and exotic animals such as monkeys, elephants, and fish. Some were even life size. In true folk-art fashion, he set out to capture not the literal animal but the fierce, untamed spirit that it symbolized.

Archuleta used a chainsaw to begin these large carvings and adorned the finished beasts with such simple but original materials as hemp, brush bristles, wool, and marbles. He was part of the grand *bultos* tradition, the carving of fully rounded figures that flourished for two and a half centuries in Mexico but had almost completely died out by 1900. Archuleta's intricate work renewed interest in nonreligious *bultos* and revived the tradition. Among those who followed him were Alonso Jimenez and Archuleta's own son Leroy (1949–), both of whom began their careers as his assistants.

As he grew older, Archuleta's reputation in the growing folk-art market rose, and he was unable to keep up with the demand for his work. "I can't satisfy the whole world, amigo," he complained to one collector. But he tried his best, turning out his unique animals until 1987. He died on January 1, 1991, in Tesuque.

Felipe Archuleta received the Governor of New Mexico's Award of Excellence in Achievement in the Arts in 1979. His work is in the permanent collections of the Museum of International Folk Art in Santa Fe, New Mexico; the Milwaukee Art Center/Museum in Wisconsin; and the Museum of American Folk Art in New York City, among others.

Further Reading

Congdon, Kristin G., and Kara Kelley Hallmark. *Artists from Latin American Cultures: A Biographical Dictionary.* Westport, Conn.: Greenwood Press, 2002, pp. 12–14.

Smithsonian American Art Museum. "Felipe Archuleta." SAAM Web site. Available online. URL: http://americanart.si.edu/search/artist_bio.cfm?StartRow=1&ID=129&skip=1 &CFID=2063433&CFTOKEN=75576119. Downloaded on August 16, 2005.

Wecter, Elizabeth. *Animal Carvers of New Mexico.* New York: Museum of American Folk Art, 1986.

Arnaz, Desi
(Desiderio Alberto Arnaz y de Acha III)
(1917–1986) *actor, bandleader, musician, singer, television producer*

The often neglected half of the most celebrated husband-and-wife team in television history, Desi Arnaz was a multitalented performer who may have left his greatest mark as one of television's most prolific and brilliant producers.

Desiderio Alberto Arnaz y de Acha III was born in Santiago, Cuba, on March 2, 1917. He came from Cuba's privileged class; both sides of his family were well-to-do landowners. His grandfather was a founding partner in the Bundaberg Rum Company, and his father, Desiderio II, was the mayor of Santiago. Desi's charmed childhood came to an abrupt end in 1933 when he was 16. A revolution overthrew President Gerardo Machado, and Fulgencio Batista came to power. The Arnaz family, friends of the former president, was stripped of its wealth, status, and property. Desi's father was thrown into jail and only released through the negotiations of U.S. officials, who claimed he remained neutral during the revolution.

The family fled to Miami, Florida, where the former privileged son found himself cleaning canary cages in a pet shop and driving a truck to help the family survive. Through sheer grit and raw talent, he joined a Cuban band as a guitarist and vocalist in 1936. His sparkling personality on stage impressed Spanish bandleader XAVIER CUGAT, who hired him in New York as lead vocalist with his famous orchestra. After only six months with Cugat, Arnaz left to form his own combo, in which he sang and played the bongo drums. The new band, which grew to an orchestra, rode to fame on the then-current conga craze, based on the syncopated Brazilian dance that swept the country in the late 1930s.

In 1939, Arnaz was cast as a Cuban bongo player in the Richard Rodgers and Lorenz Hart Broadway musical *Too Many Girls.* It was an apt title, for Desi was an irrepressible ladies' man. When Hollywood picked up the musical the following year, Desi reprised his role in the film version. One of his costars was a vibrant redhead, Lucille Ball, who had been acting in films since 1933. The two fell in love almost immediately and were married a few months later.

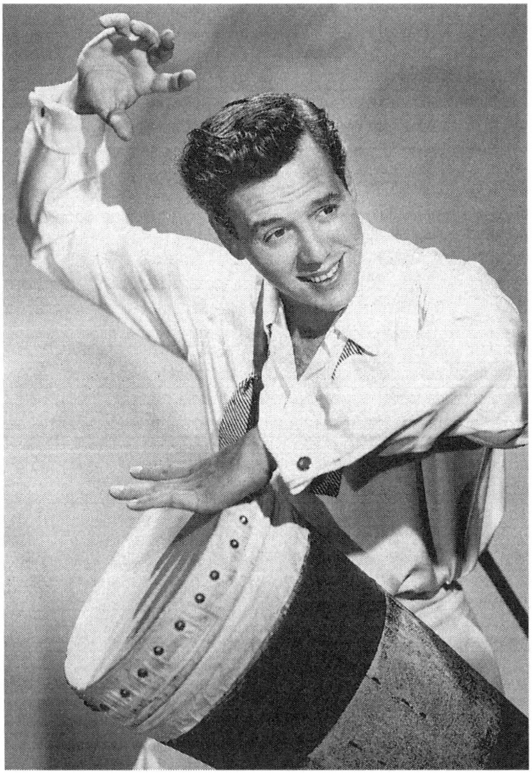

More than a conga player, bandleader, and sitcom actor, Desi Arnaz was one of the first great innovative television producers. *(Photofest)*

For the next decade, the Arnazes saw precious little of each other. He was busy traveling with his band and making an occasional movie, including the excellent war film *Bataan* (1943), his only dramatic role in a Hollywood film. Shortly after, he was drafted during World War II, but, due to a knee injury, he spent his time in service directing United Service Organizations (U.S.O.) shows for soldiers at a California military hospital. Lucy was busy with her film career, playing second leads and comic roles in dozens of movies. They later claimed to have spent $30,000 on telephone calls and telegrams during these years of separation.

In the late 1940s, Ball starred in a radio comedy *My Favorite Wife* opposite actor Richard Denning. The Columbia Broadcast System (CBS) wanted to bring the radio show to the new medium of television in 1950, with both actors reprising their roles. Ball insisted that her real husband, Desi, play her television husband on the new show. Both of them saw it as a golden opportunity to work together after years of working and living apart. But the head of programming at CBS was adamantly against Desi. He claimed viewers would never buy that Ball was married to a Cuban American. He also felt Arnaz could not act and would be unintelligible with his Spanish accent. The couple set out to prove him wrong.

They put together a vaudeville-style show and took it on the road to perform live before audiences around the country, all at their own expense. The road show was a hit, but CBS still was not convinced. The couple filmed a pilot episode, again at their own expense. Desi played Ricky Ricardo, a none-too-successful Cuban bandleader and Lucy, who retained her own first name, was his zany, show-biz crazy wife.

There were other problems to surmount before their show, named *I Love Lucy,* hit the airwaves. Most television shows were shot live in New York, but the Arnazes wanted to remain in California and do the show from there. There was as yet no permanent national, coast-to-coast cable, and CBS was against sending copies that had been filmed off a TV screen, called kinescopes, to the East Coast because they were of poor quality. Lucy and Desi said they would solve the problem by filming the episodes live. This presented a new problem of how to film a situation comedy before a live audience.

Working with technicians, Desi came up with a solution. They would film each episode in continuous action as a three-act play with multiple cameras and then edit the different camera shots later for viewing. This technique has since become standard practice in television. The Arnazes would pay the extra $5,000 that the filming would cost per episode, and in return CBS would allow them to own the shows. This proved to be a gold mine for the Arnazes. Their shows are still rerunning on television today, more than a half century after they were first shown.

I Love Lucy was a smash success after its debut in Fall 1951. It became the #3 show of the season and then went to #1 for the next three seasons. In April 1952, a research agency announced that it was the first television program to be seen in 10 million homes.

When Lucy became pregnant with their second child during the second season, Desi convinced the sponsor to let them incorporate her pregnancy into the show's story line. Never before had a real pregnant woman portrayed a woman who becomes pregnant on television. However, the network refused to allow the word *pregnant* to be used on the show. Lucy Ricardo was instead "expecting." Incredibly, the real Arnaz baby, Desi, Jr., was born the same day that the episode about the birth of little Ricky Ricardo aired. The two events gained bigger newspaper headlines than the inauguration of President Dwight D. Eisenhower!

In their five seasons on the air, the Ricardos moved to Hollywood when Desi was cast in a movie, traveled to Europe, and eventually settled in suburban Connecticut. Beginning in 1957, the couple filmed 13 one-hour specials entitled *The Lucy–Desi Comedy Hour.* This show, like *I Love Lucy,* was produced by their own production company, Desilu Productions. Under Desi's skillful direction, Desilu became television's biggest producer of shows, including such hits as the sitcoms *Our Miss Brooks, The Danny Thomas Show,* and *December Bride* as well as the ground-breaking period crime series, *The Untouchables.* They even had their own dramatic anthology series, *Desilu*

Playhouse, which Arnaz hosted and in which he sometimes starred.

While professionally the Arnazes were thriving, their marriage was falling apart. A large part of the problem was Desi's alcoholism and his womanizing, about which he wrote candidly in his autobiography *A Book* (1977). After completing their last comedy hour, the couple divorced in 1960. Desi sold his interest in Desilu Studios to his former wife in 1962. She continued as television's top comedienne in two more television series; Desi went into semiretirement and married Edith Mack Hirsch in 1963. He was executive producer of one more sitcom, *The Mothers-in-Law* (1967–69) and appeared occasionally on the show as the bullfighter Raphael del Gado.

Arnaz retired to Del Mar, California, in the 1970s. One of his rare television appearances in the 1980s was as host for the NBC comedy show *Saturday Night Live.* He was working on a second volume of autobiography, *Another Book,* when he was diagnosed with lung cancer. He died on December 2, 1986. Lucille Ball died three years later.

Desi Arnaz was a giant in early television, whose accomplishments were all too often overshadowed by his equally gifted wife. Ricky Ricardo with his crazy English and perfect straight-man timing, was a memorable creation, although Desi was never nominated for an Emmy. Unlike Lucy, he put very little stock in awards and honors. "I'm waiting for them to put in a category of bongo drummer," he said at the time, "and if they have one and don't nominate me, then I'll squawk."

His two children by Lucy, Luci Arnaz (1951–) and Desi Arnaz, Jr. (1953–), are both actors. The younger Desi portrayed his father in the movie *The Mambo Kings* (1992).

Further Reading

Arnaz, Desi. *A Book.* New York: Warner Books, 1977.

Harris, Warren G. *Lucy and Desi: The Legendary Love Story of Television's Most Famous Couple.* New York: Simon and Schuster, 1991.

Rodríguez, Clara E. *Heroes, Lovers, and Others: The Story of Latinos in Hollywood.* Washington, D.C.: Smithsonian Books, 2004, pp. 91–94.

Sands, Coyne Stevens, and Tom Gillet. *Desilu: The Story of Lucille Ball and Desi Arnaz.* New York: William Morrow, 1993.

Sinnott, Susan. *Extraordinary Hispanic Americas.* Chicago: Children's Press, 1991, pp. 177–180.

Further Listening

The Best of Desi Arnaz: The Mambo King. RCA, CD, 1992.

Further Viewing

Bataan (1943). Warner Home Video, VHS/DVD, 1991/2003.

I Love Lucy—Season One (Volumes 1–9) (1951–52). Paramount Home Video, DVD, 2002–2003.

Arreguín, Alfredo
(1935–) *painter*

A painter of rich, lush landscapes, Alfredo Arreguín's canvasses are alive with a colorful gallery of animals and plants that recall his Latino roots.

He was born in Morelia, in the Mexican state of Michoacan, on January 20, 1935. Exhibiting a gift for art at an early age, Arreguín became the youngest pupil at age nine to attend the Morelia School of Fine Art. When he was 13, he moved to Mexico City with his family; at age 23, he immigrated to the United States, settling in Seattle, Washington. Arreguín pursued art studies at the University of Washington, earning a bachelor of arts (B.A.) degree in 1967 and a master of fine arts (M.F.A.) degree two years later. He had his first solo exhibition at the Museum of Contemporary Hispanic Art (MOCHA) in New York City in 1978.

The natural world and all its splendor is Arreguín's favorite subject, and his green landscapes teem with birds, butterflies, fish, and other creatures.

His art, while sophisticated enough to please the art critics, enjoys a greater commercial appeal than many of his contemporaries. In 1985, he created a greeting card for the United Nations Children's Fund (UNICEF) that was distributed throughout Europe. He designed the White House Easter egg in 1988 and 1989. In addition, an oil triptych of flowers, *Sueño (Dream: Eve Before Adam)* (1992), is in the permanent collection of the Smithsonian Institution's National Museum of American Art (SAAM) and was rated by the Smithsonian as "one of its seven most important acquisitions from among more than 600 works of art collected by the museum in 1994."

Other paintings reside in the permanent collections of numerous museums, including the Mexican Fine Arts Center Museum in Chicago; the Tucson Museum of Art in Arizona; the National Hispanic Cultural Center in Albuquerque, New Mexico; the Tacoma Art Museum in Washington State; and the National Academy of Sciences in Washington, D.C.

Arreguín has been the recipient of many awards and honors including a Special Humanitarian Award from the Washington State Legislature Centennial Commission (1989); the OHTLI Award from the Mexican government (1997), its highest civilian honor for a nonresident; and the Distinguished Alumnus Award from the University of Washington Alumni Association (2000). He has also received two National Endowment for the Arts (NEA) grants in 1980 and 1985. Arreguín served as Seattle Arts Commissioner from 1980 to 1982 and continues to live and work in that city today.

"Alfredo Arreguín's paintings unleash our imagination and free us to envision an ideal world by celebrating both the ethereal and the tangible in the contested world around us," SAAM curator Andrew Connors has written.

Further Reading

"Alfredo Arreguín," Art and Resume. Available online. URL: http://www.jsbchorales.net/arreguín/index.html. Downloaded on April 19, 2005.

Arreguín, Alfredo, and Lauro Flores. *Alfredo Arreguín: Patterns of Dreams and Nature.* (Jacob Lawrence Series on American Artists). Seattle: University of Washington Press, 2002.

Yorba, Jonathan. *Arte Latino: Treasures from the Smithsonian American Art Museum.* New York: Watson-Guptill Publications, 2001, pp. 12–13.

Arriola, Gus (Gustavo M. Arriola)

(1917–2008) *cartoonist*

The first Latino-American cartoonist to be nationally syndicated, Gus Arriola gave millions of Americans their first taste of Latin-American life and culture in his charming, colorful comic strip *Gordo.*

Gustavo M. Arriola was born of Mexican heritage in Florence, Arizona, on July 17, 1917. When he was eight, his family moved to Los Angeles, California. After graduating from high school, Arriola got a job as an *in-betweener,* a person who draws the transitional animation in a cycle of motion between extremes in cartoons. He worked at the Charles Mintz Studio, which made cartoons for Screen Gems, a Hollywood studio. After a year at Mintz, Arriola moved on to Metro-Goldwyn-Mayer (MGM) studios, which had its own animation department. He worked as an animator on a character known as the Lonesome Stranger. A Mexican bandit in this cartoon would serve Arriola as a model for his most celebrated creation.

Three years later, Arriola left MGM and decided to try his hand at a comic strip. The main character was a Mexican bean farmer named Perfecto Salazar Lopez, better known as *Gordo,* which is Spanish for "fatso." United Features Syndicate bought the strip, and it debuted in American newspapers on November 24, 1941.

Only two weeks later, the United States entered World War II. Arriola soon stopped work on *Gordo* and joined the air force, where he worked animating training films for U.S. troops. Before he entered the service, he married Mary Frances Sevier. On evenings and weekends, he found time to start a Sunday *Gordo* strip in color.

The war ended in August 1945, and Arriola returned to civilian life. He settled with his wife in La Jolla, California, and resumed the *Gordo* daily strip the following year. Soon, the popular strip was appearing in more than 250 newspapers. In many ways, *Gordo* reinforced stereotypes of Latin Americans. Gordo was overweight, wore a big sombrero, and preferred long siestas to working in his bean fields. He had a young nephew named Pepito, a chihuahua he called Señor Dog, and a menagerie of barnyard animals that freely wandered in and out of his house. He also had a stout housekeeper, Tchuana Mama, who, after years of watching him pursue other women, became his wife.

Arriola treated Gordo and his other characters with respect and gave them a warm humanity that often transcended the stereotypes. Over time, he deepened and enriched his characters, and Gordo's broken English became noticeably better.

In 1958, Gordo largely abandoned his bean farm for a career as a tour guide, showing U.S. visitors the wonders of Mexico from his eccentric old bus, *La Comita Halley* (Halley's comet). Ironically, Arriola had never set foot in Mexico until the strip had been running for 20 years. His bold sense of design and color made the Sunday strip a treat for the eye and a favorite of readers.

The cartoonist "retired" *Gordo* in March 1985 after 44 years. During that time, he had won many awards. *Gordo* was named Best Humor Strip by the National Cartoonists Society in 1957 and 1965. In 1981, Arriola received the San Diego Comic Convention's "Inkpot Award" for Outstanding Achievement. The year he retired, the California state legislature voted a resolution honoring Arriola's professional excellence and his promotion of interethnic understanding. Gus Arriola died on February 2, 2008, after battling Parkinson's Disease.

Further Reading

Arriola, Gus. *Gordo's Critters.* Berkeley, Calif.: Celestial Arts, 1989 [reprint].

Harvey, Robert C., and Gustavo M. Arriola. *Accidental Ambassador Gordo: The Comic Strip Art of Gus Arriola.* Jackson: University Press of Mississippi, 2000.

Markstein, Don. "Gordo," Don Markstein's Toonopedia. Available online. URL: http://www.toonpedia.com/gordo.htm. Downloaded on November 28, 2004.

Azaceta, Luis Cruz

(1942–) *painter, collagist, educator*

An artist whose vivid images of violence and suffering reflect the injustices and cruelties of society, Luis Cruz Azaceta is one of today's most prominent Cuban-American painters. He was born in Marianao, Cuba, on April 5, 1942, the eldest son of an airplane mechanic. Dissatisfied with Fidel Castro's communist regime that took power in 1959, Azaceta caught one of the last commercial flights to the United States at age 18 in 1960. He settled in New York City and supported himself by working in a trophy factory. He soon began to take courses in drawing at a community center. He was accepted by the School of Visual Arts in New York and paid for his tuition by working as a clerk in a library. He graduated with a Bachelor of Fine Arts (B.F.A.) degree in 1969.

Azaceta's early paintings captured the chaos and brutality of urban life. They were first exhibited publicly at the International Art Exhibition at the Loeb Student Center at New York University. His identification with the victims and rejects of society was graphically depicted in a series of self portraits in which he painted himself as an acquired immunity deficiency syndrome (AIDS) patient, a cocaine addict, and even a cockroach.

In such later works as *Rafter Hell/Act I,* Azaceta expressed the terrible suffering of Cuban refugees, crossing the ocean to Florida and freedom in flimsy rafts and tiny boats. By the 1990s, Azaceta began to experiment with collage. He would photograph objects with a Polaroid camera and then cut the images for his collages. Everyday objects took on sharp, symbolic meaning in these works. For example, a food processor in *Immigrant* stands for the new arrivals' dream of mass consumerism but also makes a point about the mixing of cultures that takes place in the United States.

Azaceta's work earned him a National Endowment for the Visual Arts (NEVA) fellowship in 1980 and 1985. In 1986, his one-person show *Tough Ride Around the City* opened at the Museum of Contemporary Hispanic Art (MOCHA) in New York City. His more recent one-person show *Prayers—Beads—Cells* (2001) at the Arthur Roger Gallery in New Orleans included the painting series "Trax," filled with round polka-dot shapes that represent the toxic organisms spread by terrorists in post–September 11 America.

From 1981 to 1984, Azaceta taught at several institutes of higher learning, including Louisiana State University (LSU) at Baton Rouge and the University of California–Berkeley. In 2005, he was appointed the Lamar Dodd Professorial Chair of Art at the University of Georgia's Dodd School of Art. His paintings are in the permanent collections of the Museum of Fine Art in Boston; New York's Metropolitan Museum of Art and Museo de Barrio; and the New Orleans Museum of Art, among many others. Luis Cruz Azaceta is married and lives and works in a warehouse studio on Tchoupitoulas Street in New Orleans.

"Cuba gave me my values, my sense of humor, and sarcasm; in other words, a tragic-comic look at life," he has said. "The United States gave me the opportunity to become an artist, the freedom to paint the realities, anxiety, and horrors of the urban environment. The human condition."

Further Reading

Azaceta, Luis Cruz. *Hell: Luīs Cruz Azaceta: Selected Works, 1978–1993.* New York: Alternative Museum, 1993.

Cockcroft, James D., assisted by Jane Canning. *Latino Visions: Contemporary Chicano, Puerto Rican, and Cuban American Artists.* New York: Franklin Watts, 2000, pp. 109–113.

Leval, Susana Torruella. *Luis Cruz Azaceta: The AIDS Epidemic Series.* New York: Queens County Art and Cultural Center, 1990.

The University of Georgia Lamar Dodd School of Art. "Luis Cruz Azaceta Will Follow Willie Cole as the Next Lamar Dodd Professorial Chair of Art for 2005–06," The University of Georgia Lamar Dodd School of Art Web Site. Available online. URL: http://art.uga.edu/html/news.php?getLinks=getNews&getContent=getNews&contentValue=7. Downloaded on August 16, 2005.

Zuver, Marc, curator. *Cuba–USA: The First Generation—In Search of Freedom.* Washington, D.C.: Fondo del Sol Visual Arts Center, 1991, pp. 44–45.

B

Baca, Judy (Judith Francisca Baca)

(1946–) *muralist, educator, arts administrator, social activist*

Creator of the world's longest mural, Judy Baca has spent her career bringing the heritage and dreams of different peoples to life in dramatic and vivid public art. Judith Francisca Baca was born in East Los Angeles, California, on September 20, 1946. Her maternal grandparents fled Mexico in 1919 during the Mexican Revolution and settled in La Junta, Colorado, where Mexican Americans were treated as second-class citizens. Their daughter, Baca's mother, Ortencia Ferrari, moved to California in the mid-1940s and worked in a tire plant. She had a relationship with a navy man who died in World War II and shortly after gave birth to Baca. Soon, mother and daughter were joined by her grandmother and two aunts in a tiny duplex in Watts, a poor section of Los Angeles. "It was the perfect situation for creating an empowered young woman," Baca has recalled. "I was the center of everybody's life, and nobody ever told me I couldn't do things."

Baca's mother later married an Italian upholsterer, and the family moved to Pacoima, California. Baca attended a Catholic high school where her gift for art brought the shy girl out of her shell. She went on to the California State University–Northridge, where she earned a master of fine arts (M.F.A.) degree. Baca married at age 19, but the marriage did not last, and the couple divorced six years later.

She returned to her high school in the late 1960s to teach art but was soon fired for activist activities against the Vietnam War. She taught arts and crafts to children and senior citizens in 1970 with the Los Angeles Parks and Recreation Department. By 1974, Baca had established herself as an area artist and started a mural program for Los Angeles, the first of its kind in the city. She hired local people and professional artists to create murals in public places. She also brought in hundreds of youth, many of them with criminal records, and involved them in creating something positive—a mural.

Two years later, Baca founded the Social and Public Arts Resource Center (SPARC) in Venice, California, which she is still the artistic director of today. The nonprofit group's purpose was to create public art projects in ethnic communities where most residents had never seen the inside of a museum. That summer, Baca began work on what would become her most ambitious and celebrated artwork—the Great Wall of Los Angeles. She chose an unlikely site for this massive mural—the Tujunga Wash drainage canal in the San Fernando Valley. Her subject was nothing less than the history of the state of California as seen through the eyes of the many minority groups who helped create that history. She drew for inspiration on the

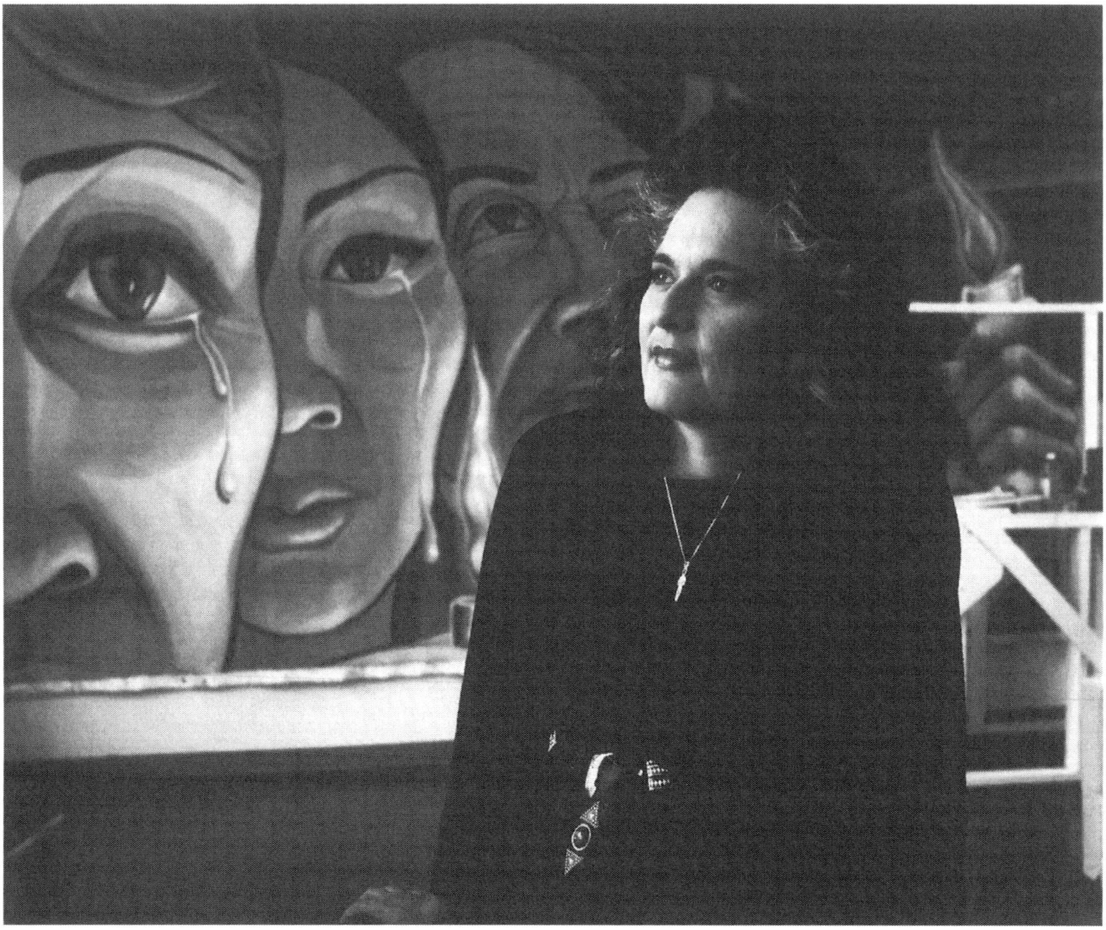

Artist Judy Baca stands before "Triumph of the Hearts," one panel in her monumental mural *World Wall: A Vision of the Future Without Fear.* *(Judith Baca)*

stories and memories of Chicanos and other ethnic peoples whom she spent months interviewing.

The mural, composed of 40 panels, was the work of hundreds of volunteers, young and old. The scenes depicted ranged from the arrival of the Spanish conquistadores to the waves of ethnic immigrants to the state in the 19th and 20th centuries. For five summers during the next seven years, the artists, under Baca's supervision, painted with acrylics on the solid concrete walls of the wash. When it was finally finished in 1984, the Great Wall was nearly a half-mile long and 13 feet high—the longest mural in the world. Big as it is, the Great Wall was just one of more than 250 murals made by more than 2,000 artists and volunteers under Baca's direction in the program's 10 years of operation.

Her next major project was not quite so colossal but in many ways more ambitious. She conceived the *World Wall: A Vision of the Future Without Fear* at a time (1998) when communism was crumbling in the Soviet Union and Eastern Europe. This 210-

foot, two-side portable canvas mural depicted such global issues as peace, cooperation, and interdependence. Since its original completion, this unique mural has traveled around the world. As the Soviet Union was in its final days, 150,000 people viewed it in Moscow's Gorky Park. As of 2001, new panels from artists in Australia, Mexico, and Canada were being added to the work.

In 1988, the city of Los Angeles started a new mural program under Baca's direction entitled *Great Walls Unlimited: Neighborhood Pride.* The program had produced 105 murals in a multitude of ethnic neighborhoods in Los Angeles County through 2003 when it ended. One of Baca's personal favorites is the Guadeloupe Mural (1988–90), in which she collaborated with hundreds of residents of the small, rural town of Guadeloupe in Santa Barbara County. The completed mural was a unique tribute to the town and its people, combining their colorful past with their hopes for the future. SPARC and Baca are currently working to restart the mural program

In recent years, Baca has been preoccupied with preserving the Great Wall of Los Angeles, which has been marred by the elements over the years. Along with restoration of the existing work, she has planned new panels to reflect the state's history since 1950, where the original mural left off.

Judy Baca, who describes herself as a "cultural attack dog," currently teaches at the University of California–Los Angeles (UCLA) and is director of the school's Cesar Chavez Digital Mural Lab, which is an experimental lab for new techniques to create murals and other large artworks.

"Muralism is the only art form that was so identified with communities of color that it came to be considered lower-class," she has said. "But in reality, muralism is a very noble art form because it talks about civic space as an amenity to our lives. We require civic spaces to come together, and we should be inspired by those spaces to become better citizens."

Further Reading

Congdon, Kristin G., and Kara Kelley Hallmark. *Artists from Latin American Cultures: A Biographical Dictionary.* Westport, Conn.: Greenwood Press, 2002, pp. 19–23.

Fernandez, Mayra. *Judy Baca* (Beginning Biographies). Lebanon, Ind.: Modern Curriculum Press, 1994.

Gruza, Agustin. "The Globe Is Her Canvas." *Los Angeles Times,* August 19, 2001, p. 1.

Judy Baca's Web Site. Available online. URL: http://www.judybaca.com/. Downloaded on September 22, 2006.

Olmstead, Mary. *Judy Baca* (Hispanic-American Biographies). Chicago: Heinemann Library, 2004.

SPARC: 30 years of Community Art Web Site. Available online. URL: http://www.sparcmurals.org/. Downloaded on September 22, 2006.

Further Viewing

A World of Art: Judy Baca. (vol. 8 of 10). Annenberg/CPB Project, VHS, 1997.

Baez, Joan
(Joan Chandos Báez, "The Queen of Folk Music")
(1941–) *folksinger, songwriter, social activist*

The first American folksinger to reach a mass international audience, Joan Baez has employed her pure, flawless soprano voice to promote peace, justice, and understanding as much as to sell records and concert tickets.

Joan Chandos Báez was born in Staten Island, one of the five boroughs of New York City, on January 9, 1941. Her father, Alberto Vicio Báez, was a Mexican-born physicist who had immigrated to the United States with his family at the age of two. He met Joan's mother, Joan Bonk, a Scotswoman who grew up in New York City, at a dance. The Báezs and their three daughters moved to California in the mid-1940s where Alberto attended graduate school at Stanford University. When he graduated, they returned to New York City. In junior high school, Joan was snubbed by other students because of her Mexican name and olive skin. By now a research physicist, Dr. Báez moved his family to Iraq, where he worked for the United Nations (UN).

In 1958, the family returned to the states and settled in Boston, Massachusetts. Dr. Báez took a teaching position at the Massachusetts Institute of Technology (MIT) in nearby Cambridge. Folk singing was beginning to undergo a revival in many American cities. In Harvard Square, Cambridge, Joan and her father went to small coffeehouses to hear folk music, and it struck a responsive chord in her. A student at Boston University, Báez learned the guitar and started to play in these same coffeehouses. Her untrained but pitch-perfect soprano gained the attention of a music promoter who got her a two-week gig at a Chicago club. Another folksinger, Bob Gibson, was so impressed by her singing that he invited her to sing with him at the Newport Folk Festival in Rhode Island in Summer 1959. She and Gibson sang two songs together to enthusiastic applause. The next summer, she returned to Newport to sing solo to even greater acclaim. Vanguard, a record label devoted to folk music, signed her to a recording contract, and her debut album, *Joan Baez,* a collection of 13 traditional folk songs, was released in December 1960. Soon after, Baez and her boyfriend Michael moved to San Francisco. On her arrival several weeks later, she was surprised to learn that her album was selling briskly and moving up the record charts. She went on tour to promote the album, taking time out to record *Joan Baez 2* (1961). The second album's popularity boosted sales of the first album, and by the time *Joan Baez in Concert,* a live album, was released in 1962, all three were best sellers. They remained on the charts for more than two years. No other American folksinger had sold so many records before. In November 1962, Joan Baez's reputation as the "Queen of Folk Music" was firmly sealed when her picture appeared on the cover of *Time* magazine.

About this time, Baez met and befriended young singer/songwriter Bob Dylan in New York City. Baez was greatly impressed by Dylan's original folk songs dealing with social issues and quickly became his champion. She helped start his career by singing his songs in her concerts. The two eventually became lovers.

Baez's sixth album, *Farewell Angelina* (1965), included four Dylan songs as well as songs by the English folk-rock artist Donovan and American folk pioneer Woody Guthrie. Baez's change of repertoire from traditional folk music to more contemporary songs coincided with her growing social activism. She sang at the historic March on Washington for civil rights led by the Rev. Martin Luther King, Jr. A live recording of the protest song "We Shall Overcome" that she sang at Mills College in Birmingham, Alabama, that same year became her first single on the pop charts. She joined in the protest movement against the Vietnam War, which the United States waged in 1965 to fight communists in Southeast Asia. That same year, she founded the Institute for the Study of Nonviolence in Carmel, California, where she lived. In 1968, while in jail briefly for protesting the war, she met peace activist David Harris. The two fell in love and married in 1968. They had a daughter, Gabriel, but the marriage ended in divorce in 1972.

In the late 1960s, Baez began to move from folk to country and rock music. She recorded a song by The Band, a rock group that was formerly Dylan's backup band. "The Night They Drove Old Dixie Down" (1971) became her biggest pop hit, going to #3 on the pop charts.

In 1972, around Christmastime, Baez visited Hanoi, the capital city of North Vietnam, the United States's enemy in the war. She described the experience in her original song "Where Are You Now, My Son?," splicing into the track the sound of American bombs dropping on Hanoi.

Baez's Latina roots were largely unknown by the public until she released an album of Spanish-language songs, *Gracias a la Vida* (*Here's to Life*) in 1974. The album was her response to the downfall of the socialist presidency of Chile's Salvador Allende Gossens and the rise of a military dictatorship in its place. She dedicated the album to her father who, she wrote, "gave me my Latin name and whatever optimism about life I may claim to have."

Her crowning moment as a songwriter came four years later with the release of the best-selling album *Diamonds and Rust* (1975). The title song, her last hit pop single to date, was autobiographical and described her complicated relationship with Bob Dylan.

In the 1980s, the few albums that Baez recorded were mostly done in Europe, where she found a new and eager audience for her music. She concentrated on the concert circuit and her many social causes, which included performing at the Live Aid concert in 1985. In the 1990s, she resumed recording in the United States and was nominated for a Grammy Award for Best Contemporary Folk Recording for the album *Play Me Backwards* (1992). Her next album, *Gone from Danger* (1997), featured songs by such young gifted songwriters as Sinead Lohan, Richard Shindell, and Dar Williams.

In her music and her life, Joan Baez continues to embody the spirit and social conscience of American folk music. Her younger sister, Mimi Farina, who died of cancer in 2001, was also a well-known songwriter and folksinger.

Further Reading

Baez, Joan. *And a Voice to Sing With: A Memoir.* New York: Summit Books, 1987.

———. *Daybreak.* New York: Avon Books, 1969.

Garza, Hedda. *Joan Baez* (Hispanics of Achievement). New York: Chelsea House, 1992.

Hajdu, David. *Positively 4th Street: The Life and Times of Joan Baez, Bob Dylan, Mimi Báez Farina and Richard Farina.* New York: North Point Press, 2002.

Heller, Jeffery. *Joan Baez: A Singer with a Cause.* Chicago: Children's Press, 1991.

Further Listening

The First Ten Years (1970). Vanguard Records, CD, 1990.

Gracias a La Vida (1974). Universal/A & M, CD, 1994.

Joan Baez—Greatest Hits. A & M Records, CD, 1996.

Further Viewing

B. B. King and Joan Baez—In Concert at Sing Sing Prison, 1972. Varied Directions, DVD, 1972.

Banderas, Antonio (José Antonio Domínguez Bandera)

(1960–) *actor*

The leading Latino male box-office star in Hollywood today, Antonio Banderas has retained his reputation as a Latin heartthrob while earning respect from critics and audiences alike as a serious and versatile actor.

José Antonio Domínguez Bandera was born in Málaga, Spain, on August 10, 1960. His father was a policeman, and his mother, a schoolteacher. As a child, Banderas's dream was to become a professional soccer player. That dream ended at age 14 when he broke his foot during a soccer game. He turned his ambitions toward acting and attended the School of Drama Art in Málaga. In 1981, he was hired by the National Theatre of Spain in Madrid where he developed his acting skills playing a variety of roles in repertory. His first break came a year later when Spanish filmmaker Pedro Almodóvar saw him in a play at the National and cast him in his next film *Laberinto de pasione* (*Labyrinth of Passion*) (1982). The two men worked well together, and Almodóvar cast Banderas in four more of his films, including the screwball comedy *Woman on the Verge of a Nervous Breakdown* (1987). The film proved a breakthrough for both

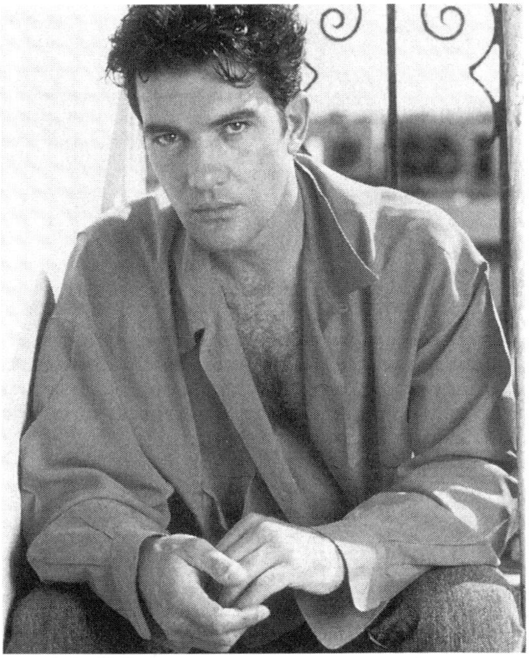

Despite his image as a Latin lover, Antonio Banderas has proven to be a serious actor, who also has a flair for comedy and self-parody. *(Photofest)*

Almodóvar and Banderas. It was an art-house film hit in the United States and was nominated for an Academy Award as Best Foreign Language Film in 1989.

On the basis of this success, Banderas decided to move to the United States and try his luck in Hollywood. In his first American film, he played himself as Madonna's love interest in her star vehicle *Truth or Dare* (1991). He had a more substantial role as a Cuban musician in New York in the 1950s in *The Mambo Kings* (1992), the film adaptation of Oscar Hijuelos's Pulitzer Prize–winning novel. Banderas did not speak English at that time and had to learn all his lines phonetically. While the film was not a hit, it boosted Banderas's image as a sexy Latin lover. Uncomfortable as many Latino screen actors before him were with this label, Banderas played against type as Tom Hanks's gay lover in the drama *Philadelphia* (1993).

He established his credentials as a leading action hero in two solid films, *Desperado* and *Assassins,* both released in 1995. *Desperado* was the second film by director ROBERT RODRIGUEZ about El Mariachi, a mysterious, guitar-playing outlaw in Mexico. In *Assassins,* Banderas was a professional hit man pitted against a top competitor, played by Sly Stallone.

Now a bona fide Hollywood star, Banderas was named one of the 50 most beautiful people in the world by *People* magazine in 1996. His marriage to Spanish actress Ana Leze, whom he married in 1988, fell apart, and in May 1996 he married American actress Melanie Griffith, his costar in the flop comedy *Two Much* (1996).

Banderas was reunited with Madonna in the long-anticipated movie version of the hit musical *Evita* (1996), based on the life of Eva Perón, wife of Argentinean dictator Juan Perón. Banderas played the pivotal role of revolutionary Che Guevara, and made an impressive debut on screen as a singer. His next major film was *The Mask of Zorro* (1998), a vastly entertaining adventure movie based on the popular masked character who fought evil in old Spanish California. Banderas managed to hold his own with costars Anthony Hopkins, as the older Zorro, and Catherine Zeta-Jones, as Hopkins's fetching, sword-wielding daughter.

Banderas's comedic abilities were more fully exhibited in another Rodriguez production, *Spy Kids* (2001). Banderas and his screen wife, Carla Gugino, played secret agents who kept their true identities from their two children. That quickly changed as the offspring became part of their next assignment. Banderas repeated his role in two successful sequels, *Spy Kids 2: The Island of Lost Dreams* (2002) and *Spy Kids 3–D: Game Over* (2003). He then completed Rodriguez's El Mariachi trilogy in the action epic *Once Upon a Time in Mexico* (2003), which reunited him with costar SALMA HAYEK. This same busy year, Banderas returned to his first love, the stage, starring on Broadway in a revival of the musical *Nine.* It was a role that was originated by another Latino actor, RAÚL JULIÁ. In October 2005, Banderas was honored with a star on the Hollywood Walk of Fame.

Banderas and Griffith have a daughter, Stella, and two children from Griffith's previous marriage to actor Don Johnson. An actor of great range, Banderas works hard at each role and has a healthy attitude toward his career. "This may sound a little harsh, but I don't care about my career," he has said. "Really, I don't like actors who are always planning what they're going to do next or always worrying about doing something that will go against the image they've created. To me, that's almost like an attack of narcissism."

Further Reading

Allison, Amy. *Antonio Banderas* (Latinos in the Limelight). New York: Chelsea House, 2001.

The Internet Movie Database. "Antonio Banderas," The Internet Movie Database. Available online. URL: http://imdb.com/name/nm0000103. Downloaded on November 30, 2004.

Tracy, Kathleen. *Antonio Banderas*. New York: St. Martin's Mass Market Paper, 1996.

Further Viewing

Desperado (1995). Columbia/Tristar Home Video, VHS/DVD, 2000/2003.

The Mark of Zorro (1998). Columbia/Tristar Home Video, VHS/DVD, 2002/2003.

Spy Kids (2001). Dimension/Walt Disney Home Video, VHS/DVD, 2004.

Barela, Patrociño

(ca. 1900–1964) santero, *folk carver*

A folk artist of great power and originality, Patrociño Barela was perhaps the first Mexican-American artist in any media to gain a national reputation. He was born into a poor Mexican family sometime around 1900 (the exact date and place of his birth are unknown).

His father Manuel emigrated from Mexico and settled in Bisbee, Arizona, where he worked as a miner in the copper mines. Patrociño's mother died when he was an infant. The family moved north to Taos, New Mexico, about 1908; there, Manuel bought a small ranch and became a shepherd, while Patrociño and his brother briefly attended school. He showed little interest in schoolwork and spent most of his time drawing and making clay models. His father saw no point in education and took his sons out of school after a few weeks. Patrociño was given the job of tending the family goats. At age 11, he ran away from home; a black family took him in as a foster child and taught him English.

After wandering from place to place and working as a shepherd, farmworker, and miner, Barela settled in Pueblo, Colorado, where he worked for seven years in a steel factory. He finally returned to New Mexico in 1930, married, and settled in Canon, just outside Taos. One day, a friend asked him to fix a damaged wooden carving of a saint, called a *santos*. Barela discovered that he had a gift for carving. Working with only a pocketknife and a chisel, he became a *santero*, a carver of wooden religious statues, a centuries-old tradition in the Southwest and Mexico. As his work matured, he turned from carving only saints to carving ordinary people but with the same expressiveness and spiritual power that he gave to his religious subjects.

In 1935, Barela began work for the Works Progress Administration's (WPA) Emergency Relief Administration hauling gravel and dirt for building in his horse-drawn wagon. A representative for the WPA's Federal Arts Project saw his carvings and was greatly impressed. He showed them to Vernon Hunter, director of the WPA in New Mexico. Hunter befriended Barela and hired him to make carvings for the Federal Arts Project (FAP). The two men became close friends.

Barela was now able to devote himself full time to his carvings in cedar and pinewood. He gained wider recognition when eight of his works were included in an exhibition of the FAP in 1936 called New Horizons in American Art, held at the prestigious Museum of Modern Art (MOMA) in New York City. *Time* magazine published a feature article about his work, calling him the "discovery of the year." MOMA went further, hailing Barela as the "most dramatic discovery made in American art for the past several years." His work was also featured at the New York World's Fair in 1939.

While Barela was part of the long Hispano (original Mexican settlers of the Southwest) heritage of New Mexico, he drew on many other influences in his work. These included the severe beauty of European romanesque art of the Middle Ages and the primitive art of the Polynesian people of the South Pacific. He was also strikingly modernistic in his bold use of semiabstract figures and negative space. Despite his sudden fame, Barela gained little monetarily from his art.

After the FAP shut down in 1943, Barela continued to create wood sculptures. New York galleries expressed interest in representing Barela's work, but because his English was poor and he could not read or write, communication was difficult. Vernon Hunter and other people tried to represent his interests, but their efforts were not successful. Unable to make a living at his art, Barela returned to shepherding. His last years were marred by alcoholism, which he battled for many years.

Patrociño Barela died tragically on October 24, 1964, in a fire that broke out in his workshop. One of his last works, a triptych (triple) carving, shows a spirit springing forth from a corpse at the moment of death.

Since his death, Barela's reputation has continued to grow. His highly personal approach to a traditional art form has had an enormous influence on many of New Mexico's contemporary Santeros. His grandson Luis was so moved after attending an exhibit of his grandfather's work in 1980 that he decided to become a carver. Today, Luis Barela is a prominent New Mexico *santero,* as is another grandson Carlos.

In 1996, the Harwood Museum of the University of New Mexico–Taos organized an ambitious traveling exhibition of Barela's work entitled *Spirit Ascendant, the Art and Life of Patrociño Barela.* Other carvings are in numerous museums including the Museum of Fine Arts in Santa Fe; the Smithsonian American Art Museum (SAAM) in Washington, D.C.; and MOMA in New York.

"His work comes from the roots of the land and Hispano society of New Mexico," wrote artist Edward Gonzales and art historian David L. Witt. "The images he made, from the erotic to the tragic to the religious, shows individuals bearing the struggles of life."

Further Reading

Congdon, Kristin G., and Kara Kelley Hallmark. *Artists from Latin American Cultures: A Biographical Dictionary.* Westport, Conn.: Greenwood Press, 2002, pp. 28–31.

Crews, Mildred T., Judson Crews, and Wendell Anderson. *Patrociño Barela: Taos Wood Carver.* Taos, N.Mex.: Taos Recordings and Publications, 1955.

Gonzales, Edward, and David L. Witt. *Spirit Ascendant, The Art and Life of Patrociño Barela.* Santa Fe, N.Mex.: Red Crane Books, 1996.

Nunn, Tey Marianna. *Sin Nombre: Hispana and Hispano Artists of the New Deal Era.* Albuquerque: University of New Mexico Press, 2001, pp. 144–149.

Yorba, Jonathan. *Arte Latino: Treasures from the Smithsonian American Art Museum.* New York: Watson–Guptill Publications, 2001, pp. 16–17.

Barretto, Ray
(Ray Bareto)

(1929–2006) *jazz and Latin percussionist, bandleader, songwriter, music director*

Credited as the first U.S.-born musician to integrate the conga drum into jazz music, Ray Barretto was in the forefront of that peculiar hybrid—Latin jazz—for more than four decades. He was born in Brooklyn, New York, on April 29, 1929, the son of Puerto Rican immigrants, and was raised from the age of four by his mother after his father left. While his mother was at night school, Ray and his siblings stayed at home alone, listening to recordings of the big bands of the 1940s. "They were our baby-sitters!" he recalls. Barretto served a hitch in the army in the early 1950s after graduating high school and was stationed in Germany. Here, he began to play the conga drums. Unlike many Latin jazz musicians, his first musical love was jazz, and he came to master the rhythms of Latin music later.

Returning home after his military service, Barretto found work playing congas in small jazz groups. His big break came in 1958 when bandleader Tito Puente hired him to replace percussionist Mongo Santamaria. Barretto stayed with Puente for four years and then formed his own group, Charanga Moderna, in 1962. He modernized the sound of traditional charanga—a style of Cuban dance music with strings, flutes, and percussion—by adding brass to the mix. The group recorded for Riverside Records but also released singles on the Tico label. One of these, an offbeat novelty instrumental "El Watusi," became a crossover top-20 pop hit in 1963. This strange record consists of two men discussing in Spanish a big mean hombre called El Watusi while Barretto's group plays a catchy if repetitive dance riff in the background. It was his only pop-charting single.

While he continued to record on his own, Barretto had great success as a session player on albums by such jazz luminaries as Dizzy Gillespie, Cannonball Adderly, West Montgomery, and Cal Tjader. He began to record for the top salsa label Fania in 1967 and later took over as the musical director of the house band, the Fania All-Stars. With this group, he made memorable recordings with a number of top Latin artists, including Celia Cruz. His duet with Cruz, "Ritmo en el Corazon," won a Grammy Award for best tropical Latin performance in 1990.

After a period of experimentation with rock and funk in the 1970s, Barretto made what many consider to be his finest album, *La Cuna* (1981) with guest players Tito Puente and Charlie Palmieri. He became musical director of the prestigious Latin music television program *Bravisimo.*

Barretto formed the Latin jazz sextet New World Spirit in 1992 and played and recorded with them until his death. In January 2006, he received the Jazz Masters Award from the National Endowment for the Arts (NEA). Two days after the induction ceremony, he suffered a heart attack and died of heart failure on February 17, 2006.

Further Reading

Chinen, Nate. "Ray Barretto, a Master of the Conga Drum, Dies at 76" [obituary]. *New York Times,* February 18, 2006, p. C11.

Jazz News. "Ray Barretto HOMAGE to Art Blakey Quartet at the Blue Note, April 8th–April 13th," All About Jazz Web Site. Available online. URL: http://www.allaboutjazz.com/php/news.php.id-2573. Downloaded on September 13, 2005.

Richard S. Ginell. "Ray Barretto: Biography," Mp3 Web Site. Available online. URL: http://www.mp3.com/ray-barretto/artists/2680/biography.html. Downloaded on August 15, 2005.

Further Listening

Best of Ray Barretto. Charly UK, CD (2 discs), 2004.

La Cuna (1981). Import [Generic], CD, 2003.

Further Viewing

Celia Cruz: Quantanamera (1974). Pioneer Video, DVD, 1998.

Bernal, Louis Carlos

(1941–1993) *photographer, educator*

One of the foremost chroniclers of Chicano culture in the Southwest, Louis Carlos Bernal's legacy lives on in the hundreds of students whom he inspired.

He was born in Douglas, Arizona, on August 18, 1941, of Mexican heritage. Drawn to photography as a young man, Bernal studied for a time with master photographer Frederick Sommer at Prescott College in Prescott, Arizona.

In 1971, Bernal was hired as a photography instructor at Pima Community College's West Campus in Tucson, Arizona, where he would teach for the next 18 years. When he was not teaching and sharing his experience with his students, Bernal was roaming the barrios of New Mexico, Arizona, and Texas with his camera. He got to know his subjects, treating them with a respect that few of them had experienced before. Bernal photographed people in their homes, surrounded by the things that they loved most—a small religious shrine, family photographs, and dusty heirlooms. He saw each subject as an individual and tried to capture the person's spirit in simple black-and-white images. It was a job that he took very serious. As he told one student, "you like to take the easy photographs, great photographers don't take the easy shots."

In 1984, Bernal, along with nine other top photographers, was invited to cover the Summer Olympic Games in Los Angeles. While others focused on capturing the athletes and the competition, Bernal was fascinated with the people in the stands, the vendors, and all the excitement, celebration, and ceremony of this special event.

Five years later, in October 1989, Bernal was riding his bicycle to Pima College when a vehicle struck him. He was seriously injured and went into a coma from which he never emerged. Four years later, on his 52nd birthday, he died. Later that year, the fine-art gallery at Pima was renamed in his honor. An annual scholarship for a photography student was also set up in his name. In 2002, a retrospective exhibit of Bernal's best work was held at the Louis Carlos Bernal Gallery. In a book of his photographs that was later published, curator and friend Ann Simmons–Myers stated: "Louis Bernal was a spirited conduit for the beauty of life in the barrio, an artist who saw portraiture as a powerful champion of the human spirit."

"The Chicano artist cannot isolate himself from the community, but finds himself in the midst of his people, creating art of and for the people," Bernal once said. "I have concerned myself with the mysticism of the Southwest, and the strength of the spiritual and cultural values of the barrio."

Bernal's work resides in the permanent collection of several museums, including the University of Arizona's Center for Creative Photography and the Palacio de Bellas Artes in Mexico City.

Further Reading

Martin, Patricia P., with Louis Carlos Bernal, photographer. *Images and Conversations: Mexican Americans Recall a Southwestern Past.* Tucson: University of Arizona Press, 1983.

Simmons-Myers, Ann, ed. *Louis Carlos Bernal: Barrios.* Tucson: University of Arizona Press, 2002.

Willett, Tom. "Artist Profile Louis Carlos Bernal," Virtual Tucson Magazine. Available online. URL: www.virtualtucsonmagazine.com/main/arts/artist/loubernal/lou.html. Downloaded on April 27, 2005.

Blades, Rubén
(Rubén Blades Bellido de Luna, "The Latino Bob Dylan")

(1948–) *Latin and salsa singer, songwriter, musician, actor, screenwriter, political activist, political administrator*

A multitalented artist of the stage, screen, concert hall, and recording studio, Rubén Blades's work is infused with a deep commitment to social and political change in Latin America and the world. He was born in Panama City, Panama, on July 16, 1948. His father, Rubén Dario Blades, was a Colombia-born conga player and a policeman. His mother, Cuba-born Anoland Benita, was a cabaret singer and met his father while performing in nightclubs. Rubén inherited his parents' love of music. While he enjoyed Latino music, he also came to love American doo-wop and rock and roll, which he listened to nightly on the radio. As a teenager, he taught himself to sing and play the guitar, but Rubén, Sr., did not want his son to pursue a career as a musician. He stressed the importance of a good education and urged Rubén to study law. His son dutifully did so, attending the University of Panama, but in his spare time, he sang with small, local bands.

By now, American domination in Central America had turned Blades against the U.S. government, and he refused to sing in English for years. He did, however, visit New York City on a school vacation and was able to record his first album there, *De Panama a Nueva York.* Returning to Panama, he completed his law degree and passed the bar exam to become a lawyer for the Bank of Panama. But music and performing was still in his blood.

In 1974, he returned to New York, this time to stay. Salsa, the spicy blending of African and Caribbean dance music, was gaining momentum in the United States among Latinos. Fania Records was the leading salsa label, and the 26-year-old lawyer took a job in the company mailroom to get his foot in the door. Fania quickly saw that Blades was a talented musician and songwriter and signed him to a recording contract. His second album for the label, *Siembra* (1978), made with trombonist Willie Colón, became a huge hit and one of the biggest-selling salsa albums ever.

Blades soon was expanding the parameters of salsa, using the music's rhythms to back lyrics, not about love and dancing, but social problems and politics. People were beginning to call him the Latino Bob Dylan. He became a champion of the *nueva canción* (New Song) movement that mixed social protest with Latin music. While this new music gained him new fans, it also made him many enemies, especially in Miami's politically conservative, fiercely patriotic Cuban-American community. Many of these Cubans had fled Castro's communist state to find freedom and prosperity in the United States. They were particularly scandalized by Blades's song "Tiburon," which sharply criticized powerful countries like the United States for interfering in the life of small developing countries. Latin radio stations in Miami banned the song, and when Blades played in Miami, he always wore a bulletproof vest.

In 1984, Blades again surprised many listeners by leaving Fania and becoming the first Latino artist to sign with a mainstream American record label, Elektra/Asylum. His first album for the label, *Buscando America* (*Searching for America*), was an innovative mix of Latin music, jazz, rock, soul, and reggae. The songs were about the difficulties of life in Latin America.

That same year, Blades made another surprising move: He temporarily halted his musical career and entered a master's program in international law at Harvard University in Massachusetts. "I needed something to humble myself," he has said, "and believe me, that school, which is no picnic, did it." When he completed his degree a year later, Blades again did the unexpected. He began to act in films. His second role, and one of his best, was egotistical New York salsa singer Rudy Veloz in *Crossover Dreams* (1985), directed by Latino filmmaker Leon Ichaso. To achieve his dream of crossover to the Anglo pop market, Veloz alienates many of his Latino friends. When his career fizzles, he is left dejected and alone, but he finds his way back to his roots.

Blades hoped to succeed where his movie character had failed. In 1988, he released his first English-language album, *Nothing But the Truth.* Critics praised the album, which included such guest artists as Lou Reed and Elvis Costello. But neither the Latino nor Anglo listening audience took to the album, and it flopped commercially. That same year, Blades scored another strong dramatic role in *The Milagro Beanfield War,* directed by actor/filmmaker Robert Redford. In other films, however, Blades found himself largely typecast as shady criminal characters (*Disorganized Crime, The Two Jakes*) or cops (*Fatal Beauty, Predator 2*).

Success in Hollywood did not cause him to forget his homeland. When the United States invaded Panama in 1989 and ousted corrupt president Manuel Noriega, Blades was opposed to American interference and said so publicly. In 1991, having returned to Panama, he founded a new reform party, *Papa Egoro* (Father Earth). Two years later, he declared himself a candidate for the presidential election of 1994. While leading politicians resented Blades's intrusion into Panamanian affairs, many ordinary people liked him, and before the election, he was leading in the polls. When election day came in May 1994, however, Blades came in second place after Ernesto Pérez Balladares although his political party did gain a number of seats in the Panamanian legislature.

Returning to the United States, Blades continued to act in films and to record his music. In 1998, he starred on Broadway with singer MARC ANTHONY in songwriter Paul Simon's ambitious $11 million musical *The Capeman.* It was the real life story of Puerto-Rican American youth Salvador Agron, who killed two white gang members in 1959 and was sentenced to death for the crime. Unfortunately, *The Capeman* was poorly received by critics and closed quickly. Blades found greater success with his own music. The album *La Rosa de los Vientos* (1996) included Panamanian musicians and songwriters, and its follow-up, *Tiempos* (1999), showed the influence of classical music on his style. Both albums won Grammys. More recently, Blades played a regular role on the short-lived dramatic television series *Gideon's Crossing* (2000) and portrayed an FBI agent in ROBERT RODRIGUEZ's action film *Once Upon a Time in Mexico* (2003).

A formidable talent who continues to remain active in a number of media, Rubén Blades moved back to Panama in 2003 and was recently appointed Panamanian minister of tourism. Reserved about his private life, Blades was married to Anglo actress Lisa Lebenzon in 1987. The couple has since divorced.

Further Reading

Cruz, Barbara C. *Rubén Blades: Salsa Singer and Social Activist.* Berkeley Heights, N.J.: Enslow Publishers, 1997.

Marton, Betty A. *Rubén Blades* (Hispanics of Achievement Series). New York: Chelsea House, 1992.

Sinnott, Susan. *Extraordinary Hispanic Americans.* Chicago: Children's Press, 1991, pp. 243–245.

Thomson Gale. "Rubén Blades," Thomson Gale, Hispanic Biographies Web Site. Available online. URL: www.galegroup.com/free_resources/chh/bio/blades_r.htm. Downloaded on April 20, 2005.

Further Listening

Rubén Blades—Greatest Hits. Fania, CD (2 discs), 2000.

Further Viewing

Crossover Dreams (1985). Congress Entertainment/New York Video, VHS/DVD, 1989/2005.

The Milagro Beanfield War (1988). Universal Home Video, VHS/DVD, 1999/2005.

Rubén Blades: The Return of Rubén Blades (1985). Winstar Home Entertainment, VHS/DVD, 2003.

Bojórquez, Charles ("Chaz")

(1949–) *painter, graffiti artist, commercial artist*

Charles Bojórquez has taken the craft of graffiti, public markings by Chicano youth, and raised it to the level of fine art. He was born in Los Angeles, California, in 1949, graduated from high school in 1967, and spent the following summer at Guadalajara University of Art in Mexico, his ancestral homeland. He returned to California to attend a state college for a year before studying at the Chouinard

Art School, now known as Cal Art. At Chouinard, he studied Asian calligraphy, the art of writing, under Chinese Master Yun Chung Chiang.

In 1969, Bojórquez began to create his own unique graffiti in the streets of East Los Angeles by blending traditional Asian calligraphy with the Los Angeles "Chalo" style graffiti inspired by gang solidarity and a strong sense of honor. He deliberately turned his back on traditional painting and gallery art for the next 15 years. "I needed to find my own voice in art that described my existence, not mentally formulated solution," he has said. "I wanted in-your-face art."

Bojórquez's graffiti did not express a message of discord and destruction that many believed. A common symbol of a skull represented not death but a spiritual rebirth. As his art developed and demanded more time and effort, Bojórquez switched from walls to the artist's canvas in 1978. The act of creating graffiti in a more formal artistic setting led Bojórquez to question the meaning of art and the public's response to it. In 1979, with his girlfriend Blade, he set off on a three-year around-the-world tour, visiting 35 countries to study in depth the culture of their art and writing.

When Bojórquez returned to the states, he continued to pursue graffiti while supporting himself with commercial art. He worked on ad campaigns and movies. His innovative movie title designs graced such films as *The Warriors, The Cheap Detective,* and parts of the *Star Wars* trilogy. He also designed logos for products such as Reebok athletic shoes and covers for music albums.

Since the 1990s, Bojórquez's art has appeared regularly in museums across the country. His paintings are noted for having the vibrant kinetic energy and deep, rich textures of his graffiti. He was one of 26 artists featured in the traveling art exhibition *Chicano Visions: American Painters on the Verge,* drawn principally from the private collection of actor/comic CHEECH MARIN, which ended its run in Chicago, Illinois, in September 2005.

"I paint names or symbols of cultural and social groups, define borders of territory, and retell conversations of conflict," Bojórquez has said. "Strengths and boundaries are what help to define us as a people, and from a local and world perspective, street language can tell us who we are and where we're going."

Further Reading

Bojórquez, Charles "Chaz." Latino Art Community Web Site. Available online. URL: http://latinoartcommunity.org/community/ChicArt/ArtistDir/ChaBoj.html. Downloaded on August 17, 2005.

———. "Los Angeles 'CHOLO' Style Graffiti Art," Graffiti Verite. Available online. URL: http://www.graffitiverite.com/cb-cholowriting.htm. Downloaded on April 24, 2005.

Yorba, Jonathan. *Arte Latino: Treasures from the Smithsonian American Art Museum.* New York: Watson–Guptill Publications, 2001, pp. 18–19.

Bratt, Benjamin
(1963–) *actor*

A handsome, virile leading man, Benjamin Bratt was one of the most visible Latino actors on television in the 1990s. He was born in San Francisco, California, on December 16, 1963, the middle son of five children. His father was a sheet metal worker of German and English descent, and his mother is a nurse and a Peruvian Indian who came to the United States at age 14 with her grandmother. A committed political activist, she taught her children to stand up against injustice and even took them to a protest that resulted in the taking over of Alcatraz prison in San Francisco Bay in 1970.

Bratt attended Lowell High School, where he excelled in athletics and endured the nickname "Scarecrow" because of his thin physique. After graduating, he studied at the University of California–Santa Barbara, where he became interested in acting and graduated with a bachelor of fine arts (B.F.A.) degree in theater. He went on to attend acting classes at the American Conservatory Theater (ACT) in San Francisco.

By 1988, Bratt was getting acting jobs in television and then landed his first film role in *One Good Cop* (1991). This and other film roles as law enforcement officers led him to be cast as Detective Rey Curtis in NBC's hit police series *Law and Order* in 1995. He left the show in 1999. Unlike many television stars who fade quickly after leaving a hit series, Bratt appeared in two high-profile films, *The Next Best Thing* and *Miss Congeniality* (both 2000) in which he costarred opposite Madonna and Sandra Bullock, respectively.

He found a more dramatic role in *Traffic* (2000), about the drug trade, directed by Steven Sodenbergh. He then surprised critics and audiences alike with his strong dramatic portrayal of real-life poet, playwright, and actor Miguel Pinero in *Pinero* (2001), directed by Latino filmmaker LEON ICHASO. More recently, Bratt has returned to more commercial fare with *Catwoman* (2004), playing opposite Oscar-winner Halle Berry. He portrayed World War II hero Henry Mucci in *The Great Raid* (2005) and starred in the television series *E-Ring* (2005), which was set in the Pentagon and costarred Dennis Hopper.

Bratt's private life has made him as well known as his work on screen. From 1997 to 2001, he dated actress Julia Roberts. He married Latina actress Talisa Soto in 2002 after meeting her during the filming of *Pinero*. They have two children, a son and a daughter. Bratt's brother Peter is a film director and producer and directed him in the movie *Follow Me Home* (1996). "My family is like a sanctuary to me," Bratt has said. "I always turn to them for support and strength."

Further Reading

The Internet Movie Database. "Benjamin Bratt," The Internet Movie Database. Available online. URL: http://www.imdb.com/name/nm0000973. Downloaded on February 2, 2005.

Rodriguez, Clara E. *Heroes, Lovers, and Others: The Story of Latinos in Hollywood.* Washington, D.C.: Smithsonian Books, 2004, pp. 233–235.

Further Viewing

Pinero (2001). Buena Vista Home Video, VHS/DVD, 2002/2005.

Brito, María

(1947–) installation and mixed-media artist, painter, sculptor

A Cuban-American artist whose installations create imaginative spaces of the body and soul, María Brito draws on her childhood and her present life as a woman in her expressive and richly symbolic art. She was born in Havana, Cuba, on October 10, 1947, and came to the United States in the wake of the Fidel Castro revolution in 1961. Unlike many other Cuban artists, she arrived in Florida alone without her family and was placed in a Miami refugee camp. Later, her family followed and her life regained some normalcy.

As a high school student, Brito was interested in art, particularly the abstract art that she saw in museums and galleries. She later attended Florida International University where she earned a bachelor of fine arts (B.F.A.) degree and a master of science (M.S.) degree. She went on to received a master of fine arts (M.F.A.) degree from the University of Miami.

Parental pressure to find a practical career moved her into the field of education. Married with children, she taught part time. She kept her interest in art, however, and attended drawing classes. Eventually, at an older age than most successful artists, she began to create her own distinctive work. By the 1980s, her work was gaining greater notice and being exhibited. She is perhaps best known for her ambitious installations, three-dimensional art that fills a room. One installation, *El Patio de Mis Casa* (*The Patio of My House,*

1990), is at first glance a typical middle-class kitchen with all the accoutrements. On closer examination, however, this kitchen has some disorientating features. Faucets and other fixtures are oddly out of place, and a baby's crib is strangely dislocated on the other side of a partition. Childhood memories haunt the present, and both the crib and the kitchen are symbols of a life that has undergone drastic change.

In another work, the mixed-media piece *Altar* (1987), a large eye mounted on a wall drips real water (tears) into a bucket that is filled to overflowing. *Self-Portrait* (1989) consists of a wheelchair with a pot holding a gnarled branch on the seat, which is meant to symbolize the subject's frustration in life.

While it often draws on her Cuban roots, Brito's art is more universal in its preoccupation than that of some Latino-American artists. She deals with struggles that face many of us, particularly women, and the roles that they often do not choose for themselves in society. "I see the installations as brackets in our reality," she has said, "the reality that we all share. . . ."

María Brito has been the recipient of a National Endowment for the Arts (NEA) Visual Artists Fellowship Grant and a Florida Arts Council Fellowship. Her solo exhibition *Las Goyescas,* based on the Spanish painter Francisco de Goya's works, appeared at the Bernice Steinbaum Gallery in Miami from September to October 2006.

Further Reading

Brito-Avellana, María. *Recent Sculptures.* New York: Museum of Contemporary Hispanic Art, 1989.

Congdon, Kristin G., and Kara Kelley Hallmark. *Artists from Latin American Cultures: A Biographical Dictionary.* Westport, Conn.: Greenwood Press, 2002, pp. 45–47.

Yorba, Jonathan. *Arte Latino: Treasures from the Smithsonian American Art Museum.* New York: Watson-Guptill Publications, 2001, pp. 20–21.

Zuver, Marc, curator. *Cuba–USA: The First Generation—In Search of Freedom.* Washington, D.C.: Fondo del Sol Visual Arts Center, 1991, pp. 32–33.

C

Camnitzer, Luis

(1937–) *installation artist. mixed-media artist, printmaker, graphic artist, writer, educator*

An artist as well known in the United States for his theories on art as for his artwork, Luis Camnitzer has been a citizen of three continents. He draws on his experiences with each culture in his conceptual, expressive work.

He was born in Lubeck, Germany, on November 6, 1937, into a Jewish family. The Camnitzers moved to Montevideo, Uruguay, when Luis was one, and he considers Uruguay his true homeland to this day. He attended the Escuela de Bellas Artes at the Universidad del Uruguay where he studied sculpture and architecture. He later received a German government grant to attend the Academy of Munich in 1957; here, he studied sculpture and printmaking. Camnitzer received the academy's Annual Printmaking Award the following year. He moved to the United States in 1964. Five years later, he began to teach art at the State University of New York (SUNY)–Old Westbury, where today he is professor of art.

When a dictatorship seized control of Uruguay in 1969, many of his old friends were imprisoned and tortured. Feeling that he had to do something to express his feelings about his homeland, Camnitzer created 35 etchings, which he called *Uruguayan Torture Series.* Rather than overtly show the torture of his countryfolk, he photographed ordinary objects and his own body parts to accompany the text. "The image and text are relatively meaningless in themselves," he has written. "Once they click together, an insight occurs about the violence. That configuration is not just about being tortured, empathizing with the victim, but also with the torturer and oneself as accomplice."

A retrospective of Camnitzer's work was shown at the Museo de Plasticas in Montevideo in 1986 and at the Venice Biennale in 1988. His first retrospective in the United States took place in 1991 at Lehman College Art Gallery in the Bronx, New York. It was entitled *They Found That Reality Had Intruded Upon the Image.*

Camnitzer is well known for his perceptive essays on the nature and purposes of art and is also the author of the well-received book *New Art of Cuba.* He was the recipient of a Guggenheim Fellowship for Visual Arts in 1982 and won first prize in an art exhibition in Tijuana, Mexico, in 1996. His art is in the permanent collections of numerous museums around the world, including the Whitney Museum of American Art in New York; the Museum of Fine Arts in Houston, Texas; the Museo Universtario, Mexico; the National Library in Jerusalem; and the Museo de Arte Moderna in Buenos Aires, Argentina.

"This art is not about me; it's about you," Camnitzer has written about his torture series. "I just set the stage."

Further Reading

Binder, Pat, and Gerhard Haupt. "Luis Camnitzer, Interview," Universes in Universe/Documenta. Available online. URL: http://universes-in-universe.de/car/documenta/11/bhf/e-camnitzer-2.htm. Downloaded on April 10, 2005.

Camnitzer, Luis. *New Art of Cuba.* Austin: University of Texas Press, 1994.

Congdon, Kristin G., and Kara Kelley Hallmark. *Artists from Latin American Cultures: A Biographical Dictionary.* Westport, Conn.: Greenwood Press, 2002, pp. 48–52.

Farver, Jane, Mari Carmen Ramirez, Gerardo Mosquera, and Luis Camnitzer. *Luis Camnitzer: Retrospective Exhibition 1966–1990.* Bronx, N.Y.: Lehman College Art Gallery, 1991.

Carey, Mariah
(Mariah Angela Carey, "Mimi" Carey)
(1970–) *pop singer, songwriter, producer*

The most successful female recording artist in the history of pop music, Mariah Carey's dazzling five-octave range, versatile artistry, and stunning good looks made her the diva of the 1990s and, since her impressive comeback, a superstar of the 2000s. She was born Mariah Angela Carey on Long Island, New York, on March 27, 1970. Her mother, an Irish-American opera singer and vocal coach, Patricia Hickey, named her after the song "They Call the Wind Mariah" from the Broadway musical *Paint Your Wagon.* Her father, aeronautical engineer Alfred Ray Carey, was part African American and part Venezuelan.

Her mother discovered her amazing singing ability when Mariah was two. She was rehearsing an opera aria when, she says, "I missed my cue, but Mariah didn't. She sang it—in Italian—at exactly the right point." She immediately began to coach her daughter in singing. Family life, however, was not all roses. Her parents separated when she was still a child, and an older sister became a prostitute.

Carey's drive to succeed in show business left her little time for school. Her friends nicknamed her "Mirage" in high school because she often missed classes. The day after graduation, she moved to New York City and supported herself with such menial jobs as sweeping hair off the floor of salons while she pursued her dream of stardom. She had begun to work as a backup singer when her big break came. Pop singer Brenda K. Starr, for whom she worked on backup, passed her demo tape on to Columbia Records head Tommy Mottola. The story goes that Mottola played the tape in his limo on the way home and was so impressed by Carey's voice that he had the driver turn around and return to the party so that he could find her.

He soon signed Carey, then 21, to a recording contract. Her first self-titled album was a monster hit and produced no less than four #1 songs—"Vision of Love," "Love Takes Time," "Someday," and "I Don't Wanna Cry." At the Grammy Awards, Carey won for Best New Artist and Best Female Vocalist.

Her next album, *Emotions* (1991), produced another #1 hit; she wrote this title song herself, as she did all her material. In June 1993, Carey wed Mottola, her mentor and boss. He was 43, she was 23. The only career glitch was her first tour, a disappointing experience. When the single "Fantasy" debuted at #1 on the pop charts in 1995, Carey became the first female singer to achieve this feat and only the second person to do so.

Unable to tolerate Mottola's abusive and controlling behavior toward her, Carey separated from him in 1997, and they later divorced. Her career continued to peak, however. By the end of the 1990s, Mariah Carey was the only recording artist to have had a chart-topping record in each year of the decade. Furthermore, she surpassed the Beatles as the artist with the most cumulative weeks at the top of the charts.

In 2000, Carey seemed destined for even greater heights when she signed an unprecedented $80 million contract with Virgin Records. But then things began to go downhill. In 2001, she suffered a nervous breakdown, much of it in public, and spent several weeks in a mental hospital. Her first Virgin release, the soundtrack of the movie *Glitter,* bombed, as did the film itself in which she starred. Carey left Virgin in 2002 and signed with Island/Def Jam Records—they gave Carey her own record label, but the resulting album, *Charmbracelet* (2002), also sold poorly.

Carey seemed to have her best days behind her when she made a stunning comeback with the album *The Emancipation of Mimi* in 2005. (Mimi is one of her nicknames.) The musical mix, which included pop and hip hop, was exciting, and more hit singles flowed from the album, including her 17th #1 song, "We Belong Together." The album and the song earned her eight Grammy nominations, and she won three, including Best Female Rhythm and Blues (R&B) Vocal Performance and Best R&B Song, both for "We Belong Together." Mariah Carey was back on top with another record to add to her long list of achievements. She now ties Elvis Presley with 17 #1 songs. Only the Beatles, with 20 top charters, have more.

Carey is active in social causes, particularly the needs of children. She is founder of Camp Mariah in Fishkill, New York, an arts center for inner-city children. She received the Horizon Award at the Congressional Foundation Awards for her work for young people.

Further Reading

Ankeny, Jason, All Music Guide. "Mariah Carey," Mp3.com. Available online. URL: http://www.mp3.com/search.php?action=Search&stype=artist&query=Mariah +Carey&x=23&y=5. Downloaded on March 2, 2006.

Nickson, Chris. *Mariah Carey Revisited: The Unauthorized Biography.* New York: St. Martin's Griffin, 1998.

Shapiro, Marc. *Mariah Carey.* Toronto, Ont.: ECW Press, 2001.

Wellman, Sam. *Mariah Carey* (Galaxy of Superstars). New York: Chelsea House, 1999.

Further Listening

The Emancipation of Mimi. Island, CD, 2005.

Mariah Carey—Greatest Hits. Sony, 2 CDs, 2001.

Further Viewing

Fantasy—Mariah Carey at Madison Square Garden (1995). Sony Home Video, VHS/DVD, 1996/2004.

Mariah Carey—Number Ones (1999). Sony, VHS/DVD, 1999/2000.

Carr, Vikki
(Florencia Bisenta de Casillas Martinez Cardona)
(1941–) *pop and Latin singer*

One of the first American pop singers to celebrate her Latino heritage in song, Vikki Carr's strong, expressive voice has made her a successful star on records and in concert for more than four decades. Florencia Bisenta de Casillas Martinez Cardona was born on July 19, 1941, in El Paso, Texas, the eldest of seven children in a Mexican-American family. The Cardonas moved to California's San Gabriel Valley when Florencia was still a small child. Her first public performance was at age four singing the Christmas carol "Adeste Fidelis" in a holiday program. Florencia sang with school bands and local groups through high school and was hired as a vocalist with Pepe Callahan's Mexican-Irish band after graduating.

As Vikki Carr, she made her solo debut in a club in Reno, Nevada, where she came to the attention of Liberty Records. The label signed her to a recording contract and in 1962 issued her first single, the teen anthem "He's a Rebel." Unfortunately, Carr's version was completely eclipsed by producer Phil Spector's version of the song, sung by the girl group the Crystals. Their version zoomed to #1 on the charts, while Carr's "He's a Rebel" flopped in the United States but became a major hit in Australia.

A modest success as a pop singer at home, Carr began to appear on Dean Martin's variety show and other television programs. Her plaintive ballad "It Must Be Him" became a #1 hit in England in 1966. The following year, it was released in the states and climbed the charts to #3, earning Carr three Grammy nominations. Two other top-40 hits followed.

A favorite at the White House, Carr sang at President Richard Nixon's inaugural ceremonies in 1973 and performed for four more presidents, including Gerald Ford who called her his "favorite Mexican dish." Carr was proud of her Mexican roots and asked Columbia Records, her new label, to allow her to make a Spanish-language album in 1972. They resisted at first, but she finally won out; *Vikki Carr en Español* became a huge seller in the Latin market. She traveled to Mexico to perform the songs and became the first nonnational to be named "Visiting Entertainer of the Year."

In 1980, Carr signed a contract with Columbia's Mexico branch and released her second Spanish album *Vikki Carr y El Amor.* It became a best seller not only in Mexico, but throughout much of Latin America. In 1985, she won the first of three Grammy Awards in Latin music categories to date for Best Mexican/American Performance for the album *Simplemente Mujer.*

Vikki Carr is well known for her continuing work for numerous charities. Since its founding in 1971, The Vikki Carr Scholarship Foundation has given college scholarships, totaling more than a quarter of a million dollars, to more than 280 deserving Latino students in her home states of Texas and California.

"I didn't like what I was reading and hearing about the image of Latinos and in particular Mexican-Americans," she has said. "The Foundation is my way of doing something."

Vikki Carr has received many awards, including the Hispanic Heritage Award in 1996 and the Texas Medal of Arts Award Lifetime Achievement Award from the Texas Cultural Trust in 2005. She is married to Dr. Pedro De Leon, her third husband.

Further Reading

Feinstein's At the Regency. "Vicki Carr," Feinstein's At the Regency Archival Web Site. Available online. URL: http://www.feinsteinsattheregency.com/biographies/carr.html. Downloaded on May 3, 2005.

Maynes, J. O. Rocky. *Hispanic Heroes of the U.S.A.: Book One.* St. Paul, Minn.: EMC Paradigm, 1976.

The Official Vikki Carr Website. http://www.vikkicarr.net. Downloaded on May 3, 2005.

Further Listening

Simplemente Mujer (1985). Sony International, CD, 1989.

Vikki Carr—Greatest Hits. Curb Records, CD, 1994.

Carrillo, Charles M.
(Charlie Carrillo)

(1956–) santero, *educator, anthropologist, art historian, writer*

A celebrated contemporary carver of devotional art in the *santero* tradition, Charles M. Carrillo is a serious student of Mexican-American culture and art who has educated the public about these subjects with his books, articles, and teaching. He was born in Albuquerque, New Mexico, on January 18, 1956.

Carrillo was attracted to the art of his people and their churches from an early age. He attended the University of New Mexico–Albuquerque where he earned a doctoral (Ph.D.) degree in anthropology, the study of human physical, cultural, and social development.

He was inspired to become a *santero* (a maker of religious carvings) during an archaeological "dig" of which he was in charge at La Capilla de

Santa Rosa de Lima in Abiquiu, New Mexico, in 1977. The *retablos,* flat pictures of saints, and *bultos,* three-dimensional statues of them, moved him deeply. Shortly after returning from Abiquiu, Carrillo began to create his own *retablos* and *bultos,* employing the same traditional methods of the artists of the colonial period.

While an intellectual and academic, Carrillo's religious fervor expressed in his religious carvings is as strong and sustaining as that of any of the simple, uneducated folk artists who preceded him in the *Santero* tradition. "If I truly didn't believe in it [Christianity], I couldn't do it," he has said. "If you don't believe, you are just a painter of images."

Carrillo's work also includes *reredos,* altar screens. One of his best-known works is the *reredos Devocion de Nuevo Mexico,* which is in the classic 19th century tradition and is painted with natural pigments from plants and minerals. Carrillo has shown his work at the Spanish Market in Santa Fe, New Mexico, where he has lived since the 1980s. His religious works are part of the permanent collections of the Denver Art Museum, the Albuquerque Museum, and the Museum of Spanish Colonial Art in Santa Fe. Among his most recent shows is *Santos of the Pueblos* (2004), exhibted at the new gallery of the Indian Pueblo Cultural Center in Albuquerque. Among the awards he has won for his art is the 2000 New Directions Award at the Spanish Market and the 2002 New Mexico Arts & Crafts Festival Poster Award.

Charles M. Carrillo has written books on New Mexican pottery and art and is the author of many scholarly articles. He is the adjunct professor in the University of New Mexico's Religious Studies Program. His wife Debbie is a well-known potter, and his children Estrellita and Roan are talented *Santeros* in their own right.

Further Reading

Awalt, Barbe, Paul Rhetts, and Diane Pardue. *Charlie Carrillo: Tradition and Soul.* Albuquerque, N.Mex.: LPD Press, 1995.

Carrillo, Charles M., and Jose Antonio Esquibel. *A Tapestry of Kinship: The Web of Influence Among Escultores and Carpineros in the Parish of Santa Fe, 1790–1860.* Albuquerque, N.Mex.: LPD Press, 2004.

Rosenak, Chuck, and Jan Rosenak. *The Saint Makers: Contemporary Santeras y Santeros.* Flagstaff, Ariz.: Northland Publishing, 1998.

Yorba, Jonathan. *Arte Latino: Treasures from the Smithsonian American Art Museum.* New York: Watson–Guptill, 2001, pp. 26–27.

Carrillo, Leo

(1880–1961) *actor, comedian*

A leading character actor in Hollywood's Golden Age, Leo Carrillo ended a long career as the costar in one of television's first and most successful Westerns, *The Cisco Kid.* He was born in Los Angeles, California, on August 6, 1880, into a distinguished Hispano family that traced its lineage back to the first Spanish conquistadores. His great-grandfather was the first provisional governor of California, and his father was the first mayor of the city of Santa Monica.

Carrillo attended St. Vincent's College in Los Angeles where he studied engineering but on graduation got a job as a political cartoonist for the *San Francisco Examiner.* Acting, however, was his first love, and he soon became a comedian on the vaudeville stage. At the time, ethnic stereotypes were popular, and Carrillo played the stereotypical funny Mexican with a bewildering array of accents and dialects. In the late 1920s, he moved into film work.

The parts he played in dozens of films of the 1930s and 1940s were often stereotyped Mexican banditos and comic characters. He always brought to each role, however, a strong sense of humanity and individuality. One of his best roles was as a Mexican bandit leader who wants to modernize his operation in director Rouben Mamoulian's musical-comedy film *The Gay Desperado* (1936). He also had strong supporting roles in such prestigious pictures as the romantic drama *History Is Made at Night* (1937) and *The Fugitive* (1947), an adaptation of a Graham Greene novel directed by John Ford.

Carrillo made his last film in 1950 and then ventured into the new medium of television. He played Pancho, the jovial sidekick of *The Cisco Kid,* the first action/adventure TV show to feature two Latinos in leading roles.

Carrillo was in his seventies when he took on the demanding work of a weekly television series. Despite the friendly relationship between Pancho and Cisco, played by DUNCAN RENALDO, off-screen the two stars did not get along. Carrillo demanded that he get as much screen time as Renaldo and that his costar could never give him a direct order in the show. So when Pancho went into town to check out the bad guys, he usually did so on his own volition. *The Cisco Kid* ran until 1955 and enjoyed a long life in reruns for many years, thanks to the foresight of its producer, Frederick Ziv, who filmed it in color.

Leo Carrillo died of cancer in Santa Monica, California, on September 10, 1961. A fine actor and a man of taste and culture, Carrillo was an active member of the Latino community and served on the California Park and Recreation Commission for years. The Leo Carrillo State Park and Leo Carrillo Beach in Los Angeles County are named in his honor.

Further Reading

Carrillo, Leo. *The California I Love.* Englewood Cliffs, N.J.: Prentice Hall, 1961.

Katz, Ephraim, Fred Klein, and Ronald Dean Nolen. *The Film Encyclopedia,* 4th edition. New York: HarperResource, 2001, p. 229.

May, Dale Ballou. *The Adobe Is My Birthstone: Leo Carrillo's Rancho de los Quiotes: A Reflection on the Man, His Era, and His Career.* San Diego: D.B. May, 1988.

Further Viewing

The Cisco Kid—Collection 1 (1950–1956). MPI Media Group, DVD (2 discs), 2004.

The Gay Desperado (1936). Tapeworm/Image Entertainment, VHS/DVD, 2000/2001.

Carter, Lynda (Linda Jean Córdoba Carter)

(1951–) *actress, pop singer*

Lynda Carter sprang to fame in the mid–1970s as the embodiment of television's most famous female superhero, and it remains the role for which she is best known. Linda Jean Córdoba Carter was born in Phoenix, Arizona, on July 24, 1951, to an Anglo father and Mexican mother. In high school, she took parts in plays and sang in a student band called the Relatives. After graduation, she went to Arizona State University but left after only one semester to pursue a career as a singer. Carter sang in several bands, most notably Just Us, with whom she toured England in 1970.

She returned to Arizona in 1972 and entered a local citywide beauty contest. Her statuesque beauty earned her the title Miss Phoenix, and when she entered the Miss World contest, she represented her country as Miss U.S.A.

Fresh from this accomplishment, Carter moved to New York City and took some acting lessons. She returned to the West Coast where she played small guest roles on several television series. In 1975, she auditioned for the leading role in the new *Wonder Woman* series and won it. A comic book superhero who first appeared in 1941, *Wonder Woman* had been adapted to television several times in the past but always unsuccessfully.

Carter shot a pilot film for *The New Original Wonder Woman,* and it debuted on the American Broadcasting Company (ABC) television network in November 1975. ABC liked the show's good ratings but was concerned that Carter in her revealing costume was too sexy for a program that would attract many young viewers. Carter was finally considered "fit" for the family hour, and the show debuted in spring 1976. *Wonder Woman* was a hit almost immediately. The World War II settings that harked back to the original comic books were nostalgic, and Carter was spectacular in the role. She worked herself into top shape so that she could perform many of her own stunts in the show. She even became a vegetarian to improve her health.

Wonder Woman was akin to an Amazon warrior but was armed with bullet-stopping bracelets and a magic lasso that forced villains to tell the truth. Under the guise of Diana Prince, an army secretary, she battled Nazis of every ilk, including an enemy Wonder Woman and a circus gorilla. Her sometimes assistant, Wonder Girl, was played by a very young Debra Winger, who would later become a major movie star.

Despite great ratings, ABC lost interest in the show after the first season, and it moved to the Columbia Broadcasting System (CBS). The series was renamed *The New Adventures of Wonder Woman,* and the action was moved forward to the 1970s, losing some of the original show's charm. It lasted one more season before being canceled.

Carter's fame as Wonder Woman earned her slots in a series of television musical variety specials in the early 1980s. She had released her first solo album, *Portraits,* in 1978. In 1983, she portrayed screen goddess Rita Hayworth in a made-for-television movie. She attempted two more television series, but both folded quickly.

Since then, Carter has appeared infrequently on television and has devoted herself to charity work and the social life of Washington, D.C., where she lives with her second husband, lawyer Robert Altman, and their two children. In September 2005, she played a con artist on companion episodes of *Law & Order* and *Law & Order: Special Victims Unit.*

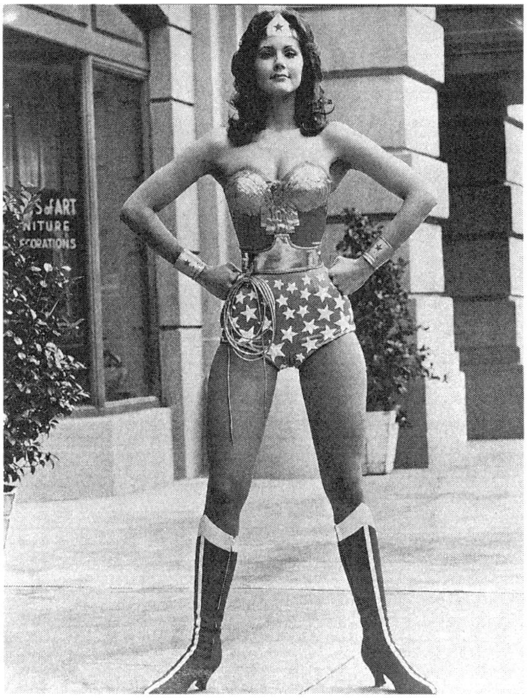

Lynda Carter strikes a heroic stance in the role for which she will always be remembered—television's Wonder Woman. *(Photofest)*

Further Reading

Cult Sirens. "Lynda Carter," Cult Sirens Web Site. Available online. URL: http://www.cultsirens.com/carter/carter.htm. Downloaded on May 3, 2005.

The Internet Movie Database. "Lynda Carter," The Internet Movie Database. Available online. URL: http://www.imdb.com/name/nm0004812. Downloaded on December 11, 2004.

Further Viewing

Wonder Woman—The Complete First Season (1976). Warner Home Video, DVD box set, 2004.

Casas, Mel
(Melesio Casas)
(1929–) *painter, educator, writer*

One of the elder statesmen of the Chicano movement of the 1960s and 1970s, Mel Casas has lost none of his wit and bite as a social critic and artist over the years. Melesio Casas was born in El Paso, Texas, on November 24, 1929. Both his parents emigrated from Mexico to the United States. His mother's ethnic background was Mexican Indian, French, and Spanish.

As a youth, Casas got a firsthand look of how two societies existed in his city—one, middle class and white, and the other, poor and Chicano (Mexican American). After completing high school, he joined the army and fought in the Korean War (1950–53), during which he was injured. He returned to the states and attended Texas Western, now the University of Texas–El Paso (UTEP), where he earned a bachelor of arts (B.A.) degree. Casas completed a master of fine arts (M.F.A.) degree from the University of the Americas in Mexico.

Casas settled in San Antonio, Texas, where he became involved with the Chicano movement and joined other Mexican-American artists whose artwork celebrated their heritage, often with heavy political overtones. To support his family—a wife and five children—Casas taught art at San Antonio College and was a book reviewer for the American Library Association's (ALA) *Choice Magazine.*

While his work is often very political in nature, he uses humor and satire to make his points. The humanscape series depicts the human body as if it were a landscape. In *Humanscape 63 (Show of Hands)* (1970), Casas recreates Michelangelo's masterpiece *The Creation of Man* from the Vatican's Sistine Chapel. In Casas's version, however, God's fingertips are tickled by a middle finger, while other hands extend out from the painting. "Here," writes one critic, "the naïvete of the image is rooted in its emotional rawness and the artist's willingness to juxtapose the sacred with the vulgar."

In other humanscapes, Casas presents images projected onto a drive-in movie screen, using this intriguing format to cast a critical and witty eye on various media, including film and advertising. Author Jonathan Yorba has called Casas "a trenchant cultural critic who conveys the message of an oppressive world."

A restless artist who is always looking for new challenges, Casas once stated when discussing a new project in an interview: "I start working with them, and I don't know what's going to happen, how they're going to come out. But I enjoy the new form because it allows me new aesthetic dangers to play with, and I don't know what's going to happen until I start doing it." Mel Casas is professor emeritus of art, design, and painting at San Antonio College.

Further Reading

Cancel, Luis R., et al. *The Latin American Spirit: Art and Artists in the United States, 1920–1970.* New York: The Bronx Museum of the Arts and Harry N. Abrams, 1988, p. 314.

Karlstrom, Paul. "Oral History Interview with Mel Casas," Smithsonian Archives of American Art. Available online. URL: http://archivesofamericanart.si.edu/oralhist/casas96.htm. Downloaded on May 1, 2005.

Quirarte, Jacinot. *Mexican American Art.* Austin: University of Texas Press, 1973, pp. 80–85.

Yorba, Jonathan. *Arte Latino: Treasures from the Smithsonian American Art Museum.* New York: Watson–Guptill Publications. 2001, pp. 28–29.

Castellanos, Carlos
(Carlos Castellanos Gómez)
(1961–) *cartoonist, illustrator*

Cocreator of the first syndicated comic strip about a Latino American by Latino Americans, Carlos Castellanos has also applied his cartooning talents to magazines, books, and advertisements. He was born in Guines, Havana Province, Cuba, on January 5, 1961. His inspiration to become a cartoonist came from seeing the character of Darren on the 1960s television sitcom *Bewitched,* who was a commercial artist. In 1981, while attending college, Castellanos began his career as a freelance illustrator.

In spring 1998, his friend Hector Cantu, associate feature editor at the *Dallas Morning News,* called him with the idea of collaborating on a comic strip about a Latino-American youth. The character they created, Baldo Bermudez, was a 15-year-old male who was caught between two cultures—that of the United States and of Latin America.

The two friends—artist and writer—worked up a month's worth of daily comic strips and sent them to numerous newspaper syndicates. Universal Press Syndicate was intrigued by the humorous strip and signed the team to a contract. *Baldo* debuted in nearly 100 newspapers in April 2000. Only three other strips in the history of Universal Press Syndicate had started with a larger circulation.

Baldo's wry and gentle humor has earned it a faithful following among both Latino and non-Latino readers. Castellanos and Cantu felt it important that Baldo have a prominent parental male figure in his life. The father–son relationship is made more intense because there is no mother present. The rest of *Baldo*'s supporting cast includes his young but wise-beyond-her-years sister Gracie, his best friend Cruz, and Tia (Aunt) Carmen who comes from the old country and lives with the family.

"Working as a humorous illustrator is very gratifying given the scope and variety of projects I get to work on," says Castellanos. "Working on *Baldo* is particularly gratifying for me in the sense that it allows me to create work that's more meaningful and personal. I'm having a blast! The support we've received from people everywhere through the years has been amazing. We hope to continue creating material that connects with people for years to come."

The Spanish-language television network Univision began work on an animated series based on *Baldo* in 2002. As of September 2006, 13 half hour episodes have been shot in Spanish and English. Castellanos and Cantu are currently looking for another distributor. Besides drawing *Baldo,* Castellanos continues to create illustrations for numerous clients including Kentucky Fried Chicken (KFC), Scholastic, Inc., and *Sports* magazine. He is also working on several personal book and television projects. Carlos Castellanos lives in West Palm Beach, Florida, with his wife and two sons.

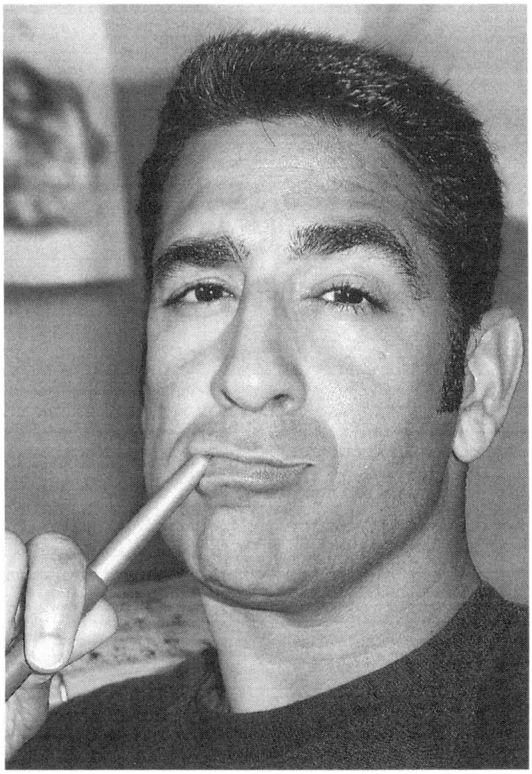

Cartoonist Carlos Castellanos's comic *Baldo* is the first U.S. syndicated comic strip about a Latino American. *(Carlos Castellanos)*

Further Reading

Cantu, Hector, and Carlos Castellanos. *The Lower You Ride, The Cooler You Are: A Baldo Collection.* Kansas City, Mo.: Andrews McMeel Publishing, 2001.

———. *Night of the Bilingual Telemarketers: A Baldo Collection.* Kansas City, Mo.: Andrews McMeel Publishing, 2002.

Carlos Castellano Illustration. Available online. URL: http://www.carloscastellanos.com. Downloaded on August 23, 2005.

The Official Baldo Web Site. Baldocomics.com. Available online. URL: http://www.baldocomics.com. Downloaded on November 28, 2004.

Charo

(María del Rosario Pilar Martínez Molina Baeza de Rasten, "The Cuchi-Cuchi Girl")

(1941–) *singer, dancer, guitarist, television personality, actress*

A talented woman who perfected playing the part as a stereotypical comic Latina beauty, Charo was one of the most visible television personalities of the 1960s and 1970s. Behind the playacting, she was, in fact, a highly accomplished classical and flamenco guitarist.

María del Rosario Pilar Martínez Molina Baeza was born in Murcia, Spain, on March 13, 1941. Her father was a lawyer whose opposition to Spanish dictator Francisco Franco led to his exile to Casablanca, Morocco, for many years. María attended a Catholic convent where she learned to play the guitar at age nine. When she was 14, she won a scholarship to study classical guitar with the Spanish master of the form, Andrés Segovia.

Besides playing the guitar, María enjoyed singing and at 16 was discovered by bandleader XAVIER CUGAT. Cugat brought her with her mother and sister to the United States to sing in his band. But because she was still a minor, María had to return to Spain for two years.

Cugat was smitten with the Spanish beauty and married her in August 1966 at Caesars Palace in Las Vegas. He was 41 years her senior. As Cugat's wife and lead vocalist, Charo received great publicity and took full advantage of it. In the long tradition of such Latina actresses as LUPE VÉLEZ and CARMEN MIRANDA, she played the part of the comic, scatterbrained Latina beauty. She quickly became a favorite on the television talk-show circuit and the popular game show *Hollywood Squares.* Her trademark phrase *"Cuchi-Cuchi"* was based on a childhood dog Cuchillo. When "Cuchi" was happy, he wiggled, and Charo repeated the movement to great effect. "Everybody thought that it was very cute when [as a child] I wiggled and say *Cuchi-Cuchi,* and they give me cookies and candy," she once explained. "Now, every time I say *Cuchi-Cuchi,* people give me money."

While she developed into a world-class flamenco guitarist and won *Guitar* magazine's readers' poll as Best Flamenco Guitarist two years in a row, most Americans knew her as the *"Cuchi-Cuchi girl"* on television. Her acting roles were limited to guest shots on a few television sitcoms and a handful of movies, including the all-star disaster film *Concorde: Airport '79* (1979).

Charo became a U.S. citizen in 1977 and divorced Cugat the following year. She married Kjell Rasten, and the couple had a son, Shel. The family moved in the 1990s to Hawaii, where Charo performed regularly at the Polynesian Palace in Honolulu and other hotels. Her son studied philosophy at the University of Southern California (USC). In 1994, she released the highly regarded album of classical and flamenco guitar pieces *Guitar Passion.*

Recently, Charo and her husband moved back to southern California. In November 2001, she opened in her own show in Las Vegas, Nevada. More recently she has resurfaced on U.S. television, appearing on VH1's *The Surreal Life* and in a commercial for GEICO car insurance.

Further Reading

Charo's Official Web Site. Available online. URL: http://www.charo.com/index2.html. Downloaded on September 14, 2006.

The Internet Movie Database. "Charo." The Internet Movie Database. Available on line. URL: http://www.imdb.com/name/nm0004819/. Downloaded on February 5, 2005.

Rivera, Lilliam. "Que les Paso? Latino Celebrities of the Seventies and Eighties Were Part of Our Lives and a Source of Pride." *Latina,* September 22, 1996, p. 96.

Further Listening

Guitar Passion. Universal Wave, CD, 1994.

Cisneros, Evelyn
(Evelyn Cisneros-Legate)
(1958–) *ballet dancer, educator, writer*

Latina-American prima ballerina Evelyn Cisneros is celebrated for her grace, power, and exotic beauty on stage. Born in Long Beach, California, on November 18, 1958, Evelyn had grandparents who were migrant workers from Mexico. The Cisneroses moved to Huntington Beach, where Evelyn was the only Mexican American in her elementary school class. The teasing she experienced at the hands of thoughtless classmates led her to withdraw into herself. To counter her shyness and give her some confidence, her mother began to take her to ballet lessons at a local shopping center. Evelyn made her mother promise that if she did not like ballet, she could quit after a year.

Evelyn's teacher, Phyllis Sear, soon recognized her gifts as a dancer and began to give her daily lessons. Her confidence turned the young dancer into a school athlete. She played volleyball and basketball and other sports, but at age 13, she had to decide whether to continue with sports or to devote all her energies to ballet. "There was this fire inside my heart that burned with the desire—the need—to dance," she later recalled.

By age 14, she was teaching beginning ballet classes, attending advanced classes, and dancing regularly with the Pacific Ballet Theatre in Los Angeles.

After auditioning for the prestigious San Francisco Ballet's (SFB) School, Cisneros was given a full scholarship for a summer session. She was made an apprentice at the SFB at age 16 and moved to San Francisco the following year. At 18, she achieved the goal to which every aspiring dancer dreams and became a principal ballerina with the company. Artistic director Michael Smuin soon created a new ballet specifically for Cisneros to dance: "A Song for Dead Warriors" and dealt with the injustices done to American Indians.

During the next two decades, Cisneros performed nearly every principal role in the SFB repertoire, including Miranda in *The Tempest,* Juliet in *Romeo and Juliet,* Princess Aurora in *Sleeping Beauty,* and the Sugar Plum Fairy in *The Nutcracker.*

"She is unashamedly theatrical in so-called abstract ballet, technically dazzling in narrative dances, womanly-irresistible in every move she makes," wrote Octavio Roca, dance critic of the *San Francisco Chronicle.* In 1982, she performed at the White House for President Ronald Reagan and Nancy Reagan. She has performed in Mexico and Spain and at the International Ballet Festivals in New Zealand (1990) and Havana, Cuba (1984 and 1988).

Among the many awards that Cisneros has received during her career are the Most Gifted Women Award in the San Francisco Bay area (1991), the Isadora Duncan Performer's Award given by the Bay Area Dance Coalition for Outstanding Performance (1989), and Achievement Award for Hispanic Women Making History (1984). She has honorary degrees from Mills College, Oakland, California, and California State University–Monterrey Bay.

Evelyn Cisneros retired from dance in January 1999 at age 40 to have a family with her third husband, fellow dancer Stephen Legate. They have two children. In November 2001, Cisneros was appointed ballet education coordinator in the SFB's education department. She also continues to work as a public speaker, a teacher, and a member of the advisory board of the Smuin Ballet/San Francisco. When she speaks at schools about her life in dance, she urges students, especially Latino-American students, to work hard to achieve their dreams. Cisneros is also the coauthor of *Ballet for Dummies* with conductor Scott Speck and hosts a Public Broadcasting System (PBS) documentary series about San Francisco neighborhoods, *Bay Windows*. She has even found time to dance in a music video by rock performer CARLOS SANTANA. In summer 2006, Cisneros was appointed academy director of Ballet Pacifica in Irvine, California.

At the time of her retirement from ballet, Cisneros said, "I am just so grateful that I have been able to do so much, more than I ever dreamed I could do, that I had such joy. That is the one thing I hope people go away with: the joy I have tried to share with the audience."

Further Reading

"Evelyn Cisneros." Ballet CD-ROM Web site. Available online. URL: http://www.pav.org/evelyn.htm. Downloaded on June 6, 2005.

Gale, Thomson. "Evelyn Cisneros." Thomson Gale Biography Online. Available online. URL: http://www.galegroup.com/free_resources/chh/bio/cisneros_e.htm. Downloaded on June 6, 2005.

Roca, Octavio. "Bowing Out Gracefully After 23 years, S.F. Ballet's Evelyn Cisneros dances her final season." The San Francisco Chronicle Online. Available online. URL: http://sfgate.com/cgi-bin/article.cgi?f=/c/a/1999/01/24/PK86713.DTL&hw=Eveyln+Cisneros&sn=001&sc=1000. Downloaded on August 23, 2005.

Ulrich, Allan. "Setting the Next Stage: Evelyn Cisneros Left Performing Ballet, But Not Her Dedication to Ballet." *Dance,* September 2004, pp. 26C–29C.

Climent, Elena
(1955–) *painter*

An artist whose small, intimate paintings of domestic life evoke a rich past and vivid childhood memories, Elena Climent recalls her Mexican upbringing in much of her work. She was born in Mexico City on March 6, 1955. Her father Enrique was a Spanish artist who fled his homeland during the Spanish Civil War. He settled in Mexico in 1939. Her mother Helen, a Jewish American, was raised in Brooklyn, New York.

When she was 16, Elena decided she wanted to follow in her father's footsteps and become an artist. Her father encouraged her talent but believed that formal training would hinder her creativity. Nevertheless, she studied in Mexico City and later in Valencia and Barcelona in Spain.

Climent had the first exhibition of her paintings at a Mexico City gallery in 1972. Later, she moved to New York City, where she lives today with her husband, Claudio Lomnitz, a college professor from Chile.

Climent is best known for her still lifes of everyday objects—photographs, plants, toys, and home altars, usually set in Mexico. She sketches her compositions in pencil and then paints them in oil. Her style falls somewhere between the precision of photo realism and realism.

One of her most celebrated series of paintings revolves around her childhood and her parents. When her mother died in 1994 (her father had died some years earlier), Climent was drawn to return to the Mexico City house in which she was raised. She spent a week there by herself, painting and taking photographs of things she would paint from the photos later.

The paintings were unique in that they depicted intimate spaces and not just household objects. Corners, shelves, and dresser drawers were lovingly captured as warm memories of her childhood in the house. Climent recreated them not only to celebrate the past, but also to come to terms with it. In their

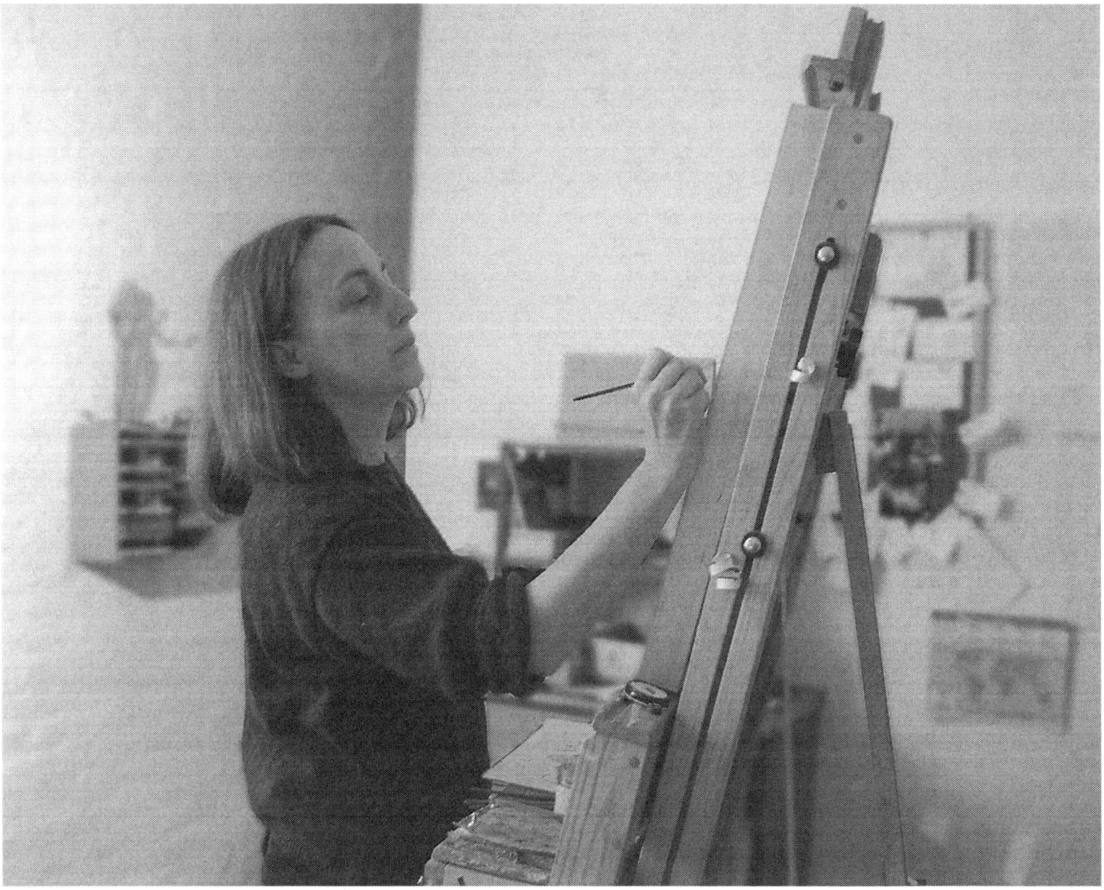

Elena Climent recalls her Mexican childhood in her intimate, domestic paintings. *(Mónica Herrera)*

quiet, intense way, the 35 paintings in this exhibit, called *To My Parents,* were meant to convey an acceptance of her parents' deaths and also her own aging from a child to a middle-aged woman. The series was exhibited at the Mary-Anne Martin/Fine Art Gallery in New York City in 1997.

More recent exhibitions have included *Latin American Still Life: Reflections of Time and Place* at the Katonah Museum of Art in New York (1999); *Windows from Here to Then* at the Mary Anne Martin/Fine Art Gallery (2000); and *Ventanas de la memoria* at the National Hispanic Cultural Center of New Mexico in Albuquerque (2001). Climent's work also appears in the permanent collections of the Milwaukee Art Museum, the Phoenix Art Museum, and elsewhere.

"I think wherever we are we reproduce ourselves," Climent wrote in notes for her *Windows from Here to Then* show. "People reflect themselves by their surroundings. We create an order around us, a mirror of what we are. I'm fascinated by what objects absorb of people."

Further Reading

AskArt. "Elena Climent." AskArt Web Site. Available online. URL: http://askart.com/biography.

asp?ID=107079. Downloaded on February 1, 2005.

Climent, Elena. *Windows from Here to There: June 7–June 29, 2000.* New York: Mary-Anne Martin/Fine Arts, 2000.

Mam/fa Newletter. "News of Elena Climent." Mam/fa newsletter Web Site. Available online. URL: http://www.mamfa.com/news/win96/elena.htm. Downloaded on May 1, 2005.

Sullivan, Edward J. "Elena Climent at Mary-Anne Martin—New York, New York." *Art in America,* December 1997, p. 97.

Colón, Willie
(William Anthony Colón Román)
(1950–) *jazz and Latin trombonist, singer, bandleader, composer, arranger, record producer*

One of the true pioneers of modern Latin jazz and salsa music, Willie Colón has been making and producing records and live music for nearly four decades. William Anthony Colón Román was born in the Bronx, New York, on April 28, 1950. His grandparents were Puerto Rican immigrants, and he learned his first songs from his grandmother, who sang him to sleep. At 12, he began to study the trumpet, but he switched to the trombone when he was 14. Three years later, the precocious young musician made his first recording for Futura Records, but the company folded before it could promote Colón's music. Soon after, he signed with Fania Records, the most successful Latin music label in New York City. Colón changed the sound of Latin music by using the trombone, not the trumpet or flute, as a lead instrument in his band and bringing in the harmonies and solo playing of jazz. The new, exciting music he made came to be called the New York Sound.

At his first Fania recording session, the vocalist did not show up, and Johnny Pacheo, owner of Fania, suggested that Colón use Puerto Rican–born singer Héctor Lavoe instead. Lavoe's distinctive voice and Colón's lively music blended well together and produced two hit singles for the Latin market, "Jazzy" and "I Wish I Had a Watermelon." Lavoe was Colón's regular vocalist through 1975 when drug addiction interrupted his career. Singer and songwriter RUBÉN BLADES, who had become friends with Colón, replaced Lavoe, leading to an even more spectacular collaboration. Their 1978 album *Siembra* was a brilliant album that solidified the New York Sound and became Fania's biggest selling record ever. When the two men worked together again in 1981, they produced *Canciones del Solar de los Aburridos,* which earned Colón his first and, to date, only Grammy Award, although he has been nominated 11 times.

Colón and Blades even costarred in a film, *The Last Fight* (1983), a boxing film. Differences on the set led to a split between the two friends, and they did not reunite on stage until a concert in San Juan, Puerto Rico, in March 1992. Since then, they have performed together numerous times.

Colón formed a new group, Legal Aliens, in the late 1980s, with several young, talented musicians. They recorded a few albums for the Sony label and still play as a group today.

Colón's music has earned him many awards. In 1991, he received Yale University's Chubb Fellowship, that institution's highest tribute. He performed at the Presidential Inaugural Ceremonies in 1993 and was invited the following year by President Bill Clinton to join the President's Committee on the Arts and Humanities. He turned down this honor to run as a Democratic candidate in the 17th Congressional District of New York State. In 1996, Colón was named one of the One Hundred Most Influential U.S. Hispanics by *Hispanic Business Magazine.* Still as committed to his music as he is to social issues and the political process, Willie Colón lives with his wife Julia and their four sons in New York City.

Further Reading

Harris, Craig. "Willie Colón," The Mp3 Web Site. Available online. URL: http://www.mp3.com/willie-colon/artists/2720/biography.html. Downloaded on September 14, 2005.

Steward, Sue, with foreword by Willie Colón. *Musica! Salsa, Rumba, Merengue, and More.* Collingdale, Pa.: Diane Publishing Company, 1999.

Willie Colón Official Web Site. Available online. URL: http://williecolon.com/work.htm. Downloaded on March 31, 2006.

Further Listening

Conciones del Solos de los Aburrides (1981). Fania Records, CD, 2000.

Siembra—Willie Colón and Rubén Blades. Fania Records, CD, 1992.

Willie Colón—The Best. Fania Records, CD, 2003.

Cruz, Celia
(Úrsula Hilaria Celia Caridad Cruz Alfonso, "The Queen of Salsa")
(1924–2003) *Latin and salsa singer*

The voice of Latin music and the queen of salsa for more than a half century, Celia Cruz remains an icon of Latino culture and spirit for several generations of listeners. Úrsula Hilaria Celia Caridad Cruz Alfonso was born in Santa Suárez, a poor section of Havana, Cuba, on October 21, 1924. There were 14 children in their family, including a number of cousins.

Celia often cared for her younger siblings and sang them to sleep. Her cousin took her to a radio talent contest, and she sang a song, winning first prize—a cake. Encouraged by her mother, Cruz entered other talent contests. She would travel from town to town on streetcars. When her money ran out, she would walk home from a competition.

Her father insisted that she pursue a more stable career path. She briefly attended a teacher's college, but she left when she was given enough work singing live on radio programs. For a time, she studied at the National Conservatory of Music in Havana.

Cruz's big break came in 1950 when she was hired as lead singer for La Sonora Matancera, Cuba's most successful big band. During the next decade, Cruz toured constantly, traveling to Mexico, Central America, and North America; she appeared on Cuban television and sang in Havana's top nightclubs. Her hallmark as a singer was a powerful raspy voice that could be heard above the strong percussive Latin rhythms of the band. This same voice, however, could express the most delicate of emotions.

Unhappy with the communist regime of Fidel Castro that took power in 1959, Cruz fled while on tour in Mexico the following year. Unlike many Cuban emigrants who settled in the Miami area, Cruz went north to live in New York City and became a U.S. citizen. In 1962, she moved to Fort Lee, New Jersey, where she lived for the rest of her life. Castro never forgave her for leaving Cuba and refused to let her return to her homeland, even for the funerals of her parents.

In 1962, she married Pedro Knight, trumpeter of Le Sonora Matancera. He became her manager and musical director. Cruz only slowly gained the popularity in the United States that she had enjoyed in Cuba. Unlike other Latin musicians and singers, she had little interest in making the crossover to an Anglo audience. She refused to sing in English, insisting that her English was not good enough, although she was quite fluent.

But Cuban Americans came to love her music, her flamboyant stage costumes, and her energetic performances onstage and in recordings. She expanded her Latin audience by adding Puerto Rican and Dominican music to her repertoire; both nationalities had sizable populations in the Northeast.

Cruz also proved that she could change with the times—forsaking the big Latin bands in the 1960s for the new, upcoming salsa bands who played this unique musical blend of traditional Afro-Caribbean rhythm and American jazz. She sang with TITO PUENTE, Johnny Pacheo, RAY BARRETTO, and WILLIE COLÓN, both live and on recordings that sold well.

Onstage, she was a human dynamo, dressed in colorful costumes, working the audience into a frenzy with her cry of "*¡Azúcar!*" ("sugar" in Spanish), and getting them to talk back to her in a call and response. Her trademark cry originated in the 1970s when a waiter in a Miami restaurant asked her if she wanted sugar in her coffee. "Chico," she replied, "you're Cuban. How can you even ask that? With sugar!" She repeated the story that night in her show, and the word gradually became an onstage trademark.

In 1973, Cruz signed with Fania, New York's top salsa record label, and began to record with the Fania All-Stars, a top group of Latin musicians. Their chemistry was perfectly captured on a two-volume album, *The Fania All-Stars Album Live at Yankee Stadium* (1976).

Through the 1980s, Cruz continued to broaden her appeal with new styles of Latin music and sang with a wide variety of younger artists, including GLORIA ESTEFAN, rocker David Byrne of the group The Talking Heads, and even operatic tenor Luciano Pavarotti.

In 1989, Cruz won her first Grammy for Best Tropical Latin Performance for the album *Ritmo en el Corazon,* a collaboration with Ray Barretto. She would later win four more Grammys, the last in 2002 for Best Salsa Album with *Na Negra Tiene Tuembao.* In all, she recorded 70 albums, 20 of which went gold, selling more than a million copies.

In the last decade and a half of her life, Cruz was paid many honors. In 1990, the main thoroughfare of Little Havana in Miami was named Celia Cruz Way. In 1994, President Bill Clinton presented her with the National Endowment of the Arts Medal. She even was given an honorary degree from Yale University.

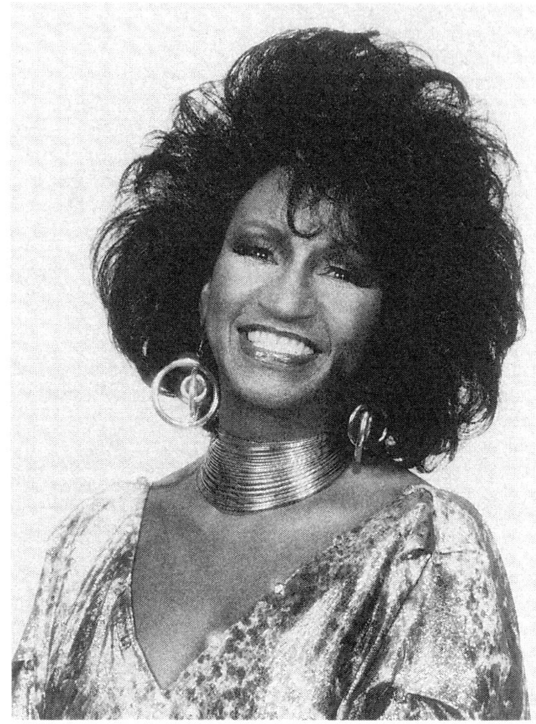

The Queen of Salsa, Celia Cruz enjoyed a popularity with Latinos that knew no age barrier. *(Photofest)*

Cruz's vivacious stage performance was captured in several films and documentaries, including two Hollywood features, *The Mambo Kings* (1990) and *The Perez Family* (1998).

She continued to play almost up until her death at age 77 on July 16, 2003, due to complication after surgery for a brain tumor. More than a half million mourners stood in line to pay their respects to the woman known as the Queen of Salsa in both New York and Miami. That October, on her birthday, the Celia Cruz Foundation was established, giving five grants to Latino students to study music. In May 2005, the Smithsonian's National Museum of American History in Washington, D.C., opened a major exhibit titled *¡Azúcar! The Life and Music of Celia Cruz.*

Further Reading

Cruz, Celia, with Ana Cristina Reymundo. *Celia: My Life.* New York: Rayo, 2004.
Marceles, Eduardo. *Azúcar! The Biography of Celia Cruz.* Translated by Dolores M. Koch. New York: Reed Press, 2004.
Rodriguez-Duarte, Alexis. *Presenting Celia Cruz.* New York: Clarkson Potter, 2004.

Further Listening

Hits Mix. Sony International, CD, 2002.
100% Azúcar!: The Best of Celia Cruz con la Sonora Matancua. Rhino Records, CD, 1997.

Further Viewing

Celia Cruz—An Extraordinary Woman. Universal Music & VI, DVD, 2003.
Celia Cruz—Azúcar! Image Entertainment, VHS/DVD, 2004.
Celia Cruz and Friends—A Night of Salsa. PBS Home Video/ Paramount Home Video, VHS/DVD, 2000/2004.

Cruz, Penélope
(Penélope Cruz Sánchez, Pe)
(1974–) *actress, social activist*

One of the leading film actresses of her native Spain, Penélope Cruz has become a rising star in American movies as well. Penélope Cruz Sánchez was born in Madrid, Spain, on April 28, 1974, into a working-class family. Her father is in the retail business, and her mother is a hairdresser and once managed a restaurant.

As a child, Cruz acted out popular television commercials for her family. She took ballet lessons at the National Conservatory and with professional dancers for nine years. At age 15, she began to act in television programs and music videos.

Cruz made her film debut at age 17 in *El Laberinto Greigo* (The Greek labyrinth, 1991). A year later, she played one of four sisters who was in love with a deserter from the Spanish army in *Belle Epoque* (1990). The film became an art-house success in the United States and won the Academy Award for the Best Foreign Language Film in 1992.

During the next five years, Cruz became one of the most popular and praised film actresses in Spain, earning the title "La Encontadora" (The Enchantress). Her film work brought her to the attention of leading Spanish filmmaker Pedro Almodóvar, who cast her in *Carne Terch* (*Live Flesh,* 1997); in the next several years, she appeared in several Almodóvar films.

In an offbeat comedy-drama *La Niña de tus ojos* (*The Girl of Your Dreams,* 1999), Cruz won a Goya, the Spanish equivalent of an Oscar, as Best Lead Actress for her performance. The success of another Almodóvar film, *Todo sobre mi madre* (*All about My Mother,* in 1999), in which Cruz played a pregnant nun, made Cruz a bankable star, and the offers from Hollywood began to roll in.

She was cast as a seductive chef in the American comedy *Woman on Top* (2000) and played a Mexican rancher's daughter who was having a forbidden affair with cowboy Matt Damon in *All the Pretty Horses* (2000). In *Blow* (2001), she played the wife of a drug dealer, acted by Johnny Depp. None of these films was as popular as *Vanilla Sky* (2001), a remake of the Spanish film *Abre los ojos (Open Your Eyes),* in which she had previously starred. The science-fiction thriller cast her opposite leading man Tom Cruise and was directed by Cameron Crowe. Cruise, who had recently divorced actress Nicole Kidman, had a much-publicized relationship with Cruz, which ended in early 2004. Her most recent collaboration with director Almodóvar, *Volver* (2006), won two prizes at the Cannes Film Festival and earned her Academy Award and Golden Globe nominations for Best Actress.

While her beauty helped make her a star, Cruz remains a deeply serious actor. Her commitment to social causes is also deep and genuine. She donated her entire salary from her first U.S. film to Mother Teresa's nuns in India. In 1997, Cruz worked among the poor in Uganda for months as a volunteer and cofounded a home and a clinic for tubercular patients and homeless girls in Calcutta, India.

"There's so much more I want to do," she has said. "I refuse to get to 50 and wait at home for the phone to ring. In Spain, actresses work until they are old. That's my plan."

Cruz dated actor Matthew McConnaughey, whom she met on the set of the adventure film *Sahara* (2005), but the couple parted in May 2006. Her sister Monica is a popular television actress in Spain.

Further Reading

Gutierrez, Eric. "Penelope's Sitting Pretty." *Latina,* June 1, 2000, pp. 88–94.

The Internet Movie Database. "Penélope Cruz." The Internet Movie Database. Available online. URL: http://imdb.com/name/nmooo4851. Downloaded on March 31, 2005.

Rodriguez, Clara. *Heroes, Lovers, and Others: The Story of Latinos in Hollywood.* Washington, D.C.: Smithsonian Books, 2004, pp. 215–217.

Scott, A. O. "From Everygirl to Everywoman." *New York Times,* September 10, 2006, pp. AR 37, 61.

Further Viewing

All About My Mother (1999). Columbia/Tristar Home Video, VHS/DVD, 2000.

Belle Epoque (1994). Columbia/Tristar Home Video, VHS/DVD, 2000/2003.

Vanilla Sky (2001). Paramount Home Video, VHS/DVD, 2003/2004.

Woman on Top (2000). Fox Home Video, VHS/DVD, 2001.

Cugat, Xavier
(Francisco de Asis Javier Cugat Mingall de Bru y Deulofeo, "Cugi," "The Rumba King")

(1900–1990) *bandleader, musician, songwriter, arranger, actor*

One of the first and most durable of Latin bandleaders to become popular in the United States, Xavier Cugat changed North American perceptions of Latin music with his bright, rhythmic orchestral sound. His music was heard in clubs, recordings, and movies for more than four decades. Francisco de Asis Javier Cugat Mingall de Bru y Deulofeo was born in Girona, Spain, a few moments after midnight on January 1, 1900. His birth at the beginning of a new century was seen as a good omen, and because of it, his father, a political prisoner, was pardoned by the Spanish government. The entire family moved to Havana, Cuba, when Cugat was three. A gifted musical prodigy, he learned to play the violin and at age 12 was the first violinist in the Havana Orchestra. When he was 15, Cugat immigrated to the United States, settled in Southern California, and was hired immediately to tour as a violinist, under the name Francis Cugat, with the great opera singer Enrico Caruso.

A perfectionist who did not feel that he could become the world's greatest violinist, Cugat eventually gave up the instrument. In the early 1920s, he was hired as a cartoonist and caricaturist by the *Los Angeles Times* and at night put together a musical band. They called themselves X. Cugat and the Gigolos. Although a talented artist, Cugat felt the pressure of working for a daily newspaper too much for him and quit his day job to concentrate on music.

His big break came in 1928 when his band was engaged by the popular Coconut Grove nightclub in Hollywood. Cugat's rhythmic Latin beat and colorful orchestrations were infectious and just the exotic antidote for a nation that was trying to forget the Great Depression. He created a craze for the Latin dance the rumba and quickly earned the nickname "The Rumba King."

In the 1940s, the Xavier Cugat Orchestra, as it was now called, was a fixture in the Starlight Roof of the Waldorf-Astoria in New York City. Soon after, the American Society of Composers, Authors, and Publishers (ASCAP) pulled the music of its members from radio in a financial dispute in the early 1940s. As Cugat had hundreds of Latin songs which his orchestra could play that were not represented by ASCAP, he soon became a huge star on radio, playing regularly on the *Camel Caravan* show.

The radio exposure led to recordings, and Cugat had 13 pop singles on the chart in a single decade. His first hit, "The Breeze and I" (1941), was adapted from a Spanish song "Andalucia." His band was featured on the soundtrack of two popular Walt Disney animated films that were intended to strengthen American ties with Latin America during World War II—*Saludos Amigos* (1943) and *The Three Caballeros* (1945). In the second film, Cugat's Orchestra backed Bing Crosby on two hit songs, "You Belong to My Heart" and "Baia," a hypnotic samba. Cugat appeared as himself, usually with his band, in a string of MGM musical films in the 1940s, including *You Were Never Lovelier* (1942) with Fred Astaire and RITA HAYWORTH, *Bathing Beauty* (1944) with Esther Williams and Red Skelton, and *A Date with Judy* (1948) with Jane Powell and CARMEN MIRANDA.

"Cugi," as he was known to his friends, loved women as much as he loved making music and was married five times. Singer Abbe Lane, who sang with his orchestra, became his fourth wife in 1952. They were a popular Hollywood couple and appeared together in the 1957 musical television series *The Xavier Cugat Show.* He divorced Lane in 1963 and three years later married singer and dancer CHARO, who was 41 years his junior.

Xavier Cugat continued to make his magical, beguiling music until he suffered a stroke in 1971 and retired. He died on October 27, 1990, of heart failure in Barcelona, Spain.

Further Reading

Cugat, Xavier. *Rumba Is My Life.* Paris, France: Didier, 1948.

"Obituary," *Current Biography 1991 Yearbook.* New York: H. W. Wilson, 1991. p. 635.

The Unofficial Xavier Cugat Web Site. Available online. URL: http://www.icdc.com/~ncassway/cugat/. Downloaded on May 5, 2004.

Further Listening

South America, Take It Away: 24 Latin Hits. ASV Living Era, CD, 1997.

Xavier Cugat: The Gold Collection. Fine Tune, CD, 1999.

Further Viewing

Roots of Rhythm (1994). New Video Group, VHS/DVD, 1997/2001.

You Were Never Lovelier (1942). Columbia Tristar Home Video, VHS/DVD, 1992/2004.

D

Dawson, Rosario (Rosie Dawson)
(1979–) *actress*

A rising star among ethnic actresses, Rosario Dawson has turned in strong performances in a wide range of films. She was born in New York City on May 9, 1979. Her mother is a professional singer, and her father a construction worker. She is one of the most multiethnic actresses in Hollywood and is a mixture of Cuban, Puerto Rican, African-American, Native American, and Irish-American descent.

At age six, Dawson worked as a waitress in a restaurant that her mother managed. She later attended an alternate school in Manhattan and considered pursuing a career as a marine biologist. That all changed when she was discovered one summer's day in 1994, sitting on the stoop of her apartment building by filmmaker Larry Clark. He asked her if she'd like to be in his new movie, and she said yes. The film, *Kids* (1995), was a no-holds-barred look at the social and sexual lives of a group of urban teens. While the film drew mixed reviews, Dawson's career as a film actress was launched.

In her third film, *He Got Game* (1998), directed by Spike Lee, she played a leading role opposite Denzel Washington, who played a convict and former basketball player. Since then, she has alternated between commercial projects (such as *Josie and the Pussycats* [2001], *Men in Black II* [2002], and *The Adventures of Pluto Nash* [2002], in which she co-starred opposite Eddie Murphy) and more serious films (such as *Love in the Time of Money* and Lee's *25th Hour,* both 2002). This last film, in which she played a drug dealer's girlfriend, earned Dawson a Best Actress award at the Eighth Annual American Black Film Festival (ABFF) in 2004.

Her more recent films include ROBERT RODRIGUEZ's *Sin City* (2005), a dark, futuristic film noir, in which she plays the leader of a group of prostitutes, and *Rent* (2005), based on the hit Broadway musical, playing the drug-addicted exotic dancer Mimi Marquez. Dawson, who broke up with actor Jason Lewis in November 2006, has recently started her own production company, Trybe.

A political activist, Dawson was arrested for disorderly conduct and obstruction at the 2004 Republican National Convention in New York City while filming *This Revolution* (2005), a political docudrama which was set during the convention.

"She's very open, and she's very easy to direct," Spike Lee has said. "She always comes to the set with great energy."

Further Reading

The Internet Movie Database. "Rosario Dawson," The Internet Movie Database. Available online. URL: http://www.imdb.com/name/nm0206257/. Downloaded on January 16, 2005.

Mendez, Juan M. "Rosario Rising." *Latina,* August 1, 1998, pp. 80–83.

Ogunnaike, Lola. "Go West, Young Mimi Marquez," *New York Times,* November 6, 2005, Arts and Leisure section, p. 3.

Rodríguez, Clara E. *Heroes, Lovers, and Others: The Story of Latinos in Hollywood.* Washington, D.C.: Smithsonian Books, 2004, pp. 231–233.

Further Viewing

Kids (1995). Pioneer Video. DVD, 1997.

25th Hour (2003). Buena Vista Home Video, VHS/DVD, 2004.

del Rio, Dolores (Dolores Martínez Asúnsolo López Negrete)

(1905–1983) *actress*

The first Latina to achieve international film stardom, Dolores del Rio was renowned for both her acting skills and her natural beauty in a career that spanned more than half a century. Dolores Martínez Asúnsolo López Negrete was born in Durango, Mexico, on August 3, 1905. Hers was a well-to-do family; her father was a banker, and leading Hollywood actor RAMON NOVARRO was her second cousin. The Mexican Revolution erupted when Dolores was five, and revolutionary Pancho Villa seized her father's bank and their home. The family fled to Mexico City, where she attended convent school and took dance lessons.

At age 16, the beautiful young girl married wealthy writer Jaime Martínez del Rio, who was 18 years her senior. He encouraged her to perform in solo ballet productions that were staged for an intimate audience of family and friends.

Hollywood film director Edwin Carewe met del Rio at a tea party in Mexico City and was impressed by her beauty and charm. He invited the couple to come to Hollywood where Dolores could pursue a film career. Mexican society was scandalized when she said that it "would be fun" to be in pictures. When her friends told her that a Mexican lady had never done something like that before, she replied, "Very well, I will be the first."

Although del Rio spoke no English at the time, this was not seen as a problem in the era of silent films. Carewe cast her in his drama *Joanna* (1925), and soon she was one of Hollywood's most popular leading ladies, appearing in such silent classics as *What Price Glory* (1926), *The Loves of Carmen* (1927), *Ramona* (1928), and *Evangeline* (1929). Her fresh and flawless beauty quickly became legendary. As one photographer of the day spoke of her face, "Wherever the light falls, it composes beauty."

With the emergence of sound films in 1929, del Rio's star began to descend. She now spoke English but with a thick Spanish accent, that gradually relegated her to stereotyped roles as exotics and impetuous Latins. Her charm and acting skills shone through, however, in *Bird of Paradise* (1932), where she played a South Sea islander whose romance with an American sailor ends in tragedy. The following year, she was the nominal star of the musical *Flying Down to Rio* (1933) but was overshadowed by the debut of dance team Fred Astaire and Ginger Rogers, who would never play supporting roles again.

Divorced from her husband in 1928, she married leading Hollywood art director Cedric Gibbons in 1930. They became one of filmdom's most fashionable couples. By the end of the 1930s, del Rio found herself relegated mostly to secondary roles. She divorced Gibbons in 1941 and dated the film director and actor Orson Welles, who played opposite her in the thriller *Journey into Fear* (1942).

With little future in Hollywood, del Rio might have been expected to retire quietly and live off her earnings, but she surprised everyone at age 37 by moving back to Mexico and beginning a new career there in film and theater. "I didn't want to be a star anymore," she later said, "I wanted to be an actress." She also wanted to play meaningful roles as real Mexican women, rarely seen in films before. The timing was right. Director Emilio Fernández and others were making socially important films in what would come to be called the Golden Age of Mexican cinema. He directed del Rio in such classic films as *Maria Candelaria* (1944), which won the Grand Prize at the Cannes Film Festival in France, and *Las Abandonadas* (1945), in which she costarred with Mexican actor Pedro Armendáriz, with whom she became romantically involved. Del Rio was nominated five times for the Silver Ariel Award, Mexico's equivalent of the Academy Awards and won twice.

She continued to play supporting roles in Hollywood films, most notably in director John Ford's *The Fugitive* (1947), in which she played an Indian woman who aids a fugitive priest, played by Henry Fonda. Still stunningly beautiful in her fifties and sixties, del Rio played Elvis Presley's Indian mother in the Western *Flaming Star* (1960), regarded by most critics as Presley's best film. She worked with Ford again on his last Western, *Cheyenne Autumn* (1964). Her last film was *The Children of Sanchez* (1978), in which she co-starred with Mexican-American actors ANTHONY QUINN and KATY JURADO. With her third husband, Lew Riley, who she married in 1959, del Rio worked tirelessly for the welfare of orphaned children. In 1975, she founded the first 24-hour nursery in Mexico for the children of working Mexican actresses.

Dolores del Rio died of liver failure in Laguna Beach, California, on April 4, 1983. She remains a much beloved actress in both her native and adopted land.

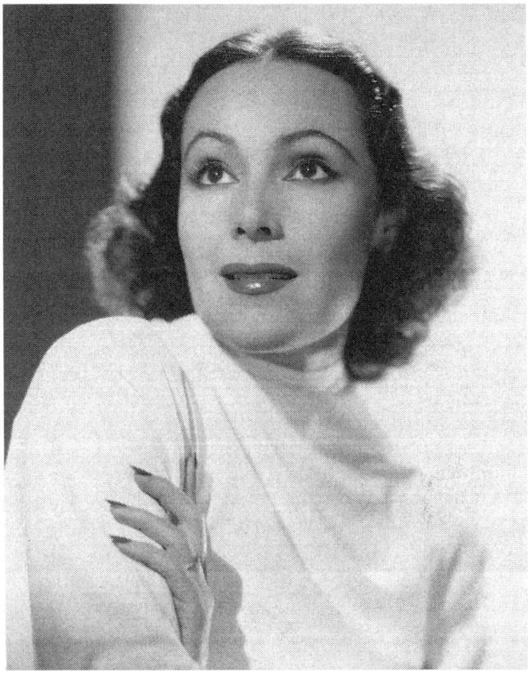

One of the most beautiful women during film's golden age, Dolores del Rio left Hollywood in the 1940s and began a second successful career in film and on stage in her native Mexico. *(Photofest)*

Further Reading

Carr, Larry. *More Fabulous Faces: The Evolution and Metamorphosis of Dolores del Rio, Myrna Loy, Carole Lombard, Bette Davis, and Katharine Hepburn.* New York: Doubleday, 1979.

Hershfield, Joanne. *The Invention of Dolores del Rio.* Minneapolis: University of Minnesota Press, 2000.

The Internet Movie Database. "Dolores del Rio." Internet Movie Database. Available online. URL: http://www.imdb.com/name/nm0003123. Downloaded on February 26, 2005.

Rodríguez, Clara E. *Heroes, Lovers and Others: The Story of Latinos in Hollywood.* Washington, D.C.: Smithsonian Books, 2004, pp. 27–29, 52–65.

Woll, Allen L. *The Films of Dolores del Rio.* New York: Gordon Press, 1978.

Further Viewing

Bird of Paradise (1932). Madacy Entertainment/Roan Group, VHS/DVD, 1998/2004.

Evangeline (1929). Image Entertainment, DVD, 2001.

Flaming Star (1960). Fox Home Entertainment, VHS/DVD, 2002/2004.

The Fugitive (1947). Turner Home Entertainment, VHS, 1990.

Del Toro, Benicio
(Benicio Monserrat Rafael Del Toro Sanchez)
(1967–) *actor*

Only the third Puerto Rican American to win an Academy Award for acting, Benicio Del Toro is one of the most gifted and prolific Latino film actors working today. Born in San Germán, Puerto Rico, on February 19, 1967, both of Benicio Monserrat Rafael Del Toro Sanchez's parents, Gustavo and Fausta Sanchez Del Toro, were lawyers, and the family moved to the town of Santurce when he was very young. Del Toro's mother died when he was nine, and he moved with his father and brother to the United States four years later. They settled on a farm in Mercersburg, Pennsylvania, and Del Toro attended the Mercersburg Academy where he excelled in baseball and art. After graduating in 1985, he entered the University of California–San Diego to study business. To audition for a school play, he changed his major to acting and fell in love with performing.

Anxious to launch an acting career, Del Toro dropped out of college and moved to New York City, where he studied at the Circle in the Square Theatre School. He won a scholarship to study with master acting teacher Stella Adler in Los Angeles (LA). His first acting job for television was a guest shot on the popular crime series *Miami Vice*. Other TV work followed. His first film role was Duke, the Dog-Faced Boy, in the comedy *Big Top Pee-Wee* (1988). A casting agent saw him in a play in LA and invited him to audition for a villainous role in the James Bond film *License to Kill* (1989). Del Toro got the part, becoming the youngest actor at that time to play a Bond villain.

During the next five years, Del Toro gave a number of praiseworthy performances in little-seen films, including *The Indian Runner* (1991), directed by Sean Penn; *China Moon* (1994), a suspenseful film noir in which he played a cop; and *Fearless* (1993), with Jeff Bridges and Rosie Perez. His breakthrough film was another film noir, the puzzling *The Usual Suspects* (1995), in which he played one of the most mysterious of a team of small-time crooks who get in over their heads when attempting to hijack a cocaine shipment. Although the role was quite small, Del Toro was singled out for an Independent Spirit Award for Best Supporting Actor.

He next played an egotistical Latin baseball player who is stalked by Robert De Niro in *The Fan* (1996). In *Fear and Loathing in Las Vegas* (1998), based on the book by journalist Hunter Thompson, he gained 45 pounds in nine weeks to play outrageous, drug-addicted Dr. Gonzo. He so immersed himself in this character that in one scene he actually burned himself with cigarettes. The film failed at the box office, but Del Toro's reputation as a leading cult actor grew.

In *Traffic* (2000), an epic drama about the drug trade in California and Mexico directed by Steven Soderbergh, Del Toro received major recognition. In a large, star-studded ensemble, he stood out as Javier Rodriguez, an honest Mexican border cop who is the film's moral center. His work earned him an Academy Award for Best Supporting Actor. The only other Puerto Rican-American actors to win Oscars before him were José Ferrer and Rita Moreno.

The Oscar did not change Del Toro's choice of roles. He continued to appear in offbeat and ambitious films. He played a jewel thief disguised as a priest in the black comedy heist film *Snatch* (2001) and was a suicidal Native American who is wrongly accused of a child's murder in *The Pledge* (2001), reuniting him with director Sean Penn, who has called him "an acting animal."

Perhaps his most challenging role to date was as an ex-con, born-again Christian whose life becomes inextricably bound to two strangers in *21 Grams* (2003). The role earned him the 2003 Audience Award for Best Actor at the Venice International Film Festival and a second Academy Award nomination.

Despite his recent star status, Benicio Del Toro continues to be an actor on the edge, always seeking out new and different roles. "I like anything that's three dimensional," he has said, "anything I can believe in—even if it's fantastic, surreal or from another planet."

Del Toro has dated Alicia Silverstone, who costarred with him in the film *Excess Baggage* (1997), and French–Italian actress Chiara Mastroianni. He remains one of Hollywood's most eligible bachelors.

Further Reading

Espinaza, Galina. "King of Cool." *Latina,* December 1, 2003, pp. 71–72.

The Internet Movie Database. "Benicio Del Toro," The Internet Movie Database. Available online. URL: http://www.imdb.com/name/nm0001125. Downloaded on November 30, 2004.

The Official Benicio Del Toro Web Site. Available online. URL: http://www.beniciodeltoro.com. Downloaded on May 12, 2005.

Further Viewing

Traffic (2000). Umvd/USA Films, VHS/DVD, 2003/2001.

21 Grams (2003). Universal Home Video, VHS/DVD, 2004.

The Usual Suspects (1995). MGM/UA Home Video, VHS/DVD, 2004/1999.

Del Toro, Guillermo

(1964–) *filmmaker, producer, screenwriter, television director*

One of the most successful creators of horror and science-fiction films today, Guillermo Del Toro is known for his stylish and disturbing use of imagery, ranging from the religious to the insect world. He was born in Guadalajara in Jalisco Province, Mexico, on October 9, 1964. He was raised by his devoutly Catholic grandmother and began to make short films while in his teens. Del Toro befriended Hollywood master makeup and special-effects technician Dick Smith, who inspired him to become a makeup supervisor in Mexican films and television. He worked in the industry in this capacity for a decade, during which time he formed his own production company, Necropia. The first feature that he produced was *Dona Herlinda and Her Son* (1986).

For the next four years, Del Toro produced and directed television programming for Cin Mexico. He finally broke into feature films as a director with *Cronos* (1992), a dazzling thriller about the hunt for a precious scarab. The film was a huge success and earned nine Mexican equivalents to the Academy Awards. It also won the International Critics Week Award at the Cannes Film Festival in France.

Del Toro eventually made the move to Hollywood, where he directed the horror film *Mimic* (1997), starring Mira Sorvino. The problems he faced making this movie led the director to turn his back on Hollywood and return to Mexico, where he formed another production company, The Tequila Gang. His next film, *El Espinazo del Diablo* (*The Devil's Backbone,* 2001) was an ambitious film set in a mysterious orphanage during the last days of the Spanish civil war. A skillful blend of drama and the supernatural, the film earned Del Toro praise from critics and audiences alike. With the clout and confidence he needed, he returned to Hollywood to direct *Blade II* (2003), the big-budget sequel to the comic-book-inspired vampire tale *Blade,* starring Wesley Snipes.

But it was another comic book that Del Toro most wanted to bring to the screen, and it took him seven years of battling the studios to do it. Del Toro wanted to cast actor Ron Perlman, with whom he had previously worked on *Cronos,* in the lead part of *Hellboy,* based on Mike Mignola's popular comic book. The studio heads rejected Perlman as not a big enough box-office draw. Del Toro refused to make the film without him and eventually got his way. *Hellboy* (2004) became another hit, and the director is developing its sequel *Hellboy 2: The Golden Army* (2008). His *El Laberinto del Fauno* (*Pan's Labyrinth* 2006), won Academy Awards for art direction, makeup, and cinematography.

"Of all the genres in cinema, horror is the one that is the most liberating in the sense that it allows you to use images and situations that are completely fantastic and not of reality," Del Toro said in an interview. "At its best, it can transcend reality and become like a fairy tale image generator; at its worst, it's fun to do." Guillermo Del Toro lives in Los Angeles, California, with his wife and children.

Further Reading

Briggs, Peter, Jeff Rebner, and Guillermo Del Toro. *Hellboy: The Art of the Movie.* Milwaukie, Ore.: Dark Horse, 2004.

The Internet Movie Database. "Guillermo Del Toro," The Internet Movie Database. Available online. URL: http://www.imdb.com/name/nm0868219. Downloaded on May 26, 2005.

The Official Guillermo Del Toro Fansite. Available online. URL: http://www.deltorofilms.com Downloaded on May 26, 2005.

Further Viewing

Cronos (1992). Vidmark-Trimark/Lions Gate Home Entertainment, VHS/DVD, 2000/2003.

The Devil's Backbone (2001). Columbia/Tristar Home Video, VHS/DVD, 2002.

Diaz, Al
(J. Albert Diaz)
(1958–) *photojournalist*

One of America's foremost Latino photojournalists, Al Diaz always focuses on the human face of a news story, whether it is a devastating hurricane or a great sports event. Albert Diaz was born in Miami, Florida, on April 9, 1958, in a Cuban-American family. He studied journalism at the University of Florida and received a bachelor of arts (B.A.) degree in 1983. While still in college, Diaz worked as a stringer photographer for the Associated Press (AP) and also served as a photographer intern for the *Gainesville Sun,* a local newspaper.

After graduating, Diaz was hired as a staff photographer at the *Miami Herald,* where he is still employed more than 20 years later. He quickly distinguished himself with expressive photographs of people, especially within Miami's large Cuban community. Diaz was part of the team of *Herald* writers and photographers whose in-depth coverage of Hurricane Andrew in 1993 earned the team a Pulitzer Prize Public Service Award.

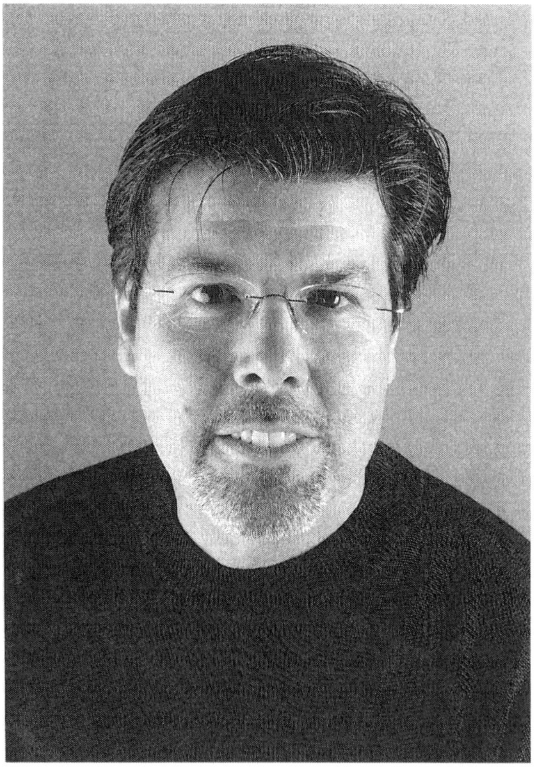

Photojournalist Al Diaz has captured on film a multitude of news and human-interest stories for the *Miami Herald* newspaper. *(Cindy Seip)*

Diaz's empathy for society's poor and downtrodden is dramatically revealed in his prize-winning photo "Precious Time," which appeared in December 2003. It shows a single mother in a Miami nursing home surrounded by her children and her mother as she suffers the final stages of cervical cancer. It won second place in the Best of Still Photojournalism contest in 2004.

Diaz has won many other awards for his photographs. In 1993, he shared a Robert F. Kennedy Journalism Award for a series on needy families in the holiday season. He won Photographer of the Year for illustration from Southern Newspapers in 1992. His photographs have appeared to date in two books—*Americanos: Latino Life in the United States* (1999) and *A Day in the Life of the United States Armed Forces* (2003).

Diaz has been a very active member of the National Association of Hispanic Journalists. He was chairperson of the group's photography contests for five years, served as chairperson of their visual task force for conventions, and was project creator of a special photography exhibit and auction.

Diaz's enthusiasm for his work is summed up in this comment he made while covering the 2004 Summer Olympic Games in Athens, Greece: "No matter what, there is always the chance to capture the magic in a great photograph of the world's greatest athletes, but I want to capture it all."

Further Reading

Diaz, Al. "Olympic Memories: Al Diaz," Sports Shooter Web Site. Available online. URL: http://www.sportsshooter.com/news/1263. Downloaded on September 27, 2005.

Journalism Award Winners. "Diaz, Albert," Latinos and Media Project Web Site. Available online. URL: http://www-new.lationsandmedia.org/jawards/bios/author-DiazAlbert.html. Downloaded on May 31, 2005.

Korman, Lewis J., and Matthew Naythons. Photographs by Al Diaz and others. *A Day in the Life of the United States Armed Forces.* New York: HarperCollins, 2003.

Miami Herald. "Al Diaz," Herald.com. Available online. URL: http://www.miami.com/mld/miamiherald/news/photos/7340119.htm. Downloaded on February 15, 2005.

Olmos, Edward James, Lea Ybarra, Manuel Monterrey, and Carlos Fuentes. Photographs by Al Diaz and others. *Americanos: Latino Life in the United States.* Boston: Little, Brown, 1999.

Diaz, Cameron
(Cameron Michelle Diaz)
(1972–) *actress, model*

Although she had no training as an actress when she landed her first film role in 1994, Cameron Diaz is today one of the highest paid and most popular actresses in Hollywood. Cameron Michelle Diaz was born in San Diego, California, on August 30, 1972. Her father, Emilio Diaz, is Cuban American, and her mother Billie is of Anglo-German-Italian and Native American descent.

She attended Long Beach Polytech High School, where she was a half-time dancer at football games. At age 16, with her parents' permission, Diaz left school to pursue a modeling career. For the next five years, she traveled and worked in Japan, Australia, Mexico, Morocco, and Paris. Her striking statuesque good looks got her work with the Elite Model Agency, and she appeared in ads for Coke and L.A. Gear.

She returned to California in 1993 to continue her modeling career. That same year, she decided to audition for the female lead in the comedy *The Mask,* starring Jim Carey. Despite the fact that she had no professional acting experience, Diaz beat the odds and won the part over hundreds of more seasoned actresses. Naïve in the extreme, she did not realize that this was a major Hollywood production and even asked someone on the set where her parents could see the film when it was released. "Cameron," came the reply, "at the theaters."

The Mask (1994) was a smash, but Diaz wisely decided to learn her craft before accepting a role in another major movie. She took acting lessons and appeared in a string of small, independent American films where she could flex her acting muscles in a low-risk environment. Among the small, offbeat pictures she appeared in were *The Last Supper* (1995), *She's the One, Feeling Minnesota,* and *Head Above Water* (all 1996).

She returned to commercial movies as a clueless bride-to-be who almost loses her man to Julia Roberts in *My Best Friend's Wedding* (1997). Although the comic foil to Roberts's leading lady, Diaz held her own and earned excellent reviews. True stardom came the following year when she played the love object of hapless Ben Stiller in the outrageous comedy *There's Something about Mary* (1998). The movie was one of the biggest box-office hits of the year, which fully justified her $2,000,000 salary.

Diaz continued to excel in offbeat comedies. She was a crazy fiancée in the black comedy *Very Bad Things* (1998) and played John Cusack's dumpy wife in the zany *Being John Malkovich* (1999), directed by Spike Jonze. In Oliver Stone's *Any Given Sunday* (1999), she played the owner of a football team.

Diaz then teamed up with Drew Barrymore and Lucy Liu in the big screen remake of the popular 1970s television series *Charlie's Angels* (2000). The same year, she was the voice of Princess Fiona in *Shrek,* one of the most successful animated films of all time. Diaz played Tom Cruise's girlfriend-from-hell in the science-fiction thriller *Vanilla Sky* (2001), which also starred PENÉLOPE CRUZ. She gained stature as a dramatic actress in the historical urban drama *Gangs of New York* (2002), directed by Martin Scorsese, in which she played a pickpocket who falls for Irishman Leonardo DiCaprio.

With the sequel *Charlie's Angels: Full Throttle* (2002), Diaz joined her friend Julia Roberts in the "Twenty Million Club," receiving the highest salary ever paid to a film actress, according to the *Guinness Book of World Records. People* magazine named her one of the 50 Most Beautiful People in the world in 2002. (She previously made the list in 1998.) More recently she starred opposite Shirley McLaine in the comedy-drama, *In Her Shoes* (2005).

At the top of her profession, Cameron Diaz is likely to remain a popular star for years to come. "Your regrets aren't what you did, but what you didn't do," she has said. "So I take every opportunity." Diaz lived for five years with video producer Carlos De La Torre and was engaged for a time to actor Jared Leto.

Further Reading

The Internet Movie Database. "Cameron Diaz," The Internet Movie Database. Available online. URL: http://www.imdb.com/name/nm0000139/. Downloaded on December 13, 2004.

O'Brien, Daniel. *Cameron Diaz.* Surrey, U.K.: Reynolds & Hearn, 2003.

Scott, Kieran. *Cameron Diaz* (Latinos in the Limelight). New York: Chelsea House, 2001.

Further Viewing

Being John Malkovich (1999). Umva/USA Films, VHS/DVD, 2002/2001.

Gangs of New York (2002). Buena Vista Home Video/Miramax Home Entertainment, VHS/DVD, 2004.

There's Something about Mary (1998). Fox Home Entertainment, VHS/DVD, 2002/2005.

Diaz, David

(ca. 1959–) *illustrator, graphic designer*

One of the leading Latino-American illustrators of children's books today, David Diaz's bold style has been compared to the paintings of 20th-century masters George Roualt and Marc Chagall. He was born in New York City or—depending on which biography you read—Fort Lauderdale, Florida, ca. 1959, where he attended school. His mother died when he was 16, and he found art a great comfort in the face of this tragedy. A high-school teacher recognized his talent and encouraged Diaz to enter student art competitions. He won several of these and worked for a time as an apprentice to sculptor Duane Hanson.

In a high-school art class, Diaz met and fell in love with Cecelia, a fellow art student. "The focus of my time in art class became seeing how much I could distract her from her weavings and batiks," he has written. The two later married.

After high school, Diaz studied at the Fort Lauderdale Art Institute and then moved to southern California with Cecelia to pursue graphic design. He worked for several design firms before setting up his own business called Diaz Icon. While he did both design and illustrative work for corporations and publishers, he grew to prefer illustration.

A cover illustration that Diaz did for a children's book caught the attention of book editor Diane D'Andrade, and she invited him to illustrate a book of poems, *Neighborhood Odes* (1992), by leading Latino author Gary Soto. His next assignment was *Smoky Night* (1994), a picture book by Eve Bunting about the recent Los Angeles riots. Diaz's powerful illustrations that combined thickly bordered paintings with photo collages perfectly fit the serious story, and the book won the 1995 Caldecott Medal, the most prestigious award in children's book publishing. Diaz was thrust into the forefront of children's book illustrators and was able to devote his energies full time to this work.

To date, he has illustrated more than a dozen children's books as well as adult books such as *Passing Strange: True Tales of New England Hauntings and Horrors* (1996) by Joseph A. Citro. Some of his books reflect minority and Latino themes, such as Eve Merriam's *The Inner City Mother Goose* (1996) and Nancy Andrews–Goebel's *The Pot That Juan Built* (2002), for which he used computer art for the first time. He has also illustrated *Feliz Navidad: Two Stories Celebrating Christmas,* by singer and songwriter José Feliciano.

Diaz uses different, sometimes experimental, techniques to meet the needs of each book he illustrates. He used photo collage extensively in Kathleen Krull's *Wilma Unlimited* (1996), silhouettes for in *Be Not Far from Me* (1998) by Eric Kimmel, and soft pastels to illustrate Sarah Weeks's *Angel Face* (2002). David Diaz lives near San Diego, California, with his wife Cecelia, who is also an artist, and their three children.

Further Reading

Bunting, Eve, and David Diaz. *Smokey Night.* New York: Voyager Books, 1999 [reprint].

Merriam, Eve, and David Diaz. *The Inner City Mother Goose.* New York: Simon & Schuster, 1996.

National Center for Children's Illustrated Literature. "Meet the Artists—David Diaz," NCCIL Web Site. Available online. URL: http://www.nccil.org/diaz.html. Downloaded on August 25, 2005.

E

Elizondo, Hector

(1936–) *actor, stage and television director, musician*

A highly respected actor, Hector Elizondo has expressed virility, strength, and intelligence in a wide range of roles on stage, screen, and television in a career spanning nearly 40 years. He was born in West Harlem in New York City on December 22, 1936. His father, Martin Echevarria Elizondo, was a Basque from Spain and was born on a cargo ship en route from Spain to Puerto Rico. In Puerto Rico he met Carmen Medina. The couple married and moved to New York City, where Hector and his sister were born.

Hector took to acting at a very young age. At 10, blues composer and pianist W. C. Handy discovered him and performed with the youth on local radio and television stations. In high school, Elizondo was a top baseball player, good enough to be scouted by the Pittsburgh Pirates for their farm team. But he decided to go to college instead and in 1954 entered the City College of New York (CCNY), studying to become a history teacher. The following year, he met his first wife. The marriage lasted less than two years, but produced a son, Rodd.

Elizondo left college to pursue a career as a musician and singer. He played conga drums in a Latin band, worked as a classical guitarist, and studied dance at the Ballet Arts Company at Carnegie Hall. When a knee injury ended his dancing career, he decided to give acting a try.

Finding roles in the New York Theater for a Latino was hard at first, but Elizondo's drive and talent eventually got him good parts Off-Broadway. His first big break was playing God in Bruce Jay Friedman's offbeat comedy *Steambath* in 1969, for which he won an Obie (Off-Broadway) Award for Best Supporting Actor. The next year, he appeared on Broadway in the comedy *Sly Fox* opposite George C. Scott and earned a Drama Desk Award nomination.

In 1970, Elizondo made the difficult transition from stage to screen. At first, he played the stereotypical villainous roles that were foisted upon many Latino actors, but he played them always with flair and vitality. He was a Mexican bandit in *Valdez Is Coming* (1971) and the most bloodthirsty of four criminals who hijack a New York City subway in the thriller, *The Taking of Pelham One Two Three* (1974).

While he did not mind being a bad guy, he resented being pigeonholed as a "Latin." "I'll be damned if they call me a Latin actor," he once said. "Nobody calls Sinatra an Italian singer. I'm an actor period."

Elizondo's commitment to his craft paid off in 1984 when he was cast as Matt Dillon's nonethnic, hard-working father in the comedy *The Flamingo Kid,* directed by Garry Marshall. Marshall was so impressed with Elizondo's talents that he has cast him in every film he subsequently made, 14 in all. He has called the actor his "good luck charm."

One of these films, *Pretty Woman* (1990), made a star of Julia Roberts and put Elizondo in the forefront of Hollywood's character actors. His portrayal of a hotel manager who befriends Roberts's prostitute is filled with insight, humor, and humanity. His 10 minutes onscreen earned him Golden Globe and an American Comedy Award nominations.

To date, Elizondo has appeared in more than 80 films, but he has been just as familiar a face to television audiences. He has appeared as a regular in six TV series, most of them unsuccessful, including *Popi* (1976), *Freebie and the Bean* (1980), and *Casablanca* (1983), an ill-advised adaptation of the classic 1942 Hollywood film in which Elizondo played the corruptible but likeable Captain Renault, played by Claude Rains in the movie. He finally found a winner of a role as Dr. Phillip Watters, chief of surgery, which he played for six seasons on the CBS medical drama *Chicago Hope* (1994–2000). The part earned him an Emmy for Outstanding Supporting Actor in 1997. He has been nominated for three more Emmys. Among his most memorable roles is the Mexican-American father of three grown daughters in the comedy *Tortilla Soup* (2001).

Elizondo is the recipient of the Diversity Award's Integrity Award and the Lifetime Achievement Award of Nosotros, an organization that is dedicated to improving the image of Latinos in the entertainment industry. Elizondo is an ardent supporter of several charities and is an active member of the LA Theatre Works, an actors' group that recreates classic radio dramas for National Public Radio (NPR). He made his directorial debut with episodes of the Latino sitcom *a.k.a Pablo* (1984), starring comedian PAUL RODRIGUEZ, in which he also appeared. He has also directed the stage show *Villa!*

Since 1969, Elizondo has been happily married to his third wife, actress and photographer Carolee Campbell, whom he met at the Actor's Studio. His son Rodd is a schoolteacher.

Further Reading

Balmaseda, Liz. "Hombres We Love: Hector Elizondo." *Latina,* October 1, 1997, p. 46.

The Internet Movie Database. "Hector Elizondo." The Internet Movie Database. Available online. URL: http://www.imdb.com/name/nm0001185/. Downloaded on December 14, 2004.

Rodríguez, Clara E. *Heroes, Lovers, and Others: The Story of Latinos in Hollywood.* Washington, D.C.: Smithsonian Books, 2004, pp. 176–178.

Further Viewing

The Flamingo Kid (1984). Anchor Bay Entertainment/MGM/UA Home Video, VHS/DVD, 1998/2003.

Pretty Woman (1990). Touchstone Video, VHS/DVD, 2000/2004.

Tortilla Soup (2001). Columbia/Tristar Home Video, VHS/DVD, 2003/2004.

Emilia, María (María Emilia Castagliola)

(1946–) *painter, installation artist, mixed-media artist, educator*

One of the most prominent Cuban-American artists of Florida's West Coast, María Emilia has a bold, expressive style that she has used to explore political, social, and feminist issues. She was born in Havana, Cuba, on September 11, 1946, and moved to the United States with her family to escape the Fidel Castro regime in 1961. Emilia attended the University of South Florida–Tampa (USFT), where she received a bachelor of arts (B.A.) degree in sociology and a master of fine arts (M.F.A.) degree. She later was an assistant professor of art at USFT. Today, she lives and works in the Tampa Bay area.

Some of her best work uses form to convey content. For example, in *A Matter of Trust,* one of her most popular works, she took secrets written down on paper by female friends and family members and sewed them shut inside envelopes. She then sewed the envelopes into a quilt pattern

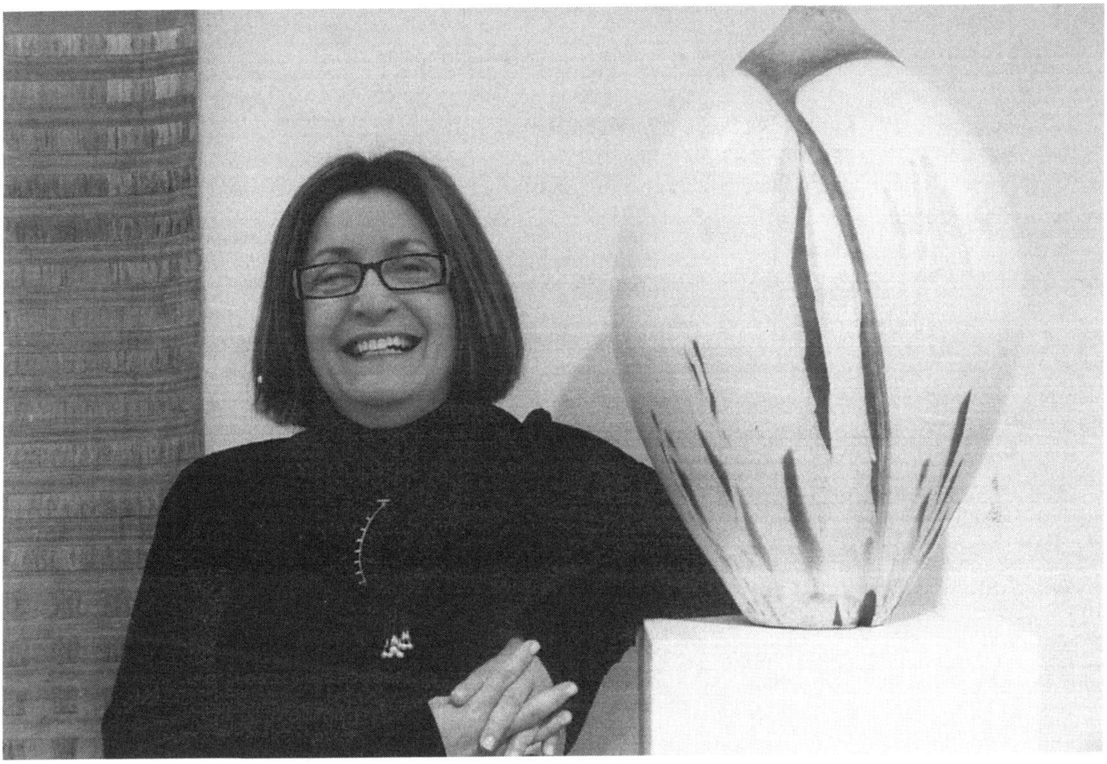

Cuban-born María Emilia poses with one of her ceramic works. She is the executive director of Florida Craftsmen, a statewide group of fine craft artists. *(María Emilia)*

of rectangles, squares, and triangles. The quilt was then sealed tight between sheets of fiberglass window screen, never to be opened. The artist has said that the quilt represents the concept of feminine bonding and is an example of female support.

Emilia's commitment to political change and the artist's role in this process is best seen in her show *In Praise of Federico Garcia Lorca,* which appeared at the Gulf Coast Museum of Art in 2002. It consisted of 12 paintings, 7 drawings, and 5 mixed-media objects, all dedicated to the life and work of the most celebrated Spanish author of the 20th century, who supported political change in his land and was killed during the Spanish civil war in 1936.

Another major work is *Flight of Fantasy* (1997), a 1,200-pound sculpture of steel panels, aluminum tubing, and neon lights inspired by Renaissance artist Leonardo da Vinci's studies of a bird in flight. It is installed at the Recreation Facility of the University of South Florida in Tampa. "My goal in this piece," she has written, "is to confirm the promise of the human potential to raise the question for unthinkable dreams and remarkable ambition."

Emilia was awarded a Florida Individual Arts Fellowship in 1997–98 and served a residency at the Cambridge Center for Science and Art in North Carolina. She was the only Tampa Bay artist to have her work included in *Cuba–USA: The First Generation—In Search of Freedom,* an exhibition of the art of 26 Cuban exiles, which toured the United States and Europe in the early 1990s.

Further Reading

Engerran, Kathy. "Flight of Fantasy," *Florida Trend,* January 2000, p. 23.

Marger, Mary Ann. "Aesthetic Synthesis." St. Petersburg Times On Line Floridian. Available online. URL: http://www.sptimes.com/news/091601/news_pf/Floridian/Aesthetic_synthesis.shtml. Downloaded on May 31, 2005.

Yorba, Jonathan. *Arte Latino: Treasures from the Smithsonian American Art Museum.* New York: Watson-Guptill Publications, 2001, pp. 30–31.

Esparza, Moctesuma

(1949–) *filmmaker, film producer, executive, documentary filmmaker*

The leading film producer of Latino-American cinema for more than three decades, Moctesuma Esparza has a lifelong commitment to Latinos and their betterment in the United States. He was born in Los Angeles, California, on March 12, 1949. His father emigrated from Mexico in 1918 during the Mexican Revolution and imparted a strong sense of social justice to his son. Because of this, Esparza was keenly aware of prejudice against Chicanos and other Latinos as a young man. "I grew to be . . . a very angry young man," he said in a 1998 interview, "angry at the injustice that existed for our people here in this country."

He entered the University of California–Los Angeles (UCLA) in 1967 and quickly became a leader in the fight for student rights that took place on college campuses across the nation in the late 1960s. Esparza was a coordinator in a walkout of March 1968 in which 20,000 students in Los Angeles (LA) went on strike for a week. Soon after, he and 12 other student leaders were arrested and indicted on charges of conspiracy to commit a misdemeanor, a felony that could have put him in prison for 45 years to life. The charges were later dropped, and Esparza returned to UCLA. After finding faculty in the history department unsympathetic to his interest in Latino history, he switched his major to film, graduating with a bachelor of arts (B.A.) degree in 1971. He earned a master of fine arts (M.F.A.) degree in Theater Arts–Film–Television two years later.

Esparza's first job out of college was helping create bilingual segments for the popular Public Broadcasting System (PBS) children's television program *Sesame Street.* Through his contacts with PBS, Esparza soon found himself producing the pilot and first season of another series, *Villa Alegre* (1970), aimed at older Latino children and their families. The series earned a Peabody Award.

During the next decade, Esparza directed and produced documentaries about the Latino experience. One of these, *Agueda Martinez: Our People, Our Country* (1977), was nominated for an Academy Award for Best Documentary, Short Subject. Although he enjoyed making documentaries, he believed he could reach a larger audience with feature-length, fictional films. His first effort *Only Once in a Lifetime* (1979) was a minor effort, but then he received a grant from the Corporation for Public Broadcasting (CPB) to develop a film about a real-life Latino hero in the Old West. *The Ballad of Gregorio Cortez* (1982) was three years in the making. When it premiered on PBS's *American Playhouse,* it was critically praised as a pioneering work about Latino-American history.

While Esparza enjoyed his relationship with PBS, he decided that working in the commercial Hollywood system would produce faster results and reach a wider audience. As an independent producer, he developed *The Milagro Beanfield War* (1988), directed by Robert Redford. This simple but charming fable about community action in a small New Mexican town featured an all-star Latino cast including Rubén Blades, Sonia Braga, and Freddy Fender. It was Esparza's most profitable movie to that date and a great critical success.

Not all of his movies have been about Latinos. In 1992, he worked with television executive Ted Turner to bring one of the Civil War's most decisive battles to the small screen. *Gettysburg* (1993), first aired on Turner Network Television (TNT), became the most watched original movie in cable history. A sequel of sorts, *Gods and Generals* (2003), released directly to theaters, was a box-office disaster.

In between these two productions, Esparza produced one of the most successful Latino-American films, *Selena* (1997), about the life and tragic death of the popular Mexican-American singer, starring JENNIFER LOPEZ. One of Esparza's most recent productions is cable television's Home Box Office (HBO) docudrama *Walkout* (2006), about the 1968 walkout of Mexican-American high school students in East LA to protest unfair treatment. Bodie Olmos, son of EDWARD JAMES OLMOS (the film's director), played Esparza.

Esparza was recently appointed to serve on the California State University Board of Trustees by California governor Arnold Schwartzenegger. In 2005, he was the recipient of a Latin Spirit Award as a filmmaker and producer. Esparza sees his goal as a producer "to transform an image Hollywood has created which was stereotypical and demeaning to an image of us as a people, as human beings of this land, who have something to offer this country and the world."

Further Reading

The Internet Movie Database. "Moctesuma Esparza," The Internet Movie Database. Available online. URL: http://www.imdb.com/name/nm0260800. Downloaded on June 14, 2005.

Nava, Yolanda. *It's All in the Frijoles: 100 Famous Latinos Share Real-Life Stories, Time-Tested Dichos, Favorite Folktales, and Inspiring Words of Wisdom.* New York: Fireside Books, 2000, pp. 40, 67, 117.

Payon, Victor. "Interview with Moctesuma Esparza." San Diego Latino Film Festival Web site. Available online. URL: http://www.sdlatinofilm.com/trands3.html. Downloaded on June 12, 2005.

Further Viewing

The Ballad of Gregorio Cortez (1982). Columbia/Tristar Home Video, VHS, 1990.

Gettysburg (1993). Ardustry Home Entertainment/Warner Home Video, VHS/DVD, 2004/2005.

The Milagro Beanfield War (1988). Universal Home Video, VHS/DVD, 1999/2005.

Estefan, Gloria
(Gloria Maria Milagrosa Fajardo)
(1957–) *pop and Latin singer, songwriter*

The first Latin performer to achieve complete crossover stardom, Gloria Estefan brought Latin-American music into the national mainstream both with her band the Miami Sound Machine and more recently as a solo artist. Gloria Maria Milagrosa Fajardo was born in Havana, Cuba, on September 1, 1957. Her father, José Manuel Fajardo, was an Olympic bronze-medal wrestler and a bodyguard for Cuban president Fulgencio Batista. When Batista was overthrown by rebel Fidel Castro in 1959, the family fled Cuba and settled in Texas. After the birth of their second daughter Becky, the Fajardos moved to Miami, Florida, where they joined the Cuban refugee community in "Little Havana."

José returned to Cuba as part of the U.S.-backed Bay of Pigs invasion. The invasion failed to overthrow Castro, and Fajardo and other Cubans who were captured were thrown into prison. It was a difficult time for the Estefan family back in Miami. It was particularly difficult for Gloria who was shy and withdrawn. Her father was later released and returned to his family. He joined the U.S. Army and served two years in Vietnam during the war there, achieving the rank of captain. Gloria attended an all-girls Catholic academy. She saw herself as fat and unattractive. "For me," she later said, "music was the only bright spot in my life. . . . I sang instead of crying."

There was much to cry about. Her father returned from Vietnam and developed the degenerative disease multiple sclerosis (MS). Gloria nursed her ailing father and sang to soothe him. After graduating from the academy, she attended the University of Miami where she majored in psychology. While in college, she attended a friend's wedding. The music was provided by a local band, the Miami Latin Boys. Their leader and percussionist, Emilio Estefan, knew Gloria slightly and invited her to sing a couple of songs with the band. He was so impressed that he immediately offered her the job of vocalist. By the time Fajardo graduated from college in 1978, she knew that music would be her life. That same year, she and Emilio married and the newly named Miami Sound Machine (MSM) released its first record album, including songs in both Spanish and English.

Slowly, the group became a Miami fixture with their bright Cuban and rhythmic dance music that Gloria sang with vibrant energy. In the early 1980s, they signed with Columbia Broadcasting System (CBS) International. They released four albums within four years for the Latin market, and all sold well in Central and South America. Then in 1984, Epic Records put out an all English-language album, *Eyes of Innocence,* whose success, while modest, proved that MSM could crossover with their music to the broader pop market. In 1985, "Conga," a single from their *Primitive Love* album, became a top-10 pop hit. Suddenly, the members of this Latin band were pop stars, their music playing on dance floors and in clubs across America.

Gradually, Gloria gained tremendous confidence as a performer and a songwriter. She had been writing songs since high school. Her ballad "Anything for You" was initially rejected by the front office at Epic for their new album *Let It Loose* (1988). The label finally relented, and the song zoomed to #1 on the pop charts. The album contained some of their biggest dance hits, including "Rhythm Is Gonna Get You" and "1-2-3." It sold 2 million copies.

Emilio retired from performance after this album and concentrated on forming a music production company for MSM and other artists. Among his clients was former MSM backup singer Jon Secada, who had launched a successful solo career.

Things could not be going better for the Estefans and their band when the unexpected happened. While traveling on tour in eastern Pennsylvania on a snowy day in 1990, their bus was struck from behind by a truck. Most of the band members suffered only slight injuries, but Gloria's back was broken. For a time, it looked as if she might never sing again. But through therapy and sheer determination, she recovered in a year and was back in the recording studio with a new album, *Into the Light* (1991). It was her second solo album and produced her third #1 hit, "Coming Out of the Dark." With this album, Estefan had moved from Latin music into a more adult contemporary sound.

Through the 1990s, Estefan continued to grow in popularity, recording more million-selling albums and performing at such spectacular events as the World Series, the Summer Olympics in Seoul, Korea, and the Super Bowl. By the end of the decade, however, her popularity with pop audiences was fading, and she wisely returned to making mostly Spanish-language records for her most loyal audience, Latinos. In 2000, she won the Latin Grammy Award for Best Music Video and two years later cohosted the Latin Grammy show. In 2004, she released *Amor y Suerte: Exitos Romanticos,* a beautiful compilation of the best of her Spanish music. In June of that same year, she announced her latest world tour would be her last tour.

Estefan's efforts for needy causes are well known. She has performed in concerts to aid hurricane victims, the families of 9/11, and the victims and families of the December 2004 tsunami in the Pacific. She has been awarded the Ellis Island Congressional Medal of Honor for her many philanthropic works.

As a songwriter, Estefan became the first Latino woman to be named Broadcast Music Incorporated (BMI) Songwriter of the Year and has been inducted into the Songwriters' Hall of Fame. She is the winner of five Grammy Awards. She also has produced albums of other Latino artists, including Shakira. She has also appeared

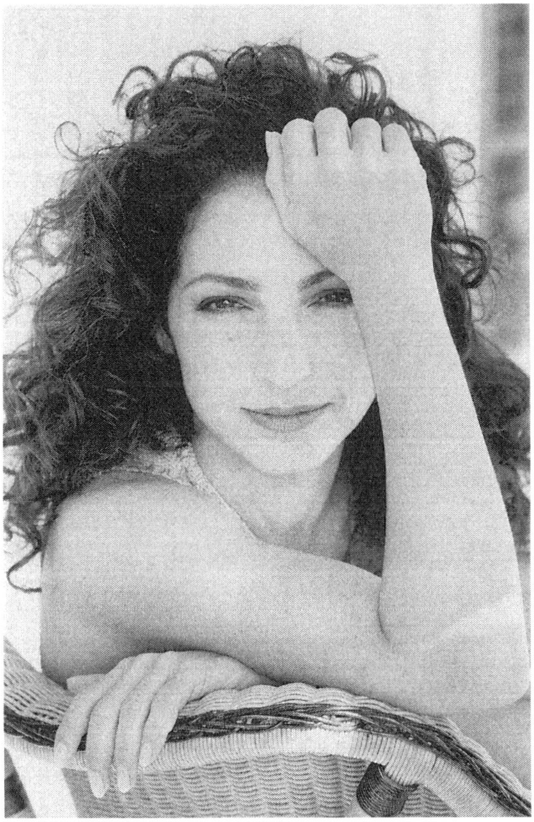

After a serious road accident nearly ended her career, singer Gloria Estefan sprang back with courage and determination to resume performing. *(Photofest)*

in numerous films, usually performing as herself and had a leading dramatic role in director Wes Craven's *Music of the Heart* (1999).

Gloria and Emilio Estefan have two children, Nayib, born in 1980, and Emily Marie, born in 1994.

Further Reading

DeStefano, Anthony M. *Gloria Estefan: The Pop Superstar from Tragedy to Triumph.* New York: Signet Books, 1997 (bilingual edition).

Lee, Sally. *Gloria Estefan: Superstar of Song* (Latino Biography Library). Berkeley Heights, N.J.: Enslow Publishers, 2005.

Phillips, Jane. *Gloria Estefan* (Women of Achievement). New York: Chelsea House, 2001.

Further Listening

Amor y Suerte: Exitos Romanticos. Sony International, CD, 2004.

Gloria Estefan: Greatest Hits. Sony, CD, 1992.

Gloria Estefan: Greatest Hits, Vol. 2. Sony, CD, 2001.

Further Viewing

Gloria Estefan—Live in Atlantis (2000). Sony Music International, VHS/DVD, 2002.

Estevez, Emilio
(Emilio Estévez)
(1962–) *actor, filmmaker, screenwriter*

A charter member of Hollywood's "Brat Pack," as well as one of its most illustrious acting families, Emilio Estevez may not have achieved the fame of his more celebrated brother, but he has shown himself to be a triple threat as a writer, actor, and director. He was born in New York City on May 12, 1962, to actor Martin Sheen and his wife Janet. The eldest of four children, Estevez's brother Ramon and Charlie Sheen also became film actors. When Emilio was six, the family moved to Malibu, California, where his father's film career began to take off. Emilio wrote stories and poems at an early age. He submitted a script to the television anthology series *Rod Serling's Night Gallery* when he was eight and got his first rejection letter. At 11, he began to make films with his father's portable movie camera. His collaborators were his brother Charlie and their friends, Chris and Sean Penn and Chad and Rob Lowe, all of whom would go on to successful acting careers.

In the late 1970s, Emilio accompanied his father to the Philippines where Sheen was starring in Francis Ford Coppola's epic Vietnam movie *Apocalypse Now* (1979). Emilio got his first movie role as a messenger in the film, but the scene did not make the final cut.

Returning to California and Santa Monica High School, Estevez wrote an original play based on a Vietnam War vet whom he had met in the Philippines; Sean Penn directed the play at school. After graduation, Estevez, who adopted his father's birth name, immediately found work acting in several television programs. His first film role was opposite Matt Dillon in *Tex* (1982), adapted from a novel by S. E. Hinton. Director Coppola chose him to star next in another Hinton adaptation, *The Outsiders* (1983), which also featured a young Tom Cruise.

Director Oliver Stone approached Estevez to star in his Vietnam War film *Platoon,* but filming was stalled when Stone could not obtain enough financial backing. Ironically, when he finally had the money several years later, he cast Estevez's brother Charlie in the leading role. *Platoon* won the Academy Award for Best Picture and made Charlie Sheen a star.

But Estevez was finding his own road to stardom. In 1984, he played a punk rocker who takes a job repossessing cars in the cult classic *Repo Man,* which costarred the inimitable Harry Dean Stanton. He also found good roles in, *The Breakfast Club* and *St. Elmo's Fire* (both 1985). The cast included such youthful actors as Ally Sheedy, Molly Ringwald, and Judge Reinhold. This group of up-and-comers was dubbed the Brat Pack by the press, and Estevez was named their unofficial leader.

Estevez was eager to make his own movies and now had the clout to do it. He wrote and starred in *That Was Then . . . This Is Now* (1985) and wrote, directed, and starred in *Wisdom* (1986). Both films were critically panned and failed at the box office. Estevez's second directorial effort, the comedy-action film *Men at Work* (1990), teamed him with brother Charlie as two sanitation workers who become mixed up in a murder.

He was more effective in another comedy-action film, *Stakeout* (1987) as cop Richard Dreyfuss's partner and was an eccentric Billy the Kid in another hit, *Young Guns* (1988). But Estevez's biggest hit to date was the Disney comedy *The Mighty Ducks* (1992) in which he played a lawyer who is drafted to coach a kids' hockey team. He went on to reprise his role in *Mighty Ducks 2* (1994) and agreed to do a cameo in the third installment, *MD3* (1996) on the condition that Disney helped finance his own film, the Vietnam drama, *The War at Home* (1996). The movie costarred his father and actress Kathy Bates but was only released in three cities before disappearing from view. Estevez was married to singer Paula Abdul from 1992 to 1994.

In 2000, he again costarred with brother Charlie in a TV film he directed for Showtime, *Rated X,* the real-life story of two brothers who direct adult films. More recently his career is on the rebound with the release of the well-received *Bobby* (2006), a film about the assassination of U.S. Senator Robert F. Kennedy, which he wrote and directed.

Further Reading

The Internet Movie Database. "Emilio Estevez," The Internet Movie Database. Available online URL: http://www.imdb.com/name/nm0000389/. Downloaded on December 5, 2004.

Riley, Lee, and David Schumacher. *The Sheens: Martin, Charlie, and Emilio Estevez.* New York: St. Martin's Press, 1989.

Wikipedia. "Emilio Estevez," Wikipedia, the Free Encyclopedia. Available online. URL: http://en.wikipedia.org/wiki/Emilio_Estevez. Downloaded on March 31, 2006.

Further Viewing

The Breakfast Club (1985). Universal Home Video, VHS/DVD, 2001/2003.

Repo Man (1984). Anchor Bay Entertainment. VHS/DVD, 2000.

Young Guns (1998). Vestron Video/Aristan Entertainment. VHS/DVD, 1999/2001.

F

Feliciano, José
(José Montserrate Feliciano García)
(1945–) *pop and Latin singer, guitarist, songwriter*

A vocalist with a distinctive style blending folk, rock, Latin, and jazz, José Feliciano burst onto the music scene in 1968 and continues to be a creative and inspiring force in pop and Latin music today. Born in Lares, Puerto Rico, on September 8, 1945, José Montserrate Feliciano García was the second of eight sons in a poor farming family. The disease glaucoma left him blind from birth. When José was five, his father abandoned their farm and moved the family to New York City, where he hoped they would find a better life.

The Felicianos settled in the Spanish Harlem section of Manhattan's Upper East Side. José quickly proved a natural musician, teaching himself the concertina, a kind of small accordion, at age six. He taught himself to play the guitar at nine by listening to rock and roll records. José made his first public appearance the same year at El Teatro Puerto Rico in the Bronx.

By the time he was in his teens, Feliciano was making the rounds of coffeehouses and small clubs in the Greenwich Village section of lower Manhattan. Most club owners were not interested in hiring a blind musician, but Feliciano devised a way to get work. After being turned down, he asked if he could stay just long enough to tune his guitar. Then he started to play passionately. When he finished, most owners were impressed enough to change their minds. The only pay that he received from these gigs was from patrons who tipped him when he passed around a hat. He gave what money he made to his parents, who were still struggling economically.

In 1962, at age 17, Feliciano dropped out of high school to pursue a music career. He took a gig in Detroit, Michigan, and eventually landed a recording contract with RCA Records. The label did not quite know how to package Feliciano's eclectic talents. His first release was a novelty song, "Everybody Do the Click." From the record's poor sales, apparently few took up the challenge. He recorded three pop albums for RCA during the next several years and all flopped.

In 1966, Feliciano attended and performed at a music festival in Argentina in South America. The audience was enthralled by his Spanish-language songs, and soon after, RCA moved him to its international label where he recorded three best-selling Spanish albums for the Latin market. However, he remained virtually unknown to American audiences. That all changed with the release in 1968 of another English-language album, *Feliciano!* The album consisted mostly of covers of popular rock and pop hits of the day, but Feliciano's passionate interpretations—a unique mixture of flamenco, folk, and jazz—were arresting and eminently listenable. One critic called them "soulful easy listening." His slow, smoldering version of The Doors's hit "Light My Fire" was released as a single and climbed to #3 on the pop charts in summer 1968. Overnight, José Feliciano became one of the most influential singers in pop music.

But within months of his newfound fame, he would become a figure of great controversy. He was invited in October 1968 to open the fifth baseball game of the World Series in Detroit. Feliciano sang "The Star-Spangled Banner," accompanying himself on his guitar, in his own slow, soulful, Latin-jazz fashion. Many listeners at the stadium and watching at home on television were enchanted by his singing, but many others took offense at his personal interpretation of the national anthem. The controversy that swirled around that moment continued to dog him for years to come. Interestingly, Feliciano's pioneering effort paved the way for other singers, such as Whitney Houston and Ray Charles, to interpret the anthem in their own way. Today, hardly anyone questions such artistic license. The live recording of Feliciano's "The Star-Spangled Banner" became one of four more hit singles that he charted in 1968. When the Grammy Awards were held the following year, he won two for Best New Artist and Best Contemporary-Pop Vocal Performance for "Light My Fire."

Feliciano recorded three albums in 1969, but his career as a hit singles' artist was about over. He continued to be a popular draw, however, in concert and on television. He guest starred on a number of TV series, including *Chico and the Man* starring FREDDIE PRINZE, for which he also wrote the theme song in 1974. It is his last charting single to date.

In 1980, Feliciano became the first recording artist signed to Motown Records's new Latin division, but he had little success with the label. He rejuvenated his fading career later in the decade by returning to Spanish-language music. His albums sold well, and four earned Grammy Awards for Best

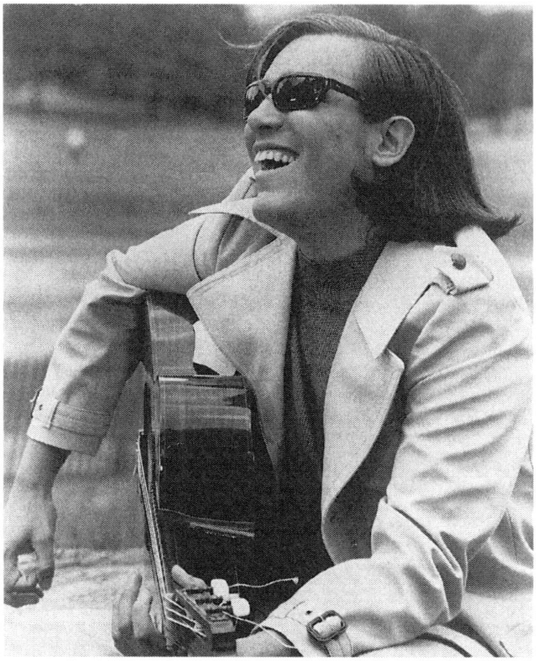

José Feliciano's joy in making music is captured in this photograph of the blind singer taken early in his career. *(Photofest)*

Latin Pop Performance. He was the first Grammy winner to win pop music awards in two language categories. Feliciano's self-penned Christmas song "Feliz Navidad" ("Merry Christmas") has become a holiday classic and was transformed into a children's book with illustrations by DAVID DIAZ.

In the 1990s, Feliciano turned his talents to a new career as a disc jockey on a weekly radio show on a Connecticut station. In 1996, an East Harlem school was renamed the José Feliciano Performing Arts School in his honor. He continues to record and play live shows. On a 2003 album, he recorded "Killing's Not the Answer," his heartfelt response to the terrorist attacks of September 11, 2001. In 2007, he released *The Soundtrax of My Life.* José Feliciano lives in Connecticut with his wife and three children. His son Jonathan is a drummer and has played in concert with his father.

Further Reading

Ankeny, Jason. "José Feliciano," All Music Guide, Mp3.com. Available online. URL: http://www.mp3.com/josé-feliciano/artists/2580/biography.html. Downloaded on August 30, 2005.

Feliciano, José, illustrations by David Diaz. *Feliz Navidad: Two Stories Celebrating Christmas.* New York: Cartwheel, 2003.

José Feliciano Official Web Site. Available online. URL: http://www.josefeliciano.com/index2.html. Downloaded on June 20, 2005.

Further Listening

Feliciano! (1968). RCA, CD, 1994.

Legendary José Feliciano. BMG International, CD (3 discs), 2001.

Señor Bolero. T. H. Rodven, CD, 1998.

Further Viewing

Guitarra Mia—Tribute to José Feliciano. Banco Popular, VHS/DVD, 2000.

Fender, Freddy (Baldemar Huerta, "El Be-Bop Kid") (1937–2006) *rock and country singer, guitarist*

One of the most successful Latino rock and country singers, Freddy Fender's road to stardom was long and difficult. Baldemar Huerta was born in San Benito, Texas, in the Rio Grande Valley on June 4, 1937. His parents were poor Mexican-American migrant farm workers whom Baldemar accompanied on their travels during the harvest season. He developed his own singing style listening to the black workers sing the blues in the picking fields and to the Tejano, Tex-Mex musicians back in the barrio, the Mexican neighborhood that he called home during the rest of the year.

At age 10, Huerta sang for the first time on radio, competing in an amateur talent contest. He won first prize, a tub of food worth $10. When he was 16, he joined the U.S. Marines and served for three years. Back in civilian life, Huerta pursued a musical career in earnest. He played regularly in rowdy Texan dance halls and clubs and landed a recording contract with Falcon Records, a local label, in 1956. His Spanish version of Elvis Presley's "Don't Be Cruel" was a #1 hit in Mexico and parts of South America. He was one of the first Latinos to record rock and roll in Spanish, although he made English records as well.

Imperial Records, a major label in Los Angeles (LA), California, signed Huerta in 1959. To achieve crossover success in the Anglo market, Huerta changed his name to Freddy Fender, taking his surname from the make of his electric guitar. His recording of "Wasted Days and Wasted Nights" became a minor hit nationwide in 1960. Fender seemed to be on the road to success when he and his bass player were arrested for marijuana possession. They were convicted and sentenced to Louisiana's notorious Angola State Prison.

His recording career finished, Fender settled in New Orleans on his release from prison and soaked up Cajun and rhythm-and-blues music while playing sporadically. By 1969, he was back in Texas working full time as a mechanic. Tex–Mex rocker Doug Sahm heard him play on a weekend gig, and recommended Fender to Houston, Texas, producer Huey Meaux. Meaux produced Fender's album *Before the Next Teardrop Falls* (1974), which gave just the right commercial sheen to the singer's heartfelt tenor. The title song, a tear-filled ballad, soared to #1 on both the pop and country charts in April 1975. Fender became the first recording artist to top both charts at the same time. His follow-up single, a remake of "Wasted Days and Wasted Nights," went top-10 pop and gave him a second #1 country hit. Fender had two more pop hits that year and was named Best Male Artist of the Year by *Billboard* magazine. Although his pop career faded by the end of 1976, he continued to be a top country artist through 1983, scoring a total of 21 chart hits.

In 1977, Fender made his acting debut, playing Mexican revolutionary Pancho Villa in the film *She Came to the Valley.* He appeared in four more movies.

In 1990, after a fallow period in the 1980s, Fender enjoyed renewed popularity as a member of the Tex-Mex supergroup, the Texas Tornados, playing with Doug Sahm, organist Augie Meyer, and accordionist FLACO JIMENEZ. With Fender on vocals and guitar, the Texas Tornados earned a Grammy Award for Best Mexican/American Performance for their first self-titled album. After a string of successful albums, the Tornados parted, but Fender joined Jimenez in a second supergroup, the Los Super Seven, which included Cesar Rosas and David Hidalgo of the rock band Los Lobos, country singer Rick Trevino, Texas rock singer Joe Ely, and bandleader Ruben Ramos. They sang mostly in Spanish, and their premiere album earned Fender a second Grammy.

Fender continued to make solo recordings but mostly in Spanish. In 2002, he won his third Grammy in the Best Latin Pop category for *La Musica de Baldemar Huerta,* an album lovingly dedicated to the traditional Mexican border music of his forefathers. Fender died on October 14, 2006, of lung cancer. An eclectic performer who embodied the best of rock, roots music, and country, Freddy Fender was a respected artist for legions of both Anglo and Latino listeners.

Further Reading

Ankeny, Jason. "Freddy Fender," All Music Guide, MP3.com. Available online. URL: http://www.mp3.com/freddy-fender/artists/59175/biography.html. Downloaded on August 30, 2005.

DeCurtis, Anthony, and James Henke. *The Rolling Stone Album Guide.* New York: Random House, 1992, p. 243.

The Official Freddy Fender Web Site. Available online. URL: http://www.freddyfender.com. Downloaded on June 12, 2005.

Further Listening

Best of the Texas Tornados. Warner Bros, CD, 1994.

La Musica De Baldemar Huerta. Back Porch, CD, 2002.

20th Century Masters—The Millennium Collection: The Best of Freddy Fender. MCA Nashville, CD, 2001.

Further Viewing

Encore Series: Freddy Fender Live. Pro-Active Entertainment, DVD, 2004.

Fernández, Rudy
(Rudy Fernández, Jr.)
(1948–) *painter, sculptor, mixed-media artist, educator*

One of the better-known Chicano (Mexican-American) artists in the Southwest, Rudy Fernández combined his people and his personal past in his intriguing mixed-media paintings and sculpture. He was born in Trinidad, Colorado, near the New Mexico border, on September 21, 1948. His father, Rudy Fernández, Sr., was a geologist, and the family traveled around the Southwest as his work dictated. They finally settled in Salt Lake City, Utah, where Rudy attended Catholic elementary school and public high school.

His father encouraged Rudy to develop his artistic gift for drawing and taught him to take pride in his Mexican heritage. In emulation of his father, he majored in geology at the University of Colorado–Boulder. One day, a geology professor saw a small painting on which he was working and urged Fernández to consider becoming an art major. He took the advice and eventually became a teaching assistant in the art department and an active member of the university's Chicano community.

After graduating Phi Beta Kappa in 1974, Fernández attended Washington State University–Pullman to work on a master of fine arts (M.F.A.) degree in sculpture. While there, he served as the head of the Chicano Student Program. In 1975, Fernández won a scholarship to study and teach at the Institute Cultural Tenochtitlan in Mexico City. He was deeply impressed by the work of Mexican artists, especially that of Frida Kahlo. Realizing that Latin-American artists were largely overlooked by American universities' curriculum, he began a long and exhaustive study of early Latin-American art, predating the invasion of the Spanish conquistadores. These images and symbols would become an integral part of his art.

Returning to Washington State University, Fernández began to work seriously at his art while employed as a consultant to the superintendent of Public Instruction for the state. In this capacity, he designed and put into force a program for public mural painting and taught independent-study art classes. He received his M.F.A. in 1977.

Fernández's work of this period often took established Latin art traditions and gave them a contemporary, often autobiographical, twist. His *Trinidad Brick Cadillac* (1974–75) was a recreation of a Southwestern reliquary that was meant to hold saints' relics, but his version contained a brick from his hometown and other personal memories of his early life. *Escape* was a traditional New Mexican devotional screen, or *reredos,* with personal images. Some of Fernández's most profound works have dealt with loss, such as his series of memento-mori (reminders of death) paintings done in loving tribute to a close brother, who died in 1995.

Fernández has had numerous solo and group exhibitions and was included in the historic touring show *Hispanic Art in the United States* (1987) that originated at the Houston Museum of Fine Arts. Since 1978, he has resided in Arizona. His works are found in the permanent collections of many museums, including the National Museum of American Art in Washington, D.C., and the Museum of Fine Arts in Santa Fe, New Mexico. "Acutely aware of the power of symbols to express himself autobiographically about his emotional journey, he continues to successfully employ his special vocabulary of emblems and images to make poignant narratives about the transitory nature of life," writes art critic Julie Sasse.

Further Reading

Carroll, Karen Lee. *Rudy Fernández, the Retable.* Worcester, Mass.: Davis Publications, 1988.

Sasse, Julie. "Private Icons, Cultural Perspectives: The Painting and Sculpture by Rudy Fernández." Resource Library Magazine Web Site. Available online. URL: http://www.tfaoi.com/aa/2aa/2aa634.htm. Downloaded on June 6, 2005.

Yorba, Jonathan. *Arte Latino: Treasures from the Smithsonian American Art Museum.* New York: Watson–Guptill Publications, 2001, pp. 36–37.

Fernández, Teresita

(1968–) *installation artist, sculptor*

A creator of monumental installations, Cuban-American Teresita Fernández captures the essence of nature and its power through her unique and interactive art. She was born in Miami, Florida, on May 12, 1968, and attended the Florida International University in Miami where she earned a Bachelor of Fine Arts (B.F.A.) degree in 1990. She then attended Virginia Commonwealth University in Richmond to obtain a master of fine arts (M.F.A.) degree in 1992. She had her first solo exhibit at the Museum of Contemporary Art (MOCA) in Miami.

Fernández's "architectural installations" do not so much represent nature as evoke it in unexpected ways. In her *Landscape Projected* (1997), viewers entered a museum room and found themselves in a garden setting. *Waterfall* (2000) is composed of tiny plastic strips of blues and whites that express the swirling power of a real waterfall. Viewers could walk under and around the 12-foot-high piece, entering into its turbulent world.

Dune (2002) is composed of thousands of irregularly shaped glass beads that create an almost mystical pattern. Fernández was inspired to create this work by several trips to White Sands, New Mexico. *Passerby* and *7:42 P.M.* (both 2002) are wall pieces that are made up of hundreds of colored acrylic cubes that have been arranged haphazardly to suggest a warm summer night.

Fire (2005), one of Fernández's most recent works, features two suspended circles, each containing thousands of colored silk threads. As a visitor walks around the two circles, the flickering threads appear like flames of fire. This stunning work was created for the Fabric Workshop and Museum in Philadelphia, Pennsylvania, where Fernández was artist-in-resident.

Teresita Fernández is the recipient of several awards and grants, including a 1994 National Endowment for the Arts (NEA) Individual Artist Grant, Visual Arts. She was artist-in-residence at Artspec San Antonio in 1998, won the Louis Comfort Tiffany Biennial Award in 1999, and earned an affiliated fellowship to the American Academy in Rome the same year. Fernández was named a MacArthur Fellow in 2005. Among her most recent exhibitions are *In Situ: Installations and Large-Scale Works* (2004) at MOCA and exhibits at the Lehmann Maupin Gallery in New York City and the Centro de Arte Contemporaneo de Málaga in Spain (both 2005).

Fernández lives and works in Brooklyn, New York. "Throughout her career she has consistently balanced the beauty and seductiveness of her works with aspects of their structure, revealing them as constructions of nature rather than illusions," wrote London gallery curator Rochelle Steiner.

Further Reading

Fernández, Teresita. *Teresita Fernández.* Philadelphia: Institute of Contemporary Art, University of Pennsylvania, 1999.

Grachos, Louis, Erin Shirreff, and Allan S. Weiss. *Teresita Fernández.* Santa Fe, N.Mex.: SITE Santa Fe, 2001.

Lloyd, Ann Wilson. "From an Architect of Desire, Many-Layered Constructions." *New York Times,* March 21, 1999, p. 41.

Steiner, Rochelle. "Teresita Fernández: Immersion." Grand Arts Web site. Available online. URL: http://www.grandarts.com/exhibits/Tfernandez.html. Downloaded on June 6, 2005.

Trainor, James. "Teresita Fernández at Lehmann Maupin—New York—Sculpture," *Art in America,* March 2003, p. 117.

Ferrer, José
(José Vincente Ferrer de Otero y Cintrón)

(1909–1992) *actor, stage director, filmmaker, producer*

The first Latino American to win an Academy Award for acting, José Ferrer was a protean talent who achieved great success on stage and screen as an actor, a director, and a producer for more than five decades. José Vincente Ferrer de Otero y Cintrón was born in Santurce, Puerto Rico, on January 8, 1909. His father was a successful lawyer who moved the family to the United States when José was six. A precocious youth, he passed the entrance exam for Princeton University in New Jersey when he was 14, but, on the advice of the college, waited a year to go there and attended a preparatory school in Switzerland. At Princeton, he was an architecture major but soon fell under the spell of the theater. He joined the Princeton dramatic society, the Triangle Club, where one of his fellow thespians was future film star James Stewart. Ferrer also formed a 14-member jazz band called José Ferrer and His Pied Pipers. They not only played local dates but also toured Europe, with Stewart on the accordion.

After graduating in 1933, Ferrer joined stage director Joshua Logan's stock company as a stage manager. He made his Broadway acting debut two years later in the small role of a policeman in the play *A Slight Case of Murder.* He gradually gained

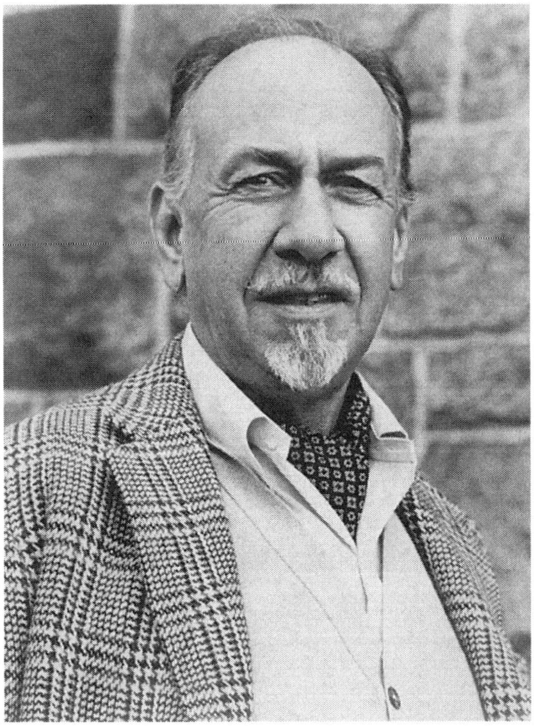

A consummate actor on stage and screen, José Ferrer was the first Latino American to win an Academy Award for acting for his signature role of the romantic hero Cyrano de Bergerac. *(Photofest)*

a reputation as a solid character actor who excelled in both comedy and drama. He played the title role in the comedy *Charley's Aunt* (1940) and the evil Iago to Paul Robeson's Othello in Shakespeare's tragedy (1942).

In 1946, in a touring company, he first took on the role for which he would be most famous, the title character in Edmond Rostand's romantic play *Cyrano de Bergerac.* With his commanding presence and flamboyant theatricality, Ferrer fully embodied the 17th-century soldier, swordsman, and poet with a large nose who yearns for the beautiful Roxanne. "There was never a better Cyrano in the world. . . . Others pale in comparison," said stage actress Helen Hayes after seeing Ferrer in the role on Broadway in 1947.

His performance won him a Tony Award as Best Actor that year. When he reprised the role in the film adaptation in 1950, he won an Academy Award as Best Actor. He became not only the first Latino American to win an Oscar for acting but the first male actor to win an Oscar for recreating a role for which he had won a Tony on the stage.

Ferrer proved to be a versatile talent and a Renaissance man of the theater. Throughout the 1940s and 1950s, he was a dominating force on Broadway as actor, director, and producer, often directing himself in plays. In 1952 alone, he directed three plays on Broadway, starring in one of them, *The Shrike,* about a psychologically abused husband. He won two Tonys, one as director and another as Best Actor in *The Shrike,* of which he would also star and direct a film version in 1955. Altogether, he directed eight films, but they pale when compared to his stage triumphs.

Ferrer did have considerable success, though, as a screen actor. Prior to playing Cyrano, he had been nominated for a Best Supporting Actor Oscar in his very first film, *Joan of Arc* (1948), in which he played the French dauphin who later becomes king, opposite Ingrid Bergman's Joan. He earned a third acting nomination in 1952 for his portrayal of French painter Toulouse Lautrec in *Moulin Rouge,* directed by John Huston. To convincingly play the very short Lautrec, Ferrer walked around on his knees for the entire film, a painful experience.

In the early 1950s, a hysterical hunt for communists in the government and the Hollywood community was under way. Like many actors, directors, and writers, Ferrer was called before a Senate investigative committee headed by Senator Joseph McCarthy. Unlike a number of his colleagues, however, Ferrer refused to sign a loyalty pledge and would not "name names" of other people in Hollywood who might be communists. His courageous stand against this modern-day witch hunt cost him dearly. He was blacklisted in Hollywood and could not find work in film or television. He was eventually removed from the blacklist through the efforts of lawyer Abe Fortas, who would later serve on the Supreme Court.

As he grew older, Ferrer was relegated to smaller character parts and leading roles in lesser films, but when a good role came along, he met the challenge—consider his work as a sadistic Turkish officer in the epic film *Lawrence of Arabia* (1962). He continued to find great success on the stage—he played Don Quixote in the Broadway musical *Man of La Mancha* in 1967. The role gave him a rare opportunity to demonstrate his singing ability. In 1985, Ferrer became the first actor to be awarded the U.S. National Medal of Art by former fellow actor President Ronald Reagan.

He was rehearsing a leading role in the Broadway play *Conversations with My Father* in 1991 when he had to leave the production due to illness. He died of colon cancer in Coral Gables, Florida, on January 26, 1992, a few weeks after his 83rd birthday.

A notorious womanizer, Ferrer was married five times, once to actress and acting teacher Uta Hagen and twice to singer/actress Rosemary Clooney, with whom he had five children. Two of his sons, Miguel Ferrer and Rafael Ferrer, are film and television actors. He was the uncle of actor George Clooney.

Further Reading

The Internet Movie Database. "José Ferrer," The Internet Movie Database. Available online. URL: http://www.imdb.com/name/nm0001207/. Downloaded on June 8, 2005.

Katz, Ephraim, Fred Klein, and Ronald Dean Nolen. *The Film Encyclopedia.* 4th edition. New York: HarperResource, 2001, p. 445.

Rodríguez, Clara E. *Heroes, Lovers, and Others: The Story of Latinos in Hollywood.* Washington, D.C.: Smithsonian Books, 2004, pp. 130–132.

Further Viewing

Cyrano de Bergerac (1950). VCI Home Video/Gotham Distribution, VHS/DVD, 1995/2003.

Joan of Arc (1948). UAV Corporation/Image Entertainment. VHS/DVD, 2002/2004.

Moulin Rouge (1952). MGM/UA Home Video, VHS/DVD, 1989/2004.

Ferrer, Mel (Melchior Gaston Ferrer)

(1917–2008) *actor, filmmaker, producer, screenwriter*

One of a handful of Latino actors groomed by the Hollywood studios as "Latin lovers" in the 1950s, Mel Ferrer never quite fit the part with his aristocratic bearing and sensitive, some would say distant, nature. He never became a major film star but gave some memorable performances and had more success in the director's chair than many actors who have attempted it.

Melchior Gaston Ferrer was born in Elberon, New Jersey, on August 25, 1917. His father was a successful surgeon and Cuban immigrant, and his mother, a glamorous socialite. His sister would follow in her father's footsteps and become a celebrated cardiologist; his brother is a surgeon.

Ferrer attended Princeton University but dropped out in his sophomore year to pursue an acting career. He acted in summer stock and then moved to Vermont, where he edited a newspaper and wrote a children's book, *Tito's Hat.* Ferrer moved to New York City and received his first acting job on Broadway dancing in the chorus of two musicals. His stage career was beginning to take off when he was stricken with polio. Unable to act on stage, he took a job as a disc jockey on a small radio station. He eventually became a director, a producer, and a writer of radio programs for the National Broadcasting Company (NBC) in New York City.

In 1945, Ferrer directed his first film, *The Girl of the Limberlost* (1945), which was a modest success at the box office. He served as legendary filmmaker John Ford's assistant on *The Fugitive* (1947), which was filmed on location in Mexico. His first film role was as a black man passing for white in *Lost Boundaries* (1949).

Ferrer is best remembered as the emotionally crippled and physically lame puppeteer opposite Leslie Caron in *Lili* (1953), which would later be adapted into the hit musical *Carnival.* He was effective as Marlene Dietrich's gunslinger lover in *Rancho Notorious* (1952), King Arthur in *The Knights of the Round Table* (1953), and the doomed Prince Andrei in the filmed adaptation of Leo Tolstoy's *War and Peace* (1956).

As a film director, he reached his peak with the thriller *The Secret Fury* (1950). He directed his third wife, Audrey Hepburn, in the jungle saga *Green Mansions* (1959) and also produced the movie version of the stage hit *Wait Until Dark* (1967), which gave Hepburn one of her best roles as a blind girl terrorized by a psychopathic killer. By then, however, the couple was separated.

Ferrer moved in the 1960s to Switzerland, where he continued to act in and sometimes direct low-budget films. He often came back to the States to act in exploitative films and made-for-television movies through the 1980s. He was a regular on the prime-time soap opera *Falcon Crest* from 1981 to 1984, playing the lawyer of matriarch Jane Wyman. Mel Ferrer died on June 2, 2008.

Further Reading

The Biography Channel. "Movie Stars: Mel Ferrer," The Biography Channel Web Site. Available online. URL: http://www.thebiographychannel.co.uk/new_site/biography.php?id=716&showgroup=. Downloaded on August 30, 2005.

The Internet Movie Database. "Mel Ferrer." The Internet Movie Database. Available online. URL: http://www.imbd.com/name/nm0002072/. Downloaded on February 23, 2005.

Katz, Ephraim. *The Film Encyclopedia,* 2nd edition. New York: HarperResource, 1994, p. 445.

Further Viewing

Lili (1953). Warner Home Video, VHS, 1991.

War and Peace (1956). Paramount Home Entertainment, VHS/DVD, 2002/2003.

Ferrer, Miguel

(1955–) *actor, drummer*

An incisive character actor with a penchant for sardonic villains, Miguel Ferrer may find his greatest success to date playing one of the good guys, a forensic examiner on a hit television series. He was born in Santa Monica, California, on February 7, 1955, the eldest son of actor José Ferrer and singer-actress Rosemary Clooney.

Although from an acting family, his first ambition was to be a drummer. He was inspired to play the drums by watching Ringo Starr, drummer of the Beatles. Ferrer worked as a studio musician for several years, playing drums on the album *Two Sides of the Moon* by the Who's drummer Keith Moon. He also played in his own band, the Jenerators, that included actor and friend Billy Mumy. It was Mumy who persuaded the reluctant Ferrer to accept a part in the National Broadcasting Company (NBC) television series *Sunshine* as, accordingly, a drummer.

Although he seemed to enjoy acting, it would be another eight years before Ferrer got further work as a professional in movies and television. His big break came in 1987 when he played an evil, cocaine-snorting executive in the sci-fi film *Robocop.* He suddenly found himself in demand as a movie villain. He played a mad scientist in *Deep Star Six* (1989), a small-time criminal enlisted by the Devil himself in the made-for-TV version of Stephen King's epic *The Stand* (1994), and a drug dealer turned informant who lives almost long enough to testify against a drug lord in the Oscar-winning film *Traffic* (2000).

Ferrer has had wide exposure in television in several series. In 1990, he was probably the only actor on television appearing simultaneously in three prime-time series. He was a Louisiana cop in *Broken Badges,* a district attorney in the excellent but short-lived *Shannon's Deal,* and a high-strung FBI forensic examiner in filmmaker David Lynch's cult series *Twin Peaks.*

He had a rare opportunity to play the leading man in another King adaptation, *The Night Flier* (1997), where he was a tabloid reporter on the trail of a vampire. More recently, Ferrer has played a more traditional chief medical examiner in Boston in the hit NBC series *Crossing Jordan* (2001–). He made his New York stage debut in 2003 in the Off-Broadway play *The Exonerated.* Ferrer still plays drums with the Jenerators, whose members include Mumy and comedian/actor Bill Murray. They have released two CDs.

Ferrer has two children from his marriage to actress Leelani Sarelle, who he divorced in 2003. His brother Rafael is also an actor and film director. Actor George Clooney is his cousin.

Further Reading

Brennan, Sandra. "Miguel Ferrer," All Movie Guide Web Site. Available online. URL: http://www.allmovie.com/cg/avg.dll. Downloaded on June 12, 2005.

The Internet Movie Database. "Miguel Ferrer," The Internet Movie Database. Available online. URL: http://www.imdb.com/name/nm0001/208/. Downloaded on November 30, 2004.

Miguel Ferrer Official Website. Available online. URL: http://www.miguelferrer.com. Downloaded on October 1, 2006.

Further Viewing

Robocop (1987). Orion/Image Entertainment. VHS/DVD. 1993/1998.

Stephen King's The Stand (1994). Republic Studios. VHS/DVD, 1997/2001.

Twin Peaks—Fire Walk with Me (1992). New Line Home Entertainment. VHS/DVD, 1995/2002.

Ferrer, Rafael

(1933–) *sculptor, painter, printmaker, performance artist, installation artist, educator*

An artist who expresses himself in a broad range of media, Rafael Ferrer's work includes art installations, paintings, and sculptures. He was born in San Juan, Puerto Rico, on January 25, 1933. He moved to the United States at age 14 to attend the Staunton Military Academy in Virginia. After graduation, he entered Syracuse University in New York State and then returned to his homeland to study art at the University of Puerto Rico–Río Piedras. Graduating in 1954, Ferrer moved to New York City, where he made his living for a time as a musician.

He first gained notice with innovative temporary installations fashioned from such common materials as leaves, hay, and corrugated metal. By the late 1970s, he had turned his attention to figurative painting and monumental sculptures. His 25-foot-high *Puerto Rican Sun* (1979) is composed of two arching palm trees surrounding a golden sun fashioned of steel. It forms a stunning archway to a community park in the Bronx, New York. In the 1980s, Ferrer's work focused on bright and colorful landscapes set in the Caribbean. Many of these vibrant, rich landscapes, alive with color, shadow, and intriguing figures, connect with places that he knew as a child. Ferrer recalls "going to deserted beaches when I was little; going through palm groves which are endless. . . . There is this combination of what you see and what you imagine." He is also known for his woodblock prints done in a traditional Japanese style, as well as lithographs, monotypes, and books. In 1972, Ferrer founded Artforum, an umbrella for anarchic thoughts and acerbic language, which continues to the present.

Ferrer has won numerous awards and grants, including three National Endowment for the Arts (NEA) fellowships (1972, 1978, 1989), a Guggenheim Award (1975), and a Pew Foundation Grant (1994). In 1978, he took a teaching position at the

School of Visual Arts in New York City. Through the mid-1980s, he was a visiting professor at several colleges, including the Skowhegan School of Painting and Sculpture in Maine.

Rafael Ferrer's works are in the permanent collections of numerous museums including the Museum of Modern Art (MOMA) in New York City, the Denver Art Museum, and the Lehmbruch Museum in Duisberg, Germany. He has had one-person and group shows at the El Museo del Barrio, the Metropolitan Museum of Art, and the Whitney Museum of American Art, all in New York City, as well as other museums.

"There is a compelling energy, unleashed by the lively paint surface in Ferrer's work," writes author Tom E. Hinson. "By stressing simplified forms, rhythmic flattened surfaces, and the supremacy of light and atmosphere, Ferrer allows his lavish pictorial surfaces and colors to simmer with emotion."

Further Reading

Cancel, Luis R., and others. *The Latin American Spirit: Art and Artists in the United States, 1920–1970.* New York: The Bronx Museum of the Arts and Harry N. Abrams, 1988, pp. 316–317.

Ferrer, Rafael. *Rafael Ferrer: March 5–April 6, 1988 Nancy Hoffman Gallery.* New York: The Gallery, 1987.

———. *Recent Work and an Installation.* Philadelphia, Pa.: Institute of Contemporary Art, 1978.

Hinson, Tom E. "Rafael Ferrer, *El Sol Asombra,*" Butler Institute of American Art Web Site. Available online. URL: http://www.butlerart.com/pc_book/pages/rafael_ferrer_b.htm. Downloaded on August 31, 2005.

Fresquís, Pedro Antonio ("The Truchas Master")

(1749–1831) santero

The *santeros* are folk artists of New Mexico who practice a tradition that goes back four centuries of painting and carving images of saints of the Roman Catholic Church. Pedro Antonio Fresquís was the first native-born New Mexican to create this beautiful religious artwork. He was born in Santa Cruz, New Mexico, of Mexican ancestry in 1749. The exact date of his birth, along with many other facts of his life, has been lost to history. Even less is known about many of the native *santeros* who came after him. Some of them are not even known by name and are identified by where they lived (The Laguna Santero) or the specific art they created (The Santero of the Mountain Village Crucifixes).

Fresquís probably learned the art of making *santos* from the Franciscan missionaries who converted his people to Christianity. The first *santos* were brought by the missionaries from Spain and Mexico as visual aids to teach the native peoples about the lives of the saints and Jesus Christ. Later, the missionaries made their own *santos.* There were two types—*retablos,* two-dimensional paintings, and *bultos,* three-dimensional statues carved out of wood.

While little is known of Fresquís's life, much is known of his art. Many of his works have been found at Truchas, a town near the capital city of Santa Fe. Because of this, Fresquís is known as The Truchas Master, and he probably lived and worked there as an adult.

His best-known *santos* are all *retablos* and the most celebrated is *Our Lady of Guadalupe,* a finely painted devotional panel depicting the Virgin Mary who, according to legend, appeared to a Native American shepherd in 1531. Like many of Fresquís's pieces, the figure of the lady is highly stylized with a long nose and oval eyes. The border is decorated with flowers and a vine design—a Fresquís trademark. Today, *Our Lady of Guadalupe* resides in the permanent collection of the Smithsonian American Art Museum (SAAM).

Like other *Santeros* who followed him, Fresquís created his *santos* to be displayed in local churches, homes, and *marades,* village space reserved for worship. The devoted Mexican Americans treated their *santos* with reverence. Many of their religious processions and celebrations centered around these holy objects. The *santeros* of New Mexico today are the spiritual descendants of Pedro Antonio Fresquís and work with the same care, skill, and reverence as he did.

Further Reading

Boyd, E. *The New Mexico Santero.* Santa Fe: Museum of New Mexico Press, 1969.

Cash, Marie Romero. *The Santero's Art of Historic New Mexico: 1760–1960, The Priscilla Timpson Collection.* Santa Fe, N.Mex.: The Gallery and Al Luckett, Jr., 1991.

The Collector's Guide: Santos of New Mexico. "Santos of New Mexico," The Collector's Guide Web Site. Available online. URL: http://www.collectorsguide.com/fa/fa077.shtml. Downloaded on June 22, 2005.

Yorba, Jonathan. *Arte Latino: Treasures from the Smithsonian American Art Museum.* New York: Watson–Guptill, 2001, pp. 38–39.

G

Gamboa, Harry, Jr.

(1951–   ) *video artist, performance artist, installation artist, photographer, writer, educator*

A multitalented artist who sees his work as a social force for the moment and not art created for the ages, Harry Gamboa, Jr., has been chronicling urban Chicano (Mexican-American) life with wit and expressive power for nearly four decades. He was born in Los Angeles, California, on November 1, 1951. Rebellious to authority from childhood, he refused to speak English in an elementary school class, and his teacher punished him by making him wear a dunce cap with the letters S–P–A–N–I–S–H written across it. Gamboa later became a student activist leader while attending the University of California–Los Angeles (UCLA) and led student walkouts in 1968 to protest the poor treatment of Chicano students.

After college, Gamboa joined with fellow Chicano artists GRONK (Glugio Nicondra), WILLIE HERRÓN, PATSSI VALDEZ, and actor Humberto Sandoval to found ASCO (Spanish for "nausea"), an experimental performance-art group.

ASCO was a controversial group that attacked racism and prejudice against Latinos in highly publicized "no movie" events. Their "films" were actually a series of stills. When a curator at the Los Angeles County Museum of Art (LACMA) declared that Chicanos do not make "real art," Gamboa and two of his colleagues spray painted their names on the side of a LACMA building, calling it the first Chicano art to be presented at the museum.

ASCO disbanded in 1987; since then, Gamboa has concentrated on making videos. He has produced more than 30 of them, as well as interactive Web sites and digital photography. His experimental videos have been heavily influenced by Hollywood B pictures, film noir, and Mexican telenovelas. One video, *L.A. Familia* (1993), was part of the 1995 Whitney Museum of American Art Biennial. His work has been exhibited in solo shows at the Smithsonian Institution in Washington, D.C. (1997), the List Visual Arts Center at the Massachusetts Institute of Technology (MIT) in Cambridge (2000), LACMA (2001), and the International Center for Photography (ICP) in New York (2003).

Gamboa has taught at several branches of the University of California, including Los Angeles, Riverside, and San Diego. A permanent collection of his media work and papers has been set up at Stanford University in California. His collective writings was published in 1998 under the title *Urban Exile*. It includes interviews with other artists, poetry, fiction, photography, and political writing.

Gamboa is married to fellow artist Barbara Carrasco. "In the context of urban hysteria," wrote Susan Otto, reviewing Gamboa's book, "he is an observer of the extended-play apocalypse who refuses to become numb."

Further Reading

Buuck, David. "Harry Gamboa and the Contemporary Avant-Garde," Jouvert Web Site. Available online. URL: http://social.chass.ncsu.edu/jouvert/v613/gamboa.htm. Downloaded on June 26, 2005.

Gamboa, Jr., Harry. Chon A. Noriega, ed. *Urban Exile: Collected Writings of Harry Gamboa, Jr.* Minneapolis: University of Minnesota Press, 1998.

Harry Gamboa, Jr. Official Web Site. Available online. URL: http://www.harrygamboajr.com. Downloaded on March 17, 2006.

Rangel, Jeffrey. "Oral History Interview with Harry Gamboa," Smithsonian Archives of American Art. Available online. URL: http://artarchives.si.edu/guides/archivos/index.cfm?fuseaction=OralHistories.detailOH&CollectionID=5475. Downloaded on June 27, 2005.

Further Viewing

Harry Gamboa, Jr.: 1990s Video Arts, Vol. 3. UCLA Chicano Studies Research Center, DVD, 2004.

Garcia, Andy
(Andrés Arturo García Menéndez)
(1956–) *actor, documentary filmmaker, film producer*

A handsome, serious leading man with an intense style of acting, Andy Garcia is as devoted to his family and the Cuban-American community as he is to his film career. Andrés Arturo García Menéndez, the youngest of three children, was born in Havana, Cuba, on April 12, 1956. His father was a successful lawyer and farmer who developed the "Garcia Number One" avocado. His mother was an English teacher. Fidel Castro came to power when Andrés was three and appropriated the family's wealth and property in his communist revolution. The Garcías fled Cuba in 1961 and settled in Miami, Florida. Unable to practice law in the United States, the senior García worked for a caterer. He saved up his money and built a million-dollar perfume company.

Andy attended Miami Beach Senior High School where he excelled in athletics, particularly basketball. In his senior year, he suffered a bout with mononucleosis that ended his athletic career and eventually led him to try acting at Florida International University. He left school in 1977 to pursue an acting career. He began to find theater work in Florida and elsewhere before moving to Hollywood the following year.

While auditioning for parts in film and television, Garcia supported himself as a waiter and loading dockworker. He received mixed messages about his ethnicity. One agent said he would only represent the actor if he lost his Spanish accent, while a casting director would not cast him because he did not look ethnic enough. When he finally began to get work in 1981, Garcia was caught in the familiar Latino actor's typecasting as either a criminal or a cop. He was a gang member in the pilot episode of the television cop drama *Hill Street Blues* in 1981, a detective on the trail of a serial killer in *The Mean Season* (1985), and a drug lord in *Eight Million Ways to Die* (1986). It was his sharp characterization in this last film that caught the attention of filmmaker Brian de Palma who offered Garcia the role of gangster Al Capone's "enforcer" Frank Nitti in his film *The Untouchables* (1987). Not wanting to be forever typecast as a gangster, Garcia held out for the role of good guy Elliott Ness's right-hand man, agent George Stare. De Palma gave in, and Garcia received excellent reviews for the role. He played another good cop investigating a very bad one in the police thriller *Internal Affairs* (1990), his first time in a leading role.

But the role that made Andy Garcia a film star was Vincent, the ruthless nephew of mob boss Michael Corleone in the long-anticipated *The Godfather, Part III* (1990), directed by Francis Ford Coppola. Garcia beat out some of Hollywood's biggest names for the part, including Robert De Niro. While the film did not measure up to expectations for most critics, Garcia got rare reviews for his volatile gangster and earned an Academy Award nomination as Best Supporting Actor.

He now found himself being offered a wider range of roles. He played a fake hero who takes credit away from a real one in *Hero* (1992), the husband of a hopeless alcoholic in *When a Man Loves a Woman* (1994), and legendary gangster Lucky Luciano in *Hoodlum* (1997). In 2000, Garcia played a part dear to his heart, the famous Cuban trumpeter Arturo Sandoval in a Home Box Office (HBO) television movie, *For Love or Country—The Arturo Sandoval Story.* He was nominated for a Golden Globe Award for his portrayal of the musician.

Another Cuban musician that Garcia admired was Israel "Cachao" Lopez, who pioneered mambo dance music in the 1930s. In 1993, he produced and directed a Spanish-language documentary about Lopez's life. Several years before this, Garcia had conceived a fictional film about three brothers in Cuba on the eve of the Castro revolution. Called *The Lost City,* it has been Garcia's pet project for the past 16 years, as he has struggled to find financing for the film. In 2005, *The Lost City,* directed by, cowritten by, and starring Garcia, was released to mixed reviews.

An unusually private man by Hollywood standards, Andy Garcia has been married to his college sweetheart, María Victoria Lorido, a photographer, since 1982. They live in Toluca Lake, California, and also have a home in Key Biscayne, Florida. Garcia is active in many social causes, particularly those affecting Cuban Americans. "You are defined by who you are, by your choices in life, in all regards, not just in doing movies," he has said.

Further Reading

The Internet Movie Database. "Andy Garcia," The Internet Movie Database. Available online. URL: http://www.imdb.com/name/nm0000412/. Downloaded on February 25, 2005.

Morey, Janet, and Wendy Dunn. *Famous Hispanic Americans.* New York: Dutton, 1996, pp. 53–63.

Ojito, Mirta. "His Homeland, His Obsession." *New York Times,* February 12, 2005, p. B7.

Further Viewing

For Love or Country—The Arturo Sandoval Story (2000). VHS/DVD, 1997/1999.

The Godfather, Part III (1990). Paramount Home Video, VHS/DVD, 2002/2005.

When a Man Loves a Woman (1994). Touchstone Video, VHS/DVD, 1997/2003.

Garcia, Jerry (Jerome John Garcia)

(1942–1995) *rock singer, guitarist, songwriter*

Founder and lead guitarist for one of the most durable bands in rock history, Jerry Garcia was, despite his reputation as a prankster and druggie, a profoundly serious musician who mastered a wide range of styles in his 30-year career. Jerome John Garcia was born in San Francisco, California, on August 1, 1942. His grandfather, Manuel Garcia, immigrated to the United States from Spain in 1918. His father was a professional musician who named him after the Broadway composer Jerome Kern. His father died in a fishing accident when Jerry was five, and he was raised by his grandparents while his mother worked as a nurse.

At 15, Garcia came under the spell of rock and roll and the electric-guitar playing of Chuck Berry. Uncertain of his future, he dropped out of high school and joined the army but was discharged in 1960 as unfit for service. He discovered folk music, which was becoming a leading form of pop music in the late 1950s, and became a skilled folk guitarist and bluegrass banjo player. He teamed up for a time with poet Robert Hunter, making bluegrass music together. Hunter would later become the main lyricist to Garcia's music. Garcia played in several folk and jug bands with names like Sleep Hill Hog Stompers and Thunder Mountain Tub Thumpers. With

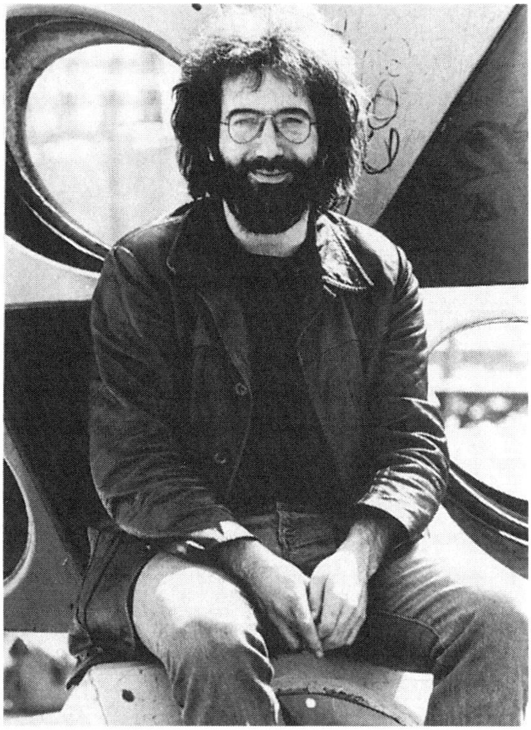

Jerry Garcia led his rock band, the Grateful Dead, for three decades and may be the only rock star to have a popular ice-cream flavor named after him. *(Photofest)*

friends Bob Weir and Ron McKunan (better known as "Pigpen"), he formed Mother McCree's Uptown Jug Champions in 1964. They switched to playing electric rock when a music-store owner offered them free equipment if they changed their style.

Garcia's befriending of jazz trumpeter Phil Lesh was a turning point in his musical career. Lesh introduced him to the world of jazz and blues and became the bass player for Garcia's new rock band, the Warlocks. The group also included his jug band buddies and Bob Sommers on drums. They played regularly at Beat writer Ken Kesey's "acid kool aid" parties (at which the drug LSD was notoriously consumed) and became one of the first so-called psychedelic rock bands of the 1960s.

The Warlocks soon changed their name to the Grateful Dead, a name which Garcia supposedly picked out randomly from a dictionary. In summer 1966, the group moved to San Francisco's Haight–Ashbury neighborhood, which would become the epicenter of the hippie movement. Their free-form eclectic rock and blues music gained national attention at the Monterey Pop Festival in 1967, and they signed a recording contract with Warner Bros. Records. "Luckily, our first record was not a huge success," said Garcia in an interview. "It gave us a chance to be slow and deliberate about our own development. It kept us interested."

The Grateful Dead were certainly different from other groups of the time. They seemed little concerned with the commercial side of recording and gained a reputation as a free-spirited band whose live performances could be exciting or boring, depending on the mood of the musicians that night. They gained a strong following at San Francisco's Carousel Ballroom, which promoter Bill Graham later took over and renamed the Fillmore West. The band's resistance to the commercial world lessened, and two albums, *Workingman's Dead* and *American Beauty* (both 1970), became best sellers.

The Dead's lineup in the 1970s changed regularly as members left and others died (Pigpen passed away in 1973 from liver disease). For a time they even had a female vocalist, Donna Jean Godchaux. Garcia was an easygoing leader who encouraged members to record on their own, something he began to do regularly after 1971. His solo albums reflected his eclectic taste and love of all kinds of music—bluegrass, rock, jazz, blues, and rhythm and blues. He formed the Jerry Garcia Band in the 1980s, but perhaps his most outstanding work on his own was the series of albums he made with master mandolinist David Grisman beginning with *Almost Acoustic* in 1988. Fans used to Garcia's one-note guitar solos with the Dead were surprised to hear his intricate acoustic work with Grisman on roots and traditional mountain music.

At the same time, the Grateful Dead was becoming a performing phenomenon. Despite having only one top–40 hit in two decades, the group developed a huge audience of faithful followers who called themselves "Deadheads" and seemed to spend much of their lives following the group from concert to concert about the country. Some supported themselves by selling Dead merchandise, everything from T-shirts to live music tapes, at concerts. While their music was a draw, the mystique of the group and their anything-can-happen concerts was equally important. As one Deadhead told an outsider, "The Grateful Dead is only fifty percent music. The other half you will *never* understand."

By the 1990s, several generations of new Deadheads had joined the tour. Many of them were not born when the group began in the 1960s. "Our audience doesn't come to see showmanship and theatrics," Garcia once said. "They realize what we are and that we're not performers and that we're a group that's earnestly trying to accomplish something and we don't quite know what it is."

Years of hard living and addictions to cocaine and heroin caught up with Garcia by the mid-1980s. In 1986, he went into a diabetic coma and almost died. He finally succumbed to a heart attack on August 9, 1995. The band he made famous continues to perform on tour without him, though they have dropped the word *Grateful* from their name. Aside from his musical legacy, Jerry Garcia is the only rock musician to have a best-selling ice cream flavor, Ben & Jerry's Cherry Garcia, and, more recently, a line of herbal teas named after him.

Further Reading

Gans, David, ed. *Not Fade Away: The Online World Remembers Jerry Garcia.* New York: Thunder's Mouth Press, 1995.

Garcia, Jerry, Jann Wenner, and Charles Reich. *Garcia: A Signpost to New Space.* New York: Da Capo Press, 2003 [reissue].

Jackson, Blair. *Garcia: An American Life.* New York: Penguin, 2000.

Troy, Sandy. *Captain Trips: A Biography of Jerry Garcia.* New York: Thunder's Mouth Press, 1995.

Further Listening

All Good Things: Jerry Garcia Studio Sessions. Rhino Records, CD [box set], 2004.

Grisman & Garcia. Acoustic Disc, CD, 1991.

The Very Best of the Grateful Dead. Rhino Records, CD, 2003.

Further Viewing

Grateful Dawg (2000). Columbia/Tristar Home Video. VHS/DVD, 2003/2004.

Grateful Dead—View from the Vault 1–3. Monterey Home Video, VHS/DVD [box set], 1990, 2001/2002.

García, Rupert
(Marshall R. García)

(1941–) *painter, graphic artist, printmaker, writer, educator*

A leading Chicano artist in the San Francisco Bay area, Rupert García has used the expressive power and bold colors of his posters and paintings to focus on injustice and racism in American society for Latinos and other minorities. Marshall R. García was born in French Camp, California, on September 29, 1941. At age 21 he entered the U.S. Air Force and served in the Air Police at home and later in Indochina at the beginning of the Vietnam War. After his discharge in 1966, he attended San Francisco State University on the GI Bill and earned a bachelor of arts (B.A.) degree in painting in 1968 and a master of arts (M.A.) degree in printmaking and silkscreen in 1970.

Based on his Vietnam experiences and his strong sense of social justice, García became a leader in the student protest movement of the late 1960s. He spoke out against the disproportionate number of Latinos and other minorities serving in Vietnam and organized protests against the war.

He discovered that he was able to express himself far more effectively in his art than with words alone. His political posters, produced between 1967 and 1975, were about the Vietnam War, racism, and injustice in American society at home and abroad. García's work combined the power of the great 20th-century Mexican muralists with the equally bold style of American pop art. His posters and paintings gained national attention in 1978 when a one-man show of his work was put on at the San Francisco Museum of Modern Art (SFMOMA). Since then, he has had numerous group and solo exhibits. Among his most recent solo exhibits were "Politics and Provocation: The Posters of Rupert García" at the Corcoran Gallery of Art in Washington, D.C. (2001) and "Rupert García: Another Look, the 1960s & 1970s" at the Rena Bransten Gallery in San Francisco (2003).

García is also a well-known teacher and writer. He has taught at numerous colleges and universities since 1969 and since 1988 has taught art at San Jose State University, School of Art and Design, where he is currently professor of art. His books include a history of Chicano muralists and a bibliography of Mexican artist Frida Kahlo. He has also written many essays. In 1993, Rupert García was awarded an honorary Doctorate in Fine Arts from the San Francisco Art Institute. He received the Arts as a Hammer Award from the Center for the Study of Political Graphics in Los Angeles in 2000.

Further Reading

Cancel, Luis R. et al. *The Latin American Spirit: Art and Artists in the United States, 1920–1970.* New York: The Bronx Museum of the Arts and Harry N. Abrams, 1988, p. 317.

Favela, Ramon. *The Art of Rupert García: A Survey Exhibit.* San Francisco: Chronicle Books, 1987.

García, Rupert. *Rupert García, 4 September–4 October 1997.* San Francisco: Rena Bransten Gallery, 1997.

———. *Rupert García: Paintings and Posters, 1967–1990.* San Francisco: Fine Arts Museum of San Francisco, 1991.

Karlstrom, Paul J. "Oral History Interview with Rupert García." The Smithsonian Archive of American Art. Available online. URL: http://www.aaa.si.edu/oralhist/garcia96.htm. Downloaded on June 30, 2005.

Garza, Carmen Lomas

(1948–) *painter, illustrator, printmaker, sculptor, educator*

A leading Chicana artist, Carmen Lomas Garza celebrates the everyday world of Chicanos (Mexican Americans) in her native Texas in her simple, brightly colored paintings. She was born in Kingsville, Texas, 30 miles southwest of Corpus Christi, in 1948. Her grandparents left Mexico during the Mexican Revolution and settled in Texas. Her early love of art was hereditary: Her mother was a painter and florist, and her grandmother crocheted, embroidered, and fashioned paper flowers. Both women encouraged Garza to be an artist, and she drew every day.

She attended Texas Arts and Industry University in Kingsville after high school; today, it is a branch of Texas A&M. After receiving her teacher's certificate in art in 1972, she earned a Master of Art (M.A.) degree from Juarez–Lincoln/Antioch Grad School in Austin, Texas, the following year. She also earned a Master of Arts (M.A.) degree in art from San Francisco State University in 1981.

Garza's response to prejudice and racism in college was different from other students and artists. She decided to react positively by recreating the colorful moments of Chicano life that she recalled growing up in Kingsville. As she began her artistic career, Garza dropped some of the techniques and styles that she learned in school. "[I wanted to] do my artwork as simple and direct as possible," she later wrote. "I really wanted to be able to communicate. I felt that I could not afford to lose my Mexican American audience."

In her deceptively "primitive" paintings, Chicana women go about their chores, cooking, cleaning, and playing with their children. Men work and recreate. Families gather to share meals and celebrations. Although she clearly is aiming her art at the Chicanos and other Latinos, she states her titles in both Spanish and English to reach an Anglo audience as well.

Garza has illustrated books about Chicano life including *In My Family* (1996). She is a master of the Mexican craft of *papal picado,* which involves folding and cutting tissue paper to create art forms. She wrote a book for children about this craft, *Making Magic Windows* (1999).

Carmen Lomas Garza was granted a National Endowment for the Arts (NEA) fellowship in printmaking in 1981 and another in painting in 1987. She has received four California Art Commission Artist in Residence grants between 1979 and 1986. In 2004, she was in the residency program of the Rockefeller Study and Conference Center in Bellagio, Italy. She currently teaches at San Francisco State University and lives in that city.

Further Reading

Congdon, Kristin G., and Kara Kelley Hallmark. *Artists from Latin American Cultures: A Biographical Dictionary.* Westport, Conn.: Greenwood Press, 2002, pp. 146–150.

Garza, Carmen Lomas. *A Piece of My Heart/Pedcito de Mi Corazon: The Art of Carmen Lomas Garza.* New York: New Press, 1994.

———. *Making Magic Windows: Creating Cut-Paper Art with Carmen Lomas Garza.* Berkeley, Calif.: Children's Book Press, 1999.

Garza, Carmen Lomas, and Harriet Rohman, David Scheiter, ed. *In My Family/En Mi Familia.* Berkeley, Calif.: Children's Book Press, 1996.

Karlstrom, Paul J. "Oral History Interview with Carmen Lomas Garza," The Smithsonian Archives of American Arts. Available online. URL: http://artarchives.si.edu/guides/archivos/index.cfm?fuseaction=OralHistories.detailOH&CollectionID=5492. Downloaded on September 1, 2005.

Gil de Montes, Roberto

(1950–) painter, sculptor, ceramist, photographer, educator

A Mexican-American artist who specializes in lyrical, colorful landscapes and intriguing male portraits, Roberto Gil de Montes has revealed a deep fascination with color and texture and their symbolic meanings throughout his career. He was born in Guadalajara, Mexico, in 1950. His family moved to Los Angeles, California, when he was five. The Gil de Montes family moved frequently during his childhood. Roberto later attended Otis Art Institute in California where he earned a master of fine arts (M.F.A.) degree.

Early on Gil de Montes was interested in ceramics and photography, which he still pursues, but oil painting soon became his central medium as an artist. Since he was part of the East Los Angeles Latino art community in the late 1970s, his art has become less ethnically oriented and more universal.

An exceptional portraitist, Gil de Montes's male figures are often mysterious and distant. In two key works, *Screen* and *Boy Behind Screen,* two male heads are shielded from the viewer by a highly textured screen or veil. The viewer is both attracted to the persons and at the same time distanced from them. Other works are more ominous, such as *Trap,* where a person is caught in a spider's web. In *Snarled,* a dead bird is entwined in a maze of twisted cords.

Gil de Montes has traveled extensively in India, a country whose exoticism clearly fascinates him. In a series of paintings, *Works Inspired by India,* his childlike figures and landscapes are filled with a bright, lyrical quality that is captivating.

He had a close friendship with fellow Chicano artist CARLOS ALMARAZ. His painting *Grid and Sound* is a homage to the painter, who died in 1989.

Gil de Montes's work was part of the national touring show *Hispanic Art in the United States: Thirty Contemporary Painters and Sculptors* in the 1980s. A video produced for a Public Broadcasting Service (PBS) television series, *Behind the Scenes with Roberto Gil de Montes,* in 1992 won the Golden Camera Award, at the United States International Film and Video Festival, and the Japan Prize, an international competition for educational television programs.

More recently, Gil de Montes joined forces with fellow artists Elsa Flores and Peter Shire to create public artworks (fountains, benches, planters) for a community park on the Paseo Cesar Chavez in Los Angeles. He is currently professor of art at the University of California–Los Angeles (UCLA). "His sole passion above all seems to be to explore paint, to find out through paint what one is capable of, what paint itself can do, and to enjoy oneself in the process," Margarita Nieto has written about the artist.

Further Reading

Beardsley, John, and Jane Livingston. *Hispanic Art in the United States: Thirty Contemporary Painters & Sculptors.* New York: Abbeville Press, 1987, pp. 173–177.

Nieto, Margarita. "Roberto Gil de Montes," Art Scene California Web Site. Available online. URL: http://artscenecal.com/ArticlesFile/Archive/Articles1996/Articles0996/RgdeMontes.html. Downloaded on July 1, 2005.

Yorba, Jonathan. *Arte Latino: Treasures from the Smithsonian American Art Museum.* New York: Watson–Guptill Publications, 2001, pp. 40–41.

Further Viewing

Behind the Scenes with Roberto Gil de Montes. First Run Features, VHS, 1992.

Gomez, Thomas (Sabino Tomas Gomez)
(1905–1971) *actor*

One of the first Latinos to be nominated for an Academy Award in acting, Thomas Gomez was a memorable character actor during Hollywood's Golden Age, adept at playing both sympathetic and villainous roles. Sabino Tomas Gomez was born on Long Island, New York, on July 10, 1905. Of Spanish descent, he was granted a scholarship to a New York drama school after finishing high school to study under veteran actor Walter Hampden. Soon after, he answered an ad for actors for the Alfred Lunt Theater group and began his professional career. His Broadway debut was playing a cadet in a production of *Cyrano de Bergerac,* starring Hampden. He appeared in a number of Broadway productions through 1940 and occasionally returned to the stage after that.

Gomez was cast as an evil Nazi in his first film role in *Sherlock Holmes and the Voice of Terror* (1942). Heavyset with brooding features and a hoarse voice, he was born to play bad guys, although he often portrayed kindlier characters with equal conviction. He did, however, refuse to play Latin or Latino characters that were stereotypical lazy men in sombreros or wicked banditos. He would only take a Latin part that he said could be played "with sympathy, or at least with humanity." He found such a role in a film noir that was set on the Mexican border, *Ride the Pink Horse* (1947). His insightful performance as a Mexican peasant earned him an Oscar nomination as Best Supporting Actor.

Gomez had key roles in several other film-noir classics. He was gangster Edward G. Robinson's right-hand man in *Key Largo* (1948) and a small-time operator trapped in the numbers racket by his lawyer brother, played by John Garfield, in *Force of Evil* (1948). Gomez appeared often on television, beginning in 1940 with an experimental broadcast of the play *A Game of Chess.* He later played Pasquale, an Italian restaurateur, in the early ethnic sitcom *Life with Luigi* (1953) and was a memorable devil in an episode of the fantasy series *The Twilight Zone* (1959–64). The actor returned to the Broadway stage after nearly a decade in the original production of the hit play *A Man for All Seasons* (1961–63).

Gomez's last film was *Beneath the Planet of the Apes* (1970), a stirring sequel to *Planet of the Apes* (1968). A lifelong bachelor and a gourmet who loved eating in good restaurants, Gomez weighed close to 300 pounds most of his adult life. Dieting at the end of his life brought his weight down to less than 150 pounds. He died on June 18, 1971, from the after effects of a car accident in Santa Monica, California.

Further Reading

Katz, Ephraim, Fred Klein, and Ronald Dean Nolen. *The Film Encyclopedia,* 4th edition. New York: HarperResource, 2001, p. 542.

The Internet Movie Database. "Thomas Gomez," The Internet Movie Database. Available online. URL: http://www.imdb.com/name/nm0327089/. Downloaded on June 9, 2005.

Further Viewing

Force of Evil (1948). Republic Studios/Lions Gate Home Entertainment, VHS/DVD, 1999/2004.

Key Largo (1948). MGM/UA/Warner Home Video, VHS/DVD, 1989/2000.

Gómez-Peña, Guillermo

(1955–) *performance and video artist, installation artist, writer, editor, educator*

A self-proclaimed trickster who confronts and assaults his audience with his challenging performance pieces, Guillermo Gómez-Peña focuses his work on the borders that divide people, cultures, and national identities. He was born in Mexico City on September 23, 1955. He came to the United States in 1978 when he was 23 years old, became a citizen, and studied at the California Institute of the Arts in Valencia.

In 1981, Gómez-Peña and choreographer Sara-Jo Berman formed a "neotribalist" group called Poyesis Genetica that performed around southern California. When the group disbanded in 1985, Gómez-Peña and Berman founded the Border Arts Workshop, which operated along the U.S.-Mexican border near San Diego. The workshop contributed performance pieces scripted by Gómez-Peña, interviewed residents on both sides of the border, and sank great staples into the ground along the border, dramatizing the connectiveness of the two countries.

Kristin Congdon and Kara Kelley Hallmark have called Gómez-Peña's performance works "raw, confrontational, politically driven and highly intellectual." In *Year of the White Bear,* one of his best-known performance pieces, he and fellow artist Coco Fusco posed in cages dressed in stereotypical Mexican costumes while their "guards" fed them by hand and walked them on leashes to the bathroom. Visitors were encouraged to pay them money to perform dances, tell stories, and pose with them for pictures. The piece uses savage satire to show how ethnic "others" are often treated little better by society than zoo animals.

Gómez-Peña is also a frequent contributor to the magazines *High Performance* and *The Drama Review.* He is the author of eight books, including his most recent, *Ethno-Techno: Writings in Performance, Activism and Pedagogy* (2005). Like most of his books, it is a collection of performance scripts, essays, poetry, and other writings. His *New World Border* (1997) won the American Book Award. Gómez-Peña was editor of the experimental art periodical *The Broken Line* and contributes regularly to *Latino U.S.A.,* a program on National Public Radio (NPR). He lives in San Francisco, where he is artistic director of La Pocha Nostra, a transdisciplinary arts organization that provides a support network and forum for artists.

Gómez-Peña was the first Chicano artist to be the recipient of the John D. and Catherine T. MacArthur Fellowship (in 1991) and received the Cineaste Lifetime Achievement Award at the Taos Talking Pictures Film Festival in 2000. His performance, installation, and video work has been featured at more than 700 venues worldwide, including the House of World Culture, Berlin, Germany (2002); the Cervantino Festival, Mexico City (2004); and the Los Angeles Museum of Contemporary Art (LACMA) in California (2005).

"I am a nomadica Mexican artist/writer in the process of Chicanization, which means I am slowly heading North," Gómez-Peña has written. "Once I get 'there,' wherever it is, I am forever condemned to return, and then to obsessively reenact my journey."

Further Reading

Congdon, Kristin G., and Kara Kelley Hallmark. *Artists from Latin American Cultures: A Biographical Dictionary.* Westport, Conn.: Greenwood Press, 2002, pp. 91–94.

Gómez-Peña, Guillermo. *Ethno-Techno: Writings in Performance, Activism and Pedagogy.* London: Routledge Press, 2005.

———. *Dangerous Border Crossers: The Artist Talks Back.* New York: Routledge, 2000.

Guillermo Gómez-Peña's Official Web Site. Available online. URL: www.pochanostra.com. Dowloaded on September 26, 2006.

Gonzalez, Myrtle

(1891–1918) *actress*

When President George W. Bush mentioned the name Myrtle Gonzalez in his proclamation for National Hispanic Heritage Month in September 2002, most Americans and many Latinos probably had never heard of her. But Myrtle Gonzalez deserved her moment in the spotlight as arguably Hollywood's first Latina film star.

She was born in Los Angeles, California, on September 28, 1891. Her father was a grocer and the descendant of a long line of Hispanos, longtime Mexicans living in California. Her mother was the child of Irish immigrants who settled in New York. Myrtle attended a convent school in Los Angeles. As a young woman she enjoyed riding and swimming.

A natural actress, Gonzales was hired at an early age as a performer with the Belasco Stock Company in Los Angeles. She moved easily from stage to screen when she signed a contract with Vitagraph Films. Interestingly, the Hollywood studios allowed Gonzales and other Latino stars to keep their Latin names and identities, a practice that was changed in the sound era. Gonzales appeared in her first silent movie in 1913, although some sources claim she made her first film a year earlier. She was successful enough to be signed later to Universal Studios, where her innocence and beauty earned her the nickname "the Virgin Lily of the Screen."

But Gonzalez was no dainty flower in silent movies. At Universal, she specialized in playing high-spirited, outdoorsy heroines in such action adventure films as *The Secret of the Swamp* (1916), *The Girl of Lost Lake* (1916), and *The Greater Law* (1917). In this last film, set in the frozen Klondike, Gonzalez fights a duel with the man who supposedly killed her brother and wins. In *The End of the Rainbow* (1916), Gonzalez's heroine works undercover in her tycoon father's lumber camp in the California Redwoods, where she exposes corruption and saves the day. Her father was played by Latino actor George Hernandez, who costarred with her in several films.

In real life, Gonzalez was not as robust as the women she portrayed on the silver screen. She had a heart condition and was in fragile health. As World War I (1914–1918) ended, a great influenza pandemic swept across the United States and the rest of the world, taking more than 22 million lives. It claimed the life of the 27-year-old actress on October 22, 1918. She was survived by her husband Allen Watt and a seven-year-old child. While information about this pioneering Latina film star is scant and few of her films have survived, she opened the doors of Hollywood to generations of Latino actors and actresses who have followed in her footsteps.

Further Reading

The Internet Movie Database. "Myrtle Gonzalez," The Internet Movie Database. Available online. URL: http://www.imdb.com/name/nm0327762/. Downloaded on June 8, 2005.

Rodríguez, Clara E. *Heroes, Lovers, and Others: The Story of Latinos in Hollywood.* Washington, D.C.: Smithsonian Books, 2004, pp. 32–34.

Gonzalez-Gonzalez, Pedro (Ramiro Gonzalez-Gonzalez)

(1925–2006) *actor, comedian*

One of the most familiar Latino-American actors in American films and television in the 1950s and 1960s, Pedro Gonzalez-Gonzalez brought good humor and personality to the stereotypical Mexican roles he played. Ramiro Gonzalez-Gonzalez was born in Aguilares, Texas, on May 24, 1925, into a Mexican-American family. His last name is a combination of his father and mother's identical surnames. His father was a trumpet player and his mother a dancer of Spanish descent. They put together a family touring company, "Las Perlitas," that entertained migrant workers and townspeople in the Southwest. Pedro had to leave school at age seven to join the troupe and never learned to read and write. A natural comic, he soon was stealing the show from the other family members. At age 17, he married 15-year-old dancer Lee Aguirre. The marriage would last 64 years until his death.

Gonzalez-Gonzalez served as a truck driver in the army during World War II (1939–45). After the war, his parents retired the act, and he worked solo as a comedian for Spanish-speaking audiences. The host of a San Antonio, Texas, telethon on which he worked suggested that he try to become a contestant on the popular television quiz show *You Bet Your Life,* hosted by comic and film star Groucho Marx. Gonzalez-Gonzalez appeared on the show in 1953. He matched Groucho quip for quip to the great delight of the audience. Actor John Wayne saw the show and immediately signed the Latino funnyman to a contract with his production company. Thus, a 40-year film career was born.

Gonzalez-Gonzalez appeared regularly in many Wayne films from *The High and the Mighty* (1954) through *Chisum* (1970), usually playing small supporting roles as a Mexican barber, bartender, or other working man. With his thick accent and funny mannerisms, he also provided comic relief in dozens of other films. He appeared regularly on television, especially Westerns such as *Gunsmoke, Cheyenne,* and *Wanted: Dead or Alive.* Because Gonzalez-Gonzalez was functionally illiterate, he memorized his lines by having his wife read them to him.

In later years, he was criticized for perpetuating the stereotype of the comic, lazy Mexican, but in his defense, he claimed he took the only roles offered to him to provide for his family. He retired from acting in 1995 and died at age 80 on February 6, 2006, in Culver City, Los Angeles, California. His career, claimed actor Edward James Olmos, "inspired every Latino actor."

His brother José Gonzalez-Gonzalez was also an actor and played similar small roles in films. His grandson, Clifton Collins, Jr., has been a film actor since 1991 and was praised for his performance as real-life murderer Perry Smith in the Oscar-nominated film *Capote* (2005).

Further Reading

The Internet Movie Database. "Pedro Gonzalez-Gonzalez," The Internet Movie Database. Available online.

URL: http://www.imdb.com/name/nm0327602/. Downloaded on February 19, 2006.

"Pedro Gonzalez-Gonzalez, 80, Film and TV Character Actor." [Obituary]. *New York Times,* February 17, 2006, p. A21.

What a Character! "Pedro Gonzalez-Gonzalez," Whata Character.com. Available online. URL: http://www.what-a-character.com/cgi-bin/display.cgi?id=982797576. Downloaded on February 20, 2006.

Further Viewing

The High and the Mighty (1954). Paramount Home Video, DVD (2 discs), 2005.

Rio Bravo (1959). Warner Home Video, VHS/DVD, 1993/2001.

Gormé, Eydie (Edith Gormezano)

(1931–) *pop and Latin singer*

A leading pop stylist with a big and expressive voice, Eydie Gormé rediscovered her Latin roots in the 1960s and 1970s, reaching out to a new audience of Latino Americans. Edith Gormezano was born in the Bronx, New York, on August 16, 1931. Her parents were Sephardic Jews, originally of Spanish descent. Her father was a tailor who came to the United States from Sicily. Her mother came from Turkey. The family spoke Spanish at home, and Eydie and her two siblings were fluent in Spanish and English.

Singing came naturally to Eydie, and she made her debut on the radio at age three. She sang with a student band in high school and after graduation worked as a Spanish interpreter with an export company. She attended night classes at the City College of New York (CCNY).

In 1950, at age 19, Gormé was hired as a vocalist by bandleader Tommy Tucker. From there she performed with Tex Beneke's band for a year before going solo in 1952. She signed a recording contract with Coral Records but had little success. Her big break came in September 1953 when comedian Steve Allen hired the vivacious singer to be a regular on his new late-night New York television variety show, *Tonight!* Within a year *Tonight!* went nationwide on the National Broadcasting Company (NBC). Eydie met and sang with singer Steve Lawrence on the show. The two fell in love and were married in December 1957. They remain today one of show business's most celebrated performing couples.

The previous year, Gormé's recording career finally took off when she signed with ABC–Paramount Records and began a string of hits that continued into the mid-1960s. In 1960, the married singers recorded *We Got Us,* their first of many duo albums. The title song won them a Grammy for Best Performance by a Vocal Group. Gormé reached the peak of her pop success in 1963 with the catchy dance hit "Blame It on the Bossa Nova."

With her pop career still in high gear, she made her first Spanish-language album *Amor* (1964) with the Mexican ensemble the Trio Los Panchos, following it with *More Amor* (1965). Gormé earned her first solo Grammy Award for Best Female Performance for the emotional ballad from the Broadway musical *Mame,* "If He Walked Into My Life" (1967).

As their record sales faded as new styles of music came on the scene, Lawrence and Gormé turned to the stage and television. In 1967, they starred in the musical *Golden Rainbow,* which ran for a year on Broadway. Their 1975 television tribute to composer George Gershwin, *Our Love Is Here to Stay,* won them an Emmy Award. Three years later, a similar special dedicated to the songs of Irving Berlin won seven Emmys, including one for Outstanding Variety or Music Program.

Gormé recorded two more Spanish albums in the 1970s—*La Gormé* (1976), which was nominated for a Grammy for Best Latin Recording, and *Muy Amigos Close Friends* (1977), a collaboration with Puerto Rican singer Danny Rivera.

Now in her 70s, Eydie Gormé continues to sing in Las Vegas clubs and other top venues with her favorite partner—her husband.

Further Reading

The Official Website of Steve Lawrence and Eydie Gormé. Available online. URL: http://www.steveandeydie.com. Downloaded on April 4, 2005.

Ruhlmann, William. "Eydie Gormé." All Music Guide Online. Available online. URL: http://www.allmusic.com/cg/amg.dll?p=amg&sql=11:qmfjzsheh2k-T1. Downloaded on April 4, 2005.

Further Listening

Amor/More Amor: Eydie Gormé and Trio Los Panchos. GL Music Co., CD, 2004.

The Best of Steve and Eydie. Curb Records, CD, 1990.

Blame It on the Bossa Nova. GL Music Co., CD, 2004.

Gronk
(Glugio Gronk Nicondra)

(1954–) *painter, performance artist, installation artist, muralist, photographer, video artist, scenic designer*

One of the most eccentric and challenging Chicano (Mexican-American) artists of his generation, Gronk has expressed his unique views on life and art in nearly every medium from painting to digital art. Glugio Gronk Nicondra was born in Mexico in 1954. His fierce individuality was inherited from his Mexican-born mother, who left his father shortly after his birth. She chose his middle name, which he later adopted as his professional name, from an article in an issue of *National Geographic* that she was reading while in labor. *Gronk* is a Brazilian Indian word meaning "to fly."

Glugio's childhood gave him little opportunity to soar. He led a hand-to-mouth existence with his mother, who had four more children out of wedlock. "Drawing was an escape for me—from poverty, from my environment," he later wrote. "It was a way of creating new worlds for myself."

While in high school in East Los Angeles (East LA), he met WILLIE HERRON and PATSSI VALDEZ who shared his artistic sensibilities. Together, they collabroated on outlandish artistic performances. Gronk also met at about the same time HARRY GAMBOA, JR., who encouraged him to contribute writings to the journal *Regeneracion.* Gronk dropped out of high school at 16 and two years later joined with Herrón, Valdez, and Gamboa to form ASCO (Spanish for "nausea"), an arts performance group whose goal was to challenge the values of establishment U.S. society, including those of traditional Chicano culture. Gronk was probably the most iconoclastic and impish of this group of iconoclasts. At one point, he called himself the Skid Row Manicurist and would roam the streets of East LA, painting the toenails of unsuspecting, sleeping street people.

In 1978, he began a unique visual diary, made up of daily drawings that he bound into books. By 1987, Gronk had collected 40 volumes of his drawings. While he continued to collaborate with his ASCO colleagues—making murals with Herrón and directing a play written by Gamboa, he also created solo installation art and many paintings. His bold, expressive style of painting owed much to German expressionism and surrealism. "Some of Gronk's paintings look like they belong on the side of a subway car," wrote John Beardsley and Jane Livingston. "Their roots are clearly in a rebellious ghetto culture." In 1985, he was one of nine Los Angeles artists included in the Los Angeles Contemporary Museum of Art's (LACMA) project "Summer 1985." The museum held a major retrospective of his work, *A Living Survey,* in 1993.

One of Gronk's most recent projects is daring even by his standards. *Gronk's BrainFlame*

(2005) is a 14-minute computer-animated piece that he created with several collaborators for the Lode Star Dome Theater in Albuquerque, New Mexico. Gronk's first excursion into digital art, the work shows, according to the Contemporary Albuquerque Web site, "the flashpoint in a creative thought." Viewers sat back in a planetarium setting and viewed the work on a 4,750-square-foot digital canvas.

During the same summer, Gronk's scenic designs for the Santa Fe Opera's production of *Ainadamar* (The Fountain of Tears), an opera by Brazilian composer Osvaldo Golijov about the life of Spanish writer Federico García Lorca, were on display at the National Hispanic Culture Center Art Museum in Albuquerque. He has designed sets for other operas in LA and Paris.

"Whether you love his work or hate it, as is likely going to be the case, you can't help feeling uplifted by the testimony of one individual's decision to meet adversity with humor and conviction," states the back cover on a book about the artist entitled *Gronk! A Living Survey.*

Further Reading

Beardsley, John, and Jane Livingston. *Hispanic Art in The United States: Thirty Contemporary Painters & Sculptors.* New York: Abbeville Press, 1987, pp. 185–189.

Contemporary Albuquerque. "Gronk: BrainFlame and Ainadamar." Contemporary Albuquerque.com. Available online. URL: http://www.contemporaryalbuquerque.com/exhibits/2005/Gronk.html. Downloaded on March 21, 2006.

Gronk. *Gronk: Grand Hotels: Paintings and Drawings: 3 February–4 March, 1989.* Los Angeles: The Gallery, 1989.

Riggs, Thomas, ed. *St. James Guide to Hispanic Artists.* Detroit, Mich.: St. James Press, 2002, pp. 261–262.

Yunez, Rene. *Gronk! A Living Survey 1973–1993.* San Francisco: The Mexican Museum, 1993.

Guerrero, Lalo
(Eduardo Lalo Guerrero, Jr., Don Edwards)

(1916–2005) *Latin singer, songwriter, bandleader, guitarist*

A pioneer of Chicano music whose repertoire ranged freely from boogie woogie and big-band music to novelty songs and social-protest anthems, Lalo Guerrero was a beloved recording artist and bandleader in Mexico and the Southwest for more than six decades. Eduardo Lalo Guerrero, Jr., was born in a poor barrio in Tucson, Arizona, on December 24, 1916. His father, a boilermaker for the Southern Pacific Railroad, emigrated from Mexico's Baja California to Arizona. His mother taught him to play the guitar; he received no formal musical training. Trips to Mexico to visit relatives in his youth inspired him to write songs.

Guerrero dropped out of high school during the Great Depression and took to the road. He ended up in Los Angeles, California, where producer Manuel Acuna heard him playing his guitar on a street corner one day in 1939 and brought him into a recording studio the next day. That same year, Guerrero played at the New York World's Fair with his band Los Carlistas, representing the state of Arizona. From that year to his death, he recorded more than 700 songs, many of which he wrote.

In the 1940s, Guerrero recorded about 200 songs for Imperial Records in Los Angeles, under the Anglo name of Don Edwards because of public prejudice against Chicanos. He led his own band in the 1950s, becoming a fixture at East Los Angeles's Paramount Ballroom for years.

In 1955, Guerrero wrote and recorded a parody of the popular hit song "The Ballad of Davy Crockett," who in his humorous version became Pancho Sanchez. The song became a minor pop hit and led to a host of similar Chicano parodies of Anglo songs including "Tacos for Two," a takeoff of "Cocktails for Two;" "Pancho Claus;" and "Elvis Perez," parodying rock idol Elvis Presley.

Inspired by the novelty records of Alvin and the Chipmunks in 1958, Guerrero created his own Chicano chipmunks, Las Ardellites, that sang in Spanish and became a children's favorite. David Seville, creator of Alvin, sued him, but the suit was thrown out of court. With the profits from his novelty records, Guerrero opened his own nightclub, Lalo, which he operated until 1972.

Guerrero's music had a more serious side. He wrote and recorded Mexican corrido ballads, traditional topical songs of the day, in honor of Chicano activist Cesar Chavez and crusading senator Robert F. Kennedy in the 1960s. His Spanish song "Canción Mexicana" became an unofficial anthem of Mexico and was recorded by many Latino singers. Playwright and filmmaker LUIS VALDEZ incorporated Guerrero's boogie-woogie band music into his play *Zoot Suit* (1980), about the 1942 Chicano–Anglo riots in Los Angeles. The exposure revived Guerrero's career.

Guerrero's son Mark is also a singer and a songwriter, and father and son collaborated on many songs and recordings beginning in the late 1970s. They often performed together in concert as Lalo Guerrero and Mark Guerrero and the Second Generation Band.

Lalo Guerrero was named a national folk treasure by the Smithsonian Institute in 1980 and was awarded the presidential Medal of the Arts by President Bill Clinton in 1997. He published his autobiography, *Lalo: My Life and Music,* in 2002. He died on March 17, 2005, at age 88 at Rancho Mirage, California. "Lalo Guerrero gave us a voice . . . that we never had before," actor EDWARD JAMES OLMOS has said. "He's a national treasure."

Further Reading

Associated Press. "Lalo Guerrero, 88, Songwriter of Mexican-American Life." [Obituary.] *New York Times,* March 19, 2005, p. A13.

Guerrero, Mark. "Lalo Guerrero—the Father of Chicano Music." Mark Guerrero's Web site. Available online. URL: http://markguerrero.net/8.php. Downloaded on June 14, 2005.

Guerrero, Lalo, and Sherilyn Meece Mentes. *Lalo: My Life and Music.* Tucson: University of Arizona Press, 2002.

Further Listening

Vamos a Bailar—Otra Vez with Lalo Guerrero (1999). Break Records, CD, 2000.

Lalo Guerrero y Sus Ardillitas. Dimsa–Orfern, CD, 2005.

Guevara, Susan
(1956–) *illustrator*

A leading contemporary illustrator of popular children's books, many of which celebrate the Latino experience, Susan Guevara adopts her style and technique to fit each book and its theme. Born in California on January 27, 1956, in a Mexican-American family Guevara grew up in a suburb of the San Francisco Bay area. Her education was desultory for many years. "After my dilettante units at several local junior colleges I finally enrolled in the Academy of Art College in San Francisco," she writes in her official Web site. After a year at art school, she moved to Paris, France, and then Belgium to further her art studies. During the next year, she studied with Flemish Impressionist painter Remy Van Sleys and took courses at the Royal Academy of Fine Art in Brussels, Belgium.

She returned to San Francisco the next year and finally earned her Bachelor of Fine Arts (B.F.A.) degree at the Art Academy in 1988 at age 32. Her first illustrated children's book, *Emmett's Snowball,* with text by Ned Miller, appeared two years later. Since then she has illustrated more than a dozen children's books by such authors as Kathryn Lasky, Arthur Levine, and Aileen Friedman. In 1995, her illustrations for Gary Soto's *Chato's Kitchen,* about the humorous adventures of Chato, a barrio cat, received an Honorable Mention for the Americas Award. This critically praised book also was named an American Library Association (ALA) Notable Children's Book for the year. A sequel, *Chato and the Party Animals* (2000), won her the Pura Belpre Award for Illustration and the first Tomas Rivera Award.

Guevara continues to pursue Latino themes in her work. Her illustrations for Chicana poet Ana Castillo's *My Daughter, My Son, the Eagle, the Dove: An Aztec Chant* (2000) were painted on amate, a kind of Mexican bark. *Isabel's House of Butterflies* (2003), with text by Tony Johnston, is about a Mexican family's relation to the Monarch butterflies who migrate to a mountain in Mexico.

Guevara also has drawn illustrations for textbooks, greeting cards, and children's magazines such as *Cricket* and *Ladybug*. She is a frequent guest lecturer at the Academy of Art College in San Francisco. Guevara lives on her own mountain in a cabin in the Sierra Nevada range in California with her dog Don Diego Felipe Briones Ramirez Guevara.

"No two of my books are in the same style," Guevara has written. "Each story is unique to its setting and characters as should be the illustrations . . . The profession [illustration] has my awe and long-standing love. It satisfies me to the bone."

Further Reading

Castillo, Ana, and Susan Guevara. *My Daughter, My Son, the Eagle, the Dove: An Aztec Chant.* New York: Dutton Books, 2000.

Johnston, Tony, and Susan Guevara. *Isabel's House of Butterflies.* San Francisco: Sierra Club Books for Children, 2003.

Rockman, Connie C. *Eighth Book of Junior Authors and Illustrators.* New York: H. W. Wilson, 2000, pp. 191–194.

Soto, Gary, and Susan Guevara. *Chato and the Party Animals.* New York: Putnam Publishing Group, 2000.

Susan Guevara's Official Web site. Available online. URL: http://www.susanguevara.com. Downloaded on June 26, 2005.

Guzmán, Luis
(1957–) *actor*

Perhaps the most famous Latino movie actor whose name is not recognized by most, Luis Guzmán has been playing bad guys with heart and good guys with an edge in films and on television for three decades. He was born in Cayey, Puerto Rico, on January 1, 1957, moved to New York City as a youth with his family, and grew up on Manhattan's Lower East Side.

After graduating from the City College of New York (CCNY), Guzmán was hired as a youth counselor at the Henry Street Settlement House in lower Manhattan. It was here that he began to act in plays and street theater and eventually found parts in small, independent films. In 1977, he landed his first role in a major feature film, *Short Eyes,* a prison drama adapted from the play by Miguel Piñero. Given a recurring role on the popular television cop series *Miami Vice* in the early 1980s, Guzmán found more film work, usually in small supporting roles as a cop or a criminal.

In the 1990s, Guzmán began to land more meaty roles in such gritty crime films as *Q & A* (1991) and *Carlito's Way* (1993), which starred Al Pacino as a Latino crime lord who is trying to reform. Guzmán has become a favorite actor for two of the last decade's most innovative American filmmakers—Steven Soderbergh and Paul Thomas Anderson. He played sizable roles for Soderbergh as escaped criminal George Clooney's pal in *Out of Sight* (1998) and as English criminal Terence Stamp's cohort in the revenge drama *The Limey* (1999). In the Academy Award–winning *Traffic* (2000), he played an undercover cop who dies in the line of duty while on the trail of a drug lord.

Anderson has cast him in less-traditional roles, for example, as a bar owner who aspires to join a film company as a porn star in *Boogie Nights* (1997). In the director's next film, Guzmán played a contestant in the game show from hell in *Magnolia* (1999) and was Adam Sandler's business partner in Anderson's dark romantic comedy *Punch-Drunk Love* (2002).

Guzmán has been a familiar face on television, most notably as Raoul Hernandez, a Latino gang leader behind bars, in Home Box Office's (HBO) riveting prison series *Oz* (1997–2003).

A committed family man, Guzmán lives in the small town of Cabot, Vermont, with his wife Angelita Galarza-Guzmán and their five children. He sees this role as family man to be as important as any role he has played in his more than 50 films. "I'm setting an example to other Latino men as a father and as an actor," he has said.

Further Reading

The Internet Movie Database. "Luis Guzmán," The Internet Movie Database. Available online. URL: http://www.imdb.com/name/nm0350079/. Downloaded on June 14, 2005.

Luis Guzmán Official Web site. Available online. URL: http://www.luisguzman.com. Downloaded on June 14, 2005.

Further Viewing

Out of Sight (1998). Universal Home Video, VHS/DVD, 2001/2003.

Oz—The Complete Second Season (1998). HBO Home Video, VHS/DVD, 2003.

Punch–Drunk Love (2002). Columbia/Tristar Home Video, VHS/DVD, 2003.

H

Hayek, Salma (Salma Hayek-Jiménez)

(1966–) *actress, filmmaker, film producer*

The first Latina to be nominated for a Best Actress Academy Award, Salma Hayek is in the top ranks of film actresses, having excelled in both big commercial films and small independent ones. In a few short years, she went from complete obscurity to fame in Hollywood and managed to keep her values intact while doing so.

Salma Hayek-Jiménez was born in Coatzacoalcos, Mexico, on September 2, 1966. Her father is a Lebanese businessman, and her mother, a Mexican opera singer. At age 12, Salma, whose name in Arabic means "peace," was sent to a convent boarding school in New Orleans, Louisiana. Setting the school clocks back and other girlish pranks got her expelled, and she went to live with an aunt in Houston, Texas. At age 17, she returned to Mexico and entered Universidad Iberoamericano in Mexico City, where she studied international relations. Bitten by the acting bug, Hayek dropped out of school and started to make the rounds of auditions. She soon landed the title role in the telenovela (Mexican soap opera) *Teresa* and became one of the most familiar faces on Mexican TV, but in time she became frustrated by the limitations of daytime drama and wanted to move into motion-picture roles in Hollywood. After moving to Los Angeles, California, Hayek made two sobering discoveries: First, her fame in Mexico meant nothing in Hollywood, where she was an unknown; second, the few roles offered to Latina actresses were mostly domestics and prostitutes.

By 1993, the acting jobs she had been offered totaled a one-line role in a film about Los Angeles gang girls called *Mi Vida Loca* and a few small parts on television. When she appeared on a Spanish-language talk show in Los Angeles hosted by comic and actor PAUL RODRIGUEZ, Hayek vented her feelings about Hollywood.

Another Rodriguez, filmmaker ROBERT RODRIGUEZ, happened to be watching and was deeply impressed by Hayek's outspokenness, intelligence, and beauty. He decided to cast her as the love interest for ANTONIO BANDERAS in his new action film *Desperado* (1995). She would become one of Rodriguez's favorite actresses—he has cast her in six more movies to date. Hayek began to receive film offers from other directors, including lead role in the romantic comedy *Fools Rush In* (1997) costarring Matthew Perry.

For the next several years, Hayek appeared in a string of serious, small independent films, including the outrageous religious satire *Dogma* (1999), which again paired her with Matthew Perry. To develop projects for her talents as an actress, she founded her own production company, Bentanarosa. One of the resulting films was *In the Time of the Butterflies* (2001), a biographical film about the Maribal sisters of the Dominican Republic, revolutionaries who opposed the dictatorship of

Rafael Trujillo, played by EDWARD JAMES OLMOS. Hayek won an American Latino Media Arts (ALMA) Award for Best Actress from the National Council of La Raza (NCLR), the largest national Latino civil-rights organization, for her portrayal of Minerva Maribal.

Another real-life Latina whose life Hayek dreamed about filming for years was the Mexican surrealist painter Frida Kahlo. She finally found the financing to coproduce *Frida* (2002), giving herself her greatest film role to date. Costarring was ALFRED MOLINA as her brilliant, philandering husband, the muralist Diego Rivera. *Frida* was nominated for six Oscars, including one for Hayaek for Best Actress. Although she did not win, the film and the role made Hayek a bankable star.

The following year, she made her directorial debut with the made-for-television movie *The Maldonado Miracle* (2002) about a religious miracle in a small town. She also reprised her role as Banderas's lover in a sequel to *Desperado,* the epic and bloody *Once Upon a Time in Mexico* (2003). After a slight comedy crime caper, *After the Sunset* (2004), opposite Pierce Brosnan, she returned to more serious dramatic roles as a Mexican woman looking for a husband in depression-era Los Angeles in *Ask the Dust* (2006), directed by Robert Towne. Starting in 2006, Hayek was the executive producer, as well as an actor, on the television show *Ugly Betty.*

A fiercely independent actress and woman who refuses to be typecast by Hollywood, Salma Hayek's greatest films may still be before her. Having had long-term relationships with actors Edward Norton and Josh Lucas, in March 2007 she announced her engagement to French businessman François-Henri Pinault, the chief executive officer (CEO) of a fashion house conglomerate. Hayek gave birth to the couple's baby girl in September 2007 and married Pinault in 2009 in Paris.

Further Reading

Duncan, Patricia J. *Salma Hayek: An Unauthorized Biography.* New York: St. Martin's Paperbacks, 1999.

The Internet Movie Database. "Salma Hayek," The Internet Movie Database. Available online. URL: http://www.imdb.com/name/nm0000161/. Downloaded on December 11, 2004.

Scott, Kieran. *Salma Hayek* (Latinos in the Limelight). New York: Chelsea House, 2001.

Further Viewing

Desperado (1995). Columbia/Tristar Home Video, VHS/DVD, 2000/2005.

Frida (2002). Buena Vista Home Video/Miramax Home Entertainment. VHS/DVD, 2003.

In the Time of the Butterflies (2001). MGM/UA Home Video, VHS/DVD, 2002/2004.

Hayworth, Rita
(Margarita Carmen Cansino)
(1918–1987) *actress, dancer, singer*

Arguably Hollywood's most glamorous female film star of the 1940s, Rita Hayworth led a tragic and misunderstood life, much of which was only revealed after her death. Margarita Carmen Cansino was born in Brooklyn, New York, on October 17, 1918. Her father was the Spanish-born dancer Eduardo Cansino, who immigrated to the United States in 1913. He met and married Irish-English dancer Volga Hayworth in 1917. The couple formed a dance act and appeared on Broadway in the lavish revue *The Ziegfeld Follies.*

The Cansinos formed a family act that Margarita joined at age 8, appearing with her parents in the silent film *La Fiesta* (1926). By age 12, she was dancing solo in Mexican clubs where a producer from Fox Pictures saw her and put her under contract to the studio. The 16-year-old dancer made her film debut in a bit part in *Dante's Inferno* (1935) under her real name. More bit parts followed, mostly as a Mexican señorita. Just as Margarita was about to move up to larger dramatic roles, Fox merged with 20th Century, another studio, and her contract was canceled.

In 1937, she married Edward Judson, 22 years her senior, who took over the management of her career. He hired a press agent and got her a seven-year contract with Columbia Studios. Harry Cohn, head of Columbia, liked the young actress but gave her a complete makeover to "Anglocize" her. Her black hair was dyed red, she underwent painful electrolysis to raise her hairline, and she was given a new name, Rita Hayworth. She appeared in secondary roles in a number of routine pictures before finding her first good role as a cheating wife in the South American adventure film *Only Angels Have Wings* (1939), directed by Howard Hawks.

She made a greater impression on audiences in *The Strawberry Blonde* (1941), a period comedy–drama where she played opposite James Cagney. Next, Hayworth was a fiery temptress for bullfighter Tyrone Power in the Technicolor film *Blood and Sand* (1942). (She took up bullfighting as a hobby.) Her considerable dancing skills were showcased in three excellent musicals in which her partners were dancing legends Fred Astaire *(You'll Never Get Rich, You Were Never Lovelier)* and Gene Kelly *(Cover Girl)*.

Hayworth's beauty made her the #2 pin-up girl for American soldiers in World War II, earning her the nickname "The Love Goddess." Her Hollywood career reached its apex in the film noir, *Gilda* (1946), in which she played the bored wife of a wealthy older man, George Macready, and the lover of his henchman, Glenn Ford, a frequent costar. The highlight of the film was the musical number "Put the Blame on Mame, Boys," in which Hayworth made the removal of a pair of elbow-length gloves into a tantalizing striptease. Her singing voice, as in nearly all her musical films, was dubbed, although she was a reasonably good singer.

By this time, Hayworth had divorced Judson and soon married film director and actor Orson Welles. The marriage was short lived, but produced a daughter, Rebecca, and one of Hayworth's—and Welles's—best pictures, the spectacular film noir *The Lady from Shanghai* (1948). Through Welles's camera lens Hayworth, her hair dyed blonde, never looked lovelier nor played a character who was more heartless.

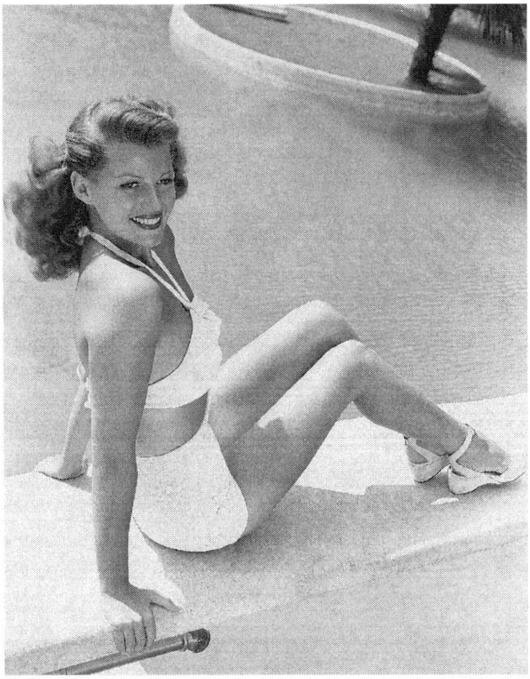

One of Hollywood's love goddesses in the 1940s, Rita Hayworth's Latin heritage was well hidden from moviegoers by the studios. *(Photofest)*

But the femme fatal image was all hype. The real Rita was quiet, shy, and something of a homebody. She summed up the dilemma of her love life succinctly when she said, "Every man I have known has fallen in love with Gilda and wakened with me." In May 1949, she married playboy prince Aly Khan, giving up her career to be his wife. The marriage lasted just two years but produced her second daughter, Yasmin.

Hayworth returned to Hollywood, where Cohn renewed her contract, but her films were inferior to her earlier ones, and in 1953, she left Columbia. She married a fourth time, to singer Dick Haymes, but again the marriage quickly soured.

Never considered much of a dramatic actress, Hayworth shone as Burt Lancaster's ex-wife in the British drama *Separate Tables* (1958), adapted from two one-act plays by Terrence Rattigan. She married the film's coproducer James Hill and found one more good dramatic role in *They Came to Cordura* (1959), a Western costarring Gary Cooper. After *The Story on Page One* (1959) her career and life hit the skids. She divorced Hill in 1961 and became increasingly erratic when seen in public. Many blamed her behavior on alcoholism. In fact, she was in the early stages of the degenerative disease Alzheimer's that attacks brain cells.

Hayworth appeared in second-rate films through the early 1970s. By 1980, however, Alzheimer's had made her a helpless invalid. Her daughter cared for her through her final years. Rita Hayworth, the love goddess of Hollywood, died at age 68 on May 14, 1987, in New York City.

Further Reading

Hill, James. *Rita Hayworth: A Memoir.* New York: Simon & Schuster, 1983.

Katz, Ephraim, Fred Klein, and Ronald Dean Nolen. *The Film Encyclopedia,* 4th edition. New York: HarperResource, 2001, pp. 609–610.

Kobal, John. *Rita Hayworth: The Time, The Place and The Woman.* New York: Berkley Publishing Group, 1983.

Leaming, Barbara. *If This Was Happiness: A Biography of Rita Hayworth.* London: Weidenfeld & Nicolson, 1989.

McLean, Adrienne. *Being Rita Hayworth: Labor, Identity, and Hollywood Stardom.* Piscataway, N.J.: Rutgers University Press, 2004.

Further Viewing

Cover Girl (1944). Columbia/Tristar Home Video, VHS/DVD, 1992/2003.

Gilda (1946). Columbia/Tristar Home Video, VHS/DVD, 1992/2004.

The Lady from Shanghai (1948). Columbia/Tristar Home Video, VHS/DVD, 1992/2000.

Separate Tables (1958). MGM/UA Home Entertainment, VHS/DVD, 2001/2004.

Hernandez, Ester
(Ester Medina Hernández)
(1944–) *printmaker, painter, muralist*

A Chicano artist fiercely committed to her people and other social causes, Ester Hernandez has challenged American society for several decades with her often controversial prints and posters. She was born Ester Medina Hernandez in Dinuba, California, in the San Joaquin Valley on December 3, 1944, the sixth child of farmworkers. Art was an important part of her background. Her mother, a Yanqui Indian from North Central Mexico, embroidered. Her grandfather was a carpenter who also made religious sculptures, and her father enjoyed photography.

Chicano farmworkers demonstrating for better working conditions led by their leader Cesar Chavez marched through Hernandez's hometown in 1965. The incident made a deep and lasting impression on her. Many local residents harrassed the marchers, but Hernandez's family welcomed them. She later took courses in Chicano studies at Grove Street College in Oakland, California, and then continued her education at the University of California–Berkeley; there, she earned a bachelor of arts (B.A.) degree in practice in art in 1976. She befriended artist RUPERT GARCIA and participated in his art classes in San Francisco.

Although she painted and created murals with the artist's group Mujeres Muralists, printmaking became Hernandez's chosen medium, mostly because she saw it as a way to make her art accessible to more people. Hernandez's prints were often angry and confrontational, as typified by *Sun Mad* (1982), a realistic depiction of a box of *Sun Maid* raisins but with the trademark Sun Maid transformed into a horrifying skeletal figure carrying a crate of grapes. It pointedly referred to the contamination of water by companies in agribusiness that in turn contaminated their grapes before they were processed into raisins. The resulting health hazard for grape pickers was serious.

Equally controversial is Hernandez's print *The Virgin of Guadalupe Defending the Rights of the Chicanos* (1973), which depicts the unearthly Virgin as a karate fighter in pants. Hernandez's social conscience has carried over from her art into her life. She has worked for the rights of the elderly and the disabled in social-service agencies. She has taught developmentally disabled adults at Creativity Explored in San Francisco for more than a decade. Hernandez is the recipient of a 1992 National Endowment for the Arts (NEA) award for theater-arts collaboration. In 1998, she received a grant from the Serpent Source Foundation of San Francisco. Her work is part of the permanent collection of the San Francisco Museum of Modern Art (SFMOMA); the Smithsonian American Art Musuem (SAAM) in Washington, D.C.; and the Frida Kahlo Studio Museum in Mexico City.

"My background has taught me that we Chicanos must continually strive for beauty and spirituality," she has said. "This beauty—found in both nature and the arts—is the seed that uplifts our spirit and nourishes our souls."

Further Reading

Congdon, Kristen G., and Kara Kelley Hallmark. *Artists from Latin American Cultures: A Biographical Dictionary.* Westport, Conn.: Greenwood Press, 2002, pp. 103–107.

Ester Hernandez Artist. Available online. URL: http://www.esterhernandez.com. Downloaded on September 6, 2005.

Mi Alma, Mi Tierra, Mi Gente: Contemporary Chicano Art. "Ester Hernandez," St. Mary's College Web Site. Available online. URL: http://www.saintmarys.edu/~events/Calendar/MoreauGalleries/artists2000–2001/Chicana2000/hernandez.html. Downloaded on March 20, 2006.

Hernandez, Juano (Huano G. Hernandez) (1896–1970) *actor*

A black Latino actor of great power and presence, Juano Hernandez achieved film stardom at age 51 in his very first major movie role. Born in San Juan, Puerto Rico, on July 19, 1896, although some sources list his birth year as 1901, his father was a sailor. After his death, Hernandez lived with an aunt in Brazil where he sang to passersby in the streets for money. Completely self-educated, he taught himself to read and write and became a professional boxer while still in his teens. He quit boxing and joined traveling circuses and carnivals as an acrobat. Hernandez toured Latin America and arrived in New Orleans, Louisiana, in 1915 continuing to tour as a vaudeville performer, he eventually found steady work with his rich baritone voice as a radio announcer and actor. He even worked for a time as a radio scriptwriter.

In 1927, Hernandez appeared in the chorus of the original Broadway production of the musical *Show Boat.* For the next 20 years, he acted on the New York stage, becoming one of the first black actors to achieve recognition in major dramatic roles. In 1949, he finally got his break in Hollywood and played a career-defining role in *Intruder in the Dust,* adapted from a novel by William Faulkner. Hernandez portrayed Lucas Beauchamp, an elderly black man in a Mississippi town who is wrongly accused of killing a white man. He barely escapes being lynched when the real killer is discovered.

A groundbreaking American film about racial prejudice, *Intruder in the Dust* was filmed entirely in Oxford, Mississippi, Faulkner's hometown. Hernandez's portrayal of a man who faces racism and injustice with dignity and strength earned him rave critical reviews, won him a Golden Globe Award for "New Star of the Year," and provided a role model for other African-American actors. "The stance and magnificent intergrity that Mr.

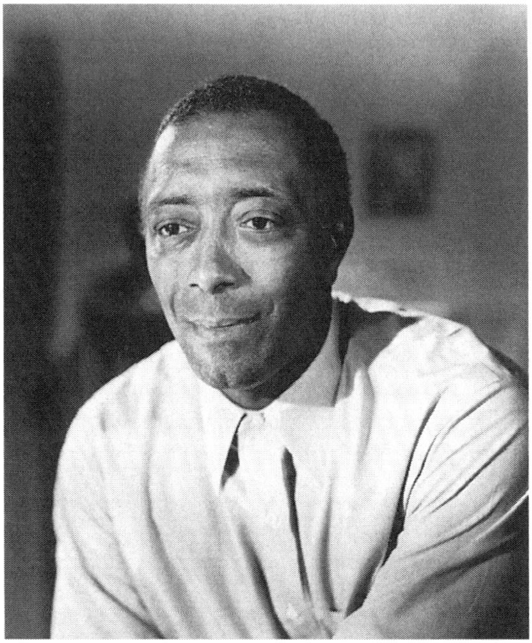

A sensitive and skillful actor, Juano Hernandez spent two decades on the stage before making a notable film debut at age 51. *(Photofest)*

Hernandez displays in his carriage, his manner and expression, with never a flinch in his great self-command, is the bulwark of all the deep compassion and ironic comment in the film," wrote the critic in the *New York Times.*

During the next two decades, Hernandez appeared in more than a score of films, usually in supporting roles. He was John Garfield's first mate and best friend in *The Breaking Point* (1950), a solid adaptation of an Ernest Hemingway novel. He was composer W. C. Handy's preacher father in *St. Louis Blues* (1958). He played Uncle Possum, a black patriarch, opposite Steve McQueen in *The Reivers* (1969), another adaptation of a Faulkner novel, and played opposite Rod Steiger in *The Pawnbroker* (1965). His last film appearance was in *They Call Me MISTER Tibbs!* (1970), which starred Sidney Poitier, a black actor who benefited from Hernandez's groundbreaking film work. Juano Hernandez died of a cerebral hemorrhage on July 17, 1970, in his hometown of San Juan.

Further Reading

Bogle, Donald. *Toms, Coons Mulattoes, Mammies, & Bucks: An Interpretive History of Blacks in American Films.* New York: The Continuum Publishing Company, 1997, pp. 154–158.

The Internet Movie Database. "Juano Hernandez," The Internet Movie Database. Available online. URL: http://www.imdb.com/name/nm0379621/. Downloaded on January 17, 2005.

Rodríguez, Clara E. *Heroes, Lovers, and Others: The Story of Latinos in Hollywood.* Washington, D.C.: Smithsonian Books, 2004, pp. 140–141.

Further Viewing

Intruder in the Dust (1949). Warner Home Video. VHS, 1993.

The Pawnbroker (1965). Republic Entertainment/Lions Gate Home Entertainment, VHS/DVD, 1994/2003.

Herron, Willie (William Herrón III)

(1951–) *muralist, commercial artist*

A powerfully expressive muralist whose public works celebrate Latino culture while criticizing the injustices done to it, Willie Herron supports his public art with a successful commercial design business. William Herrón III was born in East Los Angeles, California, in 1951. His grandfather was from Mexico, and his grandmother was a Native American from Northern California. When he was eight, his parents divorced, and he spent a lot of time with his grandparents. Herron won his first art award in the fifth grade. While still in high school, he won art scholarships to take courses in drawing at the Otis Art Institute and the Art Center College of Design.

In 1972, at age 21, he joined with fellow artists Gronk (Glugio Nicondra), Patssi Valdez, and HARRY GAMBOA, JR., to form ASCO (Spanish for "nausea"), an experimental performance art group. That same year, Herron created his first murals on walls within a block of where he lived. *The Plumed Serpent* was a portrait of the ancient Aztec god Quetzalcoatl. *The Wall That Cracked Open* was painted with local youth at the site where his younger brother was stabbed and almost killed by members of a rival gang. It depicts two youths with cracked heads coming through the wall.

Herron still favors his earliest works because he could express himself freely. "I didn't need approval and I didn't need permission from anyone because I wasn't being paid," he has said in one interview. "I was allowed the freedom . . . to just communicate how I wanted to communicate."

Through the 1970s, Herron perfected his expressive mural work around the city, often collaborating with other artists. Perhaps his most powerful mural of this period is *Black and White Moratorium Mural* (1977), created with Gronk. It is a tribute to the marchers and victims of the 1970 anti-Vietnam Chicano Moratorium in East Los Angeles (East LA), in which Latino reporter Reuben Salazar of the *Los Angeles Times* was killed by police. Herron returned to the mural in 1980 to paint him and his wife embracing in the lower right-hand corner of the artwork. Among his other well-known murals are *Advancement of Man* with Alfonso Trejo, Jr. (1975) and *Struggles of the World* (1984).

Since high school, Herron has supported himself by doing commercial design. Today, he operates a successful commercial-design studio in Laguna Hills, California, and creates logos and signs for commercial and residential customers. He has recently made murals for such clients as the Sheraton Hotel and the Art Deco Lido Cinema, both in Newport Beach, California. A versatile artist, Herron also leads his own Latino punk band, Los Illegals, that also includes poet and journalist Adolfo Guzman-Lopez.

Further Reading

Dunitz, Robin. *Street Gallery: Guide to 1001 Los Angeles Murals*. Los Angeles: RJD Enterprises, 1998.

Mural Conservancy of Los Angeles. "Willie Herron III," Mural Conservancy of Los Angeles Web Site. Available online. URL: http://www.lamurals.org/MuralistsPages/Herron.html. Downloaded on August 3, 2005.

Rangel, Jeffrey. "Oral History Interview with Willie Herron," Smithsonian Archives of American Art. Available online. URL: http://www.aaasi.edu/oralhist/herron00.htm. Downloaded on August 3, 2005.

Huerta, Salomón
(1965–) *painter*

An artist of smooth surfaces, faceless people, and enigmatic meaning, Salomón Huerta has been called an Edward Hopper for the computer age, referring to the 20th-century master of the theme of loneliness in the modern world. Huerta was born in Tijuana, Mexico, on June 22, 1965, and moved to East Los Angeles (LA), California, with his family when he was four. He attended the Art Center College of Design in Pasadena, California, graduating with a bachelor of fine arts (B.F.A.) degree in 1991. Huerta earned a master of fine arts (M.F.A.) degree from the University of California–Los Angeles (UCLA) in 1998.

When his work was included in the Biennial 2000 of the Whitney Museum of American Art in New York, fame came quickly for Huerta. The art world was intrigued by his signature portraits of unrecognizable people who were sitting or standing with their backs to the viewer. Some figures are seen standing and shown from head to toe, while others are sitting and shown only from the neck up. But all are seen from the back only.The crystal clear oil renderings of his subjects and the highly stylish clothes and background only make these faceless portraits all the more mysterious. The only suggestion of race are skin tones. Huerta seems to be asking the viewer to fill in the blanks with his or her own perceptions and prejudices.

More recently, the artist has turned to depicting houses. These paintings, considerably smaller than the head and figure portraits, are based on photographs that Huerta took while driving around the neighborhoods of South Central LA. They are renderings of lower-middle-class tract homes and bungalows where blacks and Latinos might live and are painted in a style as sharply stylized and ultrarealistic as his people. With few details or decorations to give each home individuality, these houses are somewhat cold, postmodern, and sterile, but they still exude a tantilizing hint of warmth and nostalgia. "Zeroing in on the alienating isolation at the heart of the American dream, Huerta's understated paintings make the cold calculus of upward mobility look deadly," wrote David Pagel in a review of a 2003 show at the Patricia Faure Gallery in Santa Monica, California.

Huerta's work has been exhibited in many museums in the United States, Europe, and Mexico. They include the Austin Museum of Art, Texas; Studio La Citta, Verona, Italy; and Museo de la Ciudad de Mexico. "I'm focusing visually, rather than emotionally," Huerta has said about his work. "I wanted to create images that were not typical of Latino images because I didn't want to be ghettoized."

Further Reading

Absolute Arts: Indepth Arts News. "Salomón Huerta: Paintings, Austin Museum of Art," Absolute Arts Web Site. Available online. URL: http://www.absolutearts.com/artsnews/2001/05/12/28547.html. Downloaded on August 7, 2005.

Dambrot, Shana Nys. "Salomón Huerta at Patricia Faure Gallery." *Artweek,* 32 (January 2001), p. 21.

Pagel, David. "Huerta's Home—Ruthless but Warm," *Los Angeles Times,* April 11, 2003, p. E21.

I

Ichaso, Leon

(1948–) *filmmaker, screenwriter, film producer*

A filmmaker committed to the Latino experience in America and his native Cuba, Leon Ichaso's best films are filled with anger and passion but are leavened with the saving grace of humor. He was born in Havana, Cuba, on August 3, 1948. His father, Dr. Justo Rodriguez Santos, was a director for Cuban television and a respected poet. Leon left Cuba at age 14 with his mother and sister after the revolution of Fidel Castro. After dropping out of high school in 1967, he became involved in the New York City underground film movement. He began to make experimental films with an 8-mm camera.

He eventually worked as a copywriter for an ad agency and made television commercials for Goya foods. He used the money that he earned to finance his first feature film, *El Super* (1979), which he adapted from an off-off-Broadway play. *El Super* is the comic and touching tale of a Cuban building superintendent in New York City who is homesick for Cuba. The film debuted at the Museum of Modern Art (MOMA) New Directors series and won critical praise for its skillful blend of drama and comedy.

In his next film, *Crossover Dreams* (1985), Ichaso took aim at Cuban-Americans' desire to assimilate into American culture. Rudy Veloz, played by musician and actor RUBÉN BLADES, is a salsa singer who attempts the big leap to American pop music. He ultimately fails and nearly loses everything that he had in the process. Understated and realistic, the film was a devastating examination of the dangers of assimilation for Latinos.

After the struggle to make this independent film, Ichaso decided to go mainstream and directed episodes for the hit television crime series *Miami Vice*. More television work followed—*Crime Story* and the Public Broadcasting Service (PBS) series *Tales from the Hollywood Hills* (1987). Ichaso's next film was *Sugar Hill* (1994), a thoughtful crime film starring Wesley Snipes as a drug lord who wants out. This was followed by *Bitter Sugar* (1996), an angry look at Castro's Cuba. Ichaso filmed most of the movie in the Dominican Republic but was able to sneak his crew into Cuba for a few days' shooting under the pretense of making a documentary. A failure in the United States, *Bitter Sugar* became a hit on video in Cuba.

Ichaso's next major project was an ambitious biographical film about the self-destructive Puerto Rican playwright and poet Miguel Piñero, who died in 1988. Ichaso knew Piñero personally, and in the film *Piñero* (2001), starring BENJAMIN BRATT, he captures the authentic background and foreground of Piñero's life in prison and on the street. He manages to make this depressing material bearable by injecting humor into even the darkest aspects of Piñero's life. Recently, Ichaso has been writing and directing for the hit television

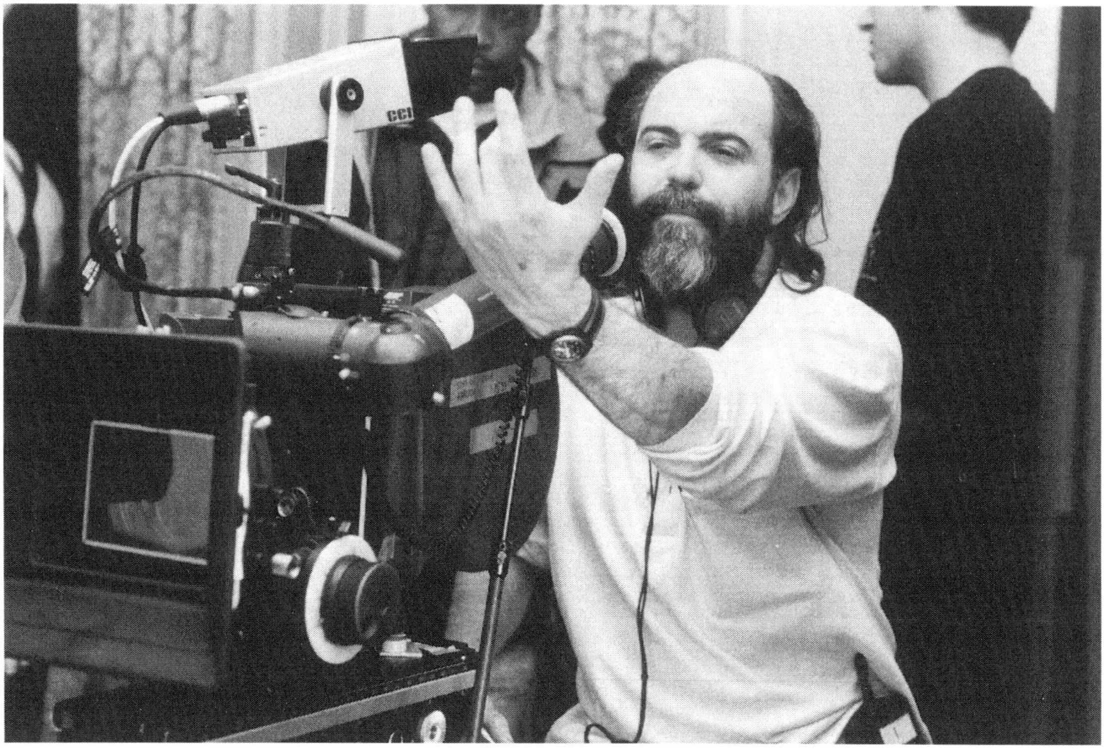

Filmmaker Leon Ichaso has examined the difficulties and pitfalls of assimilation for Latinos in such memorable movies as *El Super* and *Crossover Dreams*. *(Photofest)*

detective series *Monk* (2002–). His film *El Cantante,* starring MARC ANTHONY as Salsa singer Hector Lavoe, was released in 2006.

Further Reading

Geller, Lynn. "Leon Ichaso," BOMB Magazine. Available online. URL: http://www/bombsite.com/ichaso/html. Downloaded on July 13, 2005.

Holden, LoAnn. "Director Leon Ichaso Celebrates the Poetry of Piñero," Twnonline. Available online. URL: http://www.twnonline.org/newsarchive/020124/film_profile.htm. Downloaded on September 7, 2005.

The Internet Movie Database. "Leon Ichaso." The Internet Movie Database. Available online. URL: http://www.imdb.com/name/nm04066871/. Downloaded on July 13, 2005.

Further Viewing

Bitter Sugar (1996). New Yorker Video, VHS/DVD, 1998/2004.

Crossover Dreams (1985). New Yorker Video, VHS/DVD, 1989/2005.

Piñero (2001). Buena Vista Home Video, VHS/DVD, 2002/2005.

J

Jimenez, Flaco
(Leonardo Jimenez)
(1939–) *accordionist*

An innovator of Conjunto music, a mesmerizing blend of European polka and Tex-Mex music, Flaco Jimenez has transformed the accordion into a premier instrument of rocking, dancing roots music. Leonardo Jimenez was born in San Antonio, Texas, on March 11, 1939. His grandfather and father, Santiago Jimenez, both played the diatonic button accordion. Santiago was a pioneer of Conjunto music who first recorded for Decca Records in 1936. Leonardo began to play accordion at age five and first performed publicly with his father at age nine at dance halls and house dances around San Antonio.

As a teenager, Jimenez was influenced by country music, jazz, and the new sound of rock and roll. At 15, he was playing in a group, Los Caporales, and made his first recordings. He was nicknamed "Flaco," skinny in Spanish, which had been his father's nickname.

In the late 1960s, Jimenez met Doug Sahm, leader of the Tex-Mex rock band the Sir Douglas Quintet. The two transformed Conjunto music by giving it a country sound and a rock beat and adding a saxophone to the mix. Moving to New York City, Jimenez started to jam with a wide range of rock and rhythm-and-blues (R&B) artists, who were enchanted by his music. They included Bob Dylan, Dr. John, and guitarist Ry Cooder. Cooder included Jimenez on his classic album *Chicken Skin Music* (1976). The two also did a world tour together.

After years of playing on other artists' albums, Jimenez won his first Grammy Award in 1986 in the category Best Mexican-American Performance for the album *Ay Te Dejo En San Antonio,* whose title song was written and originally recorded by his father.

In 1990, he joined Sahm, FREDDY FENDER, and Augie Meyers to form the Tex-Mex supergroup the Texas Tornados. The group played concerts and recorded through 1996. In 1994, Jimenez was enlisted by the Rolling Stones to play on their best-selling album *Voodoo Lounge.* He won four more Grammys, including one for his 1996 solo album *Flaco Jimenez.* One of his most recent recordings, *Squeeze Box King,* was released in 2003.

Jimenez's accordion has been heard on the soundtrack of several films, including *The Border* (1982) and *Tin Cup* (1996) and on television commercials for the Texas Lottery and Chrysler Dodge. Flaco Jimenez has been inducted into the International Latin Music Hall of Fame and the National Hispanic Hall of Fame.

"American roots music is the sharing and blending of different kinds of musics, like a brotherhood thing," Jimenez said in one interview. "It makes the world rounder when there's coordination."

Further Reading

American Roots Music: Oral Histories. "Flaco Jimenez," PBS Online. Available online. URL: http://www.pbs.org/americanrootsmusic/pbs_arm_oralh_flacojimenez.html. Downloaded on July 14, 2005.

Flaco Jimenez Official Web Site. Available online. URL: http://www.flacojimenez.com. Downloaded on July 27, 2005.

Further Listening

Best of Flaco Jimenez. Arhoolie Records, CD box set, 1999.

The Best of Texas Tornados. Warner, CD, 1994.

Squeeze Box King. Compadre Records, CD, 2003.

Jiménez, Luis
(Luis Alfonso Jiménez, Jr.)
(1940–2006) *sculptor, lithographist*

The most prominent contemporary Chicano (Mexican-American) sculptor, Luis Jiménez celebrated the Chicano experience in the Southwest in his larger-than-life pop sculptures that are fashioned from plastic, fiberglass, and chrome. Luis Alfonso Jiménez, Jr., was born in El Paso, Texas, on July 30, 1940. One of his grandfathers was a carpenter, and the other was a glassblower. Luis's father emigrated from Mexico to the United States, where he started a neon-sign business. Luis worked with his father from age six. At 16, he made two 10-foot roosters for a drive-in restaurant chain.

After graduating from high school, Jiménez studied art and architecture at the University of Texas–Austin, earning a bachelor of arts (B.A.) degree in 1964. With a scholarship from the National University of Mexico, he studied in that country, gaining a deeper appreciation of his cultural heritage. He then moved to New York City to establish himself as a sculptor but was unable to interest a gallery in exhibiting his work. In a bold and desperate move, Jiménez entered the empty Castelli Gallery one day and placed three of his sculptures on display. The gallery director was impressed by his work and pointed him to another gallery, the Graham Gallery, which mounted two solo exhibits of his sculptures in 1969 and 1970.

Jiménez's New York work was often satirical and critical of American life and values. *The Barfly–Statue of Liberty* (1969) depicted a scantily dressed blonde on a barstool wearing a U.S. flag and hoisting a beer mug. More serious was *Man on Fire* (1969), which portrayed the great Aztec leader Cuautemoc, burned alive by Spanish conquistadores. The sculpture also references the Buddhist monks who immolated themselves in protest of the Vietnam War and the many Chicanos who fought and died in that controversial conflict.

Unable to fully succeed as an artist in New York, Jiménez moved to Roswell, New Mexico, in 1971. His first major recognition as an expressive spokesperson for Latinos came with his first one-person museum show at the Contemporary Arts Museum in Houston in 1974. Since then, he retained his position as a major American artist.

Much of Jiménez's work focuses on the Southwest and Chicanos' role in its history. *Vaquero* (Cowboy, 1977), a giant Mexican cowboy on horseback, is a reminder that the first cowboys were not Anglos, but Mexicans. One of his most celebrated works deals with more personal, contemporary history. *Cruzando El Río Bravo* (*Border Crossing,* 1989) shows a man carrying a woman who has a small child in her arms. The material—urethane-coated fiberglass—seems to glisten with the waters of the Rio Bravo, the river that these illegal immigrants just crossed. It is a powerful testament to his own grandmother who crossed into the United States in 1924 carrying his father. "People talked about the aliens as if they landed from outer space, as if they weren't really people," he said about these legions of courageous, illegal immigrants. "I wanted to put a face on them; I wanted to humanize them."

Jiménez lived with his family in Hondo, New Mexico, while also spending time in El Paso. He was that rare artist whose work appeals to both the museum crowd and the ordinary, working person. He created public sculptures in such diverse cities as Pittsburgh, Albuquerque, New York City, Houston, and San Diego. A major retrospective of Jiménez's work took place in 1999 at the Moody Gallery in Houston, Texas. He died tragically on June 13, 2006, when one of his sculptures accidentally fell on him in his studio.

His work is in the permanent collections of many museums including the Chicago Art Institute, the Metropolitan Museum in New York, and the Hirshhorn Museum and Sculpture Garden in Washington, D.C. Jiménez also made color lithographs and drawings. "I want my work to become an integral part of the society that surrounds it;" he said, "to generate a meaningful dialogue among members of the diverse community."

Further Reading

Baker-Sandback, Amy. "Signs: A Conversation with Luis Jiménez." *Artforum 23,* September 1984, pp. 84–87.

Cockcroft, James D., assisted by Jane Canning. *Latino Visions: Contemporary Chicano, Puerto Rican, and Cuban American Artists.* New York: Franklin Watts, 2000, pp. 51–54.

Congdon, Kristin G., and Kara Kelley Hallmark. *Artists from Latin American Cultures: A Biographical Dictionary.* Westport, Conn.: Greenwood Press, 2002, pp. 122–125.

Flores-Turney, Camille, Luis Jiménez, and Dave Hickey. *Howl: The Artwork of Luis Jiménez* (New Mexico Magazine Arts Series). Santa Fe: New Mexico Magazine, 1998.

Jiménez, Luis. *Luis Jiménez: February 17, 1985 through March 31, 1985 (Concentrations).* Dallas: Dallas Museum of Art, 1985.

Quirarte, Jacinto. *Mexican American Artists.* Austin: University of Texas Press, 1973, pp. 115–120.

Juliá, Raúl
(Raúl Rafael Carlos Juliá y Arcelay)
(1940–1994) *actor, social activist*

One of the top stage actors of his generation and a versatile screen actor, Raúl Juliá never achieved the movie stardom for which many thought him destined. Raúl Rafael Carlos Juliá y Arcelay was born in San Juan, Puerto Rico, on March 9, 1940. His father owned a popular restaurant that specialized in fried chicken. Raúl attended a well-known Jesuit-run high school in San Juan and then went on to the University of Puerto Rico where he intended to study law but was quickly won over to acting. He graduated with a bachelor of arts (B.A.) degree in drama and found work performing in a local nightclub. American actor Orson Bean saw him there, was impressed by his talent, and urged him to move to New York City to pursue an acting career.

Juliá arrived in New York in 1964 and was soon performing regularly in Off-Off-Broadway productions. His first break came two years later when he was chosen as a member of the Public Theater's Shakespeare in the Park company. He gradually worked his way from small parts to major roles. He played Edmund in *King Lear* and *Othello,* giving Shakespeare's jealous Moor a Latin temperament.

A fine singer, Juliá was as much at home in musicals as in nonmusical plays. He portrayed Valentine in a musical version of Shakespeare's *Two Gentlemen of Verona* (1971) and was Mack the Knife in the Public Theater's hit revival of Kurt Weill's *Threepenny Opera* (1976). Juliá was nominated for a Tony Award as Best Actor in a Musical as the beleaguered central character in *Nine* (1982), a Broadway musical based on the film *8 ½* by Italian director Federico Fellini.

Juliá's journey from Broadway star to movie star was slow and frustrating. It was nearly 15 years between his first feature-film role in *Been Down So Long It Looks Like Up to Me* (1971) to

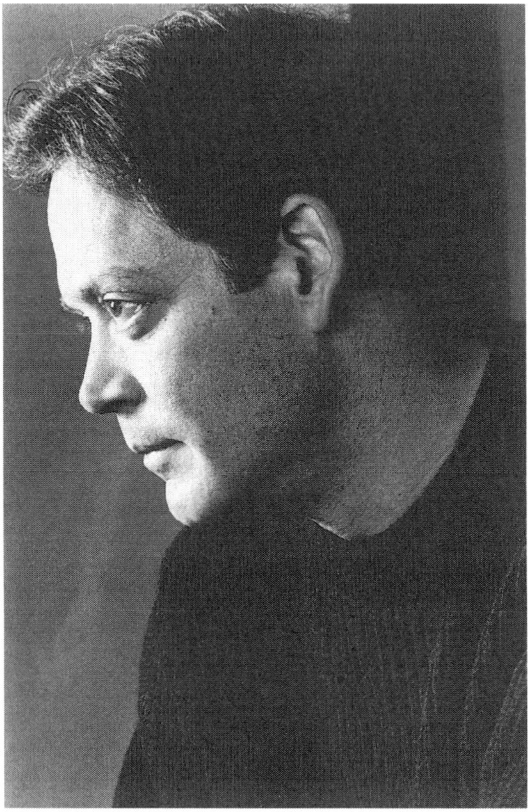

The compassion he felt for the world's underprivileged and his commitment to change is captured in this reflective photograph of the late actor Raúl Juliá. *(Photofest)*

his breakthrough role as a committed revolutionary in a South American jail in *Kiss of the Spider Woman* (1985), based on the novel by Argentinean novelist Manuel Puig.

Tall, handsome, with Latino features, Juliá's acting credentials helped him avoid the Latin-lover stereotype, but film producers still did not quite know what to do with him. "There's a subtle kind of compartment I'm put in," he once said. He had solid supporting roles in the crime thrillers *The Morning After* (1986) and *Tequila Sunrise* (1988) and was excellent as the defense lawyer in the courtroom drama *Presumed Innocent* (1990).

Although he avoided stereotypical Latino roles, Juliá seized the opportunity to play two real-life Latin-American heroes with depth and conviction. He portrayed the rebel Salvadoran priest Óscar Arnulfo Romero who had been killed by government soldiers in *Romero* (1989) as well as martyred Brazilian environmentalist Chico Mendes in the Home Box Office (HBO) cable-television movie *The Burning Season* (1994), for which he won a Golden Globe award. Juliá's choice of these roles reflected his own social activism. He was involved in a number of social causes, most prominently the Hunger Project to help eliminate world hunger. He was also deeply committed to his homeland and appeared in tourism television commercials for Puerto Rico.

Ironically, Juliá achieved his greatest fame as an actor in two comedies based on the macabre television situation-comedy series *The Addams Family.* His droll interpretation of Gomez Addams, the family's head, showed a sure touch for comedy of which many of his fans had not been aware.

Diagnosed with cancer in the early 1990s, Juliá suffered a stroke in his New York City apartment on October 16, 1994. He went into a coma and died on October 24 at age 54 in Manhasset, New York. Juliá's body was flown to Puerto Rico for a state funeral and burial. He left behind a wife and two sons.

As intelligent and kind as he was talented, Raúl Juliá once said, "I didn't come to New York to be a stereotype. I came to be an actor." In a career that was much too short, he was an actor par excellence.

Further Reading

Cruz, Barbara C. *Raúl Juliá: Actor and Humanitarian.* Berkeley Heights, N.J.: Enslow Publishers, 1998.

The Internet Movie Database. "Raúl Juliá," The Internet Movie Database. Available online. URL:

http://www.imdb.com/. Downloaded on December 5, 2004.

Stefoff, Rebecca. *Raúl Juliá* (Hispanics of Achievement). New York: Chelsea House, 1994.

Further Viewing

The Addams Family (1991). Paramount Home Entertainment, VHS/DVD, 2000.

The Burning Season: The Chico Mendes Story (1994). Warner Home Video, VHS, 1996.

Kiss of the Spider Woman (1985). Polygram Video, VHS/DVD, 2001/2005.

Romero (1989). Vidmark/Trimark, VHS/DVD, 1994/2000.

Jurado, Katy
(María Cristina Estella Marcela Jurado de García)
(1929–2002) *actress, journalist*

The first Mexican-born actress to be nominated for an Academy Award in acting, Katy Jurado rose above the stereotyped exotic roles that she was often given in Hollywood films of the 1950s and 1960s with her strong presence and fine acting. María Cristina Estella Marcela Jurado de García was born in Guadalajara, Mexico, on January 16, 1924. Some sources give her birth year as 1927 or 1929. She came from an upper-class family that she later claimed owned land in Texas for six generations. Her parents discouraged her from pursuing an acting career, but she persisted and became a respected actress in Mexican films, usually playing a glamorous socialite. Jurado supplemented her acting career by writing a film column that appeared in more than a half dozen Mexican magazines and newspapers. She was also a bullfight critic. In 1951, while attending a bullfight, she was spotted by American filmmaker Budd Boetticher who was on location for his film *The Bullfighter and the Lady*. Impressed by her sultry beauty, Boetticher immediately cast Jurado as the second female lead in his film, even though she did not speak a word of English.

The following year, her English much improved, Jurado landed her most memorable role in an American film, the former mistress of Marshall Will Kane (Gary Cooper) in the Western classic *High Noon* (1952). As writer Clara Rodriguez points out, the part of Helen Ramirez was one of the few substantial Latina film roles of the decade. The owner of the town's store and saloon, Jurado's Ramirez was an independent and spirited woman who did not need a man to get by but who understood Kane better than his Eastern bride, played by Grace Kelly. That same year, Jurado received an Ariel, Mexico's equivalent of the Oscar, for her role in Spanish filmmaker Luis Buñuel's dark comedy *El Bruto* (1952).

Largely relegated to playing exotic Mexicans and Native Americans in Hollywood Westerns, Jurado was nominated for Best Supporting Actress as Spencer Tracy's Mexican wife in *Broken Lance* (1954). She gave another outstanding performance as the wife of Marlon Brando's nemesis in *One-Eyed Jacks* (1961), the only film that Brando directed.

As she grew older, Jurado continued to be impressive in smaller character roles in such films as the Mexican-made *The Children of Sanchez* (1978) and *Under the Volcano* (1984), based on the Malcolm Lowery novel and filmed in Mexico by John Huston. She made her TV series debut as the family matriarch in the Latino sitcom *aka Pablo* (1984), starring PAUL RODRIGUEZ and HECTOR ELIZONDO.

Jurado was married to actor Ernest Borgnine from 1959 to 1964. She died of a heart attack in Cuernavaca, Mexico, on July 5, 2002.

"Some Mexicans go to Hollywood and lose a career in Mexico because they play imitation," she once said, "I didn't want this to happen to me." It never did. Katy Jurado always played from the heart.

Further Reading

The Internet Movie Database. "Katy Jurado," The Internet Movie Database. Available online. URL: http://www.imdb.com/name/nm0432827/. Downloaded on December 13, 2004.

Rodríguez, Clara E. *Heroes, Lovers, and Others: The Story of Latinos in Hollywood.* Washington, D.C.: Smithsonian Books, 2004, pp. 116–119.

Further Viewing

Broken Lance (1954). Fox Home Video, VHS/DVD, 2003/2004.

High Noon (1952). Republic/Lions Gate Home Entertainment, VHS/DVD, 2004.

One-Eyed Jacks (1961). Artemis/Unicorn Video, VHS/DVD, 1994/2002.

L

Lamas, Fernando (Fernando Alvaro Lamas)

(1916–1982) *actor, filmmaker, television director*

An actor who personified the Latin lover in 1950s Hollywood, Fernando Lamas never fully broke out of the stereotype but managed to switch later in his career from acting to directing. He was born in Buenos Aires, Argentina, on January 9, 1916. Orphaned at age four, Lamas was raised by an aunt and a grandmother. As a young man, he was an outstanding athlete, excelling at swimming and boxing. He pursued an acting career and found success on the stage and radio in his homeland. He made his film debut in Spanish-language movies in 1942. Hollywood took note, and Metro Goldwyn Mayer (MGM) signed him to their studio in 1951. He played small supporting roles in his first few films, and then he was cast as the leading man opposite Lana Turner in a remake of the operetta *The Merry Widow* (1952). The following year, he played a romantic Frenchman in love with bathing beauty Esther Williams in the musical *Dangerous When Wet.* More than a decade later, she would become his fourth wife. A ladies' man, Lamas's third wife was actress Arlene Dahl. His reputation as "First of the Red Hot Lamas" was well earned.

While rarely called on to stretch his acting muscles, Lamas's good looks, breezy personality, and rich baritone made him perfect for musicals and light comedies. He occasionally returned to the stage in New York and was nominated for a Tony Award for Best Actor in Musical for his role in *Happy Hunting* (1956), costarring Ethel Merman.

As Latin-lover roles disappeared in the 1960s, Lamas shifted to acting in low-budget European films and directed two films; one of them, *The Magic Fountain* (1961), was filmed in Spain. He played a convincing villain in *100 Rifles* (1969), a Western set during the Mexican Revolution that starred Burt Reynolds and RAQUEL WELCH.

Lamas turned to directing episodic television in his last decade, including *Falcon Crest,* a prime-time soap opera that starred his son LORENZO LAMAS. He himself was cast in an action series, *Gavilan* (1982), about a retired Central Intelligence Agency (CIA) agent but was forced to withdraw due to cancer. He died of the disease in Los Angeles on October 8, 1982.

Never more than a minor star in the Hollywood firmament, Lamas may be best remembered for the line "You look *mah*velous," which comedian Billy Crystal made the centerpiece of his Lamas-inspired character Fernando. As for his Latin-lover image, Lamas once stated: "It was a great image to have off the screen, but a pain in the ass in the movies."

Further Reading

The Internet Movie Database. "Fernando Lamas," The Internet Movie Database. Available online. URL:

http://www.imdb.com/name/nm0482881/. Downloaded on February 15, 2005.
Rodríguez, Clara. *Heroes, Lovers, and Others: The Story of Latinos in Hollywood.* Washington, D.C.: Smithsonian Books, 2004, pp. 114–116.

Further Viewing

Dangerous When Wet (1953). Warner Home Video, VHS, 2000.
100 Rifles (1969). Twentieth Century Fox Home Video, VHS, 1988.

Lamas, Lorenzo (Lorenzo y de Santos Lamas)

(1958–) *actor, television director and producer*

Son of an acting couple, Lorenzo Lamas reached fame in the 1980s as the hunk star of one of the decade's most notable prime-time soap operas.

Lorenzo y de Santos Lamas was born in Santa Monica, California, on January 20, 1958, and grew up in Pacific Palisades. His father was Argentinean-born actor FERNANDO LAMAS, and his mother is actress Arlene Dahl. His parents divorced when he was 13, and he moved to New York City with his mother. Lamas attended Admiral Farragut Academy in St. Petersburg, Florida, where he excelled as an athlete in track and wrestling. After graduation, he planned to study veterinary medicine at the University of California, but a trip to a film set where his father was working changed his mind. Encouraged by his father, Lamas took acting classes. His first break came quickly when he was cast at age 19 as one of the high schoolers in the movie musical *Grease* (1978).

His good looks and strong physique got Lamas steady television guest shots until he landed the role that made him a household word. As Lance Cumson, he played the rebellious grandson of the martriarch of a Californian vineyard on the nighttime soap opera *Falcon Crest.* With its intricate plotting and strong characters, *Falcon Crest* was a huge hit and remained on the air for nine years.

When the show's run ended in 1990, Lamas appeared in a string of mainly low-budget action films with such titles as *Snake Eater, Night of the Warrior,* and *Final Impact.* Most of them went straight to video. Lamas returned to prime time in the action–adventure series *Renegade* (1992–97), which he developed and coproduced with Stephen Cannell and occasionally directed. He played Reno Raines, who was falsely accused of murdering his girlfriend. While trying to clear his name, he teams up with two friends and becomes a bounty hunter. A student of the martial arts who has achieved the rank of black belt, Lamas had the chance to show his stuff on the series, which ran for five seasons. Since then, he has appeared in several other series, including *Air America* (1998), for which he earned his pilot's license. In 2004, Lamas has had a recurring role in the daytime soap opera *The Bold and the Beautiful* (1987–).

He is active in several charities, including Angel Flight, providing free air transport for patients who cannot afford public transportation to hospitals. Lamas has been married four times and has six children. His son A. J. Lamas is an actor and appeared in the Latino television series *American Family* (2002–04) with EDWARD JAMES OLMOS and RAQUEL WELCH.

Further Reading

The Internet Movie Database. "Lorenzo Lamas," The Internet Movie Database. Available online. URL: http://www.imdb.com/name/nm0001444/. Downloaded on January 20, 2005.
Lorenzo Lamas's Official Web Site. Available online. URL: http://www.lorenzo-lamas.com/index.html. Downloaded on July 15, 2005.

Further Viewing

Latin Dragon (2000). Universal Home Video, DVD, 2005.

Renegade—Season One (1998). Anchor Bay Entertainment, DVD, 2005.

Legorreta, Robert ("Cyclona")
(1952–) *performance artist*

A legendary Latino street performer who emerged from the Chicano (Mexican-American) art movement of the late 1960s, Robert Legorreta has spent most of his creative life in the guise of an androgynist character who, in his own words, "laces his performances with subliminal and overt messages about race, gender and identity." Robert Legorreta was born in El Paso, Texas, on September 15, 1952. While still a child, his Mexican-American family moved to East Los Angeles (East LA) to find a better life. Rock music and the charismatic performances of Elvis Presley on television in the 1950s had a powerful effect on the young Legorreta. He was also influenced by the hit novelty song "The Monster Mash" (1962), sung by Bobby "Boris" Pickett. He claimed that for him "that song transformed Halloween from an innocent candy and costume holiday for children into a subversive teenage rite of passage."

Legorreta attended East LA's Garfield High School and underwent his own rite of passage. The late 1960s was a time of political confrontation and protest for Chicanos as well as for African Americans and those opposed to the escalating Vietnam War. Legorreta's protest took the form of dressing in drag costumes with his friend and later companion, the artist Mundo Meza, and parading down Whittier Boulevard, a main thoroughfare in East LA, to shock and provoke local residents.

Gronk (a.k.a. Glugio Gronk Nicondra), an artist and playwright, who also performed street theater, was impressed by Legorreta and Meza's "psychedelic glitter queens" and wrote them into his play *Caca-Roaches Have No Friends.* Legorreta played the outrageous transvestite Cyclona in the play and adapted it as his theatrical alter ego.

Legorreta transformed Cyclona from a transvestite to an individual of ambiguous sexuality who wears heavy makeup and drapes herself in colorful fabrics. Calling himself a live art artist, he has used Cyclona to challenge his audiences to question their perceptions of gender representation and stereotypes, as well as to speak out on such issues as police brutality, gay repression, and racism. "I am perception," Cyclona declares, "perceive me as you will."

While primarily a street performer who has enlivened parades and political rallies, Legorreta has in recent years done his act in other venues. He performed on the altar of a church during the LA Riots of 1992. In summer 1998, he set off fireworks during a performance at The Village, a gay and lesbian arts complex in North Hollywood, that brought out the police. Legorreta celebrated his 40th anniversary performing as Cyclona in 2006 and is planning a farewell performance as his favorite character for the following year.

Legorreta's personal collection of papers and memorabilia on Chicano life and its representations in popular culture, *El Fuego de la Vida* (*The Fire of Life*) reside with the University of California–Los Angeles's (UCLA) Chicano Studies Research Center.

"My goal in doing everything I've done as a live art artist is to teach my people to rise above the situation of being free in a free democracy and realize that they are not living free at all," Legorreta says.

Further Reading

Hernandez, Robb. "Performing the Archival Body in the Robert 'Cyclona' Legorreta Fire of Life/La Vida De La Ruego Collection." *Aztlán: A Journal of Chicano Studies,* (Fall 2006): 113–125.

Legorreta, Robert. Personal interview with the author. September 22, 2006.

Morales, Frank. "Liberating Unleashed Latino/Gay-themed Artifacts." *Blade,* July 2004, pp. 60–61.

Leguizamo, John

(1964–) *actor, comedian, writer, filmmaker, producer*

A gifted monologist with a riveting creative energy, John Leguizamo stormed the New York theater in the early 1990s and has since become a formidable actor in film and television. He was born in Bogotá, Colombia, on July 22, 1964. His father was an aspiring filmmaker who was forced to give up that dream to support his family. He moved with them to the United States when John was four and settled in Queens, New York. There, Leguizamo senior worked as a waiter and later became a landlord. Twice, John and his brother were sent back to Colombia to live with relatives while their parents struggled to survive. When he was 10, the marriage broke up, and the two boys went to live with their mother.

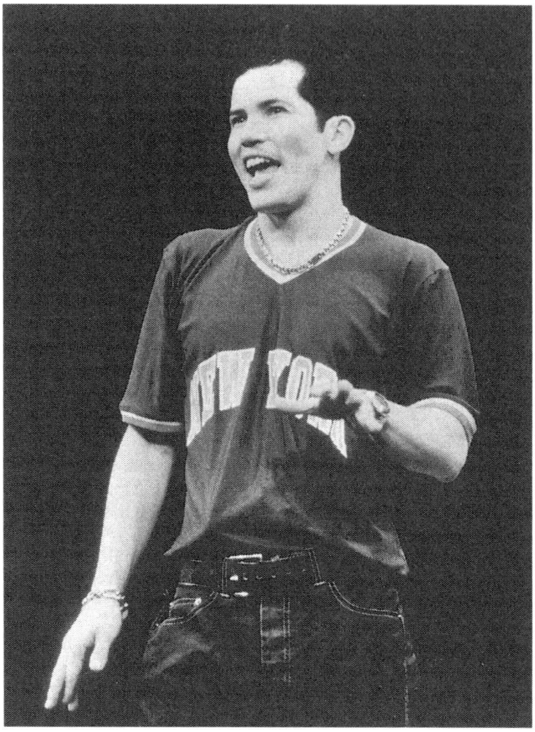

A multitalented actor and writer, John Leguizamo first made his mark on the New York stage in two mesmerizing one-person shows. *(Photofest)*

Always a comic, Leguizamo was almost thrown out of high school for his clowning. After graduating, he attended New York University (NYU), majoring in theater. He was the only Latino in his drama class and dropped out after making his first student film.

A casting director for the hit television crime show *Miami Vice* saw the film and cast Leguizamo in an episode of the series in 1984. During the next several years, he appeared in small roles in film and television, mostly as a Latino gang member or a small time-criminal. His first standout role was as a soldier in Vietnam in the war film *Casualties of War* (1989).

The lack of success and his frustration at being typecast had a positive effect on the young actor. Not able to find the kind of strong roles he wanted, he began to write them for himself. In an acting class, he began to develop a gallery of Latino characters that were based on people he knew and loved, playing them all himself. With the encouragement and help of his acting teacher, Peter Askin, Leguizamo put together a one-man show based on these characters called *Mambo Mouth,* which was produced Off-Broadway in 1991. The show was a hit. Audiences experienced a new world through Leguizamo's characters, and *Mambo Mouth* won the Off-Broadway Award (the Obie) for Best Play. The following year, it was filmed for television's Home Box Office (HBO). Leguizamo put together a second one-man show, *Spic-O-Rama,* which was staged successfully in New York in 1993 and won a Drama Desk Award and four Cable ACE Awards when it, too, was televised on HBO.

Television producers came calling, and Leguizamo developed a Latino comedy-variety show for the Fox Network, *House of Buggin,* in 1995. A critical success with two Emmy nominations, it failed to find a large audience and went off the air after one season.

Meanwhile, Leguizamo's movie career began to take off. He had a strong role as one of four Bronx teens in *Hangin' with the Homeboys* (1991); played gangster Al Pacino's assassin in *Carlito's Way* (1993); and was Tybalt, Romeo's rival, in a modern-punk version of Shakespeare's *Romeo + Juliet* (1996).

Soon after, he established his own production company and produced several Latino-themed films and a one-man television movie, *Sexaholix: A Love Story* (2002), which was nominated for an Emmy. In the hit musical film *Moulin Rouge* (2001), Leguizamo played French artist Toulouse-Lautrec. Black filmmaker Spike Lee gave him his most ambitious role to date as a womanizing hairdresser in the South Bronx in the drama *Summer of Sam* (2002), which dealt partly with the Son of Sam murders in the summer of 1977. The film, unfortunately, was a box-office failure.

Leguizamo continues to act and produce and in 2003 directed and starred in the made-for-TV boxing film *Undefeated.* During the 2005–06 season, he played a recurring role as the brilliant but troubled supervising physician Victor Clemente in the hit medical TV series, *ER* (1994–). He remains one of the most interesting and talented Latino actor/writers of his generation.

As Leguizamo has pointed out, he has no intention of playing the movie game the way Hollywood producers have played it: "I see the new Latino actor as a pioneer, opening up doors for others to follow. And when they don't open, we crowbar our way in."

Further Reading

Cohen, Ross. "Making the Rounds." *USA Weekend,* March 31–April 2, 2006, p. 10.

The Internet Movie Database. "John Leguizamo," The Internet Movie Database. Available online. URL: http://www.imdb.com/name/nm0000491/. Downloaded on December 5, 2004.

Leguizamo, John. *Freak: A Semi-Demi-Quasi-Pseudo Autobiography.* New York: Riverhead Trade, 1998.

Rodríguez, Clara E. *Heroes, Lovers, and Others: The Story of Latinos in Hollywood.* Washington, D.C.: Smithsonian Books, 2004, pp. 240–242.

Further Viewing

Casualties of War (1989). Columbia/Tristar Home Video, VHS/DVD, 1997/2004.

Hangin' with the Homeboys (1991). New Line Home Entertainment, VHS/DVD, 1994/2004.

Mambo Mouth (1991). Uni/Polydor, VHS, 1992.

Summer of Sam (2002). Touchstone Video, VHS/DVD, 2001/2003.

León, Tania

(1943–) *conductor, composer, pianist, music director*

One of the best-known women music conductors in America, Tania León has done as much for Latin-American classical music as anyone alive today. She was born in Havana, Cuba, on May 14, 1943. Although Cuban by birth, she is also of Chinese, French, Nigerian, and Spanish heritage. León took to music at an early age and studied piano, violin, and music theory at the Carlos Alfredo Peyrellado Conservatory. She earned several bachelor of arts (B.A.) degrees and a master of art (M.A.) degree in music.

In 1967, León gave up a promising career as a pianist in communist Cuba to move to the United States. Two years later, a meeting with Arthur Mitchell, director of the Dance Theater of Harlem (DTH), led her to the position of pianist for the ballet ensemble. She later became music director, a position she held until 1980. In 1970, León composed her first ballet for DTH, *The Beloved.* Other ballets and musical works followed.

Another of León's ambitions was to conduct. She made her conducting debut at the Festival of Two Worlds in Spoleto, Italy. She returned to New York, determined to succeed in a field that had very few women. León went back to school and earned a master's degree from New York University (NYU). At the invitation of music director Lukas Foss, León helped to found the Brooklyn Philharmonic Community Concert Series, which she led as conductor for 11 years. After a period of guest conducting with five orchestras, she was given the residency at the Lincoln Center Institute in New York.

In one of her more memorable concerts, León conducted the Johannesburg Symphony during DTH's tour of South Africa. León's commitment to Latino music is total. She helped establish the *Sonidas de las Americas* (Sounds of the Americas) Festival in 1994. She was also the artistic director for a concert series on Latin-American Music that is run by the American Composers Orchestra (ACO).

As a composer, León has often drawn on her Cuban and African background for inspiration. *Carabali,* an orchestral piece, refers to Africans who resisted kidnapping by the slave traders. Her first opera, *Scourge of Hyacinth,* which premiered in 1994, was adapted from a play by Nigerian writer Wole Soyinka. In December 2005, León was awarded a commission from the Fromm Music Foundation at Harvard University to write her first string quartet to be performed in spring 2007.

Like her mixed ethnic background, Tania León is at home with music from every background and country and is committed to performing and conducting all kinds of contemporary music. "I have come to a place where I have no citizenship and I have a global consciousness," she has said. "My chosen purpose in life is to be a musician, a composer, a conductor. This is the way I am making my contribution to mankind."

Further Reading

Hispanic Heritage Biographies. "Tania León," Gale Group Web Site. Available online. URL: http://www.galegroup.com/free_resources/chh/bio/leon_t.htm. Downloaded on February 8, 2005.

Mandel, Howard. "Tania León: Beyond Borders," *Ear Magazine,* January 1989, pp. 12–13.

Tania León Home page. Available online. URL: www.tanialeon.com/. Downloaded on September 20, 2006.

Further Listening

Indigena. Composers Recordings, CD, 1994.

Visiones Panamericans. Urtext Records, CD, 2002.

Limón, José
(José Arcadia Limón)

(1908–1972) *modern dancer, choreographer, educator, dance company director*

A giant in the world of modern dance, José Limón was one of the great male dancers of the 20th century. His virile, dramatic style changed the concept of male dancers and carried over into his dynamic choreography. José Arcadia Limón was born in Culiacán, Mexico, the eldest of 12 children, on January 12, 1908. His father Florencio was a musician and director of the State Academy of Music. His mother died at age 34 when José was still a child, and his father took the family to the United States amid the turmoil of the Mexican Revolution. They eventually settled in Los Angeles (LA), California, where Limón excelled in elementary school and high school. He entered the University of California–Los Angeles (UCLA) in 1926 to pursue a career as a painter. He dropped out of school at age 20 and went to New York City with three friends to pursue his art career. In New York, Limón found little success and abandoned his art. Quite by accident, he attended a modern-dance concert with his friends and was awestruck.

"What I saw simply and irrevocably changed my life," he wrote years later. "I saw the dance as a vision of ineffable power. A man could, with dignity and towering majesty, dance . . . as Michelangelo's visions dance and as the music of Bach dances." Almost immediately, he began to attend dance classes at a studio run by modern dance pioneers Doris Humphrey and Charles Weidman.

Limón became one of their star pupils and was soon dancing in their company with a virility and dramatic intensity that brought a new dimension to male dancing. Before him, male dancers were generally viewed as effete or, at their best, subordinate to the female dancers. Limón made male dancing appealing, strong, and real. When he was not dancing in Humphrey and Weidman's works, he found work as a dancer in Broadway shows, such as the hit Irving Berlin musical revue, *As Thousands Cheer* (1933). He also began to choreograph his own spirited dances, highly influenced by the rhythmic Spanish and Mexican dances that he knew from his youth.

During the 1930s, Limón began to teach dance at several colleges including Bennington in Vermont and the University of California–Berkeley. He would remain a skillful and influential teacher all his life. The year 1940 was a turning point in Limón's life and career: He left Humphrey and Weidman to strike out on his own as a dancer and choreographer. He also married their receptionist, Pauline Lawrence, who would become his business manager, accompanist, and costume designer.

In 1943, during World War II, Limón was inducted into the army. He first served as a truck driver and then directed dances and shows for the Special Services Division. When the war ended, Limón returned to civilian life and founded his own dance company, the José Limón Company, with Doris Humphrey in 1946. The following year, he became a U.S. citizen.

The fledging company became known for its bold choreography and excellent dancers. In the 1950s, the Limón Company became the first American dance company to represent the nation abroad for the State Department, making several tours of South America (1957, 1960), Europe (1957), and the Fast East and Australia (1963). In 1962, Limón and his company gave the first dance performance at the New York Shakespeare Festival Theater in New York's Central Park and the first dance performance at New York's Lincoln Center for the Arts in 1963.

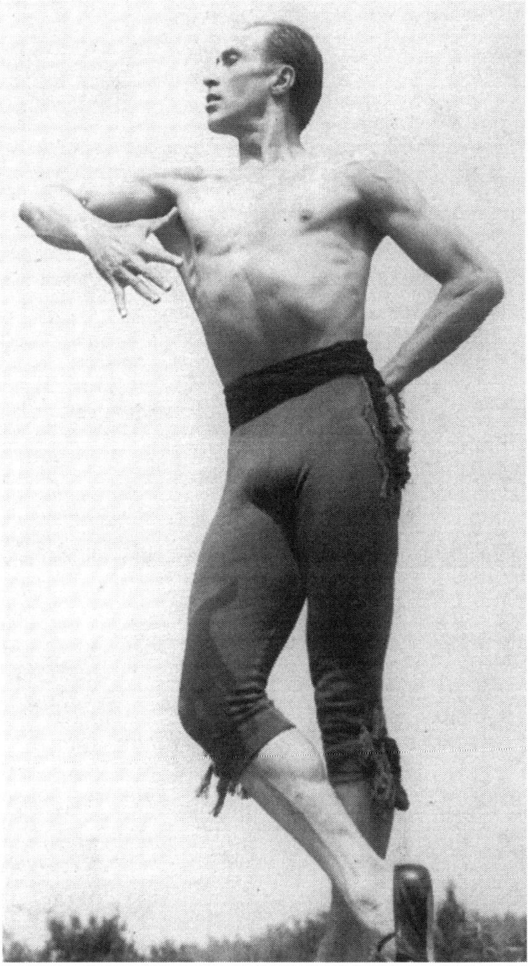

As both dancer and choreographer, José Limón brought a majesty and a dynamic masculinity to the world of modern dance that was distinctly Latin. *(Photofest)*

Limón worked tirelessly as both dancer and choreographer. From 1949 to his death in 1972, he choreographed at least one new piece a year. His most-produced piece, which is today considered his masterpiece, is *The Moor's Pavane* (1949) which retells the tragic story of Shakespeare's *Othello* in the form of a Renaissance dance. Other major works include *The Traitor* (1954), which retells the story of Judas and Christ, relating it to the communist witch hunt in America during the 1950s, and *There Is a Time* (1956), based on the part from the Bible's Book of Ecclesiastes that begins "To everything there is a season . . ." The latter work's score by composer Norman Dello Joio won the Pulitzer Prize for Music in 1957.

A devoted teacher, Limón and his wife spent their summers for many years in residence at the Connecticut College School of Dance in New London, Connecticut, and appeared at the school's annual American Dance Festival. He also was on the dance faculty at the Juilliard School of Music in New York from 1954 to his death. By the 1960s, Limón had largely stopped dancing and devoted all his energies to choreographing and teaching. He gave his last public performance in 1969. He died three years later on December 2, 1972. The José Limón Company continued on without him, the first dance company in America to survive the death or retirement of its founder. The following year, the company toured the Soviet Union. It celebrated its 50th anniversary in 1997.

Limón won many honors and awards in his lifetime, including honorary doctorates from Wesleyan University in Connecticut; Colby College in Maine; Oberlin College in Ohio; and the University of North Carolina.

At the time of his death at age 64, dance critic Clive Barnes praised Limón as one "of America's greatest choreographers . . . and as a dancer, an eagle." Limón himself once said, "I believe that we are never more truly and profoundly human than when we dance."

Further Reading

Cady, Jennifer. *José Limón* (The Library of American Choreographers). New York: Rosen Central, 2005.

Dunbar, June, ed. *José Limón*. Oxford, U.K.: Routledge, 2002.

Limón, José, Lynn Garafola, ed. *José Limón: An Unfinished Memoir.* Middletown, Conn.: Wesleyan University Press, 1999.

Pollack, Barbara, and Charles Humphrey Woodford. *Dance Is a Moment: A Portrait of José Limón in Words and Pictures.* Hightstown, N.J.: Princeton Book Co., 1993.

Shawcross, Nancy. "José Limón—Biography," New York Public Library Web site. Available online. URL: http://digilib.nypl.org/dynaweb/dhc/ findaid/limon@Generic_BookTextView/125;pt=107. Downloaded on November 29, 2004.

Sinnott, Susan. *Extraordinary Hispanic Americans.* Chicago: Children's Press, 1991, pp. 164–165.

Further Viewing

José Limón—The Modern Dance Classics (The Moor's Pavane/The Traitor/ The Emperor Jones) (1999). Videos Arts International, VHS/DVD, 1999/2002.

Lopez, Alma
(1966–) *photographer, painter, video artist*

One of the most controversial of Latina artists today, Alma Lopez uses traditional Mexican-American art forms to challenge existing attitudes toward race, gender, and sexuality. She was born in Los Mochis in Sinaloa State, Mexico, on November 14, 1966, and as a child moved to Los Angeles (LA), California, with her family. Lopez received her bachelor of arts (B.A.) degree from the University of California–Santa Barbara and then earned a master of fine arts (M.F.A.) degree from the University of California–Irvine. As a woman, an artist, and a lesbian, Lopez feels it is her role to confront the status quo, both in Latino and Anglo culture.

In recent years, she has turned from traditional painting and photography to digital, computer-generated prints, often making collages of photographs with computer technology. Many of these works are subversive images with a heightened sense of reality and fantasy. Her digital print *Our Lady* (1999) started a firestorm of controversy at the Museum of International Folk Art in Santa Fe, New Mexico, where it was part of an exhibition in 2001. Set in the form of a *retablo,* a religious painting, Lopez's Lady of Guadalupe, a Mexican version of the Virgin Mary, wears an outfit made of roses and a cape with an engraved image of the Aztec warrior moon goddess Coyolxauhqui. The model is performance artist Raquel Salinas, whose one-person performance "Heat Your Own," as well as Sandra Cisnero's essay "Guadalupe the Sex Goddess" and the artist's experience growing up with this cultural and religious icon, inspired the work. Our Lady is held up by a butterfly angel with bare breasts that is portrayed by cultural activist Raquel Gutierrez. "The two Raqueles and I grew up in Los Angeles with the image of the Virgin of Guadalupe in our homes and community," explained Lopez. She sees the figure as a strong, contemporary woman.

Others who saw it felt otherwise. The archbishop of Santa Fe claimed that the depiction was sacrilegious, portraying the Virgin "as if she were a tart." Despite the criticism from many, the museum refused to remove the print from the exhibit but agreed to close the show earlier than originally planned "in the spirit of reconciliation." Lopez herself was not discouraged by the adverse reaction to her work. She sees it as an opportunity to respond to her critics and has even published her ongoing dialogue with them on her Web site.

More recently, Lopez has created her first digital video documentary, *Bio Hair* (2005), showcasing three young lesbian women of different ethnic backgrounds who explain why they choose to wear their hair short.

Alma Lopez is the recipient of several awards including the California Community Foundation Arts Funding Initiative's Individual Artist Grant. Her work has been featured in museums and in such periodicals as *Ms. Magazine* and *Art in America.*

Further Reading

Alma Lopez's Official Web Site. Available online. URL: http://www.almalopez.net. Downloaded on August 2, 2005.

Contemporaries. "Alma Lopez 2002," Calfund Web Site. Available online. URL: http://www.calfund.org/arts/lopez.php. Downloaded on September 8, 2005.

Lopez, Alma. "Tattoo, Santa Nina de Mochis, California Fashions Slaves, and Our Lady." *Frontiers—A Journal of Women's Studies,* January 1, 2002, pp. 90–92.

Matthew, Sandra. "Icons, Heroes and Stories of Survival." *Masquerade: Women's Contemporary Portrait Photography,* edited by Christine Ralph and Kate Newton. Cardiff, Wales: Ffotogallery, 2003.

Walker, Hollis. "Our Lady of Controversy." *The New Gate Keepers: Emerging Challenges to Free Expression in the Arts,* edited by Christopher Hawthorne and Andras Szanto. New York: National Arts Journalism Program, 2004.

Lopez, George (George C. Lopez)

(1963–) *actor, comedian, writer, television producer*

Only the fourth Latino to be the star of a television sitcom, George Lopez spent two decades honing his skills as a stand-up comic and actor before achieving stardom. George C. Lopez was born in Mission Hills, California, on April 23, 1963. His father, a Mexican-American migrant worker, abandoned the family when George was two months old. His mother, who suffered serious psychological problems, turned him over to the care of his maternal grandparents when he was 10. Filled with anger and resentment at the world and at his parents, Lopez found his only escape in comedy.

Modeling himself after successful Latino comic and TV star FREDDIE PRINZE, he began to appear at local comedy clubs while still a teenager.

At age 17, Lopez played a bit part in the martial-arts movie *Fist of Fear, Touch of Death* (1980) but found little further work as a Latino in Hollywood. He continued to work the comedy-club circuit, cushioning his insecurities and depression with alcohol.

Year after year, Lopez honed his comedy act, which dealt largely with the life of Latino Americans—their families, rituals, and problems living in an Anglo society. He built up a loyal following, especially among Latinos, but true stardom eluded him until a scout for actress Sandra Bullock's production company caught his act at a nightclub. The company was seeking Latinos who could be marketed on television and Lopez's Latino-based humor made the cut. Soon, he was starring in his own television sitcom, appropriately named *George Lopez* (2002–) on ABC. In the show, he plays the manager of a Los Angeles (LA) airplane-parts factory. Besides starring in the show, Lopez is also its cocreater, producer, and one of its writers.

George Lopez gave Lopez the national exposure that has made him a star. Now a top draw on the comedy circuit, he sold out LA's Universal Amphitheater for three successive nights in October 2003—a feat achieved by only a few other comedians. His 2003 live comedy album *Team Leader* was nominated for a Grammy for Best Comedy Album in 2004. He has continued to act in films, notably in *Bread and Roses* (2000), a comedy-drama about a Latina who starts a union for janitors in East LA. More recently, he was seen in the Latino comedy *Tortilla Heaven* (2005) about the miraculous discovery of the face of Jesus on a tortilla in a small-town restaurant in New Mexico.

Lopez's autobiography *Why You Crying?* was published in 2004. On April 25, 2005, he underwent a successful kidney transplant. The donor was his wife Ana Serrano. Lopez was honored with a star on the Hollywood Walk of Fame in March 2006.

Further Reading

The official George Lopez Web Site. Available online. URL: http://www.georgelopez.com/. Downloaded on September 20, 2006.

The Internet Movie Database. "George Lopez," The Internet Movie Database. Available online. URL: http://www.imdb.com/name/nm0520064/. Downloaded on December 9, 2004.

Lopez, George. *Why You Crying?: My Long, Hard Look at Life, Love and Laughter.* Carmichael, Calif.: Touchstone, 2004.

Further Listening

Team Leader. Oglio Records, CD, 2003.

Further Viewing

Bread and Roses (2000). Studio Home Entertainment, VHS/DVD, 2001.

López, George
(George T. López)
(1900–1993) santero

One of the most celebrated *santeros* of the 20th century, George López brought a dramatic, animated style to his unique carved religious scenes and figures. George T. López was born in Cordova in northern New Mexico in a mountain valley of the rugged Sangre de Cristo Mountains on April 23, 1900. His family's roots in the area go back to 1590, and his grandfather and father were both accomplished *santeros,* creating their religious figures for churches and home altars. His father, José Dolores López, was the originator of the Cordova style of *santos,* characterized by a chip-carved technique and unadorned by paint.

In 1937, the year his father died, López carved his first significant work—a group statue of Adam and Eve and the Tree of Life. It would become a favorite biblical theme and would appear many times in his work. During this time, he worked on the railroad and was often away from home.

At age 52, López finally returned for good to Cordova and devoted himself completely to his art. While greatly influenced by his father, López developed his own highly expressive style that captured movement and action in his figures and scenes. One of his seminal works is *San Miguel el Arcángel y el Diablo* (St. Michael the Archangel and the Devil, ca. 1955–56). Almost medieval in its stark beauty, the sculpture shows St. Michael standing triumphantly over the devil, his foot atop the fallen angel's chest.

For the last four decades of his life, López was busy filling orders for local churches and for collectors who sought his work. But he made a clear distinction between his works for churches and home altars and those for secular collectors. "This block of wood is nothing more than wood," he once said. "It's the same thing to make a carving for these people [collectors] or for a church. . . . But if the priest blesses this, well, then, they are images of the Apostles in Heaven. . . . If not, they are just blocks of wood, no more."

López carved his unadorned figures from a variety of woods, including juniper, cedar, pine, and cottonwood, although aspen was his favorite medium in which to work. He collected wood himself from the mountains in which he lived and sold most of his work right out of his house. His wife Silvianita worked with him, carving small animals to decorate the figures he made. George López died on December 23, 1993.

Today, Cordova continues to be a center for *santeros.* Several of López's relatives pursue the art of *santos,* most prominently his niece Sabinita López Ortiz, who has her own workshop in the town.

Further Reading

Congdon, Kristin G., and Kara Kelley Hallmark. *Artists from Latin American Cultures: A Biographical Dictionary.* Westport, Conn.: Greenwood Press, 2002. pp. 151–153.

Martinez, Eluid Levi. *What Is a New Mexico Santos?: Creating Carved Religious Figures.* Santa Fe, N.Mex.: Sunstone Press, 1978.

Yorba, Jonathan. *Arte Latino: Treasures from the Smithsonian American Art Museum.* New York: Watson–Guptill Publications, 2001, pp. 50–51.

Lopez, Jennifer
(Jennifer Lynn Lopez, "J.Lo," "Jenny from the Block")
(1969–) *actress, singer, dancer, film producer*

A multitalented Latina whose music albums have sold millions and who is one of the highest paid actresses in Hollywood, Jennifer Lopez skyrocketed to fame in the late 1990s with a formidable combination of talent, beauty, and hard work. Jennifer Lynn Lopez was born in the Castle Hill section of the Bronx, New York, on July 24, 1969, the second of three daughters. Her parents were both Puerto Rican-born and later met and married in the United States. Her father David is a computer technician, and her mother Guadalupe is a kindergarten teacher.

Lopez attended all Catholic schools and took dancing and singing lessons from age five. She was a good athlete in high school, playing tennis and softball and participating in gymnastics. After graduating in 1986, she attended Baruch College in New York but left after a semester to pursue a career as a dancer and actress. Living on her own from age 18, Lopez earned a living working days at office jobs and performing as an actress and dancer in small theaters at night. She sometimes slept in the same dance studio where she practiced.

She auditioned for Rosie Perez, then choreographer for the hit Fox Network comedy show *In Living Color.* Lopez won the role of one of the show's famous "Fly Girl" dancers and relocated to southern California, which she initially did not like. After leaving the show in 1992, she got a job as a dancer on tour with singer Janet Jackson and also appeared in one of Jackson's music videos. Lopez landed parts in several short-lived television series, including Fox's *South Central* (1994).

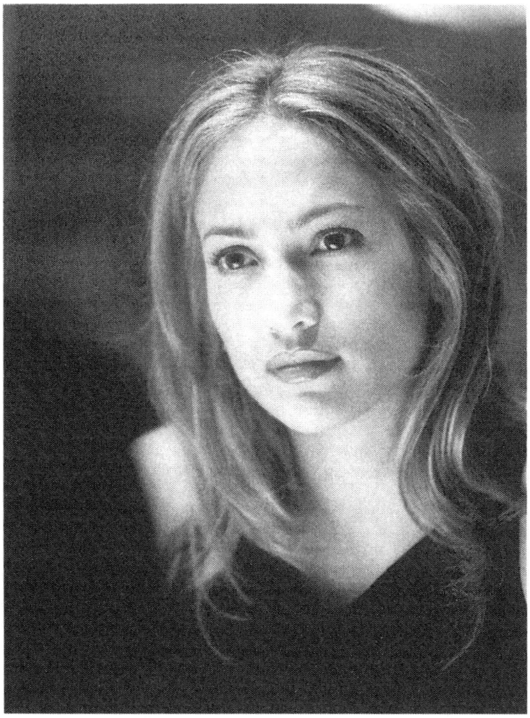

Jennifer Lopez's image as the Puerto Rican girl from down the street is a huge factor in her phenomenal success as a film actress and a recording artist. *(Photofest)*

The following year, she received her first substantial role in a major film, *My Family, Mi Familia* (1995) about the trials of a three-generation Mexican-American family in East Los Angeles, directed by GREGORY NAVA. Her beauty and on-screen charisma got her the parts of a subway investigator and love interest in the action comedy *Money Train* (1995), an elementary school teacher in Francis Ford Coppola's comedy *Jack* (1996), and Jack Nicholson's venal girlfriend in the twisty film noir *Blood and Wine* (1997).

Then came the film that lifted her to stardom and reunited her with director Nava. She played Tejena singer SELENA Quintanilla Perez in the biographical film *Selena* (1997), which co-starred JON SECADA and EDWARD JAMES OLMOS, as Selena's father. Lopez's energetic and touching performance immediately put her in the forefront of Latina actresses in Hollywood.

Her next film, *Out of Sight* (1998), was a change of pace. She played a tough but empathetic federal marshal who falls for an on-the-run criminal, played by George Clooney. Having established her film career, Lopez released her first album as a solo singer, *On the 6* (1999). The album title refers to the local subway train that she took to get to auditions in Manhattan. Critics complained that her voice was slight, but fans loved her hip-hop style, and the album became a huge hit. It was followed by *J.Lo* (2001), titled after her most popular nickname. Its release coincided with her first big romantic comedy, *The Wedding Planner* (2001), in which she played the title role. Lopez became the highest paid Latina actress to date, receiving $9 million for this film, and was the first performer from any background to have the number one record on the charts and the number one movie in America simultaneously.

Part of Lopez's appeal to audiences was her down-to-earth "Jenny from the Block" image, a song title from her third album *This Is Me . . . Then* (2002). The image was reinforced by her second romantic comedy, *Maid in Manhattan* (2002), in which she played a hotel maid and single mother who is wooed and won by a prominent Anglo politician who stays at the hotel. In the more recent *Monster-in-Law* (2005), she teamed up with actress Jane Fonda who plays a mother-in-law from hell in Fonda's first film in 15 years. Lopez's salary for this film was $15 million. Later that same year, she played Robert Redford's daughter-in-law in *An Unfinished Life.*

Not content with acting and singing, Lopez, a confessed workaholic, has funneled her wealth into several successful enterprises, including a production company to develop film projects for her, a line of perfume and clothing, and a Cuban restaurant in Pasadena, California.

Lopez's love life has been as closely followed by the public as any of her achievements on disk or screen. Her first two marriages to actors Ojani Noa and Cris Judd both ended in divorce. Among her boyfriends has been rap singer–actor–producer Sean "P. Diddy" Combs, with whom she was arrested in 1999 for involvement in a nightclub shooting. Charges against her were later dropped, and Combs was acquitted after a highly publicized trial. Lopez's affair and subsequent engagement to actor Ben Affleck was the biggest entertainment story of 2003. The engagement, which led to the twosome making two disastrous movies (*Gigli* and *Jersey Girl*), ended in 2004. In June of that year, Lopez married singer MARC ANTHONY in a wedding so secret that the wedding guests thought they were attending an afternoon party.

Her sister Linda Lopez is an entertainment reporter for Channel 11 News in New York City.

Lopez continues to be one of Hollywood's superstars. "If I could describe myself in a few words, strong would be one of them," Lopez has said. "I know what I want and I'm willing to go after it."

Further Reading

Duncan, Patricia J. *Jennifer Lopez.* New York: St. Martin's Press, 1999.

Hurst, Heidi. *Jennifer Lopez* (People in the News). San Diego, Calif.: Lucent Books, 2003.

The Internet Movie Database. "Jennifer Lopez," The Internet Movie Database. Available online. URL: http://www.imdb.com/name/nm0000182. Downloaded on December 13, 2004.

Wheeler, Jill C. *Jennifer Lopez* (Star Tracks). Edna, Minn.: Abdo & Daughters Publishing, 2002.

Further Listening

On the 6. Sony, CD, 1999.

Rebirth. Sony, CD, 2005.

Further Viewing

Maid in Manhattan (2002). Columbia/Tristar Home Video, VHS/DVD, 2004/2005.

Out of Sight (1998). Universal Home Video, VHS/DVD, 2001/2003.

Selena (1997). Warner Home Video, VHS/DVD, 2004.

Lopez, Lourdes

(1958–) ballet dancer, educator, broadcaster, arts administrator

A leading dancer with the New York City Ballet for more than two decades, Lourdes Lopez has continued to contribute to the world of dance as a teacher, television arts reporter, and an arts administrator. She was born in Havana, Cuba, on May 2, 1958, the youngest of three daughters of Felix and Marta Lopez. Her father was an army officer who opposed the revolution of Fidel Castro. In 1959, his wife and children fled Cuba, disguised as tourists. He later joined them in Miami, Florida, where the family settled.

Lopez was diagnosed as having orthopedic problems in her legs at age five, and her doctor recommended that she take dance lessons to build up her legs. She and a sister took a ballet class weekly. When her talent as a dancer emerged, Lopez began to study daily with Russian Alexander Nigodoff. At age 10, with her teacher's encouragement, she auditioned in New York for the School of American Ballet and was offered a scholarship to attend. She held off going until she was 14 and returned to Miami. George Balanchine, legendary choreographer and founder and director of the New York City Ballet (NYCB), was impressed by the young Cuban-American dancer. He hired her as an apprentice, and when she turned 16, he invited her to join his company.

At NYCB, Lopez performed many leading roles. Balanchine made her a soloist in 1981. Three years later, she became a principal dancer. She toured Europe with the company and appeared on several *Dance in America* television shows on the Public Broadcasting System (PBS).

Then in winter 1988 the nightmare that haunts every dancer happened to her. She injured her foot and underwent surgery. As she entered a long period of recuperation, Lopez was not sure that she would ever dance again. To prepare for an uncertain future, she took courses in child psychology at Fordham University and had her first child, a girl, Adriel, with her attorney husband Lionel in November 1989.

Fortunately, the injury healed and Lopez returned to the ballet in 1991. But her time away gave her a different perspective on the world of dance. She began to lecture and to demonstrate dance to school children in the region under the auspices of the ballet's education department.

In 1995, Lopez retired from NYCB, but her love of dance took her in several new directions. She became a part-time cultural arts on-camera reporter for WNBC–TV in New York. She continued to teach minority students, creating her own arts program. She was also named a senior faculty member of the Ballet Academy East.

As a TV reporter, Lopez went to her homeland of Cuba for the first time since she was an infant. This rekindled her love of Cuba and its people. She later helped found the Cuban Artists Fund (CAF), a nonprofit organization that offered funds to Cuban artists.

In September 2002, Lourdes Lopez was appointed the executive director of the George Balanchine Foundation, a public charity incorporated in 1983 shortly after the choreographer's death. In this new role, she supervises the foundation's activities and helps to develop funding.

Further Reading

The George Balanchine Foundation News & Events. "Lourdes Lopez Named Executive Director of the George Balanchine Foundation," The George Balanchine Foundation Web Site. Available online. URL: http://www.balanchine.org/05/archive/2002llopez.html. Downloaded on August 7, 2005.

Morey, Janet, and Wendy Dunn. *Famous Hispanic Americans.* New York: Dutton, 1996, pp. 90–101.

López, Ramón José

(1951–) *silversmith,* santero, *jewelry designer*

A master craftsman, whose work ranges from intricate jewelry to paintings on buffalo hides, Ramón José López is among the most versatile of New Mexican folk artists. He was born in Santa Fe, New Mexico, in 1951. His grandfather Lorenzo López, noted *santero,* carver and painter of religious objects, died two years before his birth. As a young man, López worked in the construction business and only later turned to the crafts of silversmith and jewelry making. Although known for his simple, beautiful silver and gold jewelry, he also makes traditional religious objects such as *bultos* (wooden statues) and *retablos* (painted wood religious panels or statues) using his grandfather's tools. He also has painted on buffalo hides, another traditional art form, and fashions chalices and rosary boxes for churches. He researches the traditional techniques meticulously to reflect the old masters of the past, like his grandfather. He has even revived the craft of blacksmithing in creating his artwork.

López's *Liturgical Cross* (1998), one of his most stunning pieces, has silver ornmentation like rays flashing from angles off a crucified Christ figure. On the reverse is a figure of Saint Francis. The piece resides in the Smithsonian American Art Museum (SAAM) in Washington, D.C.

López's work has earned him many honors. In 1993, he received both the Governor's Award for Excellence and Achievement in the Arts and the Santa Fe Mayor's Recognition Award for Excellence in the Arts. He was awarded a National Heritage Fellowship by the National Endowment for the Arts (NEA) in 1997.

López operates his own gallery in Santa Fe, Good Hands Gallery. His four children are also artists and craftspeople. Their work and their father's was included in a traveling exhibition *Cuando Hablen Los Santos* (When the saints speak).

"My traditional work [lets] me see how influenced I really was by my heritage, my history," he has said. "I want to achieve the quality of these old masters . . . what they captured on wood, emotions so powerful, so moving,"

Further Reading

Cockcroft, James D., assisted by Jane Canning. *Latino Visions: Contemporary Chicano, Puerto Rican, and Cuban American Artists.* New York: Franklin Watts, 2000, pp. 18–19.

Fleming, Jeanie Puleston. "Crafting a New Mexico Tradition—Wood Carving." *Sunset,* November 2000, p. 52.

Rosenak, Chuck, and Jan Rosenak. *The Saint Makers: Contemporary Santeras y Santeros.* Flagstaff, Ariz.: Northland Publications, 1998.

Yorba, Jonathan. *Arte Latino: Treasures from the Smithsonian American Art Museum.* New York: Watson-Guptill Publications, 2001, pp. 56–57.

Lopez, Trini (Trinidad López III)

(1937–) *pop and folk singer, guitarist, actor*

An energetic performer who burst onto the pop scene in 1963 with a string of folk-song remakes backed by a dynamic guitar, Trini Lopez's "overnight success" was actually years in the making. Trinidad López III was born in Dallas, Texas, on May 15, 1937. His father, Trinidad II, was a Mexican-born singer, dancer, and actor who immigrated to Texas following his marriage to Petra Gonzalez. When Trini was 11, his father gave him a spanking for hanging out with the wrong crowd of kids. He later felt guilty about the spanking and bought his son a $12 guitar. "A spanking literally changed my life," Lopez said years later.

Learning to play and sing, Lopez dropped out of high school in his senior year to find work as a performer to help his financially struggling family. Soon he was playing with his own group in small clubs across the Southwest. Under the influence of rock and roll, he wrote the song "The Right to Rock" and recorded it on a small Dallas record label. The producers wanted him to change his name professionally to something non-Latino, but he refused. Lopez's first real break was befriending rock singer Buddy Holly, who introduced him to his producer Norm Petty of Clovis, New Mexico. Petty did not want a Latino group and turned Lopez's band into an instrumental combo called the Big Beats.

Soon after, Buddy Holly died in a plane crash that also took the life of Latino rock star RITCHIE VALENS, a role model for Lopez. Holly's former

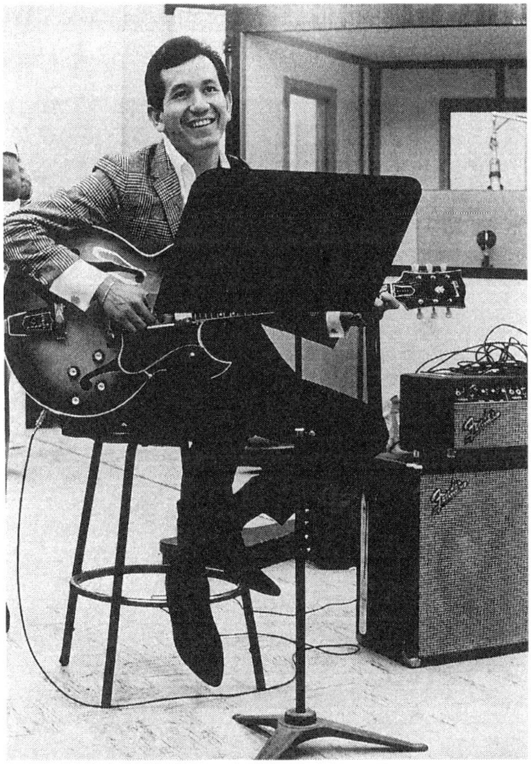

Trini Lopez almost replaced Buddy Holly after his death as lead singer of the Crickets, but he gained solo success instead singing revved-up folk songs at an LA club named PJ's. *(Photofest)*

group, the Crickets, invited Lopez to come to Hollywood to be their new lead singer. When he arrived there, however, the Crickets were enjoying their royalties and in no rush to record.

Stranded in California with no money, Lopez took a solo gig at a small club in Beverly Hills. What started as a two-week engagement ended up stretching to a year. Lopez's exciting pop interpretations of familiar folk songs was a local phenomenon. When he took his act to PJ's, a larger night spot, producer Don Costa saw him and recommended him to Frank Sinatra who had recently started his own record label, Reprise. Sinatra signed Lopez to an eight-year contract.

His first Reprise album, *Trini Lopez at PJ's,* released in 1963, zoomed to #1 on the album charts. One cut, Lopez's high octane version of the Pete Seeger folk song "If I Had a Hammer," shot to #3 on the singles' charts. Lopez had several more hits, mostly makeovers of folk and rock hits, including "Kansas City" (1963), "Lemon Tree" (1965), and "I'm Comin' Home, Cindy" (1966).

Within a year of his "overnight success," he was expanding into film and television acting. Sinatra's pal, singer Dean Martin, befriended Lopez and featured him on his television variety show. Lopez's most ambitious acting role was as the Latino member of *The Dirty Dozen* (1967), a World War II action film.

By 1968, Lopez's recording career was fading, but he continued to be a popular live performer. His role in the Ritchie Valens bio film *La Bamba* (1987), in which he sang the title song, jump-started his career. In July 2001, he was given the Living Legend Award of Nosotros, an organization of Spanish-speaking people in the film and television industries. In 2003, Lopez was inducted into the International Latin Music Hall of Fame.

Further Reading

Dahl, Bill. "Trini Lopez," Mp3.com. Available online. URL: http://www.mp3.com/trini-lopez/artists/2599/biography.html. Downloaded on September 28, 2005.

The Trini Lopez Official Web Site. Available online. URL: http://trinilopez.com/. Downloaded on March 18, 2005.

Wikipedia. "Trini Lopez," Wikipedia—The Free Encyclopedia. Available online. URL: http://en.wikipedia.org/wiki/Trini_Lopez. Downloaded on March 23, 2006.

Further Listening

Trini Lopez—Greatest Hits. Laserlight, CD, 2002.

Further Viewing

The Dirty Dozen (1967). Warner Home Video, VHS/DVD, 2001/2005.

Lucero, Michael
(Michael Luis Lucero)
(1953–) *sculptor, ceramist, educator*

Michael Lucero is a master of a multicultural style that is built largely on an artistic material that is totally ignored by most contemporary artists—clay. In Lucero's gifted hands, clay has become a treasured art medium. Michael Luis Lucero was born in Tracy, California, on April 1, 1953. His ancestors were Sephardic Jews from Spain who migrated to New Mexico to escape persecution. As a boy, he spent his summers at his grandparents' home in Las Vegas, New Mexico, where he was fascinated by the many animals, insects, and reptiles that he saw. These creatures have since become a major theme of his work.

After high school, Lucero attended Humboldt State University in northern California, where he earned his bachelor of arts (B.A.) degree in 1975. He continued his studies at the University of Washington–Seattle, earning a master of fine arts (M.F.A.) degree. He attributes his interest in ceramics and other crafts to his "funky teachers" at Seattle "who used crafty techniques" in their weaving and knitting. Moving to New York City, Lucero taught at New York University (NYU) and the Parsons School of Design before devoting himself fulltime to sculpture and ceramics.

His clay figures—including beetles, turtles, frogs, and human heads—relate directly to pre-Columbian and Chicano culture. He has also borrowed from many other cultures, including Native American (totem poles and stick figures), African (bottle trees and face jugs), 20th-century modernism, and pop culture (found objects). Lucero's multiculturalism was decidedly out of step with the art establishment of the 1970s, but today he is considered to be a distinctive and outstanding artist on the cutting edge of global culture.

While clay is his primary medium, he also creates works in bronze, glazed ceramic, and mixed media. His satirical soldier statue *Conquistador* is made of cement with a red teapot for a head. Tirelessly inventive and possessing a sharp sense of humor, Lucero delights in unlikely combinations of things—ceramic bits with baby carriages or a piece of driftwood.

Lucero's work has been exhibited widely. A major traveling exhibit opened at the Mint Museum of Art in Charlotte, North Carolina, in 1996. A retrospective of his art going back 20 years was held at the Carnegie Museum of Art in Pittsburgh, Pennsylvania, in 1998.

"The visual and formal diversity of his works is a metaphor for contemporary life and collective existence, in which there is not one predominant culture, but many voices existing simultaneously," wrote one critic, reviewing his show at the Mint Museum. Lucero himself sees his work as "reverence for high art, affection for folk art, nostalgia for nature, and curiosity about other cultures."

Further Reading

Cockcroft, James D., assisted by Jane Canning. *Latino Visions: Contemporary Chicano, Puerto Rican, and Cuban American Artists.* New York: Franklin Watts, 2000, pp. 57–58.

Leach, Mark Richard. *Michael Lucero: Sculpture 1976–1995.* Manchester, Vt.: Hudson Hills Press, 1996.

The Mint Museum of Art."Michael Lucero: Sculpture 1976–1995." Carnegie Magazine Online. Available online. URL: http://www.carnegiemuseum.org/cmag/bk_issue/1998/marapr/feat6.htm. Downloaded on August 3, 2005.

M

Marin, Cheech (Richard Antonio Marin)

(1946–) *actor, comedian, director, screenwriter, producer, filmmaker*

One-half of the most popular counterculture comedy duo of the 1970s, Cheech Marin has since become a successful character actor in film and television and a tireless promoter of Latino art and culture. Richard Antonio Marin was born in the Watts section of Los Angeles on July 13, 1946. His family is Mexican American, and his father is a 30-year veteran of the Los Angeles Police Department (LAPD). His nickname "Cheech" came from *chicharron,* a spicy fried pork-skin snack.

Marin was an English major at California State University–Northridge. After graduating, he fled to Canada to avoid the Vietnam War draft. In Vancouver, British Columbia, he met Canadian rock guitarist Tommy Chong, who he joined in a new improvisational-comedy troupe, City Works. City Works was a failure, and Chong invited Marin to form a rock band. "But we started off with comedy," recalled Marin, "and somehow never got around to playing." Their irreverent brand of hippie humor, largely focusing on drug use, was a hit with members of the sixties generation. After success in Vancouver clubs, Cheech and Chong, as they called themselves, moved to Los Angeles in the early 1970s.

Producer Lou Adler of Ode Records caught their comedy act at the Troubadour Club in LA and signed them to a recording contract. Their debut album *Cheech & Chong* (1971) was a smash and remained on the album charts for a year. A Christmas novelty, "Santa Claus and His Old Lady," became their first of nine charting singles. While some of their hit comedy records, such as "Sister Mary Elephant (Shad-Up!)," continued to mine the vein of drug humor, other songs were clever parodies of rock music, such as "Basketball Jones" (1973) and "Born in East LA" (1985), a Latino takeoff on Bruce Springsteen's "Born in the U.S.A."

In 1978, Cheech and Chong made their film debut in *Up In Smoke* (1978), playing the same drugged-out street characters that they portrayed on their records. The film became one of the year's biggest-grossing movies, and from then on, Cheech and Chong concentrated on making films. They starred in three more hit movies as themselves and then made *The Corsican Brothers* (1984), a more conventional comedy that was set during the French Revolution and was written and produced by Cheech's actress wife Rikki. The movie bombed, and the team split up in 1985.

Chong faded from the scene, but Marin moved into mainstream acting. Cheech the Druggie now became Cheech the Bus Driver on a successful series of children's educational records. In 1987, Marin wrote and directed *Born in East LA,* based on the song of the same title. While a comedy, the film dealt with such serious issues as illegal immigration

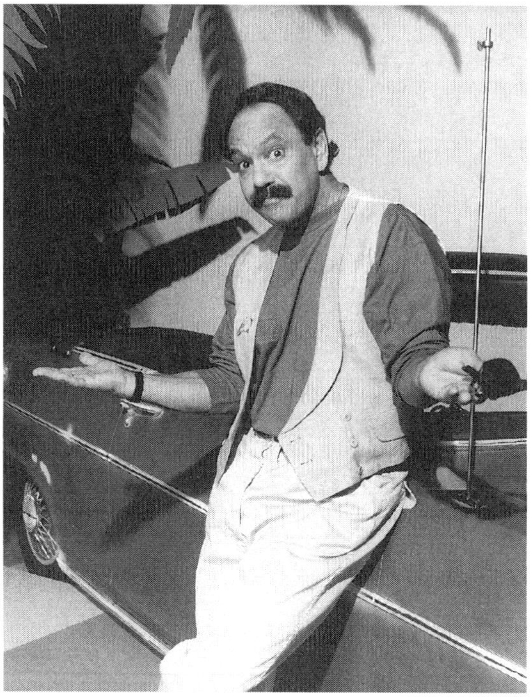

Cheech Marin strikes a characteristically funny pose. In real life, the comic actor is a serious collector and promoter of Latino American art. *(Photofest)*

and prejudice against Latinos. Marin played Rudy, a Mexican American who is mistakenly deported to Mexico as an illegal immigrant and who then must use his wits to return to the United States.

Marin found work on television as a regular in the short-lived sitcom *Golden Palace* (1992–93), a spin off of *Golden Girls,* and then costarred with Don Johnson on the hit police show *Nash Bridges* (1996–2001). He also appeared with Johnson in the romantic comedy *Tin Cup* (1996), which was set in the world of professional golf. The film turned Marin into an avid golfer; he has since played in numerous tournaments.

The previous year, Marin appeared as a villainous bartender in *Desperado* (1995), which was directed by ROBERT RODRIGUEZ. Since then, he has appeared in five more Rodriguez films.

Marin has always maintained that his druggie persona in the days of Cheech and Chong was all an act. He is a serious art collector and has one of the largest collections of Mexican and Mexican-American art in the country. Marin has written a book on the subject and has sponsored several traveling art exhibitions including "Chicano Visions: American Painters on the Verge as collected by Cheech Marin." In October 2005, he directed *Latinologues,* a Latino comedy revue on Broadway.

Marin divorced his wife Rikki in 1984 and married Patti Heid. They have two children, and he has one child from his first marriage.

Further Reading

Marin, Cheech. *Chicano Vision: American Painting on the Verge.* New York: Bulfinch Press, 2002.

Mavis, Barbara J. *Famous People of Hispanic Heritage: Gloria Estefan, Fernando Cuzq, Rosie Perez, Cheech Marin.* Hockessin, Del.: Mitchell Lane Publishers, 1996.

Sharon, Adam, and Greg Sharon. *The Cheech and Chong Bible.* Boulder, Colo.: Browne Stane Books, 2003.

Further Listening

My Name Is Cheech, School Bus Driver. Sony, CD, 1997.

Where There's Smoke There's Cheech and Chong. Rhino Records, 2 CDs, 2002.

Further Viewing

Born in East LA (1987). Universal Home Video, VHS/DVD, 2001/2003.

Tin Cup (1996). Warner Home Video, VHS/DVD, 1997.

Marisol
(Marisol Escobar)
(1930–) *sculptor*

A prominent figure in the field of pop sculpture, Marisol is as well known for her eccentricities and natural beauty as she is for her witty, often socially and politically satirical sculptures. She was born

Marisol Escobar in Paris, France, to a well-to-do Venezuelan family on May 22, 1930. Her first name is Spanish for "sea and sun," *mar y sol.* Most of her childhood was spent traveling. The family lived at different times in New York; Los Angeles (LA), California; and Caracas, Venezuela. Her mother died when Marisol was 11, and art became her comfort and security in life. In 1946, she began to take drawing classes at the Jepson School in LA. In 1949, she studied art in Paris; the following year, she moved to New York City where she took courses at The Art Students League. She also studied at the Hans Hofmann School in Provincetown, Massachusetts, where she worked with Hofmann, the famed abstract expressionist painter.

By the mid-1950s, Marisol (she had dropped her last name) was a visible member of the beat generation of avant-garde poets, musicians, and artists. Largely self-taught as a sculptor, she was heavily influenced by pre-Columbian art and its large, blocklike figures. Her first individual exhibition was held at the Leo Castelli Gallery in New York in 1958.

By the 1960s, Marisol's sculptures had grown increasingly witty and often self-alluding. Her *Self-Portrait* (1961–62) revealed seven faces that represented different sides of her and were attached to a wood blocklike torso. In *The Party,* all 13 partygoers have her face as well as pieces of her clothes.

Other works dealt with political and social issues, usually with a keen sense of humor. *LBJ* (1967) showed a giant President Lyndon Johnson holding his tiny wife and two daughters in his hand, demonstrating the lack of power women held even in the White House. A decade later, Joan Mondale, wife of Vice President Walter Mondale, decorated the vice-presidential mansion with works by Marisol.

Among Marisol's many friends was artist Andy Warhol, who dubbed her the first "glamorous girl artist" and cast her in two of his experimental films, *The Kiss* (1963) and *The 13 Most Beautiful Women* (1964). Marisol could be as eccentric as Warhol. Once, she wore a white Japanese mask to a panel discussion at the Museum of Modern Art (MOMA) in New York. When she later removed the mask, her face was made up to look like the mask.

Marisol's work was included in the important exhibition *American Sculpture of the Sixties.* In 1968, she represented Venezuela at the prestigious Venice Biennale in Italy, although she had become a U.S. citizen five years earlier. In 1991, she became the first Latina-American sculptor to exhibit her work in the National Portrait Gallery in Washington, D.C. Marisol's work is in the permanent collections of numerous museums, including the Metropolitan Museum of Art and the Whitney Museum of American Art in New York City. She continues to live and work in New York City.

Further Reading

Congdon, Kirstin G., and Kara Kelley Hallmark. *Artists from Latin American Cultures: A Biographical Dictionary.* Westport, Conn.: Greenwood Press, 2002, pp. 161–164.

Marisol. *Marisol.* Purchase, N.Y.: Neuberger Museum of Art, 2001.

———. *Recent Sculptures: March 4–28, 1998, Marlborough.* New York: Marlborough Gallery, 1998.

Sinnott, Susan. *Extraordinary Hispanic Americans.* Chicago: Childrens Press, 1991, pp. 196–198.

Martin, Ricky
(Enrique José Martín Morales)

(1971–) *Latin and pop singer, actor, songwriter*

One of the most popular Latino singers of the 1990s, Ricky Martin successfully made the rare crossover to the English-speaking pop market by the decade's end. A seasoned performer who is more than a handsome heartthrob, Martin has been an accomplished actor on stage and screen for nearly three decades.

Enrique José Martín Morales was born in Hato Rey San Juan, Puerto Rico, on December 24, 1971. His father is a psychologist, and his mother an accountant. The couple was divorced when Enrique was two. He began to sing at an early age in a choir and acted in school plays. He auditioned twice for the all-boy pop group Menudo but was turned down both times because the producers felt he was too young. He auditioned again at age 12 and was finally hired. He sang with Menudo for five years. Then, as with other members of the group, he was let go and replaced with a younger singer. Martin returned to Puerto Rico in 1989, where he completed high school and planned his future.

Interested in an acting career, he moved to Mexico, where he was cast in the hit musical *Mamá Ama El Rock* (Mama loves rock). This experience led him to a continuing role in the popular Mexican daytime drama *Alcanzar una estrella II* (To reach a star). He also appeared in a film based on the series, which earned him a Heraldo, the Mexican equivalent of an Academy Award, for acting.

Returning to his first love, music, Martin signed a recording contract with Sony Records. Sony released his self-titled debut solo album in 1991. All the songs were written by Martin and his close friend and fellow Menudo alumnus Robi Rosa. The album went gold, selling more than 500,000 copies. His second album, *Me Amaras* (Will you love me? 1993) was a collection of love ballads and earned him the Billboard Video Award for Best New Latin Artist. He was now a huge star throughout Latin America.

Martin moved to Los Angeles (LA) in late 1993, where he resumed his acting career as a Puerto Rican singer on the hit daytime drama *General Hospital*. In 1994, he made his Broadway debut as the romantic lead, Marius Pontmercy, in the long-running musical *Les Misérables*. He stayed with the show for a year. Martin's third solo album, *A Medio Vivir* (1995), produced his first U.S. pop-charting single, "Maria." He made one more Spanish-language album before releasing his first English-language record, *Ricky Martin* (1999). Two smash singles emerged from the album—"Livin' La Vida Loca," an appealing blend of salsa and pop, and "She's All I Ever Had."

These two hits made Martin a huge crossover success, a reputation secured by a second English album, *Sound Loaded* (2000), which produced the single hits "She Bangs" and "Nobody Wants to Be Lonely," a duet with CHRISTINA AGUILERA. After that, Martin fell out of favor with his English-speaking pop audience for a time. He regained some attention with *Life* (2005), his most adventurous album to date. It contains diverse sounds ranging from Middle Eastern music to rap to reggaeton, Latin-style rap music. The album fared well in the United States but was more successful in Europe.

A passionate soccer fan, Martin recorded "La Copa de la Vida" (The cup of life), the official song of the World Cup in soccer, in five languages, including English. Active in numerous social causes, he has established the Ricky Martin Foundation, an organization that has given a million dollars worth of musical instruments to Puerto Rican schoolchildren. He is also extremely active in the acquired immune deficiency syndrome (AIDS) awareness campaign for young people and the international crusade against child prostitution and child pornography. Extremely private about his personal life, Martin has had a long-standing relationship with Mexican television personality, Rebecca de Alba.

Further Reading

Bhawnani, Namrata. "I'm the King of the World," Rediff On The Net. Available online. URL: http://www.rediff.com/style/jun/20ricky.htm. Downloaded on October 18, 2005.

Duncan, Patricia J. *Ricky Martin: La Vida Loca*. New York: Warner Books, 1999.

Furman, Elina. *Ricky Martin*. New York: St. Martin's Press, 1999.

Newman, Matt. *Ricky Martin* (Galaxy of Superstars). New York: Chelsea House, 2000.

Further Listening

Best of Ricky Martin. Sony International, CD, 2001.

Life. Sony, CD, 2005.

Further Viewing

The Ricky Martin Video Collection. Sony/Columbia, VHS/DVD, 1999.

Martínez, Agueda

(1898–2000) *weaver*

One of the master weavers of Northern New Mexico, Agueda Martínez expertly combined the Spanish and Mexican tradition of weaving with Native American designs to create colorful blankets, rugs, and tapestries. She was born in Chamita, New Mexico, on March 13, 1898. Agueda first learned to weave rag rugs from her uncle Lorenzo Trujillo when she was 12. She married at age 18 and, in 1925, moved to Mendanales, a town near the capital city of Santa Fe. She lived there and in Española, New Mexico, for the remainder of her long life. Martínez led a simple rural life, tending to her crops in the summer and working at her loom in the winter.

A skilled artist, in her younger days, she could complete a 55-by–80-inch rug in a single day. One of her specialties was *jergas,* traditional New Mexican floorcloths. Using the tapestry weave technique and creating her dyes from plants and flowers in her garden, she would weave intricate geometric designs into her *jergas* instead of the simpler more traditional plaid or checkered designs. *Northern Skies* (1994), one of her best-known tapestries, is a dazzling array of stripes and diamond designs. Her *Tapestry Weave Rag Jerga* (1994) is on display at the Smithsonian American Art Museum (SAAM). Exhibited regularly at shows, her rag rugs sell for $3,000 and up.

Martínez had eight children and taught all her daughters, and later her granddaughters, how to weave "because," she said, "it's life." She also taught her craft at the Home Education and Livelihood Programs (HELP) in the towns of Hernández and Abiquiu, New Mexico.

In the year 2000 Martínez completed a particularly large weaving at her loom. The following day, she fell ill. She died three days later on June 6, 2000, in Española at age 102. Martínez was survived by 77 grandchildren, 149 great-grandchildren, and 55 great-great-grandchildren. "There is no one that can beat me at weaving because it's what I live for," Agueda Martínez once said. "It's the most important thing that I do."

Filmmaker MOCTESUMA ESPARZA made a documentary about her life, *Agueda Martínez: Our People, Our Country* (1977), which was nominated for an Academy Award for Best Documentary Short Subject.

Her daughter Eppi Archuleta is also a well-known weaver who has been declared a "national treasure" by the National Endowment for the Arts (NEA).

Further Reading

Albuquerque Journal. "Agueda Martínez, 101," The Albuquerque Journal Online. Available online. URL: http://www.abqjournal.com/2000/nm/who/23who09–19–99.htm. Downloaded on October 12, 2005.

Crossing the Threshold. "Agueda Martínez, *Northern Skies,* 1994," University Art Museum, University at Albany, SUNY Web Site. Available online. URL: http://www.albany.edu/museum/wwwmuseum/crossing/artist17.htm. Downloaded on October 11, 2005.

Yorba, Jonathan. *Arte Latino: Treasures from the Smithsonian American Art Museum.* New York: Watson–Guptill Publications, 2001, pp. 58–59.

Further Viewing

Agueda Martínez: Our People, Our Country (1977). Esparza/Katz Productions, VHS.

Martínez-Cañas, María

(1960–) *photographer, collagist, educator*

Black-and-white collages of fragments of the distant past are the focus of María Martínez-Cañas's search for her own personal past in a Cuba she never knew but still longs for. She was born in Havana, Cuba, on May 19, 1960, the youngest of three daughters. Her father was a businessman and today is an art dealer. When she was three months old, her family immigrated to Miami, Florida, and then moved to Puerto Rico in 1964. As a girl, Martínez-Cañas became fascinated with photography and cameras. She would take the family's cameras apart and put them back together again. Her parents parked their cars outside on the street so their daughter could set up the family garage as her darkroom.

When she was 18, Martínez-Cañas returned to the United States to attend the Philadelphia College of Art in Pennsylvania. She earned a Bachelor of Fine Arts (B.F.A.) degree in photography in 1982 and continued her education at the Art Institute of Chicago where she earned a Masters of Fine Arts (M.F.A.) degree in 1984. While studying there, she had her first solo exhibition of photographs at the Museo de la Universidad de Puerto Rico.

In 1985, she traveled to Spain on a Fulbright–Hayes grant to conduct research in the General Archives of the Indies in Seville. The old Spanish maps of Cuba and other islands fascinated her and she found they expressed her yearning for the land of her ancestors. On her return to the states, Martínez-Cañas began to incorporate fragments of these maps, other manuscripts, postage stamps, and other archival materials into her work. In an intricate process, she marked collages of the images with scratches and then stuck them to plastic sheets that she then printed on black-and-white photography paper. The resulting negative images are both mysterious and strangely intriguing. "Their delicacy mingles with the pattern of forms to create complex scenarios that function like road maps through a time and place that are familiar yet nowhere recognizable," wrote Carol Damian about the work.

More recently, Martínez-Cañas has turned to a more personal past in the-eries *Shadow Gardens* (1999). Photographs of the plants and flowers in the garden of her Miami home, many of them indigenous to Cuba and Puerto Rico, seem to express an inner peace. This peace serves as a safe harbor for the artist from the alienation and chaos of the modern world. Martínez-Cañas's pursuit of a natural world has resulted in the series *Hortus* and *Naturalia,* where the plant parts and flower petals mingle with various shapes and figures in complex, layered photographs.

The Museum of Art in Fort Lauderdale, Florida, held a retrospective exhibition of 110 of her images in summer 2002. Martínez-Cañas teaches photography at the School of the Arts in Miami.

"In my photography, I am talking about myself," she said in an interview. "I don't see any separation between my life as a human being and my work. They are totally connected one to the other."

Further Reading

Dews, Charles. "Snap Decisions—Photographer María Martínez-Cañas," *Latin Leaders,* February–March 2002.

Riggs, Thomas, ed. *St. James Guide to Hispanic Artists.* Detroit, Mich.: St. James Press, 2002, pp. 356–358.

Yorba, Jonathan. *Arte Latino: Treasures from the Smithsonian American Art Museum.* New York: Watson–Guptill Publications, 2001, pp. 62–63.

Mendieta, Ana

(1948–1985) *sculptor, painter, photographer, performance artist*

Arguably the most important Cuban-American artist of her generation, Ana Mendieta used her body as the central motif in her expressive art. Her tragic death was as controversial and mysterious as her life and art.

She was born in Havana, Cuba, into an affluent family, on November 18, 1948. Her father was a lawyer who originally supported Fidel Castro after he seized power in 1959. He later fell out with Castro and was imprisoned. Her mother sent Ana and her sisters to the United States under the auspices of the Operation Peter Pan program with 8,000 other Cuban children in 1961. The sisters were mistakenly placed in juvenile-delinquent camps on their arrival in the United States and later spent time in a series of foster homes in Iowa. Their mother finally was able to leave Cuba, and she joined them in 1966.

Mendieta entered the University of Iowa that same year and studied at the Center for the New Performance Arts. She earned her bachelor of arts (B.A.) degree in 1969 and a master of arts (M.A.) in painting in 1972. Five years later, she received a master of fine arts (M.F.A.) degree in multimedia and video from the University of Iowa.

One of her earlier works, *Rape/Murder* (1973), expressed her preoccupation with women's issue and the culture of violence in America. She performed this vivid performance work, a reenactment of an actual campus murder, in her apartment for friends and students. As the audience watched, Mendieta was stripped, bound, and smeared with fake blood. (She later used animal blood in many of her performance pieces.) The performance was photographed and the photographs, resembling police pictures of a crime scene, were later displayed.

That same year, she began the photograph series for which she is perhaps most celebrated, the *silueta* series (1973–77). It included pictures of her body's indentations in the earth and her torso outlined with numerous natural materials ranging from rock to snow to fire.

"I have thrown myself into the very elements that produced me," she wrote, "using the earth as my canvas and my soul as my tools."

Another series *Anima (Alma/Soul)* (1976), showed her body's form as constructed out of bamboo. She later set the image on fire and photographed it.

Mendieta always considered herself a Cuban artist in exile and was finally allowed to return to her native island for a visit. While there, she explored the ancient caves of Jaruco State Park, where she carved on the cave walls life-size figures that were derived from the mythology of the Taino people, the Native Americans who lived on Cuba at the time of Columbus. She also befriended a number of Cuban artists, including installation artist José Bedia, who later came to the United States to live and work.

By the 1980s, Mendieta was living in New York City, where she became one of the most popular and celebrated of that city's artists. Among her friends was minimalist sculptor Carl Andre, whose objective, impersonal work could not have been more different from her own.

She married Andre, who was 13 years her senior, in February 1985. The marriage was a tempestuous one with rumors of Andre's infidelities being an issue. On September 8, 1985, Mendieta fell to her death from the bedroom window of their 34th-floor apartment in the Soho district of Manhattan. Andre, who was present, claimed that his wife had committed suicide, but he was charged and tried for her murder. The trial ended in a hung jury, and he was never convicted of her death. Mendieta's violent end remains a mystery to this day.

Was her death the final act of an artist obsessed with death and violence? Mendieta herself once described her work as "a return to the mother source—I become an extension of nature. . . . My works are the irrigation veins of this universal fluid."

Further Reading

Blocker, Jane, and Ana Mendieta. *Where Is Ana Mendieta?: Identity, Performativity, and Exile.* Durham, N.C.: Duke University Press, 1999.

Clearwater, Bonnie. *Ana Mendieta: A Book of Work.* Miami Beach, Fla.: Grassfield Press, 1993.

Katz, Robert. *Naked by the Window: The Fatal Marriage of Carl Andre and Ana Mendieta.* Boston, Mass.: Atlantic Monthly Press, 1990.

Moure, Gloria. *Ana Mendieta.* New York: Rizzoli, 1998.

Viso, Olga. *Ana Mendieta: Earth Body: Sculpture and Performance, 1972–1985.* Ostfildern, Germany: Hatje Cantz Publishers, 2004.

Further Viewing

Ana Mendieta: Fuego de Tierra. Woman Made Movies (WMM), VHS, 1987.

Mesa-Bains, Amalia

(1943–) *installation artist, mixed-media artist, writer, educator, art historian, museum director*

Mexican-American artist Amalia Mesa-Bains uses traditional religious altars and other spaces to explore people's roles, particularly women, in society and life. She was born in Santa Clara, California, on July 10, 1943 into a family that nourishes creativity. Several of her uncles were wood carvers and a great uncle was a professional artist in Fresno, California.

"There was never any idleness around my home when I was growing up," she recalls. "I grew up with this quality of inventing and solving problems—with the idea I think it could work this way or that way.'"

Mesa-Bains attended San Jose State University where she earned a bachelor of arts (B.A.) degree in painting in 1966. She later received a master of arts (M.A.) degree in interdisciplinary education from San Francisco State University and an M.A. and Doctor of Philosophy (Ph.D.) degree in clinical psychology from the Wright Institute's School of Clinical Psychology in Berkeley, California, in 1983.

By the late 1970s, Mesa-Bains was working on a series of home altars, patterned after the religious altars seen in traditional Mexican-American homes. Her large-scale installations both celebrated the achievements of great women whom she admired while at the same time questioning society's role in shaping these women's public personas. They include homages to Mexican artist Frida Kahlo, the 17th-century Mexican nun Sor Juana Inés de la Cruz, and film actress DOLORES DEL RIO. The mixed-media installation, *An Ofrenda for Dolores Del Rio* (1983), is the most famous of her altarlike pieces. A lavish arrangement of silk and taffeta, old photographs and movie stills, and dried flowers, it is a moving tribute to one of Hollywood's most glamorous stars. At the same time, it challenges the stereotypes of exotic women that del Rio often played in her films.

In the 1990s, Mesa-Bains created her most ambitious series of works, *Venus Envy.* A giant installation that is housed in multiple rooms, each "chapter" of this monumental work deals with feminist issues in both text and objects. *Chapter 1: The First Hispanic Community Moments Before the End* (1984) includes a beauty salon, a museum hall, and a history classroom. *Chapter 3: Chihuatlampa, The Place of the Giant Women* (1997) honors the memory of the legendary Aztec woman warrior who Mesa-Bains sees as a symbol for all women struggling to find their place in society. Chihuatlampa's grave is depicted as an archaeological dig.

Mesa-Bains's artwork was included in several landmark Latino art exhibitions including *Chicano Art: Resistance and Affirmation* (1965–85) and *Mi Alma, Mi Terra, Mi Gente: Contemporary Chicana Art* (2000).

Mesa-Bains has taught art at California State University–Monterey Bay and is currently the director of the Visual and Public Art Institute there. She has served as a consultant to the Texas State Council on the Arts and to the Arizona Commission on the Arts. She is also a former Commissioner of Arts for San Francisco, California. Mesa-Bains is the recipient of the MacArthur Genius Award and the Service to the Field Award from the Association of Hispanic Artists in New York, both in 1992.

A prolific writer, Mesa-Bains has written many articles and books on art and artists, including a catalog she cowrote on painter PATSSI VALDEZ. She interviewed artist JUDY BACA for the archives of the Smithsonian American Art Museum (SAAM). She is considered an expert on Chicano (Mexican-American) art and frequently lectures on the subject. In 1995, Mesa-Bains suffered from a serious pulmonary disease but has since recovered.

"I have pursued a personal and collective narrative of Chicano/Mexicano history," Mesa-Bains writes. "The adoption of this form and process for more than twenty years has produced a politicizing spirituality that has served my community and given meaning to my life."

Further Reading

Mesa-Bains, Amalia. *Ceremony of Meaning: Contemporary Hispanic Spiritual and Ceremonial Art.* Santa Fe, N.Mex.: Center for Contemporary Arts of Santa Fe, 1988.

———. *Ceremony of Spirit: Nature and Memory in Contemporary Latino Art.* San Francisco, Calif.: Mexican Museum, 1993.

Kaun, Linda. *Offerings: The Altar Show.* Venice, Calif.: Social and Public Arts Resource Center, 1984.

Riggs, Thomas, *St. James Guide to Hispanic Artists.* Detroit, Mich.: St. James Press, 2002, pp. 379–381.

Miranda, Carmen
(Maria do Carmo Miranda da Cunha)
(1909–1955) *singer, dancer, actress*

A talented and energetic performer, Carmen Miranda's bright personality and outlandish headwear made her a cultural icon of the 1940s and a symbol of the all-too-brief renewed friendship between the United States and Latin America. Maria do Carmo Miranda da Cunha was born in Marco da Canavezes, Portugal, near the capital city of Lisbon, on February 9, 1909. Her family was poor and moved to Brazil to find more opportunity when Maria was a child. In Rio de Janeiro, her father operated a successful wholesale fruit business, an intriguing fact given her penchant years later for fruit-filled hats.

After attending convent school, Maria got a job in a store where she sang as she worked. Customers praised her vocal gifts, and soon she was being paid for singing on a local radio station. At age 19, she signed a recording contract with Radio Corporation of America (RCA) and quickly rose to the top of the Brazilian entertainment industry as a recording artist, live performer, and film actress.

After the film *Banana da Terra* (1939), she left Brazil and came to New York City, where she starred on Broadway in the musical revue *Streets of Paris* and introduced the song "The South American Way." More stage work followed, along with a sold-out engagement at the Waldorf–Astoria, a legendary New York hotel. Hollywood took notice of her popularity, and 20th Century–Fox signed her to a movie contract. Miranda, backed by her Brazilian band, appeared in the Fox musical *Down Argentine Way* (1940). The film, popular in the United States, was criticized in Brazil and forbidden in Argentina because it showed the country in a ridiculous way.

The arrival of Carmen Miranda in Hollywood coincided with the new "good neighbor" policy of President Franklin D. Roosevelt's administration to bring the United States and Latin America closer together as Europe entered World War II. Equally important to this political alliance was an economic motive. The United States needed to find new markets for American films that could no longer be sold in war-torn Europe.

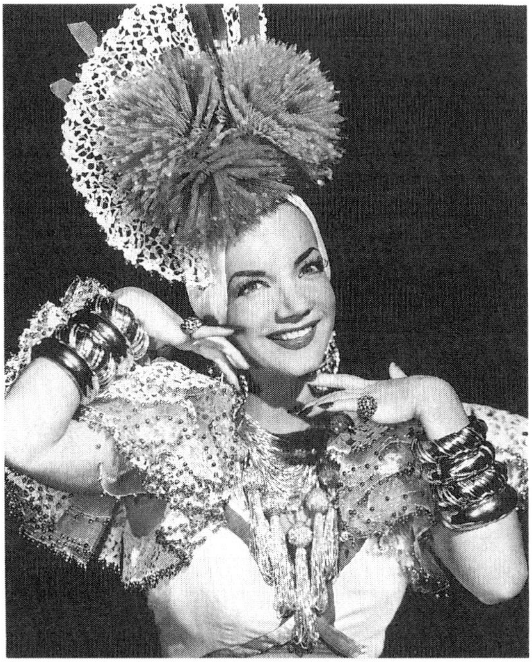

Known for her wild and crazy hats and her boundless energy, Carmen Miranda was one of the brightest stars of 1940s movie musicals. *(Photofest)*

Miranda's kooky screen personality, fractured English, and colorful costumes made her a top star in Hollywood. During the next five years, she appeared in nearly a dozen Fox musicals. Although she was never the leading lady in these movies, Miranda's musical appearances were often the films' highlight. For a time, she was the highest-paid performer in Hollywood. Perhaps her most memorable film was *The Gang's All Here* (1943), directed by movie-musical master Busby Berkeley. In her signature number, "The Lady in the Tutti-Frutti Hat," Miranda was flanked by male dancers dressed as giant bananas. As she sang and danced, her fruit-adorned hat grew bigger and bigger through Berkeley's magical camerawork until it reached the theater's ceiling. Some film critics have called the sequence one of the cinema's most surrealistic moments.

Despite her fame and carefree personality onscreen, Miranda was not a happy person. She was hurt by criticism from Brazilians that she had "sold out" in Hollywood and felt trapped by the stereotypical Latina persona that she was forced to play in her movies. As her popularity waned after 1944, she tried to expand her range by playing dual roles in the comedy *Copacabana* (1947), opposite comedian Groucho Marx. But despite some funny moments, the film bombed at the box office. She married the film's producer, David Alfred Sebastian, who physically abused her. To keep away depression and continue working, Miranda took drugs and eventually became addicted to them. In her last film, a routine comedy *Scared Stiff* (1953), she played second banana to the comedy team of Dean Martin and Jerry Lewis.

After that, Miranda's opportunities to perform were limited to nightclubs and occasional guest spots on television variety shows. It was while taping a strenuous musical number for *The Jimmy Durante Show* on August 4, 1955, that she suffered a mild heart attack. Disregarding the symptoms, she attended a party that night and went home. The next morning, she suffered a second, fatal heart attack. She was 46 years old. Her body was flown to Brazil where her death was an occasion for national mourning. She remains a figure of national importance there today, witnessed by the Carmen Miranda Museum in Rio, one of the country's most popular tourist sites, which opened in 1976.

Carmen Miranda continues to be a cultural figure of fascination for both North and South Americans. She symbolized a time of bright promise in U.S.–Latin American relations that, like her tragic career, was never fulfilled.

Further Reading

Gil-Montero, Martha. *Brazilian Bombshell: The Biography of Carmen Miranda.* New York: Dutton Adult, 1989.

The Internet Movie Database. "Carmen Miranda," The Internet Movie Database. Available online. URL: http://www.imdb.com/name/nm0000544/. Downloaded on March 1, 2005.

Katz, Ephraim, Fred Klein, and Ronald Dean Nolen. *The Film Encyclopedia.* 4th edition. New York: HarperResource, 2001, p. 952.

Rodriguez, Clara E. *Heroes, Lovers, and Others: The Story of Latinos in Hollywood.* Washington, D.C.: Smithsonian Books, 2004, pp. 83–85.

Further Listening

Brazilian Bombshell: 25 Hits (1939–1947). Asv Living Era, CD, 1998.

Further Viewing

Carmen Miranda: Bananas Is My Business (1995). Fox Lorber Home Video, VHS/DVD, 2002.

Copacabana (1947). Lions Gate Home Entertainment, VHS/DVD, 1989/2003.

Nancy Goes to Rio (1950). Warner Home Video, VHS, 1992.

Molina, Alfred

(1953–) *actor, producer*

Called a "chameleonlike [performer] who disappears into every part he plays" by movie critic Leonard Maltin, Alfred Molina has played everything from a Soviet sailor to a maniacal scientist with feeling, compassion, and depth. He was born in London, England, to working-class parents on May 24, 1953. His father, a Spanish immigrant, was a waiter, and his mother, who was Italian, was a housekeeper. Molina studied at the Guildhall School of Music and Drama in London and began to play repertory theater in his twenties.

He made his film debut in 1981, playing Indiana Jones's teacher and mentor in *Raiders of the Lost Ark.* After that, he worked primarily in British television until landing a leading role as one of two Russian sailors who spend an eventful night in Liverpool, England, in the comedy/drama *Letter to Brezhnev* (1985). But Molina did not gain wide critical attention until he gave a stirring performance as playwright Joe Orton's doomed lover Kenneth Halliwill in the biographical film *Prick Up Your Ears* (1987).

Since then, he has appeared in more than 30 films, playing a wide range of both supporting and leading roles: He was a stolid English businessman transformed by love in the comedy/drama *Enchanted April* (1992); an abusive Iranian husband to Sally Field in *Not Without My Daughter* (1991); a Cuban émigré and political prisoner in *The Perez Family* (1995); and the real-life Diego Rivera, one of Mexico's greatest artists, opposite SALMA HAYEK as his wife, artist Frida Kahlo, in *Frida* (2002).

A distinguished stage actor in his native Britain, Molina played leading roles in Tennessee Williams's *Night of the Iguana* and David Mamet's *Speed-the-Plow* with the Royal National Theater. He made his Broadway debut in the hit play *Art* (1998) and was nominated for a Tony Award as Best Actor in a Play. More recently, he played Tevye in the 2004 Broadway revival of the musical *Fiddler on the Roof* and portrayed a Catholic bishop in the movie adaptation of the best-selling novel *The Da Vinci Code* (2006).

One of Molina's screen specialties is playing outrageous villains, including the comic bad guy Snidely Whiplash in *Dudley Do-Right* (1998) and the tragic Dr. Octopus in *Spider-Man 2* (2004). He gained greater recognition in the United States when he starred in the CBS–TV sitcom, *Ladies Man* (1999–2001), which he also produced. Molina played a henpecked furniture maker in the weekly comedy, which costarred Sharon Lawrence and Betty White.

In real life, he is happily married to British actress Jill Gascoine. The couple became U.S. citizens in 2004.

Further Reading

The Internet Movie Database. "Alfred Molina," The Internet Movie Database. Available online. URL:

http://www.imdb.com/name/nm0000547/. Downloaded on February 9, 2005.

The Official Alfred Molina Web Site. Available online. URL: http://www.alfred-molina.com. Downloaded on October 14, 2005.

Further Viewing

Frida (2002). Buena Vista Home Video/Miramax Home Entertainment, VHS/DVD, 2003.

Prick Up Your Ears (1987). MGM/UA Home Video, VHS/DVD, 2000/2004.

Spider-Man 2 (2004). Sony Home Video, VHS/DVD, 2004/2005.

Montalbán, Ricardo (Ricardo Gonzalo Pedro Montalbán Merino)

(1920–2009) *actor, administrator, social activist*

A leading Mexican-American actor for more than five decades, Ricardo Montalbán's greatest contribution to his profession may be as spokesperson for Latinos in the entertainment industry. His courageous leadership has helped break long-held stereotypes and allowed Latinos to take their meaningful place in the Hollywood system.

Ricardo Gonzalo Pedro Montalbán Merino was born in Mexico City, Mexico, on November 25, 1920, the youngest of five children in a middle-class family. His parents had immigrated to Mexico from Castile, Spain, and Montalbán has always expressed equal pride in his Mexican and Spanish heritage.

His parents sent him to the United States to attend Fairfax High School in Los Angeles, California. With limited English, Montalbán struggled in school, but worked hard to master the language. Encouraged by a teacher to try out for a school play, he won the leading part and immediately decided that he wanted to make his living as an actor. A talent scout from Metro-Goldwyn-Mayer (MGM) studios caught one of his performances and offered the high school student a screen test. Montalbán turned it down, deciding to go to New York City to further his education and find work on the stage. He received small parts in summer-stock productions in the East and then had his first break playing opposite veteran actress Tallulah Bankhead in the play *Her Cardboard Lover,* his first time playing a Latin lover. Again, Montalbán was approached by MGM to take a screen test, but he again refused. This time, he needed to return to Mexico to see his ailing mother. While there, he began to appear on stage and in Mexican movies. He won a Heraldo, the Mexican equivalent of the Academy Award, for his performance in the film *La hora de la verdad* (The moment of truth, 1944). Then, for the third time, he was offered a contract by MGM and finally signed. His debut in American films was the musical *Fiesta* (1947), which was shot in Mexico and starred champion swimmer-turned-actress Esther Williams. Montalbán's dark good looks, his suave personality, and his acting ability quickly earned him the title of MGM's resident "Latin lover." He appeared twice more with Williams, most notably in *Neptune's Daughter* (1949), in which the two introduced the classic Frank Loesser song, "Baby, It's Cold Outside."

Not wanting to be stuck in a stereotype, Montalbán managed to play a surprisingly wide range of roles at MGM, including a police detective on a killer's trail (*Mystery Street,* 1950), a Latino soldier seeing snow for the first time in World War II Europe (*Battleground,* 1949), and an American Indian (*Across the Wide Missouri,* 1951). During the shooting of this Western, he suffered a serious spinal injury and was confined to a wheelchair for some time. One of his best roles during this early period was as a Mexican-American undercover cop on the trail of a criminal gang that was exploiting poor Mexicans immigrants in the grim film noir *Border Incident* (1949).

Unlike his main rival at MGM, FERNANDO LAMAS, Montalbán was no Latin lover off the set. He married Georgianna Young, sister of actress Loretta Young, in 1944. The couple remained married until Georgianna's death in 2007.

Montalbán was one of the first Latino actors to appear regularly on television. He guest starred many times on his sister-in-law's dramatic anthology series, *The Loretta Young Show,* on television in the 1950s and had the lead in *Operation Cicero* (1956), an early television movie. His screen work in the 1950s was slim but included some solid character roles, such as a Japanese Kabuki actor in love with an American woman in the Oscar-winning film *Sayonara* (1958). Montalbán made his Broadway debut in the musical *Seventh Heaven* (1955), which included future Broadway star CHITA RIVERA in a small role. Two years later, he triumphed in another musical, *Jamaica,* opposite legendary black star Lena Horne. He was nominated for a Tony Award as Best Actor in a Musical for his performance.

Despite his success on stage and screen, Montalbán was aware that roles for Latinos were limited. Many Latino actors were offered film parts only as bandits, juvenile criminals, or lazy men who wore big sombreros. "I felt like my native country had been betrayed by Hollywood," he said. To change that situation, he helped establish in 1969 Nosotros (Our Own), an organization for Latino actors and others in the entertainment industry to encourage and promote their work. As Nosotros's president, Montalbán became a public critic of the Hollywood system and its treatment of Latinos. He even attacked such fictional commercial characters as the Frito Bandito, who went around stealing Frito snack chips. Montalbán pointed out that the character could have been the Frito Amigo who gave away the chips instead of stealing them but that Hollywood only saw Mexicans as bandits.

Montalbán's outspokenness had its price. For four years, he was blackballed in the film industry and found few roles in television. But as Hollywood became more sensitive to minorities, he again found meaningful work. In 1977, he was cast as the rich non-Latino Mr. Roarke, who operated a resort where visitors wildest dreams came true, on the television series *Fantasy Island.* The show was a huge hit and made Montalbán a bigger star than he had ever been before. In 1978, he won an Emmy Award for his moving portrayal of the Sioux chief Satangkai in the television miniseries *How the West Was Won.* He gained even greater exposure as a longtime commercial spokesperson for the Chrysler Corporation, selling their product with his rich and lavish descriptions of car interiors.

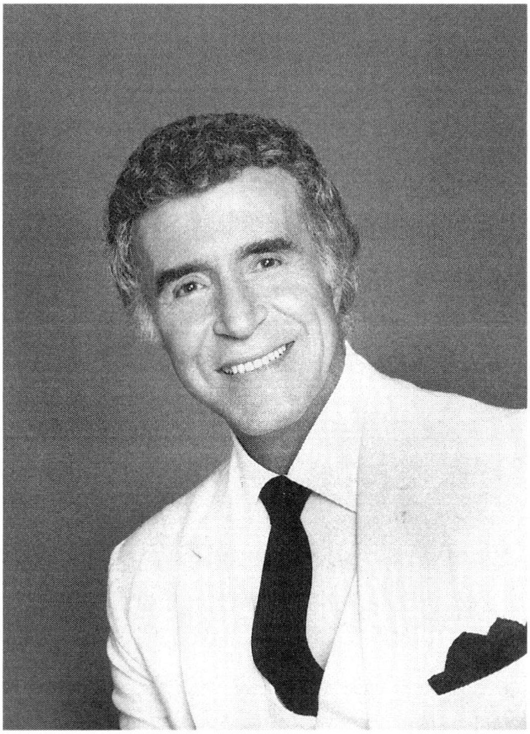

Ricardo Montalbán played a large role in the advancement of Latinos in the entertainment industry as both an actor and the founder of Nosotros, a supportive organization. *(Photofest)*

Montalbán made a triumphant return to the big screen in 1982 playing an over-the-top villain, the evil Khan, in the second movie based on the classic sci-fi television series *Star Trek.* The actor had a fondness for playing outlandish villains, none more comic that the evil master criminal in the police spoof, *Naked Gun,* who ends up being flattened by a steamroller.

While less active in films in the early 21st century, Montalbán gained a new generation of fans as the grandfather in the two sequels to the fantasy adventure film *Spy Kids,* directed by ROBERT RODRIGUEZ. Montalbán died on January 14, 2009, at his home in Los Angeles, California, and was buried next to his wife's grave.

His older brother, Carlos Montalbán, who died in 1991, was also an actor and is best known as the character "El Exigente" (The Demanding One), which he played in Savarin Coffee TV commercials for 15 years.

Further Reading

Montalbán, Ricardo. *Reflections: A Life in Two Worlds.* New York: Doubleday, 1980.

Nosotros. "Ricardo Montalbán from Stage to Screen," Nosotros Official Web Site. Available online. URL: http://www.nosotros.org/ricardo_stagetoscreen.html. Downloaded on August 29, 2005.

Rodriguez, Clara E. *Heroes, Lovers, and Others: The Story of Latinos in Hollywood.* Washington, D.C.: Smithsonian Books, 2004, pp. 112–114, 178–180.

Further Viewing

Battleground (1949). Warner Home Video, VHS/DVD, 2000/2004.

Fantasy Island: First Season (1978). Columbia/Tristar Home Video, DVD box set, 2005.

Neptune's Daughter (1949). Warner Home Video, VHS, 1989.

Star Trek II: The Wrath of Khan (1982). Paramount Home Video, VHS/DVD, 1998/2003.

Montez, Chris (Ezekiel Christopher Montanez)

(1943–) *rock and pop singer*

The first Latino rock singer to reach the top of the pop charts since RITCHIE VALENS in 1958, Chris Montez emerged a few years later as a successful suave pop crooner. Ezekiel Christopher Montanez was born in Hawthorne, California, on January 17, 1943, the youngest son in a Mexican-American family. As a boy, he sang harmony with his older brothers on traditional Mexican folk songs called *ranchera.* They also taught him to play the guitar. In his junior year at Hawthorne High, which members of the surf band the Beach Boys also attended, Montez decided to set his goals on a music career. He formed his own rock band and performed at dances. The band came to the attention of Monogram Records, a local label that signed them to a recording contract.

Montez's recording of "All You Had to Do Was Tell Me" became a modest hit in the Los Angeles (LA) area. Then, in 1962, he recorded the infectious rocker "Let's Dance." The combination of Montez's high tenor, pounding drums, and a piping organ that would not quit boosted the song to #4 on the Billboard charts and #2 in the United Kingdom. It remains one of the dance-party classics of the era. At 19, Montez was a bona-fide rock star, and he toured the country for the next few years. He had one more dance hit, "Some Kinda Fun," in early 1963 and recorded several duets with singer Kathy Young, whose recording "A Thousand Stars" was a major hit in 1960.

Montez returned to Hawthorne in 1965 and left Monogram for A&M Records, a label that was started in 1962 by Herb Alpert, leader of the instrumental group the Tijuana Brass, and his partner Jerry Moss. They transformed Montez from a hard rocker to a soft balladeer. Set to a jazzy, Latin-tinged easy-listening beat, Montez scored a top-20 hit in early 1966 with "Call Me." Using the same appealing formula, he had three more hits the same year with such pop standards as "The More I See You" and "Time after Time."

By 1967, the hits had dried up, and Montez left A&M for CBS International, where he continued to record successfully in Spanish and English for the European market. Today, he continues to perform on tour as an oldies' act in the United States, Japan, South America, and Europe. "Let's Dance" was a highlight of the soundtrack of the college comedy, *Animal House* (1978).

Further Reading

Dahl, Bill. "Chris Montez, Biography," MP3 Web Site. Available online. URL: http://www.mp3.com/chris-montez/artists/4237/biography.html. Downloaded on October 10, 2005.

Mars Talent Biography. "Chris Montez," Mars Talent Agency Web Site. Available online. URL: http://www.marstalent.com/bio_chris_montez.htm. Downloaded on October 7, 2005.

Further Listening

Chris Montez: All-Time Greatest Hits. DCC Compact Classics, DC, 1995.

Montez, Maria
(María África Gracia Antonia Vidal de Santos Silas)
(1912–1951) *actress*

The last word in exotic heroines and villains in 1940s films, Maria Montez provided war-weary moviegoers with enough escapism to make her one of Hollywood's brightest stars for a time. María África Gracia Antonia Vidal de Santos Silas was born in Barahona, the Dominican Republic, on June 6, 1912. Her father was the Spanish consul in that island nation, and she was educated at a convent school in the Canary Islands. A natural beauty, Maria pursued a career as a stage actress in France and England but with little success. She arrived in New York City in 1940 and found work as a model. She soon moved to Hollywood and was discovered by a talent scout. With little acting ability, she was signed as a contract player by Universal Films and appeared in bit parts in a half dozen films under the name 'Marie Montez.' Her big break came when she was cast as Scheherazade, the Arabian beauty and teller of tales, in *Arabian Nights* (1942). The outlandish adventure was shot in glossy Technicolor, with the desert sands of Arizona subbing for Arabia. It was a surprise box-office hit and made Maria Montez a star.

During the next five years, she appeared in a string of similar fantasy adventures, all of which were shot in color, explaining her nickname "The Queen of Technicolor." Her frequent costar was athletic actor Jon Hall.

Montez's most memorable performance was in the dual role of twin sisters in the delirious fantasy *Cobra Woman* (1944), director by Robert Siodmak. Montez's over-the-top performance as the evil Naja, high priestess of an island of cobra worshippers, has turned *Cobra Woman* into a cult classic.

By the late 1940s, postwar audiences were looking for more-realistic, contemporary films. The "sword and sandals" fantasies fell out of fashion, as did Montez. A weight problem contributed to her downfall in Hollywood. Undaunted, the actress moved to Europe with her second husband, French actor Jean-Pierre Aumont, where she appeared in a number of French, Italian, and German films. One of her more juicy roles was in the French thriller *Portrait of an Assassin* (1949) as a sadistic manager of a circus who destroys the men who love her. Among her victims was the great actor and director Eric Von Stroheim.

On September 7, 1951, the 39-year-old actress was found drowned in the bathtub of her Paris mansion, presumably the victim of a heart attack. Saved from obscurity by the kind of loyal camp worshipers that would have pleased the Cobra Woman, Maria Montez's memory lives on.

Further Reading

The Internet Movie Database. "Maria Montez," The Internet Movie Database. Available online. URL: http://www.imdb.com/name/nm0000544/. Downloaded on March 1, 2005.

Katz, Ephraim, Fred Klein, and Ronald Dean Nolen. *The Film Encyclopedia,* 4th edition. New York: HarperResource, 2001, p. 963.

Rodriguez, Clara E. *Heroes, Lovers, and Others: The Story of Latinos in Hollywood.* Washington, D.C.: Smithsonian Books, 2004, pp. 95–97.

Further Viewing

Arabian Nights (1942). Universal Home Video, VHS, 1993.

Portrait of an Assassin (1949). Vanguard Films/Image Entertainment, VHS/DVD, 2003/2000.

Morales, Esai

(1962–) *actor, social activist*

A consistently good film actor whose career has had its ups and downs, Esai Morales is also a champion of numerous social causes, not the least being the plight of Latino actors. He was born in Brooklyn, New York, on October 1, 1962, to Puerto Rican parents who separated while he was still a small child. His mother was a union organizer, instilling in him a deep commitment to society's disadvantaged. She disapproved, however, of his acting ambitions, and while she was on a visit to Puerto Rico, he ran away and became a ward of the state at age 13. He entered New York's High School for the Performing Arts while living in a group home.

After graduating, Morales pursued stage work and appeared in plays at the Ensemble Studio Theater (EST) and the Shakespeare Festival in the Park. His first film role was as a gang leader opposite Sean Penn in the excellent drama *Bad Boys* (1983). His most memorable film role to date was as the jealous, troubled older brother of rock singer RITCHIE VALENS in the screen biography *La Bamba* (1987), directed by LUIS VALDEZ. But Morales had a difficult time finding other good roles on screen. He succinctly summed up the pigeonholed parts that Latino actors were usually handed in Hollywood as "the Hispanic Three H's: to be humble, horny or hostile."

He found somewhat better opportunities in television and guest starred through the 1980s in numerous dramatic series including *Fame,* the second edition of *The Twilight Zone,* and *Miami Vice.* He found a good film role in *My Family, Mi Familia* (1995), the saga of a Mexican-American family, in which he played another black-sheep son. The all-star Latino cast also included JIMMY SMITS, JENNIFER LOPEZ, and EDWARD JAMES OLMOS.

In 2001, Morales was cast as the upright and honest Lt. Tony Rodriguez on the hit police drama *NYPD Blue* (1993–2005). He remained with the series until it ended. He played another strong Latino role, a single father, in director GREGORY NAVA's series *American Family* (2002) for the Public Broadcasting System (PBS).

Morales is one of the most socially active actors in Hollywood. He has devoted his time and energies to numerous causes including acquired immune deficiency syndrome (AIDS) relief, environmental issues, and the antismoking campaign. His commitment to the Latino acting community led him to cofound with Jimmy Smits and Sonia Braga the National Hispanic Foundation for the Arts (NHFA) in 1997. He is vice president of the Screen Actors Guild's national board of directors and has testified in congressional hearings on the problems facing Latinos in the entertainment industry.

Further Reading

The Internet Movie Database. "Esai Morales," The Internet Movie Database. Available online. URL: http://www.imdb.com/name/nm0005246/. Downloaded on March 22, 2006.

NYPD Blue. "Esai Morales," NYPD Blue Official Web Site. Available online. URL: http://www.nypdblue.

Moreno, Rita
(Rosa Dolores Alverio)
(1931–) *actress, singer, dancer*

The first performer and only woman to date to win the four crowns of the entertainment industry—an Academy Award, a Tony, an Emmy, and a Grammy—Rita Moreno triumphed over years of Hollywood stereotyping to emerge as one of the most admired of Latina actresses. Rosa Dolores Alverio was born in Humacao, Puerto Rico, on December 11, 1931. While still an infant, her parents divorced, and she was put in the care of a relative while her mother, a seamstress, went to New York in search of work. When Rosita, as she was called, was five, she came to New York to join her mother in the Washington Heights section of Manhattan. Although they had little money, her mother paid for her to take dance lessons from actress RITA HAYWORTH's uncle.

Barely in her teens, Rosita helped to support her family by dancing and singing in the toy section of Macy's department store. She made her Broadway debut at 13, but the play closed within a week. A few years later, she went to Hollywood and was hired to dub voices in Spanish for foreign versions of American films. But she really wanted an acting career and made her screen debut as a tough Latina in the reform-school drama *So Young, So Bad* (1950) under the name Rosita Moreno. Soon after, Metro-Goldwyn-Mayer (MGM) signed her as a contract player under the name Rita Moreno. She was cast in an Esther Williams water musical, *Pagan Love Song* (1950), after claiming that she could swim. In fact, she could not and almost drowned during filming.

Her contract at MGM was canceled after a year, and Moreno struggled as a freelance actress for different studios. She quickly found herself confined to two kinds of roles—fiery Latin spitfires or more complacent Indian maidens. She went to New York to reignite her stage career in *Camino Real,* a new play by Tennessee Williams. The playwright complained that her voice was not right for the part, and she was dumped after only one week's rehearsal.

It was back to Hollywood where, out of economic necessity, Moreno accepted the stereotypical roles that she detested. She later said that she played most of these roles "barefoot with my nostrils flaring" and was dubbed "Rita the Cheetah" by film critics. Amid all the dross, she landed two decent roles in the 1950s, as the starlet Zelda Anders in the classic movie musical *Singin' in the Rain* (1952) and as the Burmese slave girl Tuptim who is in love with a Burmese servant but married to the king in *The King and I* (1956). This second film was choreographed by Jerome Robbins who became a good friend. In 1957, Robbins asked Moreno to audition

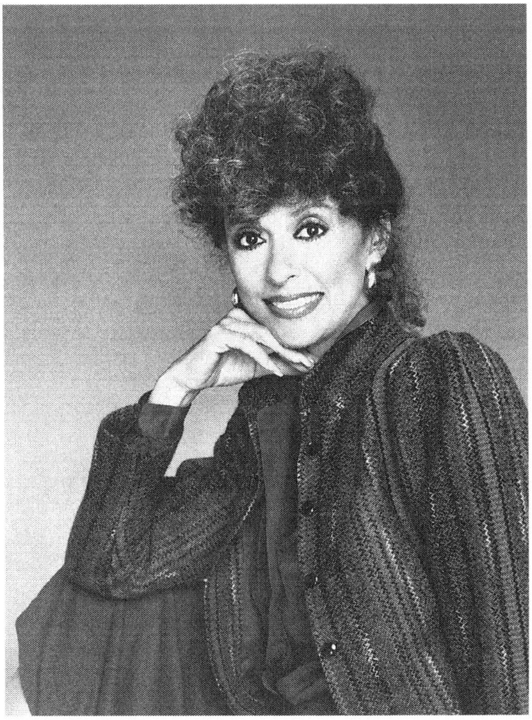

Stuck for years in stereotyped ethnic roles, Rita Moreno survived to become a respected star of film, television, and the Broadway stage. *(Photofest)*

for the female lead Maria in the new Broadway musical that he was directing. It was called *West Side Story* and was a modern-day version of Shakespeare's *Romeo and Juliet* about Puerto Rican and white gangs in New York City. Moreno was busy with film work and did not take Robbins's offer.

Three years later, Robbins was codirecting the film version of *West Side Story* (1961) and again asked Moreno to audition, this time for the part of the fiery Anita, Maria's best friend. She auditioned and won the part. Although CHITA RIVERA had been riveting in the role on Broadway, Moreno was every inch her equal in the film and transformed the tempestuous Anita into a full-bodied dramatic character. The film went on to win 10 Academy Awards, including an Oscar for Moreno as Best Supporting Actress. She was only the second Puerto Rican to win an Oscar for acting (José Ferrer was the first).

But winning an Oscar did not open the door to better role offers for the actress in Hollywood. She was still stuck with the stereotypical ethnic roles that she had played for years. After making a couple of more pictures, Moreno did not appear in another film until 1968. Instead, she returned to Broadway and starred in Tennessee Williams's *The Rose Tattoo.* This time the playwright was happy to have her in his play. In 1965, Moreno married cardiologist Leonard Gordon, to whom she is still happily married. They have a daughter, Fernanda Luisa, who was born in 1967.

Moreno returned to films but chose her roles with extreme care. She had a brief but memorable part as an exotic hooker in *Carnal Knowledge* (1971). The same year, she starred in the Public Broadcasting System (PBS) children's series *The Electric Company.* In 1972, the show's soundtrack album in which she performed, won a Grammy Award for Best Children's Album.

Moreno has a sense of humor about her Hollywood past and performed comedy routines at parties in a thick Spanish accent. Playwright Terrence McNally heard her routine, and it inspired him to include a similar character in his new play about a gay bathhouse, *The Tubs.* When the comedy, retitled *The Ritz* (1975), went to Broadway, McNally offered the role of the third-rate but energetic Latina singer Googie Gomez to Moreno. It was a part that she was born to play. The show was a hit and earned Moreno the Tony Award for Best Supporting Actress in a Play. She reprised the role in the film version in 1976. In 1977, she won an Emmy Award for her guest appearance on television's *The Muppet Show.* She won a second Emmy the next year, guest starring as a stripper on the detective series *The Rockford Files.*

The actress returned to top form on film as one of eight middle-aged married people in the comedy *The Four Seasons* (1981), directed by Alan Alda. She was a regular on the short-lived sitcom *Nine to Five* (1982–83) and put out her own best-selling exercise video in 1990. More recently, she garnered good reviews on cable television as the nun Sister Peter Marie Remondo in the Home Box Office (HBO) gritty prison drama *Oz.* She played playwright Miguel Piñero's mother in the biographical drama *Piñero* (2001), with BENJAMIN BRATT.

Less active in recent years and with two grandchildren, Moreno is a devoted spokesperson for osteoporosis awareness. When she received a much-deserved star on the Hollywood Walk of Fame in 1995, Moreno later reported, "I had been dreaming of this since I was six!" A pioneering Latina actress who never gave up, Rita Moreno serves as a role model for a new generation of Latino actors and actresses.

Further Reading

Crafts, Fred. "The Show Must Go On for. . . ." The *Register-Guard,* Eugene, Ore. August 10, 2003, p. L3.

The Internet Movie Database. "Rita Moreno," The Internet Movie Database. Available online. URL: http://www.imdb.com/name/nm0001549/. Downloaded on March 1, 2005.

Suntree, Susan. *Rita Moreno: Puerto Rican Singer and Actress.* New York: Chelsea House Publications, 1992.

Further Viewing

The Four Seasons (1981). Goodtimes Home Video/Universal Home Entertainment, VHS/DVD, 1997/2005.

The Ritz (1976). Warner Home Video. VHS, 1996.

West Side Story (1961). MGM/UA Home Video, VHS/DVD, 1998.

Moroles, Jesús

(1950–) *sculptor, installation artist*

One of the leading contemporary Latino sculptors in the United States, Jesús Moroles crafts his monumental stone sculptures from granite, a material so hard that few other sculptors would attempt to work with it. He was born in Corpus Christi, Texas, on September 22, 1950, the oldest of six children. His father José Elizondo Moroles immigrated to the United States from Monterrey, Mexico. When Jesús was still a child, the family moved to Dallas, where they lived in public housing. Both his parents encouraged Jesús's interest in art, and when he was older, they sent him to Rockport, Texas, along the Gulf Coast, to apprentice with his uncle, a master stonemason. While working with his uncle to build a seawall on the coast, Moroles took courses in commercial art at the Crozier Technical School. In 1969, he was drafted into the air force during the Vietnam War and served four years in the military.

On his return to Texas in 1973, Moroles studied art at El Centro Junior College in Dallas and earned an Associate of Arts (A.A.) degree in 1975. He then attended North Texas State University–Denton (now the University of North Texas). While studying there, he apprenticed with the well-known Latino sculptor LUIZ JIMÉNEZ in El Paso. Moroles graduated in 1978 with a bachelor of fine arts (B.F.A.) degree. Determined to be a sculptor, he traveled in 1979, to Pietrasanta, Italy, where he worked for a year in a foundry and studied European techniques of marble sculpting.

On his return to the states, Moroles chose granite as the medium in which he would work. Hard and unyielding, granite fascinated and challenged him. "It would take me over," he said later. "And it barely showed what I'd done. I hadn't scratched the surface. It was really in control of me. I just fell in love with it."

Instead of trying to carve the granite, Moroles discovered a unique method of hammering steel wedges into the rock to split it into slabs. He would then use power tools to polish some surfaces and leave others rough. In his *Granite Weaving* (1989) the stone appears to be woven and shows the artist's fascination with creating different textures.

To facilitate his difficult work, Moroles established an "art factory" in Rockport, Texas, in the early 1980s. The Moroles Studios employ most of his family, including his brother Hilario, his brother-in-law Kurt Kangas, his parents, and his sister Suzanna, who serves as his business manager.

While Moroles's works tend to be abstract, they also have a close connection with the ancient Mexican past and its present. His monumental *Georgia Stele* (1999), with its towering stone slabs, resembles ancient Mayan buildings, but at the same time, it invokes the modern American skyscraper. His largest single work is the *Houston Police Officers Memorial* (1991) in Houston, Texas. Standing 120 feet by 120 feet, it included five earthen stepped pyramids, four of them appearing to be partly excavated from the ground as at some Aztec or Mayan archaeological dig.

In 1996, Moroles founded the Moroles Cultural Center in Cerrillos, New Mexico, south of Santa Fe. This space serves as an exhibition, performance, and studio space for Latino artists in the

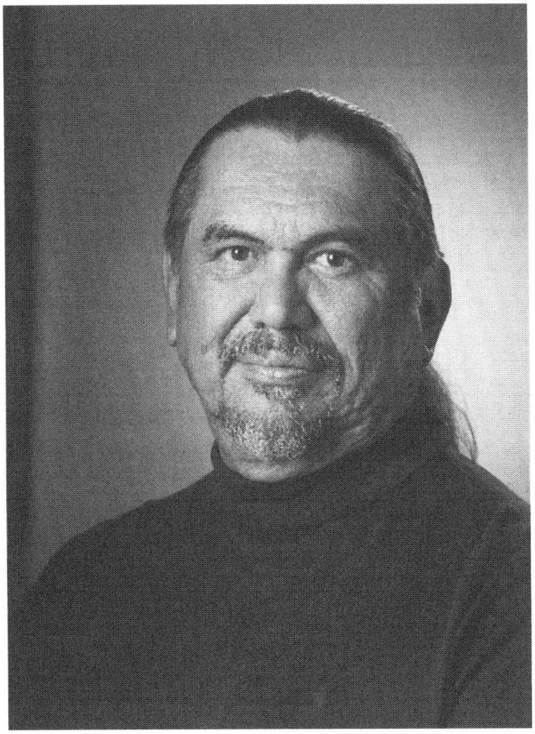

Jesús Moroles is best known for his monumental granite sculptures that evoke both the past and future of Mexican Americans and their world. *(Dennis Murphy)*

region. He also maintains a studio in Barcelona, Spain.

Jesús Moroles was the recipient of a National Endowment for the Arts (NEA) grant in 1989. Among the honors he has received are the Artists Award of the American Institution of Architects (AIA) (1995) and the University of North Texas Distinguished Alumnus Award (1996). He has had 130 one-person exhibitions. Among the most recent were shows at Artyard, Denver, Colorado; the Blue Star Contemporary Art in San Antonio, Texas; and the LewAllen Contemporary Gallery in Santa Fe, New Mexico.

"Moroles's work tests the limits of stone," wrote Kristin Congdon and Kara Kelley Hallmark. "Using granite, he explores new relationships of texture and form."

Further Reading

Congdon, Kristin G., and Kara Kelley Hallmark. *Artists from Latin American Cultures: A Biographical Dictionary.* Westport, Conn.: Greenwood Press, 2002, pp. 190–192.

Cockcroft, James D., assisted by Jane Canning. *Latino Visions: Contemporary Chicano, Puerto Rican, and Cuban American Artists.* New York: Franklin Watts, 2000, pp. 38, 54–57.

Jesús Moroles Official Web Site. Available online. URL: http://www.moroles.com. Downloaded on January 17, 2006.

Yorba, Jonathan. *Arte Latino: Treasures from the Smithsonian American Art Museum.* New York: Watson–Guptill Publications, 2001, pp. 72–73.

Muniz, Vik

(1961–) *photographer, mixed-media artist*

With his eccentric recreations of familiar images from art history and newspaper, all made from an array of ordinary and mundane materials, Vik Muniz is one of the most distinctive and original photographers working in the United States today. He was born in Sao Paolo, Brazil, in 1950. He was educated in Brazil before coming to New York City in 1983 to become an artist. From the start of his career, Muniz aligned himself with other photographers who were more concerned in the image itself and not what it might represent. He uses everyday materials to create these images, from wire and string to chocolate syrup, spaghetti marinara, and fake blood. He has even used the circular bits of paper made by a hole puncher to fashion his images. Once the image is completed he photographs it to document its existence, giving it a reality beyond the imagination that created it.

Among Muniz's best-known work is the "Sugar Children" series (1996). He used granulated sugar on black paper to form portraits of the children of sugarcane workers that he met while on a visit to St. Kitts in the Leeward Islands. After he photographed each portrait, he wiped it off the black paper so as to create the next. Muniz did this to show the transitory nature of life on the sugar plantations where the labor is hard and unending from one generation to the next. He has called the sugar he used as "the sweetest group of human beings" he ever met. This touch of sly humor is typical of Muniz, who delights in teasing his audience.

"Through his witty images Muniz honors, questions and subverts the traditions of representational art, treading the line between reality and illusion, representation and abstraction, idea and image, means and ends," writes a curator for the Miami Art Museum in Florida.

In a more recent series called *Pictures* that he has worked on for more than a decade, Muniz created images and portraits with various materials. In *Portraits of Magazines* (2003), for example, he used cut pieces of old magazines to fashion portraits of well-known Brazilians.

Muniz has had many solo exhibits and his work enjoys an international appeal. In 2005, he had shows at the Cardi Gallery in Milan, Italy; the Pennsylvania Academy of the Fine Arts in Philadelphia; and the Koyanagi Gallery in Tokyo, Japan, among other venues. *Reflex,* a major retrospective of 100 of his works from the late 1980s to the present opened at the Miami Art Museum in Florida in early 2006.

Further Reading

Muniz, Vik. *Clayton Days: Picture Stories.* New York: Frick Art Museum/The Clayton Corporation, 2000.

Muniz, Vik, and Andy Grundberg. *Reflex: A Vik Muniz Primer.* New York: Aperture, 2005.

Stainback, Charles Ashley. *Seeing Is Believing.* Pointe-Claire, Quebec, Canada: Arena Editions, 1998.

Vik Muniz Official Web Site. Available online. URL: http://www.vikmuniz.net/main.html. Downloaded on January 17, 2006.

Yorba, Jonathan. *Arte Latino: Treasures from the Smithsonian American Art Museum.* New York: Watson–Guptill Publications, 2001, pp. 74–75.

Further Viewing

Worst Possible Illusion: The Curiosity Cabinet of Vik Muniz (2003) Mixed Greens, VHS, 2006.

N

Nava, Gregory
(1949–) *filmmaker, screenwriter, producer*

One of the most prominent Latino filmmakers in the United States, Gregory Nava has managed to survive in the commercial world of movies and television without compromising his values and his vision. He was born on April 10, 1949, in San Diego, California, where his father was a defense-plant worker. Of Mexican and Basque heritage, Nava grew up believing many of the Latino stereotypes that he saw on television and in the movies. "I remember as a kid hating Mexicans because they killed Davy Crockett—then suddenly realizing I was Mexican," he said in one interview. "That was a hard thing to live with."

He attended the University of California–Berkeley and after graduating went to the University of California–Los Angeles (UCLA) film school. He made several short student films, including *The Journal of Diego Rodriguez Silva,* based on the life of Spanish author Federico García Lorca. With his then wife, fellow filmmaker Anna Thomas, he wrote his first directed feature film, the medieval drama *The Confessions of Amans* (1977). It won the Best Feature Award at the Chicago International Film Festival, but it was barely seen commercially. In 1979, Nava cofounded the Independent Feature Project (IFP), a nonprofit organization that supports and encourages independent filmmaking from diverse cultural backgrounds.

It took Nava several years to produce his next film, *El Norte* (1983), also cowritten with Thomas. The film was a stark and moving story of a brother and a sister who flee the political terrors of their native Guatemala and make the long, arduous journey to a new life in the United States. In the end, this new life brings heartache, humiliation, and ultimately death (for one of them). *El Norte* was an art-house hit and earned Nava and Thomas an Academy Award nomination for Best Original Screenplay. He was the first Latino to be so honored. More recently, *El Norte* was named an American classic by the Library of Congress.

Nava's next effort, *A Time of Destiny* (1988), was a revenge drama set in World War II (1939–45) and based on the Verdi opera *La forza del destino.* Despite a big name cast that included William Hurt and Timothy Hutton, it was a commercial and critical failure. Such was not the case for *My Family, Mi Familia* (1995), Nava's stirring 60-year saga of a Mexican-American family in East Los Angeles (LA). It had one of the most distinguished Latino casts of any Hollywood movie, including EDWARD JAMES OLMOS, JIMMY SMITS, ESAI MORALES, and a then little-known JENNIFER LOPEZ. Latino Americans flocked to see the film, and Hollywood studios realized the great potential of the Latino moviegoing audience. *My Family,*

Mi Familia received a Jury Prize Award at the San Sebastian International Film Festival in Spain.

The film's success gave Nava the clout to make two more films in quick succession. *Selena* (1997) was a solid biography of the life and tragic death of the Tejena singer Selena, portrayed by Jennifer Lopez. The film made her a star. *Why Do Fools Fall in Love* (1998) was about the life of another charismatic performer, doo-wop African-American singer Frankie Lymon, and the three women in his life who, after his death, fight each other in court over the rights to his estate. The film gave Halle Berry one of her first strong dramatic roles.

Nava's next project was the most ambitious of his career. He proposed to the Columbia Broadcasting System (CBS) an hour-long dramatic television series about a Mexican-American family living in East LA. With Edward James Olmos signed on as the family patriarch, it looked as if the show, *American Family,* would soon be on the air, but after a pilot episode had been filmed, CBS withdrew from the deal, claiming that it had no slot for the series in its schedule. Nava frantically tried to sell the pilot elsewhere, but no commercial network was interested. Finally, an executive at the Public Broadcasting System (PBS) read a newspaper column about the stranded show and agreed to air it. Moving to noncommercial PBS presented major challenges for Nava. He cut his own fee as creator and director as well as that of everyone else involved in the production. *American Family* ran for the 2000–01 season on PBS, becoming the first Latino-themed dramatic series on noncable television.

Nava's latest film, the crime thriller *Bordertown* (2006), starred Jennifer Lopez as an investigative reporter looking into the murder of Mexican female factory workers. It also featured ANTONIO BANDERAS and MARTIN SHEEN. Nava is currently developing *Zapata,* a biographical film about the famous freedom fighter of the Mexican Revolution, Emilio Zapata.

"I guess I'm a reluctant pioneer," Nava has said about himself. "I don't know why I'm always in this position, but I'm always this guy who is doing something that to me seems very logical, makes a tremendous amount of sense. But it has never been done before."

Further Reading

The Internet Movie Database. "Gregory Nava," The Internet Movie Database. Available online. URL: http://www.imdb.com/name/nm0622695/. Downloaded on December 3, 2004.

Meisler, Andy. "A Hispanic Drama, Rejected Once, Finds a Home," *New York Times,* December 16, 2001, section 2, p. 33.

Rodriguez, Clara. *Heroes, Lovers, and Others: The Story of Latinos in Hollywood.* Washington, D.C.: Smithsonian Books, 2004, p. 196.

Further Viewing

American Family—The Complete First Season (2000–01). Fox Home Video, DVD box set, 2003.

El Norte (1983). Fox Home Video, VHS, 1983.

My Family, Mi Familia (1995). New Line Home Video, VHS/DVD, 1997/2004.

Selena (1997). Warner Home Video, VHS/DVD, 1997.

Norton, Barry (Alfredo Carlos Biraben)
(1905–1956) *actor, filmmaker*

A boyishly appealing leading man of late silent and early sound films, Barry Norton starred in one of the least-known Hollywood horror classics, made for a Spanish-speaking audience. Alfredo Carlos Biraben was born in Buenos Aires, Argentina, on June 6, 1905. His family was wealthy, and Biraben grew up in a life of leisure. His interest in acting brought him to Hollywood in 1926 where Fox Pictures quickly signed him. The studio changed his name to the Anglo-sounding Barry Norton to hide his Latin background, which was not seen as an asset for a film actor. In his third film later that year, he gained critical praise as a World War I American private known as a "Mama's boy," in the war comedy–drama *What Price Glory?* Norton played leading roles in a number of other silent films, including *Four Devils* (1928), a lost film directed by master German-born filmmaker F. W. Murnau.

When sound films came later, in 1928, Norton's career went into a tailspin. Although his voice was perfectly acceptable for sound, his English was poor. Norton found himself relegated to leading roles now only in Spanish-language films with Spanish and Latino casts. Making foreign-language versions of Hollywood films was a common practice in the days when the technique of dubbing dialogue in other languages had not yet been perfected.

Often, the Spanish version was made cheaply and proved inferior to the English original. A remarkable exception was the Spanish version of the horror film *Dracula* (1931), in which Norton played the young leading man, Jonathan Harker. The English-speaking actors filmed the movie during the day, while the Spanish cast and crew came onto the same sets to shoot in the evenings.

For most critics who have seen both versions, non-Latino director George Melford and his Spanish-speaking cast surpassed the English-speaking version, despite the star presence of Bela Lugosi as Dracula. While the English version is largely static and filmed like a stage play, the Spanish version has a mobile camera that gives many scenes an eerie life. The scenes between Dracula and his female victims are far more sexually charged, undoubtedly helped by looser censorship for a film intended for a foreign market.

Barry Norton continued to make Spanish-language movies in Hollywood and Mexico, some of which he directed. By the mid-1930s, he was relegated to playing bit parts in Hollywood movies. His skill as a dancer held him in good stead, and he appeared in many movie ballroom scenes. He occasionally even worked as a dance instructor for such stars as Humphrey Bogart.

One of Norton's last screen roles must have been bittersweet for the once popular star: He played a priest in the 1952 remake of his first triumph, *What Price Glory?* Barry Norton died of a heart attack in Hollywood on August 24, 1956.

Further Reading

Erickson, Hal. "Barry Norton," MSN Movies. Available online. URL: http://beta.tv.msn.com/celebs/celeb.aspx?c=229295. Downloaded on October 11, 2005.

The Internet Movie Database. "Barry Norton," The Internet Movie Database. Available online. URL: http://www.imdb.com/name/nm0636161/. Downloaded on October 11, 2005.

Further Viewing

Dracula [Spanish version] (1931). Universal Home Video, DVD (part of *Dracula—The Legacy,* 2 discs), 2004.

Novarro, Ramón (José Ramón Gil Samaniego)

(1899–1968) *actor, filmmaker, producer*

One of the most popular romantic actors in the silent film era, Ramón Novarro's fame today unfortunately rests mainly on the shocking events surrounding his death. José Ramón Gil Samaniego was born in Durango, Mexico, on February 6, 1899. His family claimed to have traced its roots back to the Aztec leader Montezuma, who was killed by the invading Spanish conquistadores. José's father was a successful dentist, and his mother was the descendant of wealthy landowners. Actress DOLORES DEL RIO, six years his junior, was his cousin.

As a child José was sensitive and creative. He put on plays for family and friends in a marionette theater. When he was still in his teens, he moved to Los Angeles, California, to become a performer. He struggled for several years as a vaudeville performer and singing waiter. In 1917, he entered movies as an extra, an actor with no lines who appeared as a background player in films. For the next five years, he appeared as an extra in more than 100 films. He received his first screen credit as Ramón Samaniego in *Mr. Barnes of New York* (1922). Director Rex Ingram was impressed by his performance and cast the actor in a leading role in the adventure film *The Prisoner of Zenda* that same year. Ingram suggested he change his name to something that would look better on a movie marquee. He chose Navarro, the last name of a good friend, but a secretary mistyped it as "Novarro," and that is how it stayed.

Ingram directed Novarro in four more films, including the adventure movie *Scaramouche* (1923). Novarro's good looks, charm, and acting talent made him a star. He received 1,300 fan letters a week in 1923. Novarro was billed as "the new Valentino," but he never quite achieved actor Rudolph Valentino's popularity, although he was probably the better actor. He reached his career peak in 1925 when he starred in the title role in the biblical-age epic *Ben–Hur,* one of the great international hits of the 1920s. He had a pleasant voice (he sang quite well) and survived the transition to sound films at the end of the decade. Nonetheless, his popularity faded in the early 1930s. One of his last leading roles in Hollywood was opposite Greta Garbo in the spy drama *Mata Hari* (1931). In 1962, Novarro appeared in a play on Broadway, *Infidel Caesar,* but it played one preview, failed, and never officially opened.

He found leading roles in foreign films, mostly in Mexico, where he directed and starred in several movies. Novarro was also active in the Los Angeles Latino community. He built a theater in his spacious home that he called Teatro Intimo (Intimate Theatre) and produced shows with Spanish-speaking actors. He also participated in and supported benefits for relief aid to Mexico during natural disasters. He returned to Hollywood films in 1949 and appeared in small roles for the next decade.

The secret of Novarro's life was that he was homosexual. Unlike other gay Hollywood stars, including his screen rival ANTONIO MORENO, Novarro refused to give in to studio pressure to enter into a sham marriage to hide his sexuality. Nevertheless, as a leading man in film he had to keep his homosexuality quiet, and living a double life eventually drove him to drink. In his later years, Novarro was arrested several times for driving under the influence.

On October 31, 1968, Novarro made the fatal mistake of allowing two young hustlers into his home in the Hollywood Hills. They attacked him, ransacked the house for a large sum of money they believed he had hidden, and left the 69-year-old actor bound and dying from a savage beating. The two men, who were brothers, were caught, tried, and convicted of murder but served no more than nine years for their crime. It is possible that Novarro's homosexuality, still unacceptable by society, was a mitigating factor in their trial.

Further Reading

Ellenberger, Allan R. *Ramón Novarro: A Biography of the Film Idol, 1899–1968.* Jefferson, N.C.: McFarland & Company, 2000 [reprint].

The Internet Movie Database. "Ramón Novarro," The Internet Movie Database. Available online. URL: http://www.imdb.com/name/nm0003895/. Downloaded on February 25, 2005.

Soares, Andre. *Beyond Paradise: The Life of Ramón Novarro.* New York: St. Martin's Press, 2002.

Further Viewing

Ben-Hur (1925). Warner Home Video, DVD (4 discs, including 1959 version of film), 2005.

Mata Hari (1931). Warner Home Video, VHS/DVD, 1998/2005.

O

Ochoa, Victor
(Victor Orozco Ochoa)
(1948–) *muralist, painter, graphic artist, illustrator, educator, arts administrator*

A pioneer and leading figure in the Chicano (Mexican-American) art movement in San Diego, California, Victor Ochoa's bold and expressive murals capture the power and determination of Mexican Americans and other ethnic groups as they struggle for their place in American society. Victor Orozco Ochoa was born in Los Angeles, California, on August 2, 1948, and attended San Diego State University, where he earned a bachelor of arts (B.A.) degree in 1974. Ochoa soon joined the struggle for Chicano civil rights in California. In 1970, he helped found the Centro Cultural de la Raza, a community-based arts center that supported Chicano, Mexican, and Indian art and culture. As director of the Centro from 1970 to 1973 and again from 1988 to 1990, Ochoa oversaw the creation of numerous murals on the walls of buildings, bridge pillars, and other public spaces throughout the San Diego area. Brightly colored and larger than life, these murals celebrated Chicano and Indian history and culture while sometimes criticizing the society that suppressed these groups.

Among the most famous murals Ochoa himself has created is *Geronimo,* which covers part of the Centro's wall in Balboa Park. He portrayed the famous Apache Indian leader armed with a rifle in an aggressive stance. Ochoa sees Geronimo as a freedom fighter with whom he, a champion of Chicano rights, can identify. The Indian is flanked by figures of Chicano cultural achievement—a folk dancer, a potter at his wheel, an actor dressed as Death, and two musicians playing the mandolin and guitar.

Ochoa's outspokenness as an artist and a political activist has made him both friends and enemies in the San Diego community. After years of serving the Centro Cultural de la Raza as an artist-in-residence, he was removed from that position, and his materials were confiscated by a new conservative board of directors. Yet, he continues to have an impact and influence in the community as an educator and artist. Since 1988, he has taught "Mexican-Chicano Art and History" at Grossmont College in El Cajon, California, and instructs high school students in art at the MAAC Community Charter School in nearby Chula Vista.

Ochoa has created more than 100 murals. He has also made many graphic prints and posters, illustrated several books by Chicano writers, and designed sets for theatrical productions. "Art," he once declared, "is part of the solution of issues in society and Chicano art has been the expression of our people's struggle."

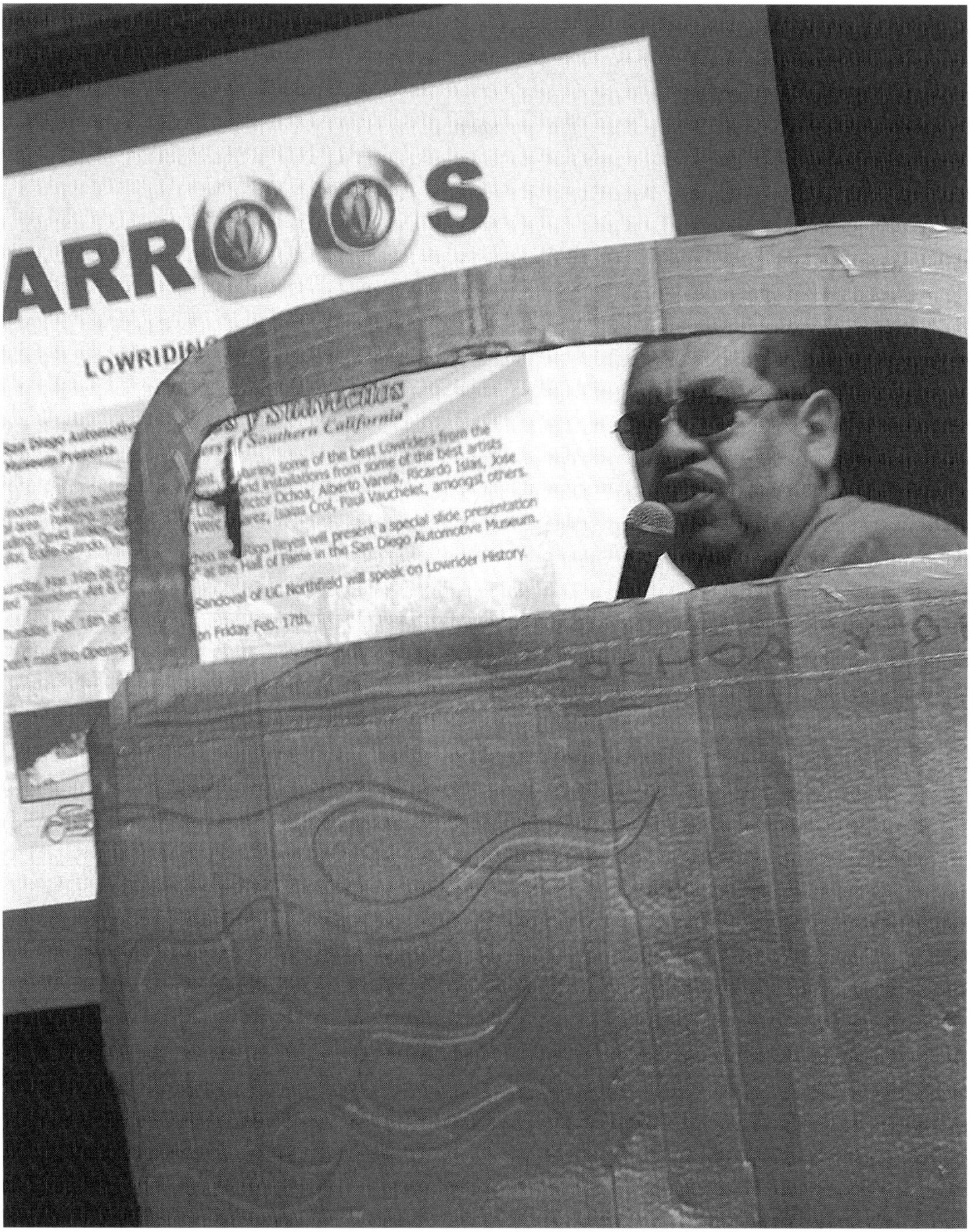

Artist Victor Ochoa enjoys his lowrider car at the San Diego Automobile Museum. Through the magic of a powerpoint presentation, Ochoa put himself in the driver's seat of this 2006 exhibition that he cocurated. *(Victor Ochoa)*

Further Reading

Calaca Press. "The Work of Chicano Artist Victor Orozco Ochoa," Calaca Press Web Site. Available online. URL: http://calacapress.com/chicanozauruz/chiczaur.html. Downloaded on January 18, 2006.

Cockcroft, James D., assisted by Jane Canning. *Latino Visions: Contemporary Chicano, Puerto Rican, and Cuban American Artists.* New York: Franklin Watts, 2000, pp. 31, 34.

Velz, Manual J., Victor Ochoa, illus. *Bus Stops and Other Poems.* San Diego, Calif.: Calaca Press, 1998.

Victor Ochoa's Official Web Site. Available online. URL: http://chicanozauruz.com. Downloaded on March 23, 2006.

Olmos, Edward James

(1947–) *actor, director, screenwriter, producer, social activist, filmmaker*

Arguably the most respected and gifted Mexican-American actor of his generation, Edward James Olmos uses his talents to provide a role model for young people, especially Latinos. He was born in East Los Angeles (East LA), California, on February 24, 1947. As a youngster, he wanted to be a professional baseball player but then fell in love with rock and roll at age 13. By 15, Olmos was the lead singer in a rock band that he helped form. Several bands later, he was performing in the better nightclubs along Hollywood's Sunset Strip. A friend suggested he try acting, and he began to attend classes. He started to win bit parts on television and in plays and made his big screen debut in a small role in the independent film *Aloha, Bobby & Rose* (1974). The role of a wino in his second film *Alambristra!* (The illegal, 1977) won him a Golden Camera prize at the Cannes Film Festival in France.

By this time married with two children, Olmos supported his family by running a furniture-moving business while appearing sporadically in films. His big break finally came at age 31, when he was cast in the play *Zoot Suit* (1978), written and directed by Luis Valdez. Olmos played El Pachuco, the play's narrator and the alter ego of the central character, one of a group of Mexican-American youths who are falsely arrested for a gang murder in 1940s LA. Based on a real incident, the trial led to the infamous zoot-suit riots, named after the elaborate dress of young Latinos. Originally performed in California, the play moved to Broadway for a brief run in spring 1979, and Olmos's powerful performance earned him a Theatre World Award and a Tony Award nomination for Best Featured Actor in a Play. He also starred in the 1981 film adaptation.

Olmos's next project was another reenactment of a little-remembered incident from Mexican-American history. *The Ballad of Gregorio Cortez* (1982) was the story of a Mexican ranchhand who was accused of murder in Texas in 1901 and became the object of the longest manhunt in Texas history. Olmos, who coproduced the film as well as starred in it, spent two years promoting the work, especially to Latino audiences. He even exhibited it for free in one LA theater to attract an audience.

Olmos's first big commercial success came in 1984 when he was cast as the taciturn Lieutenant Martin Castillo on the hit NBC crime show *Miami Vice* (1984–89). The role made him a star, despite the fact that he had few lines. "I was the highest-paid actor-per word-in the history of television!" he once joked. The role earned him an Emmy in 1985 for Best Supporting Actor.

Olmos used his clout as a television star to pursue another film project about a Latino hero, this time a contemporary one. In *Stand and Deliver* (1988), he played high-school math teacher Jaime Escalante, a Bolivian immigrant who uses calculus to turn his underprivileged Latino students into responsible, successful men and women. To play the middle-aged Escalante, Olmos gained 40 pounds, thinned his hair, and suffered two hours of makeup preparation daily during shooting. It was all worth

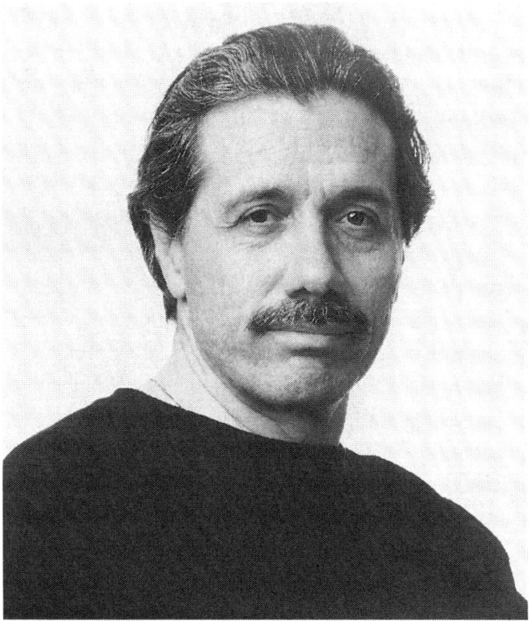

Edward James Olmos is known for choosing roles in which he strongly believes, such as his Academy Award–nominated turn as high school math teacher Jaime Escalante in *Stand and Deliver. (Photofest)*

the effort. *Stand and Deliver* became a surprise hit, and Olmos received an Academy Award nomination for Best Actor, the first time a Mexican-American male actor had been so honored. The film was the first Hollywood feature to be scripted, directed, produced, financed, and acted by Latinos.

In July of the same year of the film's release, Olmos was featured on the cover of *Time* magazine in an issue focusing on "the new spirit of Hispanic culture." His next major project, in which he starred as well as directed, was *American Me* (1992), an unflinching look at the Chicano youth gangs of LA and its effects on one Mexican-American family. The film was not as successful as *Stand and Deliver,* partly because its R restricted rating due to violence prevented the very youths whom Olmos wanted to reach from seeing the film.

Three years later, he starred in another Latino family saga, *My Family, Mi Familia* (1995), directed by GREGORY NAVA. The film depicted six decades in the life of a Mexican-American clan. Nava and Olmos were reunited in 2000 in one of the first television dramatic series about Latinos, *American Family.* Olmos played Jess Gonzalez, a barber, the grizzled, politically conservative patriarch of an East LA family. The show ran on the Public Broadcasting System (PBS) for one season.

Olmos has portrayed a wide range of memorable characters in other films, ranging from a concentration-camp survivor in *Triumph of the Spirit* (1989) to Rafael Trujillo, the real-life dictator of the Dominican Republic, in *The Time of the Butterflies* (2001), which costarred SALMA HAYEK.

While Olmos is dedicated to the craft of acting, he feels an even greater devotion to social activism. For years, he has regularly visited schools and detention centers across the country to speak to young Latinos and other youth, bringing them a message of hope by stressing the importance of education and personal responsibility. "If I can do it," he tells his audiences, "so can you."

A strong opponent of war, Olmos protested the use of the Puerto Rican island of Vieques as a bomb-testing site by the U.S. Navy. In April 2001, he was arrested for trespassing on the site and sentenced to 20 days in jail. The U.S. government ended the use of the island for its tests in 2003.

Olmos divorced his first wife, Kaija, the daughter of singer/actor Howard Keel, in 1992. He married actress Lorraine Bracco in 1994. The couple divorced in 2002, and he married Puerto Rican-born actress Lymari Nadal.

Further Reading

Carrillo, Louis. *Edward James Olmos* (Contemporary Biographies). Orlando, Fla.: Steck-Vaughn, 1997.

The Internet Movie Database. "Edward James Olmos." The Internet Movie Database. Available online. URL: http://www.imdb.com/name/nm0001579/. Downloaded on December 9, 2005.

Martinez, Elizabeth Coonrod. *Edward James Olmos* (Hispanic Heritage). Brookfield, Conn.: Millbrook Press, 1994.

Further Viewing

American Family: The Complete First Season (2002). Fox Home Video, DVD box set, 2003.

The Ballad of Gregorio Cortez (1982). MGM Home Entertainment, VHS, 2000.

Stand and Deliver (1988). Warner Home Video, VHS/DVD, 1994/1998.

Zoot Suit (1982). MCA Home Video, VHS/DVD, 1998/2003.

Osorio, Pepón (Benjamin Osorio Encarnación)

(1956–) *sculptor, installation artist*

Pepón Osorio's first career as a social worker in Latino communities strongly influenced the focus and nature of his visual art—from chandeliers to the model of a family's home after a fire. Benjamin Osorio Encarnación was born in Santurce, Puerto Rico, in 1956. He attended the Universidad Inter-Americana in Puerto Rico and at age 20 came to the United States. He enrolled at Lehman College in the Bronx, a borough of New York City, where he earned a bachelor of arts (B.A.) degree in sociology and a master of arts (M.A.) degree from Columbia University. Osorio got a job working at the Bronx child-abuse prevention unit of the Human Resources Administration. He came to know and admire the Latino families with whom he worked daily. His art, which he began to produce in 1985, is a reflection of them and their lives.

While visiting a housing project in Manhattan's Lower East Side where poor Puerto Ricans lived, he was surprised to see chandeliers hanging in several buildings' lobbies. He viewed them as a symbol of wealth and beauty amid poverty and squalor. As a result, he created *El Chandelier* (1988), an outrageously ornate six-foot-tall chandelier festooned with objects, toys, and gems that symbolize the lives and dreams of these hard-working immigrants. The work is part of the permanent collection of the Smithsonian American Art Museum (SAAM) in Washington, D.C.

Not all of Osorio's work sits in museums. *Tina's Home* (2000) is a model representing the house of a family that was burned one night in a fire. The artist spent weeks with the family, learning about their loss and how they cope with it. The house and its story have traveled the country and are put on "home visits": It is brought into a home for a week or longer and its story retold to the family. Osorio got the idea for "home visits" from the religious tradition of the visiting saint in Latin America. As a child, he recalled an image of the Virgin of Guadeloupe coming to his house and his family donating money to the church for this honor.

Tina's House has more than one message for those who it resides with. "One level is about losing your immediate possessions," he said in an interview. "On another level it's about restoring faith, which is what happens immediately after you lose something. And simultaneously, it's about possessing contemporary art, and how a work of contemporary art can take a major space in your home . . . you welcome it, you live with it for a week, and then you have to move it on, in faith, that it will be taken well care of wherever it goes."

Osorio's work has been exhibited in numerous museums including the El Museo del Barrio and the Whitney Museum of American Art, both in New York City. He has received fellowships from the Rockefeller Foundation, the National Endowment for the Arts (NEA), and the Lila Wallace Art Partners International Artist Program. Osorio currently lives and works in Philadelphia, Pennsylvania. "My principal commitment as an artist is to return art to the community," he has said.

Further Reading

Art: 21. "Pepón Osorio," PBS Web Site. Available online. URL: http://www.pbs.org/art21/artists/osorio/. Downloaded on January 17, 2006.

Blatherwick, David. "Pepón Osorio (Badge of Honor): Ronald Feldman Fine Arts, New York, Art 25—June 1." *Parachute: Contemporary Art Magazine,* January 1, 1997, pp. 65–66.

Congdon, Kristin G., and Kara Kelley Hallmark. *Artists from Latin American Cultures: A Biographical Dictionary.* Westport, Conn.: Greenwood Press, 2002, pp. 207–210.

Yorba, Jonathan. *Arte Latino: Treasures from the Smithsonian American Art Museum.* New York: Watson–Guptill Publications, 2001, pp. 78–79.

P

Page, Anita
(Anita Pomares)
(1910–2008) *actress*

A stunning blonde screen goddess of the silent and early talkie era, Anita Page returned to the movies after a 60-year hiatus, making hers one of the longest careers in Hollywood history. Anita Pomares was born in Flushing, New York, on August 4, 1910. Her father immigrated to the United States from El Salvador. After graduating from Washington Irving High School, she became an extra in movies, playing nonspeaking roles in crowd scenes. After several small roles, Metro-Goldwyn-Mayer (MGM) signed her to a long-term contract in 1926 under her new name Anita Page. She starred opposite some of Hollywood's biggest leading men, including RAMON NOVARRO (*Navy Blues,* 1927; *The Flying Fleet,* 1928) and Lon Chaney (*While the City Sleeps,* 1928). But it was her role opposite Joan Crawford in *Our Dancing Daughters* (1928) that made her a star. The following year, Page appeared as one-half of a sister singing-and-dancing act in *The Broadway Melody* (1929). The novelty of the film, the first all-talking musical feature, made it a huge hit. It went on to win the Academy Award for Best Picture, the second movie to achieve this honor. In the film, which costarred Bessie Love, Page sang the song "You Were Meant for Me," which became a #1 pop hit and her theme song for the rest of her career.

Page was now considered a Hollywood love goddess and received 10,000 fan letters weekly. The only star to receive more mail at the time was Greta Garbo. Among Page's many male admirers was Italian dictator Benito Mussolini, who proposed marriage several times. Page rejected Mussolini and married songwriter Herb Nacio Brown, the man who wrote "You Were Meant for Me," in 1934. They apparently were not meant for each other, and the marriage was dissolved a year later.

Page continued to star in films through the mid-thirties. She was classic comic Buster Keaton's love interest in both *Free and Easy* (1930) and *Sidewalks of New York* (1931). After making *Hitch Hike to Heaven* (1936), she married a naval officer and retired from the screen. Page lived for 40 years in Coronado, California, with her husband, Admiral Hershel A. House, and two daughters.

In 1996, well into her eighties, Page returned to the screen in character roles in mostly low-budget horror films with such titles as *Witchcraft XI: Satan's Blood* (2000) and *The Crawling Brain* (2002). Until her death on September 6, 2008, her official Web site, The Anita Page, claimed that she was available for bookings. "Please send us a description of what you have in mind and we will let you know if Ms. Page is interested in doing it."

Further Reading

The Anita Page. The Official Anita Page Web Site. Available online. URL: http://www.anitapage.com. Downloaded on October 20, 2005.

The Internet Movie Database. "Anita Page," The Internet Movie Database. Available online. URL: http://www.imdb.com/name/nm0656105/. Downloaded on March 23, 2006.

Rodriguez, Clara E. *Heroes, Lovers, and Others: The Story of Latinos in Hollywood.* Washington, D.C.: Smithsonian Books, 2004. pp. 12–14.

Further Viewing

The Broadway Melody (1929). Warner Home Video, VHS/DVD, 2000/2005.

Pelli, César

(1926–) *architect, educator*

One of the most successful and innovative architects in the world today, César Pelli designs every kind of building to match its intentions and environment. His towering, glass-encased structures are among the most admired in the contemporary world of architecture.

He was born in Tucumán, Argentina, on October 12, 1926. Drawn to architecture from an early age, Pelli attended the Universidad de Tucumán, where he received a bachelor of arts (B.A.) degree in architecture in 1950. He immigrated to the United States two years later and studied at the School of Architecture at the University of Illinois–Urbana Champaign, receiving a master of arts (M.A.) degree in architecture in 1954.

He began his professional career as a project designer for the architect Eero Saarinen, remaining with him for 10 years. He became a naturalized citizen in 1964. In 1968, Pelli became a partner in the architectural firm of Design, Green Associates in Los Angeles (LA), California. He remained there for eight years before opening his own firm with two colleagues, César Pelli & Associates, in New Haven, Connecticut, in 1977. During the next three decades, Pelli's firm earned an international reputation for excellence.

Unlike other great contemporary architects, Pelli does not have a signature style. He tailors each design to match the context of climate, site, and purpose, and his first goal is to please each client, usually presenting the client with several designs from which to choose. If there is a single characteristic of many of the buildings that Pelli has designed, it is probably his focus on the exterior, which he usually casts in glass. A dazzling variety of styles of glass make his buildings visually stunning. "I am interested in expressing the exteriors of buildings as enclosures for controlled living environments," he has written.

Pelli's firm has designed an impressive array of buildings from residential homes to museums, arts centers, and government centers. Some of his best-known works include the Winter Garden at Battery Park in New York City; the Washington National Airport; the U.S. Embassy in Tokyo, Japan; and the Edificio Republica in Buenos Aires in his native Argentina. His most famous building is undoubtedly the Petronas Towers in Kuala Lumpur, Malaysia. Built in 1997, this sleek skyscraper with its 32,000 windows was at that time the tallest building in the world, although the Sears Tower in Chicago, Illinois, has the highest occupied floor in the world.

In 1989, César Pelli & Associates, now called Pelli Clark Pelli Associates, was the recipient of the American Institute of Architects (AIA) Firm Award. Two years later, Pelli became the first Latino American to be named one of the 10 most influential living architects by the AIA. His firm was named the AIA Gold Medal winner in 1995 for "a singular body of work of lasting influence on the theory and practice of architecture."

Pelli was the dean of the Yale School of Architecture from 1977 to 1984. His book *Observations for Young Architects* (1999) explains his working manner and philosophy on architecture. "My works are formulated in the spirit of the presence," Pelli has said.

Further Reading

Crosbie, Michael J. *César Pelli: Buildings and Projects 1988–1998.* Boston, Mass.: Birkhauser, 2000.

Giovannini, Joseph, and Hiroyukia Suzuki. *Section Thru a Practice: César Pelli & Associates.* Ostfildren, Germany: Hatje Cantz Publishers, 2003.

Gray, Lee Edward. *Pattern and Context: Essays on César Pelli* (College of Architecture monograph series). Charlotte: University of North Carolina, 1992.

Pelli, César. *Observations for Young Architects.* New York: Monacelli Press, 1999.

Peña, Elizabeth
(1961–) *actress*

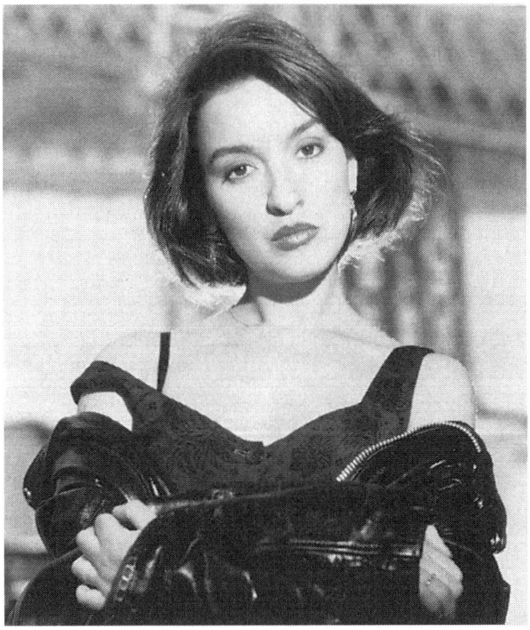

Elizabeth Peña, daughter of a Cuban-American playwright and director, has displayed her versatility in a wide range of film roles. *(Photofest)*

A versatile actress who can convey both vulnerability and strength convincingly, Elizabeth Peña has played an impressive string of leading and supporting film roles from abused wives to independent professional Latinas. She was born in Elizabeth, New Jersey, on September 23, 1961. Her father, Mario Peña, is a prominent Cuban-American novelist, playwright, actor, and director who founded New York City's Latin American Theatre Ensemble (LATE) in 1970. The family moved to New York when Elizabeth was still a child.

Eager to follow in her father's footsteps, she attended New York's High School of the Performing Arts. While still a student there, Peña began to act professionally in repertory theater and appeared in several television commercials. At age 17, she made an auspicious film debut as a rebellious teen in the Latino comedy *El Super* (1979), directed by LEON ICHASO. She appeared in a number of small, independent films in the next five years, culminating in *Crossover Dreams* (1985), another Ichaso film, in which she played the girlfriend salsa singer RUBÉN BLADES loses as he attempts to cross over to the English-speaking music market.

But despite these successes, Peña herself was unable to crossover to big-budget Hollywood films. In desperation, she gave her demo tape to a security guard whom she knew at a Hollywood studio. He gave it to a casting director; less than an hour later, Peña was summoned back to the studio to audition for director Paul Mazursky, who was casting for his comedy *Down and Out in Beverly Hills* (1986). Peña won the role of Carmen, the Latino maid in a dysfunctional upper-middle-class family, who is having an affair with head-of-the-household Richard Dreyfuss. The film was a hit, and Peña's Hollywood career was off and running.

The following year, she was part of a stellar Latino cast in *La Bamba* (1987), the biopic of rock singer RITCHIE VALENS, playing Valens's abused sister-in-law. She was also excellent as the mysterious girlfriend of haunted Vietnam vet Tim Robbins in the horror movie *Jacob's Ladder* (1990).

But despite these good roles, Peña complained about the stereotyping that limited her and other Latina actresses in Hollywood. "I'm usually offered the roles of the prostitute, the mother with 17 children, or the screaming wife getting beaten up," she has said.

She had better luck on television, where in the 1980s she starred in three short-lived series, including the excellent *Shannon's Deal* (1989), in which she played unorthodox lawyer Jamie Sheridan's no-nonsense secretary. The pilot of the series was written by John Sayles who seven years later cast Peña as a Mexican-American social worker in a Texas border town in *Lone Star* (1996), which he wrote and directed. The role earned her an Independent Spirit Award.

Peña has continued to appear in a wide range of films from the Jackie Chan action movie *Rush Hour* (1998) to the perceptive Latino comedy/drama *Tortilla Soup* (2001). In the latter film, she played an ugly-duckling schoolteacher who finally finds happiness. She also starred in the television series *Resurrection Boulevard* (2000–02) about a Latino family. The role won her an ALMA Award for Outstanding Actress in a New Television Series. Elizabeth Peña is married and has two children.

Further Reading

Buchanan, Jason. "Elizabeth Peña," The All Movie Guide Web Site. Available online. URL: http://www.allmovie.com/cg/avg.dll. Downloaded on November 25, 2005.

The Internet Movie Database. "Elizabeth Peña," The Internet Movie Database. Available online. URL: http://www.imdb.com/name/nm000161. Downloaded on December 3, 2004.

Sperling, Seana. "An Interview with Elizabeth Peña," Acid Logic.com. Available online. URL: http://www.acidlogic.com/elizabeth_pena.htm. Downloaded on March 24, 2006.

Further Viewing

Down and Out in Beverly Hills (1986). Buena Vista Home Entertainment, VHS/DVD, 2002.

Lone Star (1996). Sony Pictures/Castle Rock Entertainment, VHS/DVD, 1999.

Tortilla Soup (2001). Columbia/TriStar Home Video, VHS/DVD, 2002.

Perez, Rosie (Rosa Maria Perez)

(1964–) *actress, dancer, choreographer, producer*

A diminutive, dynamic performer from the streets of her native Brooklyn, Rosie Perez is a triple threat as an actress, dancer, and choreographer. Rosa Maria Perez was born in the Bushwick neighborhood of Brooklyn, New York, on September 6, 1964. Of Puerto Rican heritage, she left New York after high school to attend Los Angeles Community College in California, where she studied marine biology. A producer from the popular television music show *Soul Train* saw her disco dancing at a Los Angeles club and invited her to appear as a dancer on his program. She left college behind and danced on *Soul Train* for several years. Her love of dancing led Perez to try her hand at choreography. Soon, she was choreographing live stage shows and music videos for such recording artists as Diana Ross, Bobby Brown, and rapper LL Cool J.

Filmmaker Spike Lee saw her dancing in the Los Angeles club Funky Reggae and was impressed. He cast her in his film, the racial drama *Do the Right Thing* (1989), despite the fact that she had no prior acting experience. Perez played Lee's girlfriend in the film and performed a riveting dance routine during the opening credits. It was a memorable screen debut and led to

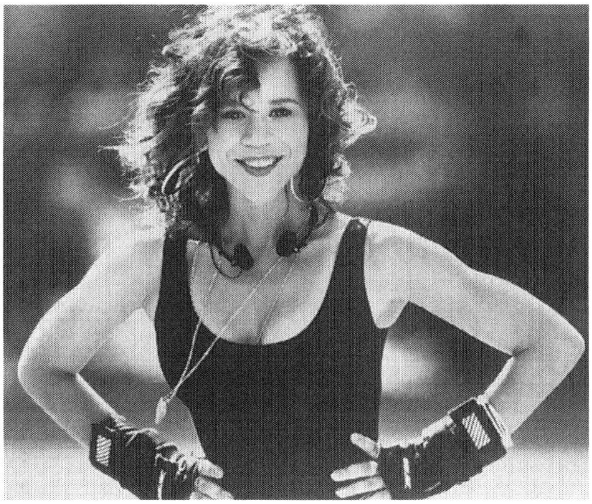

Actress Rosie Perez began her career in show business as a dancer and choreographer. *(Photofest)*

other roles, but Perez continued to work mainly as a choreographer. She was hired to choreograph the famous Fly Girls on the Fox television comedy sketch show *In Living Color* (1990–94), and she received an Emmy nomination for her work. She has since nurtured the career of another Latina Fly Girl, JENNIFER LOPEZ.

Perez was usually cast as a comic, often explosive, Puerto Rican in such films as *White Men Can't Jump* (1992) and *It Could Happen to You* (1994), but when given a solid dramatic part, she proved that she could rise to the occasion. In *Fearless* (1993), she gave a heart-wrenching performance as a guilt-ridden mother who survives the plane crash that killed her baby. The role earned Perez an Academy Award nomination for Best Supporting Actress.

But such acting opportunities were rare for the actress. She usually found herself cast as what she called a "feisty, foul-mouthed, working-class Latina." She generally found better roles in television and produced the critically acclaimed Home Box Office (HBO) television film *Subway Stories: Takes from the Underground* (1997), in which she also acted. During the filming, she met writer/director Seth Ziv Rosenfeld, whom she married in 1999. The couple separated in 2001. Perez also coproduced and starred in the independent film *The 24-Hour Woman* (1999), in which she was cast as a TV talk-show producer who was trying to juggle work and family.

The following year, Perez declared publicly that she would not accept roles that she found demeaning to her Latino heritage. A committed social activist, Perez was arrested in January 2000 for disorderly conduct after a New York City rally protesting U.S. Navy bomb tests on Vieques, a tiny island off the coast of Puerto Rico.

In 2004, she acted in *Lackawanna Blues,* a TV movie based on the life of Ruben Santiago, Jr. A year later, Perez produced *Yo Soy Boricua! Pa' Que Tu Lo Sepas!* (I'm Boricua, just so you know), a PBS documentary that cofeatured Perez with Ramon Rodriguez and JIMMY SMITS.

Further Reading

Finn, Robin. "'Do the Right Thing' Is More Than Her Movie Debut." *New York Times,* July 7, 2006, p. B2.

The Internet Movie Database. "Rosie Perez," The Internet Movie Database. URL: http://www.imdb.com/name/nm0001609/. Downloaded on March 23, 2006.

Marvis, Barbara J., and Barbara Tidman. *Famous People of Hispanic Heritage: Gloria Estefan, Fernando Cuza; Rosie Perez; Cheech Marin.* Hockessin, Del.: Mitchell Lane Publishers, 1996.

Rodriguez, Clara E. *Heroes, Lovers, and Others: The Story of Latinos in Hollywood.* Washington, D.C.: Smithsonian Books, 2004. pp. 208–211.

Further Viewing

Do the Right Thing (1989). MCA Home Video, VHS/DVD, 1992/1998.

Fearless (1993). Warner Home Video, VHS/DVD, 1995/2004.

Phillips, Lou Diamond (Louis Diamond Upchurch)

(1962–) *actor, filmmaker, screenwriter, producer*

Having made one of the most promising Hollywood debuts of any young actor in the 1980s, Lou Diamond Phillips's career quickly took a nosedive until he experienced a comeback in a most unlikely venue—the Broadway stage. Louis Diamond Upchurch was born at Subic Bay Naval Station in the Philippines on February 17, 1962. His father, a naval-aircraft mechanic, was stationed there at the time. His first and middle name came from the legendary marine gunnery sergeant Lou Diamond. Phillips's ethnic background is one of the richest in Hollywood: He claims Spanish, Filipino, Chinese, Scottish/Irish, Hawaiian, and Cherokee Indian descent.

The family returned to the states when Louis was still a child and settled in Flour Bluff, Texas, a town near Corpus Christi. Lou's parents divorced, his mother remarried, and he took his stepfather's last name. After high school, Phillips turned down a scholarship to the U.S. Naval Academy at Annapolis, Maryland, to attend the University of Texas–Arlington where he would be close to family and friends. He developed a passion for acting and performed in plays and independent local films in college. He even cowrote the screenplay for one film, *Trespasses* (1983). When he graduated in 1986, Phillips joined a Fort Worth theater company and acted in their productions for four years.

He made a career-defining debut in major feature films in 1987, giving a dynamic performance as 1950s Latino rock star RITCHIE VALENS in the biopic *La Bamba* (1987). The film, which was directed by LUIS VALDEZ, also starred ESAI MORALES and ELIZABETH PEÑA. *La Bamba* was a surprise hit and remains one of the most successful movies about Latinos to date. Phillips followed it with another fine performance in *Stand and Deliver* (1988), in which he played an East Los Angeles (East LA) gang member who is turned on to math by an inspiring high-school teacher played by EDWARD JAMES OLMOS. The role earned Phillips a Golden Globe nomination for Best Supporting Actor in a Film. In his next movie, the Western *Young Guns* (1989), he was equally impressive as a charismatic young outlaw. It looked as if Phillips was posed on the brink of stardom, but then something went wrong.

Through a combination of bad luck, poor choices, and the perennial problem of finding good roles as an ethnic actor, Phillips found himself relegated to box-office bombs that went straight to video. He tried his hand at producing (*Dakota,* 1988) and directing (*Sioux City,* 1994), but these films failed as well.

Just when it looked as if his career would never recover, he was cast as the king of Siam in a Broadway revival of a musical classic, *The King and I,* in 1996. Phillips seemed an unlikely choice for the role, which still bore the indelible stamp of the original king, Yul Brynner. But Phillips surprised audiences and critics alike with a powerful performance in which he made the role his own. It earned him a Tony nomination for Best Actor in a Musical. The same year, he made an impressive return to the screen, costarring with Denzel Washington and Meg Ryan in the Desert Storm drama *Courage Under Fire* (1996). Since then, Phillips has been busy acting in films of varying quality and making numerous guest appearances on such television series as *24, Resurrection Boulevard,* and *George Lopez.*

Phillips and his second wife, model Kelly Preston, divorced in 2006. He has twin daughters from that marriage.

Further Reading

Brennan, Sandra. "Lou Diamond Phillips," All Move Guide. Available online. URL: http://www.allmovie.com/cg/avg.dll. Downloaded on February 28, 2006.

The Internet Movie Database. "Lou Diamond Phillips," The Internet Movie Database. Available online. URL: http://www.imdb.com/name/nm0001617/. Downloaded February 13, 2005.

Further Viewing

Courage Under Fire (1996). Fox Home Video, VHS/DVD, 2001/2000.

La Bamba (1987). Sony Home Video, VHS/DVD, 1999.

Stand and Deliver (1988). Warner Home Video, VHS/DVD, 1994/1998.

Portillo, Lourdes

(1944–) documentary filmmaker, screenwriter, producer

One of the most compelling Latino documentary filmmakers working today, Lourdes Portillo has used her camera to celebrate the lives of Latinos and expose injustices against them. She was born in Chihuahua, in the state of Chihuahua, Mexico, on November 11, 1944. When she was 21 and living in San Francisco, California, a friend who was a filmmaker asked her to help complete a documentary. It proved to be a life-changing experience. "I knew from that moment what I was going to do for the rest of my life," she writes on her Web site. "That never changed. It was just a matter of when I was going to do it."

A few years later, she worked an apprenticeship at the San Francisco branch of the National Association of Broadcast Engineers and Technicians (NABET). This led to her first professional job as a camera assistant on the television movie *Over, Under, Sideways, Down* (1977).

Portillo graduated from the San Francisco Art Institute in 1978 and the following year made her first documentary, *Después del Terremoto* (After the earthquake, 1979), the riveting story of a Nicaraguan refugee living in San Francisco.

Her next film, *Las Madres: The Mothers of Plaza de Mayo* (1985), was the first of several collaborations with writer/director Susana Muñoz. It told the grim but ultimately triumphant story of the mothers of missing or murdered political detainees in Argentina during the tyranny of the military junta that ran the country in the 1970s. The mothers' weekly marches in front of the presidential palace in Buenos Aires led to a national resistance movement that helped end the military regime. The film was nominated for an Academy Award for Best Documentary in 1985 and received 20 other international awards.

The success of *Las Madres: The Mothers of Plaza de Mayo* helped Portillo and Muñoz obtain funding from the Public Broadcasting Service (PBS) to make their next film, *Las Ofrendas: The Days of the Dead* (1989). The film was about the special religious holiday on which families go to visit and picnic in cemeteries where loved ones are buried.

Portillo's most recent film is her most chilling. *Señorita Extraviada* (Missing Young Woman, 2001) is an investigation into the disappearance and murder of more than 200 young women in the Mexican border town of Juárez. A mecca for men who want to cross the border to work in the United States, it has proven to be one of the most dangerous cities in Mexico for women. The film won the Special Jury Prize at the Sundance Film Festival. It also won the NÉSTOR ALMENDROS Prize at the Human Rights Watch International Film Festival.

Portillo's other films include *El Diablo Nunca Duerme* (The devil never sleeps, 1994) which she wrote and *Corpus: A Home Movie for Selena* (1999) which she produced and directed. She sees her mission as "channeling the hopes and dreams of a people."

Further Reading

The Films and Videos of Lourdes Portillo. Official Web Site. Available online. URL: http://www.lourdesportillo.com/. Downloaded on December 2, 2005.

Fregoso, Rosa Linda, ed. *Lourdes Portillo: The Devil Never Sleeps and Other Films (Chicano Matters).* Austin: University of Texas Press, 2001.

POV. *"Señorita Extraviada,"* PBS.org. Available online. URL: http://www.pbs.org/pov/pov2002/senoritaextraviada/index.html. Downloaded on March 23, 2006.

Further Viewing

Las Ofrendas: The Days of the Dead (1989). Direct Cinema Limited, VHS, 1989.

Señorita Extraviada (2001). Women Made Movies (WMM), VHS, 2001.

Prinze, Freddie (Frederick Karl Pruetzel)

(1954–1977) *actor, comedian*

The first Latino to star in his own television sitcom, Freddie Prinze's sudden rise to fame while still in his teens ultimately ended in tragedy. He was born Frederick Karl Pruetzel in New York City on June 22, 1954. His father Karl was a Hungarian Jew (though his death certificate lists his birthplace as Germany), and his mother Maria was a Puerto Rican Catholic. Later, Prinze would jokingly call himself a "Hungarican." A chubby child, his mother enrolled him in ballet class to help control his weight. Creative and bright, he applied to Fiorella La Guardia High School of the Performing Arts without telling his parents. He was accepted and studied drama, continued ballet, and discovered his gift for comedy. In his senior year, he quit school to become a stand-up comedian.

Prinze's rise was truly meteoric. At 16, he got a regular gig doing stand-up at the Improv Club in New York. He changed his name to Freddie Prinze so that he could call himself the "Prince of Comedy." In 1973, he made his television debut on one of the last episodes of *The Jack Paar Show.* That December, he appeared on *The Tonight Show* with Johnny Carson, the prized goal of every young stand-up comic. Carson was so impressed by Prinze's abilities that he invited him to sit down after his routine and talk with him, an unheard of honor for a comic appearing on the show for the first time. Prinze would appear many more times on *The Tonight Show* and even serve as a guest host in Carson's absence.

Now a hot property, Prinze auditioned for and won the role of Francisco "Chico" Rodriguez in the NBC sitcom *Chico and the Man.* In the show, Chicano (Mexican-American) Chico forms an unlikely partnership with Ed Brown, a crotchety old Anglo who runs a garage. The role of Ed was played by veteran actor Jack Albertson, who became a close friend to Prinze.

Chico and the Man debuted in September 1974 and was an immediate hit. The following year Prinze recorded a comedy album *Loooking Goood,* which was his catch phrase on the show. In October 1975, he married Kathcrine Cochran. In 1976, as the sitcom was entering its third season, Prinze starred in the made-for-TV movie *The Million Dollar Rip-Off.*

It seemed that the world was Prinze's oyster, but inside, he was a deeply unhappy young man who was unable to cope with the pressures of overnight success and celebrity. A doctor prescribed Quaaludes to relieve his depression, and Prinze became addicted to the drug. In November 1976, he was arrested for driving under the influence (DUI). Soon after, his wife filed for divorce, fearing his drug addiction was a threat to her safety.

Prinze appeared at President Jimmy Carter's Inaugural Ball in January 1977. He did a taping of *Chico and the Man* on January 27. The next day, from his hotel room, he made a series of calls to friends and family members, saying good-bye. After receiving one of these calls, his manager Dusty Snyder rushed to his hotel room to talk Prinze out of committing suicide. He was unable to do so, and after calling his estranged wife, Prinze took a handgun out from under a sofa and shot himself in the head as a horrified Snyder looked on.

Prinze was rushed to a hospital and, after surgery, put on life support. The next day, with no hope of his recovery, his family gave the order to remove him from life support. Freddie Prinze was 22 years old. The suicide note he left read in part: "I must end it. There is no hope. I will be at peace."

Years later, at his mother's persistent request, Prinze's death was reruled as "accidental shooting due to the influence of Quaaludes." The evidence was based on his prior history of faking suicide and the fact that suicides rarely killed themselves in front of another person.

In December 2004, his son actor FREDDIE PRINZE, JR., unveiled a star in honor of his father on the Hollywood Walk of Fame.

Further Reading

Abrams, Lea. *Freddie Prinze* (Latinos in the Limelight). New York: Chelsea House, 2002.

The Internet Movie Database. "Freddie Prinze," The Internet Movie Database. Available online. URL: http://www.imbd.com/name/nm0697905/. Downloaded on December 9, 2004.

Pruetzel, Maria. *The Freddie Prinze Story.* Dallas, Tex.: Master's Press, 1978.

Further Viewing

Chico and the Man (Television Favorites, 1974). Warner Home Video, DVD, 2005.

Prinze, Freddie, Jr.

(1976–) *actor*

One of the most appealing and popular of the young generation of Latino film actors, Freddie Prinze, Jr., has recently followed in his famous father's footsteps and starred in his own television sitcom. He was born in Los Angeles (LA), California, on March 8, 1976. His father was comedian and television star FREDDIE PRINZE, who separated from his mother Katherine Cochran-Prinze when he was still an infant. Prinze, Sr., shot himself and died in January 1977.

Freddie moved to Albuquerque, New Mexico, with his mother and grandmother. He spent his summers living with his paternal grandmother in Puerto Rico, her homeland. Italian on his mother's side, Prinze is not immediately identifiable as Latino.

Prinze graduated from high school in 1994 and moved to LA to pursue an acting career. He landed small roles in several television sitcoms, including *Family Matters* in 1995, made his motion-picture debut in *To Gillian on Her 37th Birthday* (1996), and had a leading role in the made-for-television movie *Detention: The Siege at Johnson High* (1997) about a Columbinelike takeover of a high school by an armed and disgruntled dropout.

The same year, Prinze starred in the mystery–serial-killer film *I Saw What You Did Last Summer* (1997). It was about a group of teens who dispose of a body after a hit-and-run accident and are then killed off one by one by a mysterious killer who knows of their crime. Prinze was one of the film's lucky survivors and appeared in the inevitable sequel *I Still Know What You Did Last Summer* (1998).

Prinze's breakthrough film was *She's All That* (1999), a delightful teen romantic comedy. In it, he played a high school jock who accepts a bet with a friend that he can turn a plain-looking art student into the prom queen in eight weeks. Other teen comedies followed including *Down to You* (2000), *Heads Over Heels* (2001), and *Summer Catch* (2001), in which he played an aspiring pitcher at a baseball camp. Prinze also appeared in two live-action *Scooby-Doo* films (2002, 2004) that were based on the popular television cartoon series.

In 2005, Prinze debuted in his own ABC sitcom, *Freddie,* playing chef Freddie Moreno who copes with the three women in his life—his niece, his sister-in-law, and his grandmother. He is only the fifth Latino to star in a television sitcom. The first was his father who starred in *Chico and the Man* (1974–77).

Prinze married actress and frequent costar Sarah Michelle Gellar in September 2002.

"[Acting is] the only thing I'm good at," he confesses. "I know how to create and make people feel something. Honestly, if I didn't do this, I would just have some minimum-wage job in New Mexico."

Further Reading

The Internet Movie Database. "Freddie Prinze, Jr.," The Internet Movie Database. Available online. URL: http://www.imdb.com/name/nm0005327/. Downloaded on March 23, 2006.

Jordan, Victoria. *Freddie Prinze, Jr.: A Biography.* New York: Simon Spotlight Entertainment, 2000.

Shapiro, Marc. *Freddie Prinze, Jr.: The Unofficial Biography.* New York: Berkley Publishing Group, 1999.

Further Viewing

I Know What You Did Last Summer / I Still Know What You Did Last Summer (1997, 1998). Sony/Columbia Tristar Home Video, VHS/DVD, 2000/2003.

She's All That (1999). Walt Disney Video/Miramax, VHS/DVD, 2000/1999.

Puente, Tito
(Ernesto Antonio Puente, Jr., "The King of Mambo," "El Rey")
(1923–2000) *Latin and jazz bandleader, percussionist, composer, arranger*

The most renowned and influential Latin bandleader in the United States, Tito Puente was largely responsible for fusing American jazz and Afro-Cuban rhythms to form a kind of new dance music—salsa. Ernesto Antonio Puente, Jr., was born in New York City's Spanish Harlem on April 20, 1923. His father Ernest, Sr., was originally from Puerto Rico and worked as a foreman in a razor-blade factory. As a boy, Ernesto would beat out rhythms on boxes and windowsills. His mother Ercilia started him on piano lessons at age seven, but it was the drums that were his real love. He began to play percussion in local bands on weekends as a young teenager. At age 15, he dropped out of high school and went to Miami Beach for the winter to play in a band. He returned to New York and was hired as a drummer by Latin orchestra leader Jose Curbelo. He created a sensation by introducing the timbales, a pair of open-bottomed drums, which he played from a standing position. At the time, other drummers played sitting. Puente made the timbales the main beat keeper in Latin dance music.

In 1942, Puente's career was interrupted when he was drafted into the U.S. Navy during World War II (1939–45). He served for three years in the South Pacific on an aircraft carrier. While there, he taught himself to play the saxophone. When the war ended, Puente returned to civilian life with a Presidential Commendation for serving bravely in nine battles. He attended the Juilliard School of Music under the GI Bill, which paid for his schooling. He studied orchestration, composition, and conducting.

In 1948, he formed his own 10-piece band, the Piccadilly Boys. At the Palladium in New York, where the band played regularly, Puente helped popularize the latest Latin dance craze, the mambo, earning himself the title "The King of Mambo." The band recorded on Tico Records in 1949 and had their first hit record, "Abaniquito." Later that year, the band signed with RCA Victor Records and had a long string of hits. Puente lived up to his title "The King of Mambo" in 1956 when he beat Perez Prado and his band in a contest judged by the public.

In 1958, Puente's album *Dance Mania* became a best seller and to date remains the biggest-selling salsa record, although the term was not used to describe this music until the 1970s.

Puente's growing interest in American jazz led him to perform and record with such jazz figures as bandleader Woody Herman, trombonist

Buddy Morrow, and trumpeter Doc Severinson, with whom he collaborated on the album *Puente Goes Jazz.* A prolific composer, Puente published more than 400 compositions in his career. His music gained a whole new audience of middle-class white youth when CARLOS SANTANA and his rock band Santana recorded his 1950s composition *"Oye, Como Va"* as a single in 1971. It went to #13 on the pop charts. Six years later, Puente played in concert with Santana at New York's Roseland Ballroom.

In 1979, Puente won his first Grammy Award for Best Latin Recording for his album *Homenaje a Beny Moré* (A Tribute to Benny Moré, 1978). He went on to be nominated for Grammys seven more times and won three more times. His album *Mondo Birdland* (2000) won a Latin Grammy at the first awards given for Best Traditional Tropical Album. He recorded his 100th album in 1992, the first Latino popular musician to do so.

Puente brought Latin music to places where it had rarely been heard before, including the Metropolitan Opera (1967) and Japan, which he toured in 1979. He played through the 1980s on college and university campuses. He made memorable appearances on *The Simpsons* and *The Bill Cosby Show* and played himself in the movie *The Mambo Kings* (1992). President Jimmy Carter, who invited Puente to play at the White House in 1979 to perform for National Hispanic Month, called him "The Goodwill Ambassador of Latin American Music."

Puente's last years were filled with honors: In August 1990, he was honored with a star on the Hollywood Walk of Fame; in 1994, he received the American Society of Composers, Authors, and Publishers (ASCAP) Founders Award; and two years later, he became the first Latino popular musician to receive his own exhibition at the Smithsonian National Museum of American History in Washington, D.C. The exhibition commemorated his 60th year as a musician. New York's Columbia University awarded him an honorary degree in 1999.

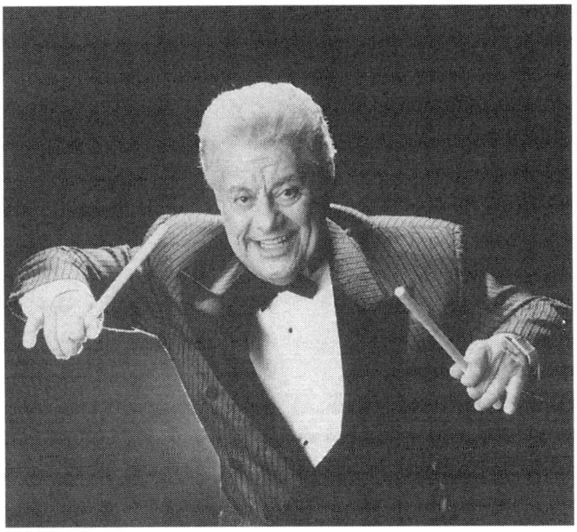

A superb percussionist, bandleader Tito Puente's skills with the timbales, which he played standing up, made these open-bottom drums a leader in the rhythmic section in every Latin band. *(Photofest)*

While undergoing heart surgery at a New York hospital on May 31, 2000, Puente died at age 77. His son Tito Puente, Jr., is also a percussionist and his daughter Audrey is a television meteorologist. "In a day when pop singers fake their way to the top and when for many artists, success is the child of hype, Puente is one of only a handful of musicians who deserved the title 'legendary,'" wrote author Mark Holston.

Further Reading

Hispanic Heritage—Biographies. "Tito Puente," Thomson Gale Web Site. Available online. URL: http://www.galegroup.com/free_resources/chh/bio/puente_t.htm. Downloaded on February 8, 2005.

Loza, Steven. *Tito Puente and the Making of Latin Music.* Chicago: University of Illinois Press, 1999.

Olmstead, Mary. *Tito Puente* (Hispanic American Biographies). Chicago: Raintree, 2004.

Puente, Tito, and Jim Payne. *Tito Puente's Drumming with the Mambo King* [book and CD]. New York: Hudson Music, 2000.

Further Listening

Dance Mania (1958). Sony International, CD, 1991.

The Essential Tito Puente. RCA, CD [2 discs], 2005.

King of Kings: The Very Best of Tito Puente. Buddha, CD, 2002.

Further Viewing

The Mambo Kings (1992). Warner Home Video, VHS/DVD, 1995/2005.

Tito Puente—Live in Montreal (1983). Image Entertainment, VHS/DVD, 2003.

Q

Quesada, Joe

(1962–) *comic-book artist, writer, editor*

One of the most gifted and influential of the new breed of comic book artists of the 1990s, Joe Quesada has more recently expanded his influence as editor-in-chief of Marvel Comics, the largest comic-book publishing company in the United States. Joseph Quesada was born in New York City on December 1, 1962, and grew up in a Cuban-American family in Jackson Heights, Queens. After high school, he attended the School of Visual Arts in New York and earned a bachelor of arts (B.A.) degree in illustration. Although Quesada loved to draw, his greatest passion was music. In the 1980s, he made his living as a professional musician, playing guitar in a band called Idle Chatter.

He got his first job in the comics industry in 1991, working as a colorist for Valiant Comics. From there, he moved to DC Comics, the second largest comic-book publisher in the United States. At DC, Quesada helped create the superhero Azrael, a kind of angel of death who later replaced for a time Batman, one of DC's greatest superheroes.

After working for nearly every major comic publisher from Dark Horse to Marvel, Quesada joined forces with artists Jimmy Palmoitti and Laurie Bradach in 1994 to create Event Comics. Their leading superhero was Ash (a.k.a. Ashley Quinn), whose day job was firefighter. (Steven Spielberg's production company Dreamworks is developing Ash into a feature animated film.)

In 1998, Event worked out a deal with Marvel to revitalize some of their older superheroes under the imprint Marvel Knights. Quesada and his team of artists brought a fresh look to such Marvel characters as Daredevil, the Black Panther, and the Punisher.

Marvel Knights was so successful that Marvel offered Quesada the position of editor-in-chief in September 2000. Within a year of taking the job, Quesada increased sales of Marvel comics by more than 75 percent. As editor, he has become, like his predecessor Stan Lee, a tireless ambassador for comic books as a popular art form. He has appeared many times on television news and talk shows and even appeared in a cameo role as a pizza delivery man in the comedy *Jay and Silent Bob Strike Back* (2001).

In spring 2002, Quesada initiated a crossover of DC and Marvel's two most popular superhero teams, the Justice League of America and the Avengers. He returned to drawing and writing with *Daredevil: Father Premiere,* a full-length graphic novel that was published in 2006.

"We are the world's storytellers!" he declared in his keynote address at the San Diego Comic Convention in July 2001. "When we're on our game, we do it better than television, novels, and the movies and we do it monthly, year in and year out over a huge number of titles! We are mythmakers, the architects of legend."

Further Reading

Joe Quesada Official Web Site. Available online. URL: http://www.joequesada.com. Downloaded on January 26, 2006.

Quesada, Joe. *Daredevil: Father Premiere.* New York: Marvel Comics, 2006.

Quesada, Joe, Alithan Martinez, and Sean Chen. *Iron Man: The Mask in the Iron Man.* New York: Marvel Comics, 2001.

Quinn, Anthony (Antonio Rudolfo Oaxaca Quinn)

(1915–2001) *actor, producer*

A charismatic actor of great power and a Hollywood star for five decades, Anthony Quinn was known for playing a wide range of ethnic roles, but few of his admirers knew that his ethnicity was Mexican American. Antonio Rudolfo Oaxaca Quinn was born in Chihuahua, in the state of Chihuahua, Mexico, on April 21, 1915. His father was a Mexican-Irish migrant worker, and his mother was Mexican. As a boy, he would follow his parents across California picking lettuce and grapes alongside them. "It was a marvelous, rambling existence," he recalled years later. "Like gypsies, we vagabonded from one home to the next, but one stop was much like another."

The family relocated to East Los Angeles (East LA), California, when Quinn was still young. He earned money shining shoes and selling newspapers. He later entered dance contests and would sell the trophies that he won for cash. As a young man, he tried various jobs, including butcher, prizefighter, and even a street-corner preacher, working for famed evangelist Aimee Semple McPherson.

Quinn's first passion, however, was for art. At age 11, he won a statewide sculpturing contest with a bust of Abraham Lincoln. A few years later, he won a scholarship to study with architect Frank Lloyd Wright. It was Wright who first encouraged Quinn to try acting to retrain his tongue after surgery for a speech impediment.

By the early 1930s, Quinn had performed in several plays and had abandoned his ambition to be an architect. His film career began in 1936, and Paramount Studios soon signed him on as a contract player. He appeared in bit parts, mostly as gangsters and Indians. He played an Indian in *The Plainsman* (1936), directed by Cecil B. DeMille, and fell in love with the director's adopted daughter Katherine. The couple married a year later. DeMille continued to cast Quinn in small roles in other films that he directed, but he did little more to further in son-in-law's acting career.

For the next 15 years, Quinn remained stuck in small, supporting parts, playing every kind of ethnic role imaginable. He was an Arab sheik in *The Road to Morocco* (1942), Indian chief Crazy Horse in *They Died with Their Boots On* (1941), and a Filipino soldier in *Back to Bataan* (1945). Between 1947 and 1949, when Marlon Brando left the original production of Tennessee Williams's play *A Streetcar Named Desire* on Broadway, Quinn, who had played the role both during Brando's vacation and on tour, replaced him as the animalistic Stanley Kowalski, bringing his own charisma to the role.

Then, at age 36, he finally got his big film break, playing a Mexican bandit and brother of revolutionary Emilio Zapata in *Viva Zapata!* (1952), directed by Elia Kazan. Zapata was played brilliantly by Marlon Brando, but it was Quinn, the venal brother, who walked off with an Academy Award for Best Supporting Actor.

Quinn, now a star, went from one screen triumph to another. He was memorable as the brutal circus strongman Zampano in the classic Italian film *La Strada* (1954), directed by Federico Fellini. Fellini said that Quinn filled up the screen like a panorama.

He was painter Paul Gaugin in *Lust for Life* (1956), opposite Kirk Douglas as painter Vincent van Gogh. The role earned Quinn a second Best Supporting Actor Oscar. Quinn was nominated as Best Actor in 1957's Oscar race for *Wild Is the Wind* but did not win. He was the American screen's third Quasimodo in a new adaptation of Victor Hugo's classic novel *The Hunchback of Notre Dame* (1957) and played an Eskimo in *The Savage Innocents* (1959). He directed *The Buccaneer* (1958), a remake of a film his father-in-law first directed, but it was not successful, and he never directed another picture.

Quinn continued to play solid roles through the early 1960s, most notably as the washed-up but honorable prizefighter in *Requiem for a Heavyweight* (1962) and the Greek peasant with an insatiable love of life in *Zorba the Greek* (1964). Nominated for a Best Actor Oscar for *Zorba,* again Quinn did not win, but Zorba proved to be a career-defining role for him and the one for which he is best remembered. He reprised the part 25 years later in a play adaptation that he helped produce on Broadway.

As Quinn grew older, he was less discriminating in his choice of roles and was often undisciplined in his acting, yet he worked constantly, and the power of his personality shone through even in the worst of pictures. He was a frequent guest on television and even starred in a short-lived dramatic series *The Man and the City* (1971–72), in which he played the mayor of a southwestern city.

Unlike many of the earthy characters he portrayed, Quinn was a thoughtful and sensitive man who was a serious sculptor and painter and wrote two well-regarded autobiographies. He also, like Zorba, had a lust for life. He was married three times and fathered 13 children. His third wife, whom he married at age 82, had been his secretary. Anthony Quinn was still a star when he died of throat cancer in Bristol, Massachusetts, on June 3, 2001, at age 86. Five of his 13 children, including Danny Quinn, are actors.

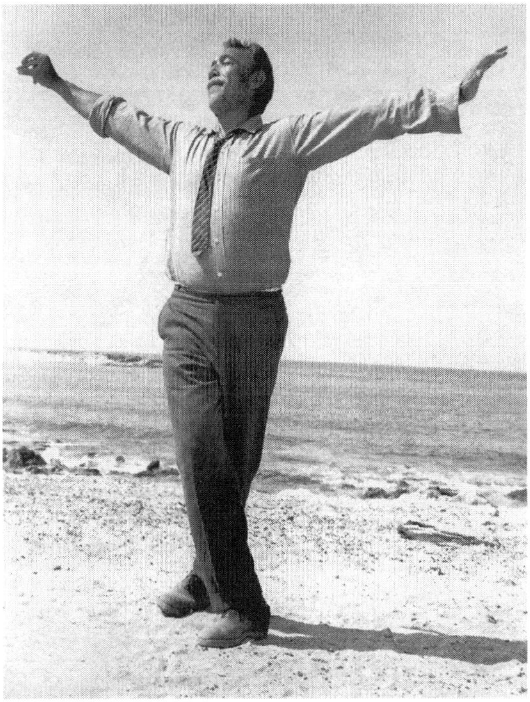

Of his many film performances, Anthony Quinn is still best known as the life-loving *Zorba the Greek,* seen here in his memorable dance on a beach. *(Photofest)*

Further Reading

Amdur, Melissa. *Anthony Quinn* (Hispanics of Achievement). New York: Chelsea House, 1993.

Katz, Ephraim, Fred Klein, and Ronald Dean Nolen. *The Film Encyclopedia.* 4th edition. New York: HarperResource, 2001, pp. 1,118–1,119.

Kuspit, Donald, Jay Parini, and Tom Roberts. *Anthony Quinn's Eye: A Lifetime of Creating and Collecting Art.* New York: W. W. Norton, 2004.

Marill, Alvin H. *The Films of Anthony Quinn.* New York: Lyle Stuart, 1975.

Quinn, Anthony. *The Original Sin: A Self-Portrait.* Boston: Little, Brown, 1972.

Quinn, Anthony, and Daniel Paisner. *One Man Tango.* New York: HarperCollins, 1995.

Further Viewing

La Strada (1954). Homevision./Criterion, VHS/DVD, 2000/2003.

Lust for Life (1956). Warner Home Video, VHS/DVD, 1998/2006.

Requiem for a Heavyweight (1962). Sony Home Video, VHS/DVD, 1958/2002.

Zorba the Greek (1964). Fox Home Video, VHS/DVD, 1985/2004.

Quintero, José (José Benjamin Quintero)

(1924–1999) *theater director, producer*

One of the founding fathers of the modern Off-Broadway theater movement, José Quintero was also the definitive interpreter of the works of one of America's greatest playwrights, Eugene O'Neill. Born in Panama City, Panama, on October 15, 1924, José Benjamin Quintero's father, a Spanish immigrant, was a successful cattleman and brewer. José attended Catholic high school, where he considered entering the priesthood. That changed when he saw a Bette Davis film and decided that he wanted to be an actor. He persuaded his father to send him to the United States, where he entered Los Angeles (LA) City College in California. Only an average student, Quintero spent most of his free time watching movies. He saw his first play, the family comedy *Life with Father,* in LA. "I didn't understand a word of English except God," he later wrote. "I was intensely religious at the time, and the slangy use of the word depressed me."

He later transferred to the University of Southern California (USC) and earned a bachelor of arts (B.A.) degree in 1948. He continued his studies at the Goodman Theater Dramatic School in Chicago, where he met the young actress Geraldine Page, one of several stage actors in whose careers he would play a crucial role. In summer 1949, a group of Goodman drama students, including Quintero, traveled to Woodstock, New York, to set up a summer theater. While working on a stage adaptation of *Alice in Wonderland,* Quintero discovered that he loved directing more than acting. When the summer ended, the group moved to New York City, where they established themselves as the Loft Players.

Out of this theater group evolved The Circle in the Square, a theater that found a home in the abandoned Greenwich Village Inn in 1951. Quintero became the theater's resident director, directing 17 of its first 21 productions. The theater specialized in revivals of plays that had failed initially on Broadway. Quintero's first great success was a revival of Tennessee Williams's *Summer and Smoke* with Geraldine Page in the leading role. It made her a star.

In 1956, Quintero turned to the work of Eugene O'Neill, the only American playwright to have won the Nobel Prize and who had died in relative obscurity three years earlier. The sensitive, emotional director felt an immediate kinship with the brooding playwright and mounted a revival of his last produced play on Broadway, the epic *The Iceman Cometh* (1946). Set in a New York saloon, the play dealt with the importance of dreams that people pursue in life. The central figure of Hickey, a traveling salesman who attempts to get the saloon's denizens to give up their dreams and face reality, was brilliantly played by Jason Robards, Jr., who would star in several more O'Neill plays under Quintero's direction.

The Iceman Cometh was a smash that at once solidified the Off-Broadway renaissance and brought a critical reevaluation of O'Neill's reputation. Later in 1956, Quintero brought O'Neill's other masterpiece, unproduced at the time of his death, to the Broadway stage. *Long Day's Journey Into Night* was a largely autobiographical family drama in which O'Neill looked unsparingly at his parents, older brother Jamie (played by Robards), and himself.

During the next three decades, Quintero directed nearly a dozen more O'Neill works, including the posthumously published *A Moon for the Misbegotten* (1972) that continued the sad story of O'Neill's brother Jamie, again played by Robards. It earned Quintero his only Tony Award for Best Direction. (He was nominated three other times.)

Not everything Quintero touched turned to gold. Among his more disappointing failures was the production of Tennessee Williams's last play, *Clothes for a Summer House* (1980). After the play closed, Quintero left New York and moved to Sarasota, Florida, although he continued to direct plays in New York.

He also directed occasionally for television, including an Emmy-winning adaptation of the Broadway production of *A Moon for the Misbegotten* in 1975. His only major movie credit, *The Roman Spring of Mrs. Stone* (1961), starred Vivien Leigh as a middle-aged woman and a very young Warren Beatty as her Italian lover.

In 1987, Quintero, who had been diagnosed with throat cancer, had his larynx removed and lost his voice for a year. He continued to direct, using a mechanical voice box. His last two Broadway productions were triumphant revivals of *The Iceman Cometh,* with Robards reprising the Hickey role, and *Long Day's Journey into Night* (1988); this last production earned Quintero his fourth and last Tony nomination.

José Quintero died of cancer in a New York hospital on February 26, 1999. A gifted director who always served the playwright's words and the actor's art, he once said, "Part of my soul belongs to O'Neill."

Further Reading

Quintero, José. *If You Don't Dance, They Beat You.* Boston: Little, Brown, 1974. Reprint, New York: St. Martin's Press, 1988.

Rothstein, Mervyn, and Richard Servo. "José Quintero, Director Who Exalted O'Neill, Dies at 74." [Obituary]. *New York Times,* February 27, 1999, p. A12.

Further Viewing

A Moon for the Misbegotten (Broadway Theatre Archives). Image Entertainment, DVD, 2002.

R

Renaldo, Duncan
(Renault Renaldo Duncan)
(ca. 1904–1980) *actor, producer*

Out of the biggest stars of early television, Duncan Renaldo thrilled a generation of young viewers as the first and most popular Latino TV cowboy, the Cisco Kid. Born Renault Renaldo Duncan, his date of birth and birthplace remain something of a mystery. A foundling who never knew his parents, Renaldo claimed to be born in Spain on April 23, 1904. Some sources doubt this and say he was born in Romania or elsewhere. Whatever his background, Renaldo arrived in the United States as a stoker on a Brazilian coal ship in the early 1920s. When his 90-day seaman's permit ran out, he stayed on, making a precarious living as a portrait painter.

Renaldo got his start in Hollywood as a producer of short features and, in 1928, was signed as a contract player by Metro–Goldwyn–Mayer (MGM). He was cast as a Latin lover in several films, but his most famous early role was as the young sidekick to an African explorer in the early sound classic *Trader Horn* (1931), the first feature film to be shot almost entirely on location in Africa.

In 1932, Renaldo's film career came to an abrupt halt when he was arrested as an illegal immigrant and was sentenced to 90 days in jail. He was later pardoned and released. Returning to movies, he appeared in dozens of inexpensive action films and serials, adventure movies for children that had been made in a string of episodes to be shown weekly in theaters. Each episode ended in a desperate situation for the hero that brought viewers back the next week to find out what happened.

Renaldo's big break came in 1945 when he was cast as the Cisco Kid in several Western films. Cisco was a good-natured Mexican bandit, loosely based on the protagonist in an O. Henry story, "The Caballero's Way." CESAR ROMERO and GILBERT ROLAND had previously played the Cisco Kid in Westerns. Romero's Cisco was a bit of a dandy, and Roland's was roguish and rough. Renaldo turned Cisco into a clean-cut gentleman who was known for his good deeds. When pioneering television syndicator Frederic Ziv decided to bring the Cisco Kid to the small screen, Renaldo won the part.

One of the first Western series on television, *The Cisco Kid* ran in syndication from 1950 to 1956. It was also one of the first filmed series to be shot in both black-and-white and color, although few viewers at the time had color sets. Renaldo, wearing his black outfit and a big sombrero, astride his horse Diablo, was a dashing hero to both young Anglo and Latino viewers. The star had his vain side and stipulated in his contract that he would never be required to take off his sombrero on the show; this way, he would hide his receding hairline. LEO CARRILLO provided the comic relief as Cisco's sidekick Pancho.

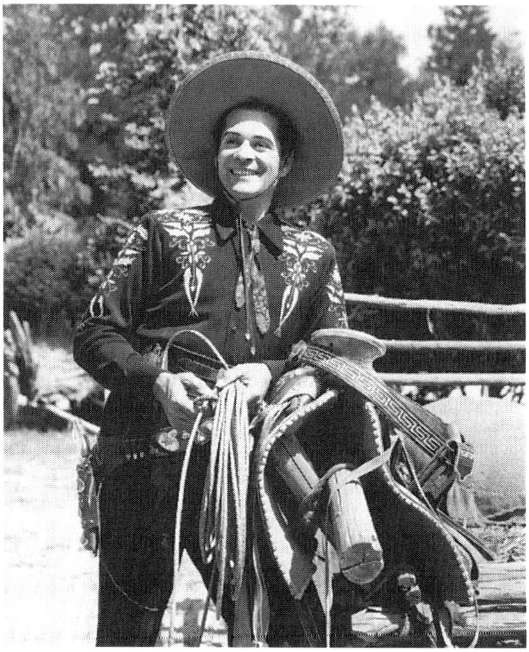

Duncan Renaldo will forever be remembered as the king of Latino cowboys, the Cisco Kid. The series was one of television's first Westerns and the first filmed series to be shot in color. *(Photofest)*

Renaldo retired when the series ended, although *The Cisco Kid* was broadcast in reruns for years, thanks to the fact that it was filmed in color. In 1980, the actor received a Special Lifetime Achievement Award from the Latino film organization Nosotros for "providing a positive Hispanic role model for Americans." Renaldo died the same year on September 3 of lung cancer in Goleta, California.

Further Reading

Erickson, Hal. *Syndicated Television: The First Forty Years 1947–1987.* Jefferson, N.C.: McFarland & Company, 2001, pp. 93–94.

The Internet Movie Database. "Duncan Renaldo," The Internet Movie Database. Available online. URL: http://www.imdb.com/name/nm0719121/. Downloaded on February 26, 2005.

Katz, Ephraim, Fred Klein, and Ronald Dean Nolen. *The Film Encyclopedia.* 4th edition. New York: HarperResource, 2001, p. 1,145.

Further Viewing

The Cisco Kid—Collection 1 (1951–1956). Mpi Media Group, DVD box set, 2004.

Trader Horn (1931). MGM Home Entertainment, VHS/DVD, 1994.

Rivera, Chita (Dolores Conchita Figueroa del Rivero)

(1933–) *actress, dancer, singer*

One of the premier performers of the Broadway musical stage, Chita Rivera's dazzling career spans five decades of hit shows. Dolores Conchita Figueroa del Rivero was born in Washington, D.C., on January 23, 1933. Her father, Pedro del Rivero, was a Puerto Rican American who played clarinet and saxophone in the U.S. Navy Band and died when she was seven. Her mother Katherine Figueroa was of mostly Scottish heritage and worked in the Pentagon. At age 11, Dolores began ballet lessons. She was one of two students from the ballet school who was chosen to audition for the American School of Ballet in New York City. She was accepted and given a scholarship to attend.

After graduating from Taft High School in the Bronx, New York, Dolores accompanied a friend to a Broadway audition for the Irving Berlin musical *Call Me Madam* (1952). She ended up auditioning herself and won a part in the chorus, appearing under the name Conchita Del Rivero. The following year, she became the first Latina to be a principal dancer in a Broadway musical, the classic show *Guys and Dolls.* She performed as a featured performer under the name Chita Rivera for the first time in the musical *Seventh Heaven* (1955), which lasted on Broadway for little more than a month. Two more featured roles in musicals followed before Rivera got her big break, playing the fiery Anita, a Puerto Rican girl whose boyfriend is a gang leader, in the hit musical *West Side Story* (1957). This modern retelling of the Shakespeare play *Romeo and Juliet* was set among the youth gangs of New York City and made Rivera a star. During the production, she met Tony Mordente, a dancer in the show. They married in December 1957 and had a daughter, Lisa Mordente, the following year. The couple has since divorced.

Rivera went on to star in another hit musical, *Bye Bye Birdie* (1960). She played Rose, the long-suffering secretary and fiancée of the manager of a rock star. The role earned her the first of eight Tony nominations for Best Featured Female in a Musical.

Rivera was now appearing regularly on television variety shows, the first Latino stage dancer to do so. Her film career, however, never got off the ground. She lost the role of Anita in the film version of *West Side Story* (1961) to another talented Puerto Rican–American actress, RITA MORENO. She was also passed over for the film adaptation of *Bye Bye Birdie* (1963). Her first film role was as the second female lead in the film version of the musical *Sweet Charity* (1969). She had recurring roles on the sitcom *The New Dick Van Dyke Show* in 1973 and the long-running soap opera *One Life to Live* in 1982. Van Dyke was her costar in *Bye Bye Birdie.*

Rivera remained a star on Broadway, however, appearing next in the short-lived musical *Bajour* (1964). She toured in *Sweet Charity* and played the part of Jenny in an Off-Broadway revival of the Kurt Weill musical *The Threepenny Opera.* Except for a one-night musical benefit, however, she was not seen on Broadway again for eight years.

In 1975, Rivera made her triumphant Broadway return in the John Kander-Fred Ebb musical *Chicago.* She played torch-singer and man-killer Velma Kelly, appearing opposite her friend and fellow dancer Gwen Verdon. The role earned her a second Tony nomination for Best Actress in a Musical. When the musical was made into a hit film in 2003, Rivera had a small role in it.

The traditional Broadway musical in which Rivera specialized fell on hard times in the 1980s. She reprised the role of Rose in *Bring Back Birdie* (1981), an ill-conceived sequel to *Bye Bye Birdie* that closed after two performances. She then brought some star luster to the disappointing magical musical *Merlin* (1983). The following year, Rivera reunited with Kander and Ebb in *The Rink* (1984). Although it was not the team's best work, Rivera was in top form and finally earned her first Tony for Best Actress in a Musical.

At age 60, when many musical performers are looking to retirement, Rivera came back to Broadway as the mysterious title character of *Kiss of the Spider Woman* (1993), a musical set in a Latin-American prison and based on a novel by Manual Puig. The role earned her a second Tony. Eight years later, she confirmed her status as a Broadway legend when she starred in a revival of the musical *Nine* (2003), collecting her eighth Tony nomination.

Chita Rivera became the first Latina American to be a recipient of the Kennedy Center Honors in the performing arts in 2002 and won the Astaire Award for Lifetime Achievement in 2003. In December 2005, the ever-youthful performer opened on Broadway in *Chita Rivera: The Dancer's Life,* a show that charts the highs and lows of her career through five decades.

Further Reading

Gold, Sylviane. "On Broadway What Becomes a Legend Most? Chita Rivera's New Show Revisits Her Struggles and Triumphs." *Dance Magazine,* December 1, 2005, pp. 108–109.

The Internet Broadway Database. "Chita Rivera," The Internet Broadway Database Web Site. Available online. URL: http://www.ibdb.com/persn, asp?ID=57887. Downloaded on September 1, 2005.

The Internet Movie Database. "Chita Rivera," The Internet Movie Database. Available online. URL: http://www.imdb.com/name/nm0729234. Downloaded on January 17, 2005.

Further Listening

Bye Bye Birdie (1960). Sony, CD, 2000.
Chicago (1975). Arista, CD, 1996.
West Side Story (1957). Sony, CD, 1998.

Further Viewing

Broadway's Lost Treasures. Acorn Media, DVD, 2003.

Rodriguez, Adam

(1975–) *actor*

A veteran of three failed television series, Adam Rodriguez finally found success as one of the stars of the hit Columbia Broadcasting System (CBS) crime series, *CSI: Miami.* He was born in New York City on April 2, 1975, into a family of Puerto Rican and Cuban heritage. He grew up in suburban New City, where he played baseball in high school. His dream of playing pro ball ended when he suffered a serious vertebra injury. With no clear direction for the future, he entered community college, where he acted in plays, including a part in a professional production at the Papermill Playhouse in New Jersey.

At age 19, Rodriguez began to train to become a stockbroker, but before he took the licensing exam, he decided that acting was what he really wanted to do. He took more acting classes and worked at different times as a bellman and a construction worker to pay the bills.

In 1996, his father was watching the Emmy Awards on television when he recognized an old military pal who had become a police officer and was now a producer for the hit show *NYPD Blue* (1993–2005). Rodriguez's father got in touch with his old friend, and this led to Adam being cast in a bit part on an *NYPD Blue* episode. Executive producer Steven Bochco liked Rodriguez and cast him in a leading role in his new cop show *Brooklyn South.* Unfortunately, the show quickly folded, and Rodriguez took a role in *Roswell* (1999–2002), a sci-fi series about aliens living in Roswell, New Mexico. He played an attorney whose girlfriend, unbeknownst to him, is an alien. *Roswell* quickly gained a cult following, but it was not enough to save it from cancellation after two seasons. Rodriguez next played a wheelchair-bound medical examiner in the short-lived medical mystery-horror series *All Souls* (2001).

He auditioned for *CSI: Miami,* a spin-off of the successful *CSI: Crime Scene Investigation,* without having watched the original. Rodriguez landed the part of underwater-crime recovery specialist Eric Delko, part of the CSI team headed by Horatio Caine, played by David Caruso who was one of the original stars of *NYPD Blue.* With its exciting Miami locales, twisty plots, and often graphic violence, *CSI: Miami* became the breakout new hit show of the 2002–03 television season.

"Innately, everybody has a morbid curiosity," Rodriguez said in a 2005 interview, explaining the show's success. "And beyond that, it's the same thing that's made Sherlock Holmes popular—people tune in to solve the mystery every week. Maritally single, he divides his time between Los Angeles (LA), where most of *CSI: Miami* is actually shot, and Puerto Rico, where he owns a condominium.

Further Reading

Hatty, Michele. "Meet Exhibit A: Adam Rodriguez." *USA Weekend,* February 11–13, 2005, p. 12

The Internet Movie Database. "Adam Rodriguez," The Internet Movie Database. Available online. URL: http://www.imdb.com/name/nm0735226/. Downloaded on March 27, 2006.

Laezman, Rick. "Adam Rodriguez on Success and Girlfriends from Outer Space . . ." *Latino Leaders,* December 2001. LookSmart Available online. URL: http://www.findarticles.com/p/articles/mi_mOPCH/is_6_2/ai_113053335. Downloaded on September 21, 2006.

Further Viewing

CSI: Miami: The Complete First Season (2002). Paramount Home Video, DVD box set, 2004.

Rodriguez, Johnny
(1952–) *country singer*

The most successful Latino country singer, with a total of 45 charting hits, Johnny Rodriguez rose from a life of petty crime and poverty to the top of the music industry. He was born in Sabinal, Texas, 90 miles from the Mexican border, on December 10, 1952. The ninth of 10 children in a Mexican-Irish family, Rodriguez was exposed to a great variety of music from an early age. "My parents favored Latin music; my older brothers preferred country; my friends were into rock and roll, I loved it all," he recalled in one interview. When he was seven, his older brother gave him his first guitar.

Rodriguez was on a path to success: He was captain of the high-school football team, and he had his own band, the Spocks, named after Dr. Spock from the TV series *Star Trek.* Then his father died of cancer, and his world fell apart. He expressed his anger at his loss through criminal acts. He was arrested four times in two years and was sent to prison.

Rodriguez never lost his love of music, however, and when Texas Ranger Joachin Jackson heard him sing in jail, he introduced him to the music promoter Happy Shahan. Shahan got Rodriguez a job on his release: a singing stagecoach driver at the Alamo Village, a tourist attraction in southern Texas. There, he came to the attention of country singer Tom T. Hall, who urged him to go to Nashville, Tennessee, the center of the country-music industry. Rodriguez took his advice and arrived in Nashville in 1971 with $14 and his guitar, which he kept in a plastic bag because he could not afford a case. Hall hired him as the lead guitarist in his band. He also brought him to the Mercury Records studios where he auditioned and was immediately signed to a recording contract. Rodriguez's first single, "Pass Me By (If You're Only Passing Through)," became the first of 14 consecutive country hits. His next single, "Ridin' My Thumb to Mexico" (1973), went to #1 on the country charts and became a minor pop hit. Two more #1 country hits followed.

By 1975, Rodriguez was a major country star, with three #1 singles in a row that year. Unhappy with Mercury's handling of his career, he switched to Epic Records in 1979 and had one top-10 country hit, "Down the Rio Grande," before experiencing a three-year slump in his recording career. He made an impressive comeback in 1983 with the top-10 county hits "Foolin'" and "How Could I Love Her So Much" before his career again ebbed. Rodriguez had his last country-charting single in 1988. Aside from two albums in the early 1990s, he has been largely inactive as a recording artist.

Rodriguez, who has never married, lives in a 100-year-old log cabin on a 27-acre farm outside Nashville. He remains active in several social causes, including the Enrichment Center, an organization that raises money for disabled Texas youth.

Further Reading

Huey, Steve. "Johnny Rodriguez," Mp3.com. Available online. URL: http://www.mp3.com/johnny-rodriguez/artists/1497/biography.html?q=Johnny%20Rodriguez. Downloaded on March 27, 2006.

"Johnny Rodriguez." Great American Talent Web site. Available online. URL: http://www.gatalent.com/Acts/Johnny_Rodriguez./johnny_rodriguez.html. Downloaded on January 3, 2006.

Malone, Bill C., and Judith McCulloh. *Stars of Country Music: Uncle Dave Macon to Johnny Rodriguez.* Champaign: University of Illinois Press, 1975.

Further Listening

The Hits. Mercury Nashville, CD, 1997.

Rodriguez, Michelle
(Mayte Michelle Rodriguez)
(1978–) *actress*

One of the most promising of the new generation of Latina film actresses, Michelle Rodriguez combines sex appeal with a physical agility that has made her an action heroine in movies and on television. Mayte Michelle Rodriguez was born in Bexar County, Texas, on July 12, 1978. When she was eight, the family moved to the Dominican Republic, her father's homeland, and then relocated to Puerto Rico, her mother's homeland, two years later. When she was 11, the family returned permanently to the United States, settling in Jersey City, New Jersey.

Rodriguez's teen years were troubled, her rebellious nature intensified by her parents' divorce. She dropped out of high school (she has since received her high-school equivalency) and went to work at Toys 'R' Us. Interested in acting, she found extra work in a few films, including Spike Lee's *Summer of Sam* (1999).

After being laid off from her full-time job, Rodriguez responded to a magazine ad for auditions for a new movie about a female boxer. She tried out along with 350 other actresses and, despite her lack of acting experience, landed the part after a round of grueling auditions, including five weeks of working out in a Brooklyn gym to get in shape for the role. The movie, *Girlfight* (2000), was well received by the public and the critics. For her performance, Rodriguez won the Best Actress Award at the Deauville Festival of American Cinema and the Female Breakthrough Performer Award from the Las Vegas Film Critics.

Her film career off and running, Rodriguez next starred in the highly popular *The Fast and the Furious* (2001) about the world of street racers. Despite the fact that she was 23 at the time, she did not have a driver's license and learned to drive during filming to participate in the movie's numerous car-chase scenes. Rodriguez went on to battle zombies in *Resident Evil* (2002) and to fight gangsters who were trying to free a drug kingpin from jail in *S.W.A.T.* (2003).

In 2005, she made her television series' debut when she joined the cast of the hit show *Lost* (2004–), which is about a group of survivors of a jet crash on a remote island. While on location in Hawaii for the show in December 2005, Rodriguez was arrested for allegedly driving while under the influence. Her costar on *Lost,* Cynthia Watros, was arrested on the same road and on the same charge within 15 minutes of Rodriguez's arrest. Rodriguez was convicted and served a five-day jail sentence in April 2006. She left *Lost* after one season when her character was killed off and is working on a clothing line with friend and fashion designer Anand Jon.

On being asked why she always plays the 'tough girl' she replied: "Well, could you really imagine me playing the girlfriend that needs rescuing. Or the . . . girlfriend?"

Further Reading

Actress of the Week. "Michelle Rodriguez," AskMen.com. Available online. URL: http://www.askmen.com/women/actress_100/148_michelle_rodriguez.html. Downloaded on March 27, 2006.

The Internet Movie Database. "Michelle Rodriguez," The Internet Movie Database. Available online. ULR: http://www.imdb.com/name/nm0735442/. Downloaded on January 16, 2006.

Rodriguez, Clara E. *Heroes, Lovers, and Others: The Story of Latinos in Hollywood.* Washington, D.C.: Smithsonian Books, 2004, pp. 230–231.

Further Viewing

The Fast and the Furious (2001). MCA Home Video, VHS/DVD, 2002/2003.

Girlfight (2000). Sony Pictures, VHS/DVD, 2001.

Rodriguez, Paul (Pablo Leobardo Castro Rodriguez)

(1955–) *comedian, actor, filmmaker, producer, screenwriter*

A pioneering standup comedian who draws on Latino life for his material, Paul Rodriguez was the second Latino comic to star in his own television situation-comedy series. Pablo Leobardo Castro Rodriguez was born in Culiacan on the west coast of Mexico, on January 19, 1955. He was the youngest of five children of migrant-worker parents who immigrated to the United States when Paul was three. The family followed the crops as they were ready to harvest across California and north to Washington State. The Rodriguezes eventually settled in Boyle Heights, a neighborhood in East Los Angeles (East LA). When he passed his citizenship test, Pablo changed his name to Paul.

Rodriguez had a reputation as a class clown in high school and dropped out before graduating to join the U.S. Air Force. He served for a time in Iceland, where he monitored the movement of Soviet submarines. After serving for four years, he left the military and returned to the states. He attended Long Beach State University on the GI Bill and earned an Associate of Arts (A.A.) degree in two years. He abandoned his goal of studying law to become a comedian.

Rodriguez began to appear at comedy clubs in the LA area, most notably The Comedy Store, where he also worked as a doorman. Rodriguez's use of Latino life and culture for comedy material was something new at the time, and his popularity with Latino audiences grew. He hired a manager who set up a tour of college campuses. When his manager died suddenly, Rodriguez was so upset that he dropped out of show business for a time.

When he returned, it was as a warm-up comic for a Norman Lear sitcom, *Gloria,* a spin-off of *All in the Family.* The show quickly folded, but producer Lear liked Rodriguez's humor and decided to build a new sitcom around his life as a Latino comic. The largely autobiographical series, *a.k.a. Pablo,* debuted in 1984. The extensive cast included a number of talented Latino actors and actresses, more than had ever been seen before on one television show. They included KATY JURADO, who played Rodriguez's mother, and HECTOR ELIZONDO, who portrayed his uncle. The series lasted only six episodes before the American Broadcasting Company (ABC) canceled it.

Rodriguez returned to television in the adventure series *Grand Slam* (1990) and the sitcom *Trial and Error* (1997), neither of which lasted a season. His most successful foray into television, outside of a handful of Home Box Office (HBO) comedy specials, was *El Show de Paul Rodriguez* (1990–94), a Spanish-language talk show that appeared on Univision, the Spanish-language network. Rodriguez hosted the show, interviewed Latino celebrities, and performed in comedy sketches.

In 1994, he made his directorial debut with the film *A Million to Juan,* based on "The Million Pound Bank Note," a short story by Mark Twain, which he also coadapted and in which he starred. He continued to appear in supporting roles in other films such as *Crocodile Dundee in Los Angeles* (2001) and *Tortilla Soup* (2001), a Latino comedy/drama in which he played ELIZABETH PEÑA's comical but charming boyfriend.

Rodriguez has long been known as a committed fundraiser for numerous charities including the National Hispanic Scholarship Fund, Project Literary, and Farm Aid. His son Paul Rodriguez, Jr., is one of the world's top professional skateboarders. He won the gold medal in 2004 and 2005 at the X Games Street Skateboard Finals.

Further Reading

The Internet Movie Database. "Paul Rodriguez," The Internet Movie Database. Available online. URL: http://www.imdb.com/name/nm0735467/. Downloaded on January 16, 2006.

Morey, Janet, and Wendy Dunn. *Famous Hispanic Americans.* New York: Dutton, 1996, pp. 156–167.

Paul Rodriguez Official Web Site. Available online. URL: http://www.paulrodriguez.com/home.htm. Downloaded on March 27, 2006.

Further Viewing

Paul Rodriguez—Live in San Quentin (2004). Fox Home Video, DVD, 2005.

Tortilla Soup (2001). Sony Pictures, VHS/DVD, 2002.

Rodriguez, Robert
(Robert Anthony Rodriguez)
(1968–) *filmmaker, screenwriter, producer*

The most commercially successful Latino American filmmaker in Hollywood history, Robert Rodriguez is a modern master of the action/adventure movie and a director of wit, imagination, and boundless energy. Born in San Antonio, Texas, on June 20, 1968, into a Mexican-American family of 11 children, Rodriguez was a creative child who loved to draw cartoons and was inspired to become a filmmaker after seeing director John Carpenter's futuristic thriller *Escape from New York* (1981) when he was 12. Using his family's old Super-8 film camera, he began to make his own short movies, enlisting his brothers and sisters as his cast and crew. Exhibiting a thriftiness and resourcefulness that would serve him well in the future, Rodriguez abandoned the film camera for a video camera because videotape was less expensive than film.

His friends and neighbors began to refer to him as "the kid who makes movies." After high school, he won a scholarship to attend the University of Texas–Austin. There, he made a name for himself by inventing a popular comic strip, *Los Hooligans,* based on the antics of his siblings. It ran for three years in a local paper.

But Rodriguez was turned down repeatedly for the university's film school because of poor grades.

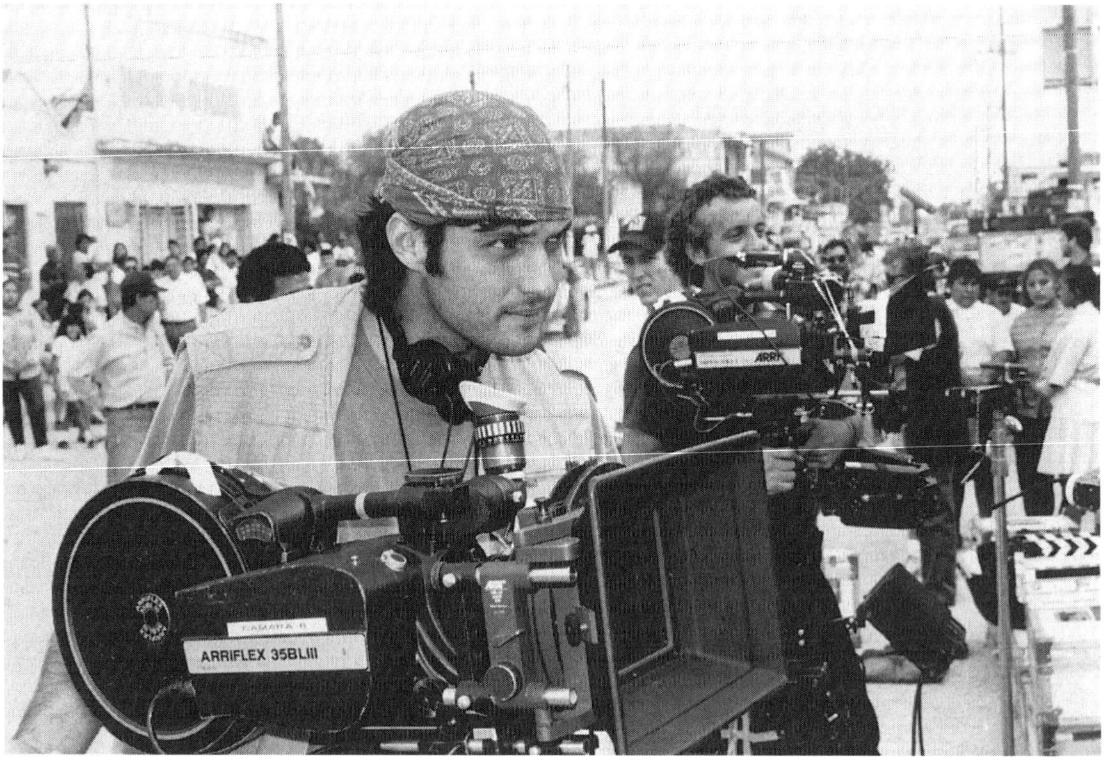

Rejected for film school because of low grades, Robert Rodriguez has gone on to become the most commercially successful of Latino filmmakers in Hollywood. *(Photofest)*

Undaunted, he continued to make student films. His most ambitious short, *Bedhead* (1991), starred one of his sisters as a girl who develops psychic powers after receiving a bump on the head. The whimsical film won several awards at film festivals, and Rodriguez's career as a director took off.

To raise money for his first feature film, he spent a month as a guinea pig in a research hospital. With the $7,000 he earned, he shot *El Mariachi* (1992), the story of a young Mexican guitar player (mariachi) who is mistaken for a dangerous killer by a gang of criminals. *El Mariachi*'s tight budget brought out all Rodriguez's resourcefulness. He shot the film working around the clock for 20 days in a Mexican border town with a cast of friends and a pickup crew that often doubled as cast. Rodriguez's commentary for the film on the DVD version is a virtual master class on how to make a good movie on a shoestring. He later wrote a book about the experience.

Rodriguez intended *El Mariachi* for the Spanish video market, but chosen for the prestigious Sundance Film Festival, it was such a hit that Columbia Pictures made him a distribution offer. A sleeper hit in release, Rodriguez's $7,000 feature ended up making more than $2 million at the box office.

He was immediately hired to direct the cable television film *Roadracers* (1994). The same year, he directed one of four episodes that made up the anthology film *Four Rooms,* produced and written by his friend and fellow rebel filmmaker Quentin Tarantino. The film proved a flop, but critics singled out Rodriguez's episode as the best part of it.

Rodriguez's next film was a sequel to *El Mariachi* entitled *Desperado* (1995), with ANTONIO BANDERAS playing the title role and introducing SALMA HAYEK as his love interest. The story more or less picks up where the first film ended, with El Mariachi, now turned gunman, seeking vengeance on the man responsible for the death of his girlfriend. Rodriguez's inspiration was the violent 1960s–70s "spaghetti Westerns" of Italian director Sergio Leone. "I wanted to try . . . it with Latin actors and Latin characters, which I hadn't ever seen growing up," he said in a 1995 interview. "And I had a feeling that if I didn't make it no one else would."

With a budget of $7 million instead of $7,000, Rodriguez filled *Desperado* with elaborately staged action sequences that were often brilliant if excessively bloody. Many viewers were left breathless, but some missed the spirited imagination behind *El Mariachi* that did more with less.

Rodriguez's next two pictures were in the horror/sci-fi genres. *From Dusk Till Dawn* (1996) was a combination vampire movie and crime thriller that starred Tarantino (who wrote the script) and television star George Clooney in his first major film role. *The Faculty* (1996) was about alien teachers in a high school; it was Rodriguez's least financially successful film to date.

The director surprised everyone with his next project—a family action/adventure movie about two youngsters who discover that their parents are former secret agents. Rodriguez says that he was inspired to make *Spy Kids* (2001) when young children were telling him how much they enjoyed his earlier films, which were intended for adults. He decided to make a film just as exciting but less violent for these young people and their parents. *Spy Kids* was such a popular and critical success that Rodriguez made two sequels during the next two years.

During this time he also filmed the final chapter of the mariachi trilogy, the epic *Once Upon a Time in Mexico* (2003). Both Banderas and Hayek repeated their roles from *Desperado,* but again the film's over-the-top violence and gore brought as much criticism as Rodriguez's skillful direction brought praise.

Rodriguez's next project would be his most challenging. A fervent fan of *Sin City,* a series of graphic novels by Frank Miller, Rodriguez persuaded the author to let him adapt the comic to the big screen. The filmmaker was so devoted to recreating the graphic novels faithfully that he made Miller codirector on the film. When the Directors Guild of America refused to allow this, Rodriguez resigned from the guild, causing him to lose the directorial assignment on the film *John Carter of Mars.*

Sin City (2005) received mixed reviews. Critics were again turned off by the excessive violence, but other viewers who knew the graphic novels were impressed by Rodriguez's loving recreation of their dark, noirish milieu. Part of this is a result of his use of digital video, which Rodriguez has used for all his films since *Spy Kids 2.*

Rodriguez sees digital video as opening up a new creative era for filmmakers. "[N]ow that film's been almost fully explored it's time for a new medium and it's exciting that it hasn't been defined enough yet for people to really know its full potential," he has said. "So to be in on that from the ground floor is just a real privilege."

Further Reading

Miller, Frank, and Robert Rodriguez. *Frank Miller's Sin City: The Making of the Movie.* TroubleMaker Publishing, 2005.

"Robert Rodriguez," God Among Directors Web Site. Available online. URL: http://www.godamongdirectors.com/rodriguez/index.shtml. Downloaded on January 23, 2006.

Rodriguez, Robert. *Rebel Without a Crew: Or How a 23-Year-Old Filmmaker with $7,000 Became a Hollywood Player.* New York: Plume Books, 1996.

Further Viewing

Frank Miller's Sin City. Buena Vista Home Video/Dimension, VHS/DVD, 2005.

Robert Rodriguez's Mexico Trilogy (El Mariachi, Desperado, Once Upon a Time in Mexico) (2003), Sony Pictures, DVD box set, 2005.

Spy Kids. Dimension/Walt Disney Home Video, VHS/DVD, 2001.

Rodríguez, Santiago

(1954–) *classical pianist, educator*

One of the first Latino American classical musicians to reach prominence, Santiago Rodríguez has been celebrated for the technical proficiency and deep feeling of his piano playing. He was born in Cárdenas, Cuba, in 1954. He began to study the piano when he was four. When Fidel Castro came to power, his parents sent Santiago and a younger brother to the United States, where they lived in an orphanage in New Orleans, Louisiana. The young musician continued his piano lessons there and, at age 10, made his public debut in a concert with the New Orleans Philharmonic. He attended the University of Texas–Austin, where he received his bachelor of arts (B.A.) degree. He then earned his master of music (M.M.) degree from the Juilliard School of Music in New York City.

Rodríguez first came to public attention when he was named the silver medallist at the Van Cliburn International Piano Competition in Fort Worth, Texas, in 1981. He was soon giving recitals at Lincoln Center's Avery Fisher and Alice Tully Halls and performed at the world-renowned Ravenna Festival in Italy.

Rodríguez's tempestuous style drew him to the works of the great Russian romantic composer Sergei Rachmaninov (Rachmaninoff). His recordings and live performances of Rachmaninov's extensive works for the piano have led him to be called one of the foremost interpreters of that composer's work. When completed, his *Rachmaninov Edition* recordings will include all the composer's work for the piano. The *American Record Guide* has praised his recordings of Rachmaninov and others for their "blazing conviction, tremendous technical strength, unswerving concentration and galvanic excitement."

Rodríguez is the recipient of the Avery Fisher Career Grant and the Shura Cheravsky Recital Award. He was recently awarded the 2005 Ignacio Cervantes Lifetime Achievement Award for

Piano. He is currently professor of piano and artist-in-residence at the University of Maryland's School of Music in College Park, Maryland. Rodríguez has played as a soloist with such leading ensembles as the Chicago Symphony, the Tokyo Symphony, and the London Symphony Orchestras.

Further Reading

Faculty Biography. "Santiago Rodríguez." University of Maryland School of Music Web Site. Available online. URL: http://www.music.unmd/edu/bios/santiagorodridguez.html. Downloaded on January 3, 2006.

Pegolotti, James. "Santiago Rodríguez Biography." The Danbury Times Web Site. Available online. URL: http://www.danbury.org/concert/rodprog.htm. Downloaded on January 4, 2006.

Further Listening

Piano in Hollywood: The Classic Movie Concertos. Elan Records, CD, 1996.

Santiago Rodríguez Performs Rachmaninov. Elan Records, CD, 2000.

Rodríguez-Díaz, Angel
(Angel Luis Rodríguez-Díaz)
(1955–) *painter, muralist*

The master of a style of painting, which he calls "modern baroque," Angel Rodríguez-Díaz combines superrealism and the surreal in his work, creating some of the most haunting images in contemporary American art. Born in San Juan, Puerto Rico, on December 6, 1955, Angel Luis Rodríguez-Díaz later moved to San Antonio, Texas, where he continues to live and work today. Rodríguez-Díaz's presence as a Puerto Rican in a state dominated by Mexican Americans, has given him a unique perspective on Latinos and himself. It may account for the theme of identity, both lost and found, that runs through much of his work.

In his series of *luchadores* (traditional masked Mexican wrestlers), the wrestlers are shown in strange settings, posed in front of mirrors and stage curtains. They are dramatic but are never shown fighting. "Ultimately, these paintings all comment on the politics of identity (and the identity in politics)," wrote art critic Tephanie Yanique in one review.

Identity is further questioned in some of Rodríguez-Díaz's more surreal portraits. In one, two arms rise up before a portrait of a Latino man. The palms, facing the viewer, contain staring eyes. In another painting, a masked giant seizes in his hand an attacking Superman and chides the superhero with these words in a cartoon dialogue bubble: "But the way to mastery lies not in simple brute strength."

Among Rodríguez-Díaz's most celebrated portraits is that of a real person—Chicana poet and novelist Sandra Cisneros, who is a fellow San Antonian. Proud and defiant, Cisneros stands between a blood-red sky wearing a black, sequined Mexican dress. Entitled "The Protagonist of an Endless Story" (1993), this powerful painting casts Cisneros as the main character in one of her stories. The portrait is part of the collection of the Smithsonian American Art Museum (SAAM) in Washington, D.C.

Rodríguez-Díaz also has created murals. His *Birth of a City* mural in the newly constructed Development and Business Services Center in San Antonio is composed of 13 canvases that are mounted on acoustic panels; it depicts a nighttime portrait of the city that is made out of a collage of photographs that are spliced together and painted over by the artist. He enhanced the final mural with computer design and programming. In 2004, Rodríguez-Díaz painted a mural for the lobby of the San Antonio City Hall. The same year, he won a competition to produce the first image featuring women for San Antonio's Catholic Cathedral.

One of his most recent works is a self-portrait included in the exhibition *Retratos: 2,000 Years of Latin American Portraiture* (2006) at the San

Antonio Museum of Art. The painting shows the artist only partially reflected in a hand mirror that is lying on a tabletop. Like so many of Rodríguez-Díaz's provocative paintings, it is, according to a review in the *San Antonio Express–News,* "pushing beyond the limits of mere representation."

Further Reading

"One Stop for River City: Angel Rodríguez-Díaz." *City of San Antonio Design Enhancements* (quarterly newsletter), September–November 2002, pp. 1–2.

Yanique, Tephanie. "Re-representations: Angel Rodríguez-Díaz," GlassTire: Texas Visual Arts Online. Available online. URL: http://glasstire.com/ReviewsDetail.asp?id=160. Downloaded on January 30, 2006.

Yorba, Jonathan. *Arte Latino: Treasures from the Smithsonian American Art Museum.* New York: Watson–Guptill Publications. 2001, pp. 82–83.

Roland, Gilbert
(Luis Antonio Damaso de Alonso)
(1905–1994) *actor*

Ruggedly handsome and athletic, Gilbert Roland brought a swashbuckling excitement to the role of Latin lover that he often played in his long film career. Luis Antonio Damaso de Alonso was born in Chihuahua, Mexico, on December 11, 1905. His father, who was born in Spain, was a professional bullfighter, and as a child, Luis worked in the bullring. During the Mexican Revolution (1910–20), the family moved to El Paso, Texas, where Luis played hooky from school to go to the movies and see his favorite actors. At age 14, he left home, hitched a ride on a freight train and arrived in Los Angeles (LA), California, determined to become a movie actor.

He soon found work as an extra, a person who appeared in crowd scenes in silent films. During a break in shooting, he crossed a set to fetch a glass of water for a fellow extra when an agent spotted him in costume and was impressed by his looks. Before he knew it, Alonso was signed to a contract and was playing the love interest of star Clara Bow in *The Plastic Age* (1925). He came up with his screen name by combining the last names of his favorite stars—John Gilbert and Ruth Roland. Like Gilbert, Roland became a screen idol, making love to such beautiful leading ladies as Norma Talmadge (*Camille,* 1926), Mary Astor (*Rose of the Golden West,* 1928), and Mae West (*She Done Him Wrong,* 1932). His off-screen affair with Talmadge wrecked her marriage to a studio executive.

Unlike some Latino actors and actresses, Roland made a smooth transition to sound films with his manly voice and fluent English. While he accepted Latino parts, he insisted on script changes if the character that he was playing was a stereotype of a Mexican American.

Roland served in the U.S. Army during World War II (1939–45) and returned to the screen to portray the Western hero the Cisco Kid in a string of B movies. For the most part, however, Roland was relegated to supporting roles in postwar movies, gaining critical praise for playing a Cuban revolutionary in *We Were Strangers* (1949) and a playboy movie star in *The Bad and the Beautiful* (1952), one of the best movies ever made about the inner workings of Hollywood.

Retaining his good looks and virile physique, Roland continued to appear in films well into his seventies. His last movie was the Western *Barbarosa* in 1982.

Gilbert Roland was married for several years to actress Constance Bennett. He married Guillermina Contu in 1954, and the marriage lasted until his death from prostate cancer in 1994. He was 88 years old.

Further Reading

The Internet Movie Database. "Gilbert Roland," The Internet Movie Database. Available online. URL: http://www.imdb.com/name/nm0738042/. Downloaded on March 24, 2006.

Rodriguez, Clara E. *Heroes, Lovers, and Others: The Story of Latinos in Hollywood.* Washington, D.C.: Smithsonian Books, 2004, pp. 88–91.

Wikipedia. "Gilbert Roland," Wikipedia, the Free Online Encyclopedia. Available online. URL: http://en.wikipedia.org/wiki/Gilbert_Roland. Downloaded on November 29, 2005.

Further Viewing

The Bad and the Beautiful (1952). MGM Home Entertainment/Turner Home Entertainment, VHS/DVD, 1999/2002.

We Were Strangers (1949). Sony Home Video, DVD, 2005.

Roman, Phil

(1930–) *animator, filmmaker, producer*

One of the most successful animators and producers in the history of television animation, with six Emmys to his credit, Phil Roman's 50-year career stretches from Disney cartoons to *The Simpsons.* He was born in Fresno, California, on December 21, 1930, to Mexican immigrants who worked as grape pickers. When he was 11, Roman's mother took him to see Walt Disney's *Bambi* (1942). The experience was so overwhelming that he decided then and there to become an animator. In high school, he took correspondent art courses through the mail. One of them was taught by *Peanuts'* cartoonist Charles Schultz, who years later would become his collaborator.

After graduation, Roman took the money that he had saved by working at a local movie house and boarded a bus to Los Angeles (LA). Once there, he enrolled in the Hollywood Art Center School, where he was accepted on a working scholarship. When the Korean War broke out in 1950, Roman left school, joined the U.S. Air Force, and served three years as a radio mechanic, mostly in France. On his discharge, he returned to the art school and finished his studies. In 1955, he fulfilled a childhood dream and was hired as an assistant animator at the Disney Studios for 99 cents an hour. His first assignment was animating the cells for the feature *Sleeping Beauty* (1959).

Realizing that it would take him 10 years to be promoted to a full animator at Disney, Roman left after two years and was hired by Imagination, Inc. in San Francisco. This animation studio made mostly television commercials. One of Roman's assignments was directing commercials starring Star-Kist Tuna's Charley Tuna. At Imagination, Roman learned the animation business from the ground up. After two years, he returned to Hollywood and during the next several years worked in the animation departments of Warner Bros. and Metro-Goldwyn-Mayer (MGM), as well as the independent and innovative animation studio United Productions of America (UPA). While at MGM, he worked with master animator Chuck Jones on the Oscar-winning animated short *The Dot and the Line* (1965). The following year, he animated the mean-spirited Grinch in Jones's television adaptation of Dr. Seuss's classic children's story *How the Grinch Stole Christmas.*

In 1970, Roman began a 13-year association with Bill Melendez Productions. During that period, he moved up from animator to codirector and then director of 16 animated *Peanuts* television specials beginning in 1973 with *A Charlie Brown Thanksgiving.* He won Emmy Awards for two of them.

With about 30 years of experience in animation, Roman was ready to start his own production company. In 1984, he founded Film Roman, Inc. While still working with Melendez, he directed two television specials based on the popular comic-strip cat Garfield. On his own he directed seven more Garfield specials, four of which won Emmys.

In 1992, Film Roman began to produce what has since become the longest-running animated series and sitcom in television history, Fox Television's *The Simpsons* (1989–). The company was becoming one of the giants in the industry, producing such animated series as *The Mask* (1995–97) and *The Critic* (1994–95), a short-lived but memorable show about the trials and travails of a television movie critic. Then Roman helped to create an entirely different kind of animated series for Fox. *King of the Hill* (1997–) was about a Texas propane salesman and his family. Unlike *The Simpsons, King of the Hill* was drawn realistically, and the characters were far closer to real people, although the show could be just as irreverent and funny as any other adult animated series.

Film Roman fell on hard financial times in the late 1990s, and Roman resigned as chairman of the board, although he remained the company's largest shareholder. He created a new company, Phil Roman Entertainment, that he used to champion the continued use of cell animation, despite a growing trend in the industry toward computer-generated animation. In 2000, he brought to life the Christmas novelty song *Grandma Got Run Over by a Reindeer* as an animated television movie. In 2002, his two companies joined together to produce both computer and cell animation.

Phil Roman was the subject of a 2005 documentary *An Animated Life: The Phil Roman Story* that was directed by Kenny and Kyle Saylors.

Further Reading

Gettleman, Jeffrey. "Animator Roman Going Head to Head with His Own Name." *Los Angeles Times,* April 16, 1999, p. 6.

Hispanic Heritage. "Phil Roman," Gale Biographies. Available online. URL: http://www.gale.com/free_resources/chh/bio/roman_p.htm. Downloaded on January 24, 2006.

The Internet Movie Database. "Phil Roman," The Internet Movie Database. Available online. URL: http://www.imdb.com/name/nm0738736/. Downloaded on January 25, 2006.

Phil Roman Entertainment Web Site. Available online. URL: http://www.philromanent.com. Downloaded on March 27, 2006.

Further Viewing

The Critic: The Complete Series (1994). Sony Pictures, DVD box set, 1994.

Garfield: Holiday Celebrations (1985). Fox Home Entertainment, DVD, 2004.

It's the Easter Beagle, Charlie Brown (1974). Paramount Home Video, VHS/DVD, 1995/2003.

The Simpsons: The Complete Fifth Season (1993). Fox Home Entertainment, DVD box set, 2004.

Romero, César
(César Julio Romero, Jr.)
(1907–1994) *actor, dancer*

A handsome, debonair leading man and supporting player in a movie career that spanned six decades, César Romero found his greatest success playing a green-haired, white-faced supervillain on television. César Julio Romero, Jr., was born in New York City on February 15, 1907. His parents were wealthy transplanted Cubans who ran a sugar-import business. He proudly claimed that famed Cuban liberator and poet José Martí was his ancestor, although he may only have been a family friend and not blood related.

Starting out as a professional ballroom dancer, Romero made his Broadway stage debut in 1927 and six years later began his long film career in Hollywood. He supported with his earnings his large family, whose sugar business had been lost during the depression.

Romero made love to Marlene Dietrich in *The Devil Is a Woman* (1935), befriended child star Shirley Temple in *Wee Willie Winkle* (1937), and danced with Betty Grable in *Springtime in the Rockies* (1942). Probably his best dramatic role was the swaggering Spanish conquistador Hernán Cortés in the historical epic *Captain from Castile* (1948). As good film roles became rarer for the aging actor in the 1950s, he turned to television, where he starred as a government agent in the espionage series *Passport to Danger* (1954).

But Romero's most memorable role was as the villainous Joker in the campy *Batman* series (1966–68). Surprised to be offered the part, Romero made the most of it, making the giggling Joker the most outrageous of the gallery of outrageous villains who appeared on the hit series. He did, however, refuse to shave his trademark moustache, and it could be seen under the Joker's white face makeup.

After many of his contemporaries had retired, Romero continued to work in films and television into his eighties. At 78, he played Peter Stavros, a Greek billionaire and Jane Wyman's love interest, on the prime-time soap opera *Falcon Crest.*

Romero never married and lived with his sister until her death. A homosexual, he suffered none of the angst suffered by such gay Latino actors as ANTONIO MORENO and RAMON NOVARRO. He lived the gay life quite openly, if discreetly, and was accepted by his peers, although the public knew nothing of his sexual preference.

Romero was a Hollywood social fixture and one of the most beloved members of the acting community until his death from bronchitis and pneumonia at age 87 on January 1, 1994.

Further Reading

Hadleigh, Boze. *Hollywood Gays: Conversations with Cary Grant, Liberace, Tony Perkins, Paul Lynde, César Romero, Brad Davis, Randolph Scott, James Coco, William Haines, Donald Lewis.* Melbourne, Australia: Barricade Books, 1996.

The Internet Movie Database. "César Romero," The Internet Movie Database. Available online. URL: http://www.imdb.com/name/nm0003110/. Downloaded on February 26, 2005.

Wikipedia. "César Romero," Wikipedia, the Free Encyclopedia. Available online. URL: http://en.wikipedia.org/wiki/Cesar_Romero. Downloaded on February 26, 2005.

Further Viewing

Batman—The Movie (1966). Fox Home Entertainment, VHS/DVD, 2001.

Captain from Castile (1948). Fox Home Entertainment, VHS, 1997.

Springtime in the Rockies (1942). Fox Home Entertainment, VHS, 1998.

Romero, Frank

(1941–) *painter, muralist, graphic designer, printmaker, museum curator*

A founder of the Chicano (Mexican-American) art movement in the 1970s with his fellow artists in Los Four, Frank Romero, in the words of one writer, "brought the barrio [poor Mexican-American neighborhoods] in the museum." He was born in Los Angeles, California, on July 11, 1941, to parents of Mexican and Spanish heritage. Interestingly, this pioneer of Chicano art spoke English at home and only learned Spanish as an adult. While still in high school, Romero earned a scholarship to the Otis Art Institute in Los Angeles. He also studied at the California State University–Los Angeles. After that, he worked as a graphic designer in the office of Charles Eames. In 1968, fellow artist and friend CARLOS ALMARAZ convinced him to come with him to New York City. The two men lived there for a year. Romero found the New York art scene, with its focus on conceptual and abstract art, to be without feeling or life. He soon returned to Los Angeles.

He arrived home at a time of great social unrest. The anti–Vietnam War movement was fusing with the fight for rights among African Americans, women, and Chicanos. Romero and Almaraz, who also returned from New York, wanted to do their part as artists in their people's struggle. In 1973, they joined with fellow artists Roberto de la Rocha and Gilbert Sánchez Luján to found Los Four, an artists' group dedicated to celebrating and publicizing Chicano culture and art. Together, they made 20 murals and public installations throughout the Los Angeles area.

While Almaraz and Luján pursued more political issues in their individual art, Romero and La

Rocha were, in Romero's words, "more concerned with art issues." Los Four focused public attention on the Chicano lifestyle in its portrayal of low-rider cars and motorcycles, festive occasions, and Chicano history.

In 1974, the Los Angeles County Museum of Art (LACMA) featured the four artists in a major exhibition. It was a historic occasion for Los Four and Chicano art. After a decade of working together, the group finally disbanded in 1983. Romero's reputation rose higher as an individual artist after a one-man show at the Arco Center for the Visual Arts in 1984. Interestingly, his work became more political from that point forward. His best-known painting, and one of his most powerful, is *The Death of Rubén Salazar* (1986). This ambitious work is a tribute to Salazar, the courageous *Los Angeles Times* reporter who had been critical of the Los Angeles police in their tactics against demonstrators. On August 29, 1970, Salazar was in the Silver Dollar Bar in Los Angeles following an anti-Vietnam demonstration. Sheriff's deputies began to fire tear gas into the bar, and a tear gas canister hit the journalist in the head, killing him. The officers involved in the killing were later exonerated but not by the Chicano community—it saw Salazar's death as a crime. Romero's boldly colored painting shows the almost robotic deputies firing into the bar while Salazar's name appears magically on a nearby movie marquee.

Romero's work is not all grimly political. *Going to the Olympics,* a 100-foot mural to honor the 1984 Los Angeles Summer Olympic Games, shows a line of his typically cartoonish cars cruising down the freeway. Romero created the broad strokes of the cars by painting them with a broom. Other of Romero's murals have celebrated the area's colorful past, such as *Santa Monica Pier Circa 1930* (1984) and *Homage to the Downtown Movie Palaces* (1990).

Romero is also a printmaker and lithographist. He was the curator of the exhibition *Murals of Aztlan* at the Los Angeles Craft and Folk Art Museum, where he is a board member.

The California State University–Los Angeles, his alma mater, mounted a major exhibition of his work in 1998. His paintings were also included in *Chicano Visions: American Painters on the Verge* (2001) at the San Antonio Museum of Art in Texas. That same year, Romero was artist-in-residence at Fullerton College in California. He was awarded a City of Los Angeles Individual Artist Fellowship in 2002 to create new work. His show *Drawings in the Shower, Paintings in the Car,* which includes a series of ceramic platters—a new medium for the artist—appeared at the Double Vision Gallery in Los Angeles in 2002. A large, jovial man with an impish sense of humor, Romero says of his lengthy and uneven career, "I've been around so long, I've been famous five or six times."

Further Reading

Beardsley, John, and Jane Livingston. *Hispanic Art in the United States: Thirty Contemporary Painters & Sculptors.* New York: Abbeville Press, 1987, pp. 232–235.

Congdon, Kirstin G., and Kara Kelley Hallmark. *Artists from Latin American Cultures: A Biographical Dictionary.* Westport, Conn.: Greenwood Press, 2002, pp. 235–237.

La Murals. "Frank Romero," La Murals Web site. Available online. URL: http://www.lamurals.org/MuralistPages/RomeroF.html. Downloaded on January 19, 2006.

Riggs, Thomas, ed. *St. James Guide to Hispanic Artists.* Detroit, Mich.: St. James Press, 2002, pp. 522–523.

Romero, Frank. *Urban iconography = Iconografila urban.* Los Angeles: Harriet & Charles Luckman Fine Arts Complex, California State University, 1998.

Ronstadt, Linda
(Linda Marie Ronstadt)
(1946–) *pop singer, songwriter, actress*

The most successful female pop vocalist of the 1970s who defined the emerging sound of country rock, Linda Ronstadt has since applied her pure, natural voice to a wide range of styles from operetta to tin pan alley to the Mexican songs of her ancestors. Linda Marie Ronstadt was born in Tucson, Arizona, on July 15, 1946. Her great-grandfather was a German immigrant who settled in Sonora, Mexico, and married a Native American woman. His son, Frederico Ronstadt, moved to Tucson as a teenager, where he became a successful businessman and amateur bandleader and musician. Frederico's daughter, Ronstadt's aunt, Luisa, became a celebrated singer and dancer of Hispanic folk music and appeared opposite Marlene Dietrich in the film *The Devil is a Woman* (1935).

With a love of music in her blood, Linda Ronstadt formed a folk trio in high school with her sister and her brother and called themselves the Three Ronstadts. After graduating, she attended Arizona State University (ASU) where she met guitarist Bob Kimmel. The two dropped out of ASU after a year and went to Los Angeles to pursue music careers. There, they formed the soft-rock group the Stone Poneys with keyboardist and songwriter Kenny Edwards. The group eventually landed a recording contract with Capitol Records and recorded three albums. The second album produced a top-15 pop hit, "Different Drum" (1967), written by Michael Nesmith of the rock group the Monkees. The Stone Poneys had little further success, and Ronstadt went solo in 1968. Her first two albums were more country than rock, and the second, *Silk Purse* (1970), produced a top-30 hit, "Long Long Time," which earned her her first Grammy nomination.

For her third album, entitled simply *Linda Ronstadt,* she engaged a new backup group led by Glenn Frey and Don Henley, who would later form the most successful country-rock group of the decade, the Eagles.

Despite a few more minor hit singles, Ronstadt was unsatisfied with Capitol and signed with Asylum Records in 1973. Her big breakthrough came a year later when she hired Peter Asher, formerly half of the British singing duo, Peter and Gordon, as her manager and record producer. Under Asher's guidance, Ronstadt made *Heart Like a Wheel* (1974), a vivid mix of rhythm-and-blues and rock songs that perfectly matched her pure but versatile voice. The album sold more than a million copies and produced three hit singles, including the #1 "You're No Good." For the rest of the decade, Ronstadt produced one hit album after another and a long string of hit singles, most of them remakes of hit songs by the Everly Brothers ("When Will I Be Loved"), Motown artists ("Heat Wave," "The Tracks of My Tears"), and Buddy Holly ("It Doesn't Matter Anyway," "That'll Be the Day," "It's So Easy").

She did not forget her love for country and won a Grammy for Best Female Country Vocal in 1975 for her interpretation of a Hank Williams song, "I Can't Help It." Her mesmerizing version of Roy Orbison's "Blue Bayou" earned her another Grammy for Best Song two years later.

In an effort to update her sound, Ronstadt released an album of punk and New Wave music, *Mad Love* (1980), with mixed results. It did produce what would be her last top-10 single for six years, "Hurt So Bad." Ronstadt's musical spirit of adventure would take her in new and surprising directions. In 1980, she appeared as the female lead in New York's Public Theater production of the Gilbert and Sullivan operetta *The Pirates of Penzance.* Ronstadt's acting and singing made the show a huge hit, and she reprised her role in the film version in 1983. That same year, she produced *What's New,* an album of prerock pop classics, working with legendary arranger Nelson Riddle, best known for his work with Frank Sinatra. "The songs just seduced me," she said later. "I just had to record them. It was total obsession."

Ronstadt's obsession caught on with both young and old fans, and *What's New* sold more than two million copies. Ronstadt and Riddle made two more albums of pop standards. In 1984, Ronstadt tried her hand at grand opera, singing the role of Mimi in a New York production of Puccini's *La Boheme.* Many critics felt her untrained voice was not up to singing opera, and she did not repeat the experiment.

She next turned her vocal talents to the music with which she had grown up as a child, the Mexican folk and love songs that she had learned from her father and her aunt. Her Spanish album *Canciones de Mi Padre* (Songs of my father, 1988) introduced this forgotten world of Mexican and Southwestern music to a largely Anglo audience. In a tribute to her aunt, Ronstadt used her words in her introduction to the album, another best seller. She followed its release with a concert tour of Southwestern music and dance.

In the late 1980s, Ronstadt collaborated more and more with other artists whose work she admired. These included Dolly Parton and Emmylou Harris as well as James Ingram and Aaron Neville. Both her duets with Ingram ("Somewhere Out There," 1986) and Neville ("Don't Know Much," 1989) were #2 hits and were among her last hit singles to date.

Ronstadt continued to record contemporary adult material through the 1990s with diminishing success. She still records and tours to this day. Taking a cue from a duet she recorded with Dolly Parton, "I Never Will Marry," Ronstadt has remained single. Among the men with whom she has had relationships are former California governor Gerry Brown, actor and director Albert Brooks, and filmmaker George Lucas.

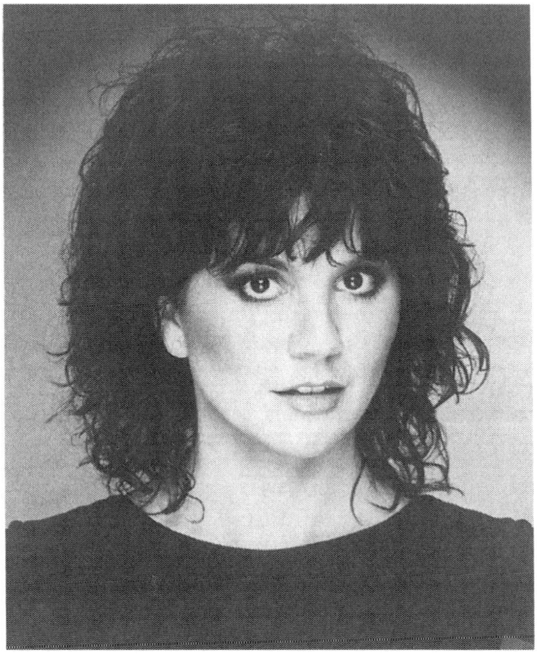

Pop singer Linda Ronstadt's Mexican ancestry was little known until she recorded the album *Canciones de Mi Padre* (Songs of My Father) in 1988. She also dedicated it to her aunt, a celebrated Latina folk singer and dancer. *(Photofest)*

Further Reading

Amdur, Melissa. *Linda Ronstadt* (Hispanics of Achievement). New York: Chelsea House, 1993.

Bego, Mark. *Linda Ronstadt: It's So Easy: An Unauthorized Biography.* New York: Eakins Press, 1990.

Erlewine, Stephen Thomas. "Linda Ronstadt," Mp3.com. Available online. URL: http://www.mp3.com/linda-ronstadt/artists/4562/biography.html?q=LInda%20Ronstadt. Downloaded on March 27, 2006.

Lewry, Peter. *Linda Ronstadt: A Musical Life.* London: Helter Skelter Publications, 2005.

Further Listening

Canciones de Mi Padre (1987). Asylum Records, CD, 1990.

'Round Midnight (collection of her three albums with Nelson Riddle). Elektra, CD (2 disks), 1990.

The Very Best of Linda Ronstadt. Elektra, CD, 2000.

Further Viewing

Linda Ronstadt—Canciones de Mi Padre: A Romantic Evening in Old Mexico (1991). Elektra/Warner Home Video, VHS/DVD, 1992/2004.

The Pirates of Penzance (1980). MCA/Kultur Video, VHS/DVD, 1992/2002.

S

San Juan, Olga
(1927–) *actress, singer, dancer, comedian*

A lively performer who personified the Latina spitfire on radio, stage, and screen in the 1940s and 1950s, Olga San Juan never achieved the notoriety of LUPE VÉLEZ nor the stardom of CARMEN MIRANDA, but she managed to live up to her nickname as "The Puerto Rican Pepper Pot." She was born in Brooklyn, New York, into a Puerto Rican family on March 16, 1927. She began dance lessons at the age of four and by seven was a member of the Latino dance ensemble, Infantile Ballet Valencia. With this group, San Juan performed at the White House before President Franklin Delano Roosevelt. By age 10, she was singing and dancing with the Hispanic Theater in the Bronx, New York.

After several years of performing on local radio and in nightclubs, San Juan was spotted by a talent hunter for Paramount Pictures and offered a contract. She appeared in her first picture, *Romance Caribbean,* in 1943. Through the end of the decade, she appeared in a number of movies, mostly musicals, as a Latina entertainer or comic love interest. One of her best films was *Blue Skies* (1946), which starred Fred Astaire and Bing Crosby and had a score by Irving Berlin. It was one of the top-grossing films of the year. Among her other films were *Out of This World* (1945), *Variety Girl* (1947), *One Touch of Venus* and *The Countess of Monte Cristo* (both 1948).

San Juan married film actor Edmond O'Brien in 1948 and made her last major film appearance in director Preston Sturges's last Hollywood film, the Western satire *The Beautiful Blonde from Bashful Bend* (1949). The film also starred Betty Grable and CÉSAR ROMERO. In 1951, San Juan appeared on Broadway in the Lerner–Lowe Western musical *Paint Your Wagon* as Jennifer Rumson, the daughter of a crusty prospector who strikes it rich in the gold fields of California. She won the Donaldson Award which was given by New York theater critics for her sparkling performance. San Juan's last film appearance was as a prostitute in the crime thriller *The Third Voice* (1960), which starred her husband. The couple divorced in 1976. Her son Brendan O'Brien is a film actor, comedy writer, and musician. Her daughter Maria O'Brien is also an actress and has done extensive work on television.

Further Reading

The Internet Movie Database. "Olga San Juan," The Internet Movie Database. Available online. URL: http://www.imdb.com/name/nm0760676/. Downloaded on January 5, 2006.

Katz, Ephraim. *The Film Encyclopedia,* 1st edition. New York: G. P. Putnam Sons, 1979, p. 1015.

The New York Times. "Olga San Juan," The New York Times Movies Web Site. Available online. URL: http://movies2.nytimes.com/gst/movies/filmography.html?p_id=62873. Downloaded on March 30, 2006.

Further Viewing

The Beautiful Blonde from Bashful Bend (1949). Fox Home Video, VHS, 1995.

Blue Skies (1946)/*Birth of the Blues* (1941) [double feature]. MCA Home Video, VHS/DVD, 2003.

Santamaria, Mongo (Ramón "Mongo" Santamaria)

(1922–2003) *percussion player, bandleader, composer*

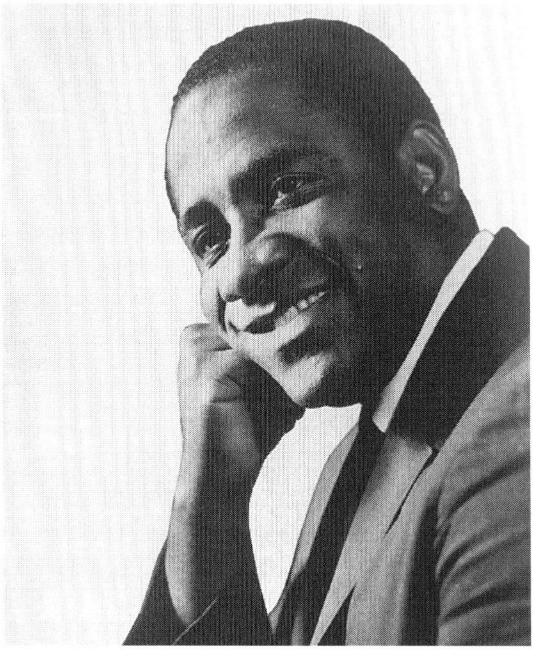

Bandleader and percussionist Mongo Santamaria brought Latin jazz and soul to the pop charts in 1963 with the infectious instrumental "Watermelon Man." *(Photofest)*

A master of the Cuban drums called *conguero,* Mongo Santamaria was a pioneer of Latino jazz who brought color and life to traditional Latin *charanga* music with blaring brass, jazzy woodwinds, and kinetic piano.

Ramón "Mongo" Santamaria was born in Havana, Cuba, on April 7, 1922. As a youth, he took up the violin but later turned to drums. Obsessed with music, Santamaria dropped out of school and got a job playing at Havana's renowned Tropicana Club. In his mid-20s, he moved to Mexico City to play for a dance group. Two years later, in 1950, he moved to New York City where he played with the Perez Prado orchestra. Santamaria became noticed as a composer when his composition "Afro Blue" was recorded by jazz musician John Coltrane in 1951. He soon joined TITO PUENTE's band and from 1957 to 1960 played with vibraphonist Cal Tjader's group. Although he was not Latino, Tjader was in the forefront of the Latin jazz movement.

Santamaria founded his own group in 1961 and was playing in a Cuban club in the Bronx, New York, when an accident gave him his biggest crossover success. That night, according to Santamaria, there were only three people in the audience, and he felt free to improvise. The band played "Watermelon Man," a new tune by jazz pianist Herbie Hancock who was sitting in with the group as a substitute player. They had so much fun with the sultry rhythmic tune that the song became a part of their repertoire. They recorded it in 1963. It rose to the top 10 on the pop charts that year. Music writer David McGee has called "Watermelon Man" "one of the signposts pointing toward soul and funk, in addition to being many Americans' first exposure to a world beat sensibility." Santamaria signed with Columbia Records in 1965 and enjoyed a string of successful commercial albums and several more pop hits.

In the 1970s, Santamaria returned to his Afro–Cuban rhythmic roots. One of his best albums in this period was *Afro–Indio* (1975), a potent collaboration with Colombian flautist and sax player Justo Almario. Santamaria continued to be a powerful force in Latin jazz into the 1990s, recording for the Milestone label, a subsidiary of Fantasy Records, in 1995. He was active almost up to the time of his death on February 1, 2003, from the effects of a stroke. The grand master of the *conguero* was 85 years old.

Further Reading

Drummerworld. "Mongo Santamaria," Drummerworld.com. Available online. URL: http://www.drummerworld.com/drummers/Mongo_Santamaria.html. Downloaded on March 24, 2006.

Gerard, Charley. *Music from Cuba: Mongo Santamaria, Chocolate Armeneros, and Other Stateside Cuban Musicians.* Westport, Conn.: Praeger Publishers, 2001.

Ginell, Richard S. "Mongo Santamaria," Mp3 Web Site. Available online. URL: http://www.mp3.com/mongo-santamaria/artists/100572/biography.html. Downloaded on August 15, 2005.

Further Listening

Afro Roots. Prestige, CD, 1989.

Skin on Skin: The Mongo Santamaria Anthology 1958–1995. Rhino, CD (2 discs), 2000.

Santana, Carlos
(Devadip Carlos Santana; Carlos Augusto Alves Santana)

(1947–) *rock guitarist, singer, songwriter*

One of the few rock artists of the 1960s to still be a creative force in the music industry at the start of the 21st century, Carlos Santana, with his self-named band and on his own, has created a unique fusion of rock, Latin music, jazz, and blues. He was born in the tiny Mexican village of Autlán de Navarro in Jalisco on July 20, 1947. The middle child of seven children, he grew up in abject poverty in a mud house without running water or electricity. His father was a mariachi violinist and taught Carlos the instrument when he was five. The boy turned to the guitar when he was eight. At age 12, he moved with his family to Tijuana on the Mexican–U.S. border. He began to play bass and his guitar for money in clubs and bars. When his family moved to San Francisco, California, in the early 1960s, Santana stayed behind in Tijuana for a time but later joined them in the United States.

The Santanas lived in the Spanish-speaking Mission District of San Francisco where Carlos attended high school. He graduated in 1965 and the following year formed the Santana Blues Band with keyboardist Gregory Rolie, bassist David Brown, and others. Despite their name, Santana had no leader. Santana was only made the nominal leader to get around a requirement of the musicians' union. A chance meeting with rock promoter Bill Graham got the group a gig in San Francisco's Fillmore, the premier rock club on the West Coast. Their unique blend of Latin music, rock, and African rhythms quickly led to a recording contract in 1968 with Columbia Records.

Their first album, *Santana* (1969), had not yet been released when the group appeared at the Woodstock Music Festival in summer 1969 in upstate New York. Their dazzling performance was a highlight of the three-day festival and was captured on film in the Academy Award–winning documentary *Woodstock* (1970). When their first album was released that fall, it sold more than a million copies and produced the top-10 hit single "Evil Ways." Their next album *Abraxas* (1970) produced the biggest single of their career, "Black Magic Woman." Another hit, "Oye Come Va," had been written and recorded years earlier by salsa bandleader Tito Puente and made him a superstar with a younger generation of listeners.

Despite their success, jealousies and other problems soon broke the group apart. Santana retained the rights to the group name and soon hired musicians to play with him. But the adventurous musician was beginning to move in different directions in his life and music. He became interested in the Eastern religion of Hinduism and became a disciple of the guru Sri Chinmoy who gave him the name Devadip, which means "the eye, the lamp, and the light of God." Santana befriended fellow Chinmoy disciple John McLaughlin, the guitarist for the Mahavishnu Orchestra. The two musicians formed a duo in 1972 and released the album *Love Devotion Surrender* (1973).

Santana had a deep interest in jazz and collaborated on albums with drummer Buddy Miles and Tuyriya Alice Coltrane, the widow of jazz saxophonist John Coltrane. At the same time, he continued to play dates and record albums with his group, but as the decade went on their commercial success diminished.

In 1979, Santana released his first true solo album, *Oneness: Silver Dreams—Golden Reality,* which was largely instrumental. Through the 1980s, he continued to collaborate with a variety of musicians and singers—jazzman Herbie Hancock and other jazz artists on the double album *The Swing of Delight* (1980) and Willie Nelson and organist Booker T. Jones on the Tex–Mex flavored best seller *Havana Moon* (1983). "Blues for Salvador" (1987), from the album of the same name, won Santana his first Grammy for Best Rock Instrumental Performance. The previous year, he had debuted as a film composer writing the score for *La Bamba,* a biographical film about the first Latino rock star, RITCHIE VALENS.

In 1990, Santana signed with Polydor Records, but after releasing *Santana Brothers* (1994) with his brother Jorge and nephew Carlos Hernández, little was heard from the rock master for nearly five years. Then in 1999, he made one of the most spectacular comebacks in the history of rock with the album *Supernatural.* It was a winning combination of Santana instrumentals with a number of songs sung by younger performers including Dave Matthews, Lauryn Hill, and Wyclef Jean. *Supernatural* was a monster hit, selling more than 10 million copies. Carlos Santana, at age 52, was one of the biggest names on the rock scene. The album went on to win a handful of Grammys, including Best Rock Album of the Year, while "Smooth" with Rob Thomas on vocals, one of two #1 singles from the album, won Best Song of the Year.

In late 2005, Santana released his 38th album, *All That I Am.* In January 2006, he made a surprise appearance, playing at the 75th birthday of the late Bill Graham at the Fillmore West in San Francisco where his career first took off more than 35 years ago.

He has been married since 1973 to Deborah Santana, who recently published a memoir about her life and marriage. Their eldest child Salvador has his own rock band. Santana contributes much of his success to his family. "A lot of my peers got too carried away with themselves—their houses, their egos, their motorcycles," he said in a 2005 interview. "I stayed true to my heart, which is my connection to my wife of 32 years, my mom, my sisters and my children. I'm here because of them."

Further Reading

Leng, Simon. *Soul Sacrifice: The Santana Story.* Richmond Hill, Ont.: Firefly Publishing, 2000.

Santana, Deborah. *Space Between the Stars: My Journey to an Open Heart.* New York: One World/Ballantine, 2005.

Santana Official Web Site. Available online. URL: http://www.santana.com. Downloaded on January 23, 2006.

Shapiro, Marc. *Carlos Santana: Back on Top.* New York: St. Martin's Griffin, 2002.

Further Listening

The Essential Santana. Sony, CD (2 discs), 2002.

Supernatural. BMG/Artista, CD, 1999.

Further Viewing

Santana—Supernatural Live. VHS/DVD, 2000.

Woodstock—The Director's Cut (1970). Warner Home Video, VHS/DVD, 1994/1997.

Schifrin, Lalo
(Boris Claudio Schifrin)
(1932–) *film composer, classical composer, conductor, pianist, arranger*

One of Hollywood's most distinctive and successful film composers since the 1960s, Lalo Schifrin brought a new sound to movies and television that was an intriguing blend of jazz, Latin rhythms, and the dissonance of contemporary classical music. Boris Claudio Schifrin was born in Buenos Aires, Argentina, on June 21, 1932. His father was the concertmaster and first violinist of the Teatro Colón orchestra for three decades. His uncle was the orchestra's first cellist. Immersed in the world of classical music from an early age, Schifrin studied piano from age six to sixteen with Enrique Barenboim, father of pianist and conductor Daniel Barenboim. Schifrin wrote his first classical composition at 14, but two years later discovered American jazz. He soon fell under the spell of such masters of the form as Charlie Parker and Thelonius Monk.

He studied composition in Buenos Aires with the modern composer Juan Carlos Paz and in 1952 went to France to study at the Paris Conservatory. He returned to Buenos Aires within a year and began to write music for Argentinean theater and television. He wrote his first film score for a short art film. Then, in 1957, he met one of his heroes, jazz trumpeter and bandleader Dizzy Gillespie, who performed in Buenos Aires as part of a U.S. State Department tour. When he heard Schifrin play his own music, Gillespie was so impressed that he offered him a job as an arranger and musician.

Schifrin took the offer and arrived in the United States in 1958. Among the memorable works he composed for Gillespie was a five-movement suite, *Gillespiana.* Soon, he was in demand as an arranger for XAVIER CUGAT and such jazz greats as bandleader Count Basie and organist Jimmy Smith. Schifrin settled in Hollywood in the early 1960s and concentrated on composing for television. He scored episodes of numerous series ranging from such anthology series as *Alfred Hitchcock Presents* to such Westerns as *The Virginian.*

After scoring two minor feature films, he was given his big break writing the music for *The Cincinnati Kid* (1965), a drama about gambling in Depression-era New Orleans. Schifrin skillfully blended American blues and roots music with jazz rhythms and dissonant modern music to dazzling effect. His next memorable score was for *Cool Hand Luke* (1967), a grim but lively story of life on a Southern chain gang. For the main character Luke, played by Paul Newman, he wrote a poignant, understated theme for classical guitar.

Schifrin's most famous film score was for the crime thriller *Bullitt* (1968), starring Steve McQueen as a San Francisco detective. Schifrin's heart-pounding music for the classic car chase up and down the streets of San Francisco is the perfect blend of music and image. In an interview, he claimed to have used Latin dance rhythms in the sequence to simulate the speeding cars. After that, gritty urban crime dramas became one of Schifrin's specialties. He scored the first two of Clint Eastwood's popular *Dirty Harry* movies as well as two of his Western films. The actor/director and film composer became good friends and share a love of jazz.

Schifrin's music was just as pervasive on television as on the big screen. His bold, angular theme music for the spy series *Mission: Impossible* (1966–73) is arguably the most recognizable theme in television history and certainly one of the best. He also wrote memorable themes for such shows as *The Man from U.N.C.L.E., Mannix,* and *Medical Center,* for which he used a Moog synthesizer to recreate the sound of a wailing ambulance siren.

Throughout his busy film career, Schifrin has kept his hand in classical composing and conducting. Among his numerous orchestral compositions are a dramatic cantata, two concertos, and *A Jazz Suite on the Mass Texts.* His *Latin Jazz Suite* includes movements devoted to the rhythms of Cuba, Brazil, and his native Argentina. He has conducted his own music and that of other composers with a number of major orchestras, including the Los Angeles (LA) Symphony and the London Philharmonic.

Nominated for six Academy Awards and the winner of four Grammys (21 nominations), Schifrin was the recipient of the Film Music Society's career achievement award in 2000. His son Ryan is a film director. Talking about film, Schifrin has said, "The producer is its lungs, the director is its brains, the cameraman is its eyes, and the composer is its ears, and we should not be aware of any one detail too much."

Further Reading

The Internet Movie Database. "Lalo Schifrin," The Internet Movie Database. Available online. URL: http://www.imdb.com/name/nm0006277/. Downloaded on January 13, 2006.

The Official Web Site of Lalo Schifrin. Available online. URL: http://www.schifrin.com/main.htm. Downloaded on March 24, 2006.

Thomas, Tony. *Music for the Movies.* Cranbury, N.J.: A. S. Barnes & Co., 1973, pp. 214–220.

Further Listening

Bullitt: New Recordings (1968). Wea International, CD, 2001.

The Cincinnati Kid (1965). Aleph Records, CD, 2002.

Latin Jazz Suite. Aleph Records, CD, 1999.

Music from Mission: Impossible (1966). Hip-O Records, CD, 1996.

Secada, Jon
(Juan Secada)
(1961–) *pop and Latin singer, songwriter, actor*

A Latin singer whose appealing blend of Latin music, rhythm and blues (R&B), and pop made him a music pop star in the early 1990s, Jon Secada has since enjoyed considerable success as a stage actor and songwriter. Juan Secada was born in Havana, Cuba, on October 4, 1961. Leaving Cuba with his family at age nine, his family settled in Miami, Florida, where his parents opened a coffee shop. Secada attended Hialeah High School and, after graduation, entered the University of Miami where he earned a bachelor of arts (B.A.) degree and then a master of arts (M.A.) degree in jazz vocal performance.

His first professional job was singing backup on tour for GLORIA ESTEFAN and the Miami Sound Machine. He also began to write songs for her, six of which made it into her comeback album, *Coming out of the Dark* (1991), following her recovery from a serious bus accident. Among the songs he cowrote was the #1 title hit.

It was not long before Secada was coming out of the shadow of Estefan and making his own music. He signed with SBK Records in 1992, and they produced his first solo album in English, *Jon Secada* (1992). It sold six million copies worldwide and made him an international star.

Secada followed this with his first Spanish-language album, *Otro Dia Mas Sin Verte* (Just another day without seeing you, 1992), which won a Grammy for Best Latin Pop Album and became the #1 album in the Latin market. A second English album, *Heart, Soul and a Voice* (1994), was a million seller. He won a second Grammy for his next Spanish album *Amor* (1995). He also sang the song "If I Never Knew You" in the Disney animated film *Pocohantas* (1995).

That same year, Secada widened his horizons by appearing in the Broadway revival of the popular 1950s musical *Grease.* He enjoyed the experience and returned to Broadway in the revival of the musical *Cabaret* (2003), tackling the challenging role of the Emcee. More recently, he starred in the national tour of the Webber–Rice musical *Joseph and the Amazing Technicolor Dreamcoat* (2004). His latest ambition is to write a Broadway musical.

By the late 1990s, Secada's recording star faded, but his most recent English album *Same*

Dream (2005), was praised by some critics as refreshing and original. He continues to write hit songs for such artists as RICKY MARTIN and JENNIFER LOPEZ. "Musical composition has always been my first love," he said in a 2004 interview. "Good songs are the essence of it all . . . at the end of the day it's all about the music."

In October 2005, Secada performed at Guantanamo Bay in his native Cuba. "It's very emotional for me to touch Cuban soil," he said about the experience.

Secada has been married to Maritere Vilar since February 1997. They have two children. His first marriage ended in divorce.

Further Reading

Erlewine, Stephen Thomas. "Jon Secada," Mp3 Web Site. Available online. URL: http://www.mp3.com/jon-secada/artists/21557/biography.html. Downloaded on January 13, 2006.

Marvis, Barbara. *Famous People of Hispanic Heritage: Giselle Fernandez, Jon Secada, Desi Arnaz, Joan Baez.* Hockessin, Del.: Mitchell Lane Publishers, 1995.

Novas, Himilce. *Secada!* New York: Signet Books, 1997.

Further Listening

Jon Secada—Greatest Hits. Virgin Records, CD, 1999.

Selena
(Selena Quintanilla Pérez)
(1971–1995) *pop and Latin singer*

The brightest star in the world of Tejano music, Selena was on the brink of crossing over to major pop success when tragedy took her life at age 23. Selena Quintanilla Pérez was born in Lake Jackson, Texas, a suburb of Houston on April 16, 1971. Her Mexican-American father, Abraham Quintanilla, ran a restaurant. When Selena was nine, her talent for singing became apparent, and Abraham decided to foster her career. He formed a family band called Los Dinos, after a doo-wop group to which he belonged in his youth. Selena was the vocalist, her brother AB played bass guitar, and her sister Suzette played the drums. Los Dinos performed regularly at the restaurant. The music they played and sang, Tejano, was a Texas melding of country, Mexican music, polka, and pop. The songs were in Spanish, which Selena did not speak at the time. She learned the lyrics phonetically and only later learned to speak Spanish fluently.

When the restaurant went bankrupt, the family moved to Corpus Christi, Texas, in 1981, and Abraham began to book Los Dinos at parties and weddings. At her father's prodding, Selena quit school in the eighth grade to keep up with the demands of performing. She later earned her high school diploma through a correspondence school. In 1987, Selena, now 15, won the Tejano Music Award for Female Entertainer of the Year. She would win that honor eight more years in succession.

She was soon signed to a recording contract by Capitol Records and recorded for their EMI International label. Her Spanish-language albums sold phenomenally; the title track from *Ven Conmigo* (1987) was the first Tejano song to sell 500,000 copies and go gold. Selena began to branch out in new directions by 1992. She started her own clothing line and later opened boutiques and beauty salons in San Antonio and Corpus Christi. She had been designing her own clothes since age 10. In April 1992, she married her guitarist Chris Perez.

Although a sexy and exciting performer that led many to compare her to Madonna, Selena appealed to all members of the Latino community, young and old. On and off stage she supported traditional family values and spoke out against drug abuse and dropping out of school.

Selena appeared in concert at Houston's Astrodome in 1994 before an audience of 61,000. It was the biggest audience ever to hear Tejano and the second-largest audience to attend a concert at the Astrodome. That year, she won her first Grammy Award for Best Mexican-American Album, *Selena Live!* and made her motion picture debut in a cameo performance as a background mariachi singer in the comedy *Don Juan DeMarco* (1995).

Columbia was ready to produce her first English-language album, *Dreaming of You,* in early 1995. "I've always believed in the saying good things come to those who wait and we've been waiting patiently," Selena said about this album. "I'm sure everything is gonna turn out okay." But it did not. On March 31, 1995, Yolanda Saldivar, president and founder of Selena's fan club and manager of her two boutiques and beauty salons, met with the star in a Corpus Christi motel room. Selena's father had earlier accused Saldivar of embezzlement from fan club funds and Selena wanted her to turn over missing financial papers for tax purposes. A distraught Saldivar pulled out a 38-caliber pistol during their emotional meeting. Selena ran from the room. Saldivar pursued the singer and shot her in the back. Selena died an hour later in a local hospital. At her trial in October of that year, Saldivar insisted that the shooting was an accident. She was, however, convicted of first degree murder and sentenced to life in prison.

As many as 50,000 fans turned out to view Selena's body in Bayfront Plaza Convention. Then-Texas governor George W. Bush declared April 16 "Selena Day." Her English album *Dreaming of You* was released posthumously and debuted at #1 on the Billboard album charts, the second album to have the highest chart debut in history (Michael Jackson's *HIStory* beng the first). In the months after her death, more than 600 infant girls in south Texas were named Selena.

A biographical film *Selena* (1997), coproduced by her father, directed by GREGORY NAVA, and starring JENNIFER LOPEZ as Selena, further burnished the legend of her short and brilliant career.

Further Reading

Brennan, Sarah. "Selena," mp3.com. Available online. URL: http://www.mp3.com/selena/artists/24143/biography.html?q=Selena. Downloaded on March 24, 2006.

Novas, Himilce, and Rosemary Silva. *Remembering Selena: A Tribute in Pictures & Words.* New York: St. Martin's Griffin, 1995.

Further Listening

Dreaming of You. EMI International, CD, 1995.

Selena—Greatest Hits. EMI International, CD, 2003.

Further Viewing

Selena (1997). Warner Home Video, VHS/DVD, 2001/2002.

Selena Live—The Last Concert (1995). Image Entertainment, DVD, 2003.

Serrano, Andres
(1950–) *photographer*

Andres Serrano considers himself an artist first and a photographer second. His search for art and meaning has taken him to the most unlikely of places—from the city morgue to the home of the Grand Wizard of the Ku Klux Klan. Along the way this quiet and reclusive artist has been thrown into the public spotlight in one of the hottest controversies to stir up the art world in the last two decades.

He was born in New York City on August 15, 1950, to Cuban–Afro and Honduran parents. He attended the Brooklyn Museum Art School from 1967 to 1969, but his gestation period as an artist was unusually slow. Serrano did not begin to take the photographs that brought him fame and notoriety until the early 1980s.

In 1985, he had his first solo exhibition at the Leonard Perlson Gallery in New York City. This show, *Tableaux,* revolved around themes that would become central to his work—the use of symbols and their significance and a fascination with religious imagery. Born Roman Catholic, Serrano no longer attends church but still considers himself to be sympathetic to Christianity.

This may sound odd to many traditional Catholics who saw or heard about his photographic series *Fluids* (1985–90). In it, Serrano explored the expressive use of various fluids, especially body fluids, in art and life. The most controversial of these pictures was *Piss Christ* (1987), a photograph that he took of a crucifix of Christ which he then dropped into a bucket of his own urine. Shocked museumgoers called it sacrilege. The controversy grew even more when it was learned that Serrano had received a $15,000 grant from the National Endowment for the Arts (NEA) in 1997 as his series was traveling the museum circuit.

U.S. senators Alfonse D'Amato and Jesse Helms on the floor of the Senate both condemned the grant, and Serrano's use of it. When *Piss Christ* appeared at the National Gallery in Australia, two patrons attacked it with baseball bats. It was saved from destruction, but the museum quickly closed Serrano's exhibition. Unlike other NEA recipients who have been under attack for their work, Serrano has refused to let the controversy politicize his work. He claims that his issues are with the Catholic Church and not God and Jesus.

Serrano has gone on to create less controversial but still challenging new series of photographs. In 1990, he unveiled two series, *Nomads,* depicting homeless people from the streets of New York City, and *Klansmen,* portraits of Ku Klux Klan members in their white robes and hoods, which he shot in Georgia. The juxtaposition of the two groups makes Serrano's point that both, in their way, are outcasts from normal society. "I like the tension between the two," he said in a 1991 interview. "They are extreme poverty and extreme prejudice."

In 1992, Serrano took his camera to a morgue and photographed the bodies deposited there over a three-month period. More recently, his show *America* (December 2003–January 2004) at the Paula Cooper Gallery in New York, consisted of portraits of Americans, ranging from a firefighter to a young beauty pageant winner.

The photographer, who lives in Brooklyn, is grateful that he has so far escaped the label of being a Latino or Hispanic artist. "My work is intensely personal," he says. "I don't think that because I am Hispanic I should therefore do Hispanic work. . . . Is it Hispanic to photograph the Klan?"

Further Reading

Congdon, Kirstin G., and Kara Kelley Hallmark. *Artists from Latin American Cultures: A Biographical Dictionary.* Westport, Conn.: Greenwood Press, 2002, pp. 249–253.

Fosco, Coco. "Shooting the Klan: An Interview with Andres Serrano," Communityartsnetwork readingroom. Available online. URL: http://www.communityarts.net/readingroom/archivefiles/2002/09/shooting_the_kl.php. Downloaded on January 18, 2006.

Wikipedia. "Andres Serrano," Wikipedia, the Free Encyclopedia. Available online. URL: http://en.wikipedia.org/wiki/Andres_Serrano. Downloaded on March 24, 2006.

Shakira
(Shakira Isabel Mebarak Ripoll)
(1977–) *pop and Latin singer, songwriter, record producer, actress*

One of the brightest pop stars at the start of the 21st century, Shakira's international success extends to Latin and North America as well as Europe. It is based not only on her seductive, intense alto voice but also on her abilities as a songwriter, producer, and dancer. Shakira Isabel Mebarak Ripoll was born in Barranquilla, Colombia, on February 2, 1977, an only child. Her father, a Lebanese, had eight children by his ex-wife. Her mother, who is also her manager, is Spanish-Catalan. Her name in Arabic means "woman full of grace." Interested in music from childhood, Shakira wrote her first song at age eight. She attended a Catholic school and began to sing and dance there. "I was known in school as 'the belly dancer girl' because every Friday I would do a number I learned," she said in a 2005 interview. "That's how I discovered my passion for live performance."

The nuns did not stop her dancing, but at age 13 they refused her membership in the school choir because her voice was "too strong." The rejection only strengthened her resolve to sing. She entered a television singing competition for children and won. Then, an executive in Sony's Colombia division heard her sing and arranged an audition for her in Bogotá with his bosses. She was immediately signed to a three-album contract. It looked like the young singer's dreams were about to come true. However, her first two albums were flops, and she herself was dissatisfied with their production. She abandoned recording temporarily and tried acting in a Colombian television soap opera, *El Oasis,* for which she also sang the theme song.

Shakira admitted that her acting ability was limited, but the exposure increased her celebrity. More confident, Shakira returned to the recording studio in 1995 and produced *Pies Descalzos, Sueños Blancos* (Bare feet, white dreams), which included more of a rock beat and touches of the Arabic music she had loved and listened to from childhood. "I was always very sure of what I wanted to hear," she has said of her growing creative control in the studio.

The album was a commercial success, and she turned to GLORIA ESTEFAN's producer-husband Emilio to produce her next album. Under Estefan's expert guidance, Shakira's music matured on *¿Dónde Están Los Ladrones?* (Where are the thieves? 1997). The album was a skillful mix of American rock, electronic music, and an array of Latin styles from Colombia *cumbia,* rhythmic dance music, to Jamaican dance-hall music. Her singing was beginning to be noticed in the United States.

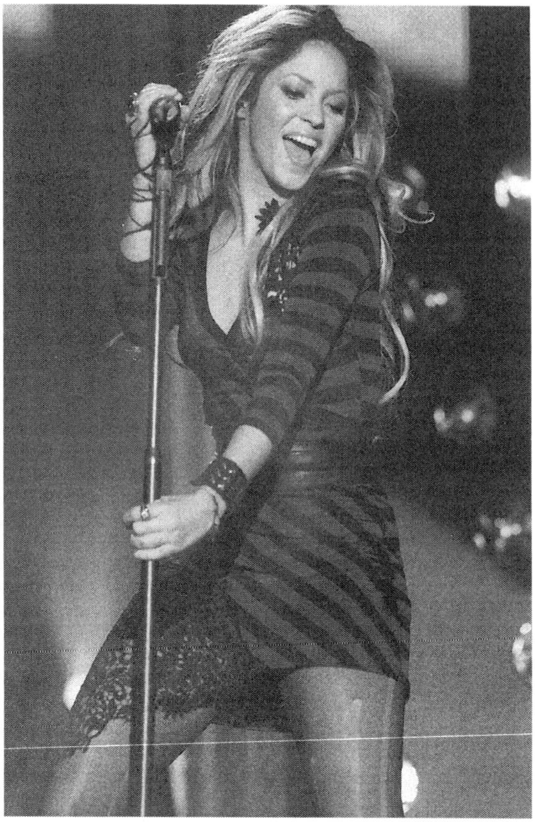

The Colombian-born Shakira is one of the true international stars of the music world today. Her name means "woman full of grace" in Arabic, the language of her Lebanese father. *(Photofest)*

She solidified her success with *Laundry Service* (2001), her first English-language album, which contained new English versions of earlier Spanish songs she had recorded and four new Spanish songs. Shakira learned enough English to be able to sing the lyrics, although some music critics found her English less than adequate. Nevertheless, the energetic "Whenever, Wherever" became an international hit, while another track, the ballad "Underneath Your Clothes" went #1 in Canada and top 10 in the United States. *Laundry Service* sold three million copies in the United States and 10 million worldwide.

Shakira followed it with *Fijacion Oral, Vol. 1* (Oral fixation, 2005), another Spanish-language album with a dazzling eclectic reach. The single "La Tortura" (The Torture), which she sang with Spanish singer Alejandro Sanz, became the most successful Latin-speaking single ever in the United States and spent a record-breaking 25 weeks at the top of the Latin charts. The album was nominated for a Grammy for Best Latin Rock Album and Shakira in 2005 became the first performer to sing completely in Spanish at the MTV (Music Television) Video Music Awards.

That fall she released *Oral Fixation, Vol. 2,* her second English-language album, with nine new songs and two English versions of songs from the previous album. Shakira, who is fluent in Spanish, Portuguese, and now English, moves easily from one language to another in her music.

She has made the Bahamas her permanent residence but also has a home in Miami, Florida, and returns regularly to Colombia. She is engaged to Argentinean Antonio de la Rúa.

"Believe it or not, I'm a very shy person," Shakira has confessed. "The stage is the only place where I feel uninhibited. The audience becomes like a huge mirror in which I look at my feelings reflected and they respond to me. We become like one. That's the magic of a good performance."

Further Reading

Diego, Ximena. *Shakira: Woman Full of Grace.* New York: Fireside, 2001.

Huey, Steve. "Shakira," Mp3.com. URL: http://www.mp3.com/shakira/artists/146698/biography.html. Downloaded on January 16, 2006.

Katz, Gregory. "Shaking It up with Shakira," *USA Weekend,* December 9–11, 2005, pp. 5, 7.

Pareles, Jon. "The Shakira Dialectic," *New York Times,* November 13, 2005. Arts Section, pp. 1, 35.

Further Listening

Laundry Service. Sony, CD, 2001.

Oral Fixation, Vol. 2. Sony, CD, 2005.

Further Viewing

Shakira—Live and Off the Record. Sony, DVD with CD, 2004.

Sheen, Charlie (Carlos Irwin Estévez)

(1965–) *actor*

A successful and handsome leading man of films and television who is adept at both drama and comedy, Charlie Sheen's personal life has brought him as much attention as his on-screen life, often to his detriment. Carlos Irwin Estévez was born in New York City on September 3, 1965. His father, MARTIN SHEEN (born Ramón Gerardo Antonio Estévez), half Spanish-American, is a successful actor. Charlie made his screen debut at age nine in a small role in a made-for-TV movie *The Execution of Private Slovik* (1974), which starred his father.

A star of the baseball team at Santa Monica High School, Sheen was a poor student with a bad attendance record and was expelled a few weeks before graduation. He turned his focus to film acting, following in the footsteps of his father and older brother EMILIO ESTEVEZ. He uses *Sheen* professionally; his daughters are surnamed *Estévez.*

Sheen had a few good small roles in several films beginning in 1984 until director Oliver Stone cast him in the major role of a soldier with a conscience in his Oscar-winning Vietnam drama *Platoon* (1986). Stone also cast him in his next film, *Wall Street* (1987), as an amoral yuppie whose mentor is the ruthless businessman Gordon Gecko, played by Michael Douglas, who won an Oscar for the role. Martin Sheen played Charlie's blue-collar father in the film. Sheen again hit a home run in *Eight Men Out* (1988), a baseball drama about the real-life "Chicago Black Sox" scandal of 1919. He then proved himself an adept comic actor in another baseball film, *Major League* (1989), and in the zany war-movie satire *Hot Shots!* (1991).

Through the 1990s, Sheen continued to find screen success in more modest pictures, playing Clint Eastwood's police partner in *The Rookie* (1990) and reprising his flyboy role in the wild sequel *Hot Shots! Part Deux* (1993). But Sheen's messy personal life was gaining more headlines than his acting. His engagement to actress Kelly Preston ended in 1990 when he accidentally shot her in the arm. In the 1990s, it was revealed that he was a regular customer of "Hollywood Madame" Heidi Fleiss, and he testified at her much-publicized trial. In 1997, he was charged with beating adult-movie actress/girlfriend Brittany Ashfield and was sentenced to probation. The following year, he was hospitalized for alcohol and cocaine abuse.

Sheen, with help from his family, especially his father, emerged clean and sober in 1999 and was hired to replace Michael J. Fox in the political television sitcom *Spin City*. He was awarded a Golden Globe for best comedic actor in television for the role in January 2002. "This is so surreal," he said when accepting the award. "It's like a sober acid trip."

Spin City was soon canceled, but Sheen returned to television in 2003 in another sitcom, *Two and a Half Men*. He plays a "bad boy" bachelor and jingle writer whose life is turned upside-down when his brother and a 10-year-old nephew move into his beachfront home. The show is a hit, and Sheen's fading career has been revitalized. In August 2006, he won an Emmy for this role as Outstanding Lead Actor-Comedy Series.

Sheen's second marriage, to actress Denise Richards, ended in divorce in January 2006. He has two daughters from that marriage and a third daughter from a previous relationship. He is the author of a book of poetry *Peace of My Mind*.

Further Reading

The Internet Movie Database. "Charlie Sheen," The Internet Movie Database. Available online. URL: http://www.imdb.com/name/nm0000221/. Downloaded on January 16, 2006.

Riley, Lee, and David Shumacher. *The Sheens: Martin, Charlie, and Emilio Estevez*. New York: St. Martin's Press, 1989.

Ruternberg, Jim. "Charlie Sheen's Redemption Helps a Studio in Its Struggles," *New York Times*, February 4, 2002, p. C1.

Further Viewing

Hot Shots! (1991). Fox Home Video, VHS/DVD, 1997/2002.

Platoon (1986). Live/Artisan, VHS/DVD, 1997.

Wall Street (1987). Fox Home Video, VHS/DVD, 1996/2000.

Sheen, Martin (Ramón Gerardo Antonio Estévez)

(1940–) *actor, political activist*

Playing the president of the United States in the most successful political dramatic series in television history, Martin Sheen has been a respected actor on stage, screen, and television for more than four decades. His fondness for political roles underlies his own strong liberal convictions, which have made him one of the most active (and arrested) political activists in the Hollywood community. Ramón Estévez was born in Dayton, Ohio, on August 3, 1940, the seventh of 10 children. His father, Francisco Estévez, was a Spanish immigrant who came to the United States via Cuba. His mother, Mary Ann Phelan, was an Irish immigrant. The couple first met at a citizenship class in Dayton.

Ramon's left arm was crushed by forceps during his birth, and he has had limited lateral movement in that arm ever since. After high school, Estévez deliberately flunked the entrance exam to

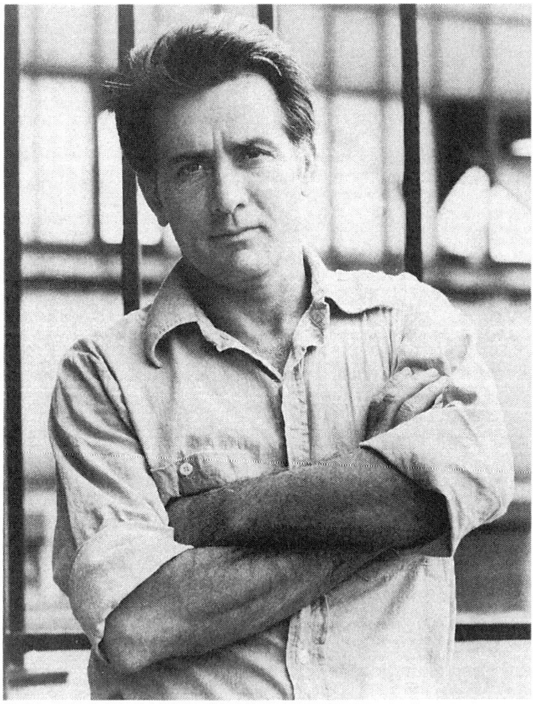

Martin Sheen was a respected film actor for more than three decades when he achieved his greatest fame playing U.S. president Josiah Bartlett on television's *The West Wing* in 1999. *(Photofest)*

the University of Dayton so that he could follow his dream of becoming an actor, an ambition to which his father was very much opposed.

Estévez moved to New York City and found roles in Off-Off Broadway plays while supporting himself in a variety of jobs, including soda jerk, messenger, and janitor. He often ate meals at the Salvation Army center.

He changed his name to avoid being typecast as a Latino, taking the last name "Sheen" in admiration of Bishop Fulton J. Sheen, a leading Catholic spokesperson and early television personality. In 1961, the year he began to appear in small roles on television, Sheen married Janet Templeton. The marriage has lasted more than 45 years.

In 1964, Sheen got his big break appearing opposite Patricia Neal and Jack Albertson in the family drama *The Subject Was Roses* on Broadway. His earnest performance as a troubled son earned him a Tony nomination for Best Supporting or Featured Actor in a Drama.

Sheen made his screen debut in *The Incident* (1967), a gritty urban drama in which he played one of two young thugs who terrorize a group of people in a New York City subway car. More film roles followed, but he did not gain wide attention until 1973 when he played a homicidal young man on a killing spree in the Midwest in *Badlands.* Sheen, his costar Sissy Spacek, and director Terrence Malick gained critical kudos for the film, and Sheen won the Best Actor Award at the San Sebastian Film Festival in Spain.

While he continued to appear in films throughout the decade, Sheen found far more good roles on television, appearing in a number of impressive made-for-television movies and miniseries. In *That Certain Summer* (1972), he played a young gay man in one of the first serious television movies about homosexuality. In *The Execution of Private Slovik* (1974), he played the only American soldier to be executed for desertion in World War II (1939–45). The same year, he played Robert Kennedy in *The Missiles of October,* based on the Cuban missile crisis of 1962. He also played Robert's brother, President John F. Kennedy, to good effect in the miniseries *Kennedy* (1983). He played a very different political figure, a dangerous demagogue running for president, in the movie *The Dead Zone* (1983).

Sheen's most ambitious film, however, is probably the Vietnam epic *Apocalypse Now* (1979) in which he played a soldier sent deep into enemy territory to find a renegade American officer (Marlon Brando) and to assassinate him. The film, directed by Francis Ford Coppola, was shot on location in the Philippines and faced numerous crises. One of the most serious crises was when Sheen suffered a heart attack and had to leave the picture for several months.

All the actor's political characterizations seemed like a long dress rehearsal for his starring role as President Josiah "Jeb" Bartlett in the television series *The West Wing,* which debuted in fall 1999. Well written and superbly acted by a large ensemble of talented actors, *The West Wing* became a huge hit and remained on the air until spring 2006. Sheen's strong performance as a troubled but dedicated president earned him four Emmy nominations for Outstanding Leading Actor in a Drama and the National Council of La Raza's (NCLR) ALMA Award for Outstanding Actor in a Television Series in 2001.

Although he has not identified widely in public with his Latino heritage as some other actors have, including son Emilio Estevez, Sheen says he is as proud of his Spanish roots as he is of his Irish roots.

It has been a standing joke that when he finishes playing a president on television, Sheen will run for the office in real life. The joke may not be so farfetched. Sheen's commitment to political and social issues is legendary in Hollywood. A dedicated pacifist, he has been arrested more than 70 times for participating in various demonstrations against war and the military. "I love my country enough to suffer its wrath," he has said. In June 2001, he was sentenced to three years probation for trespassing on an air-force base against the construction of a defense system.

Sheen is no stranger to more traditional political campaigns and vigorously supported the failed candidacy of former attorney general Janet Reno for governor of Florida against sitting Republican governor Jeb Bush in 2002.

Besides Estevez, Sheen's other three children—Charlie Sheen, Renee Estévez, and Ramon Estévez—are all working actors. Sheen played son Charlie's father in the film *Wall Street.*

Further Reading

Hargrove, Jim. *Martin Sheen: Actor and Activist* (People of Distinction). Chicago: Children's Press, 1991.

Katz, Ephraim, Fred Klein, and Ronald Dean Nolen. *The Film Encyclopedia,* 4th edition. New York: HarperResource, 2001, p. 1248.

Riley, Lee, and David Shumacher. *The Sheens: Martin, Charlie, and Emilio Estevez.* New York: St. Martin's Press, 1989.

Sinnott, Susan. *Extraordinary Hispanic Americans.* Chicago: Children's Press, 1991, pp. 213–215.

Further Viewing

Apocalypse Now (1979). Paramount Home Video, VHS/DVD, 1992.

Badlands (1973). Warner Home Video, VHS/DVD, 1995/1999.

Kennedy (1983). Starmaker-Anchor Bay/Lance Entertainment, VHS/DVD, 1989/2001.

The West Wing—The Complete First Two Seasons (1999–2001). Warner Home Video, DVD box set, 2004.

Sierra, Paul

(1944–) *painter, commercial artist*

A painter of radiant, swirling landscapes and dark, enigmatic figures, Paul Sierra's art is a unique blend of exotic expressionism and shadowy surrealism. He was born in Havana, Cuba, on July 30, 1944. His father was a lawyer and expected his son to become a doctor, but Paul was interested in art and drew from childhood. In high school, he also became interested in filmmaking. In 1961, two years after Fidel Castro's rise to power, the Sierra family fled Cuba for the United States. They lived a short time in Miami, Florida, before settling in Chicago, Illinois, where Sierra's father worked as a lawyer for the Union Tank Car Corporation.

In 1963, Sierra enrolled at the School of the Art Institute of Chicago, where he studied under Puerto Rican artist Rufino Silva, who became his mentor and friend. Feeling that he had learned all he could at the Art Institute, he left in 1966, married, and got a job as an ad layout artist. He has since expressed regret about leaving school before he had established himself as a fine artist.

Sierra did not find himself as an artist until he married his second wife. (His first marriage, which produced a daughter, ended in divorce.) The couple spent their honeymoon in Puerto Rico where Sierra rediscovered his childhood memories of island life. He soon began to paint the rich tropical landscapes that have since been a major theme in his work. However, he has pointed to such American and British artists as Jackson Pollock and Francis Bacon as influences in his work as well. "Although I grew up in Cuba," he writes on his Web site, "my artistic and emotional links to my Latin roots are intertwined with the influence of North American art and culture."

The swirling auras that surround Sierra's landscapes and figures create a magical atmosphere that is often disturbing. In a number of his large paintings, human figures are trapped by water, representing a natural environment that they struggle to overcome. "[His art] speaks to our most secret feelings and fears," writes art critic Victor M. Cassidy. "His images rarely sooth or delight, but they are very hard to forget."

Sierra's work is in the permanent collections of numerous museums including the Smithsonian American Art Museum (SAAM) in Washington, D.C.; the Museum of Contemporary Art in Chicago; and the Brauer Museum of Art at Valparaiso University in Indiana. He is closely connected with the Halstead Gallery in Chicago, an artists' cooperative.

Despite his commercial success, Sierra remains modest about his achievements. "I only hope to live long enough to make a good painting," he has said.

Further Reading

Beardsley, John, and Jane Livingston. *Hispanic Art in the United States: Thirty Contemporary Painters & Sculptors.* New York: Abbeville Press, 1987, pp. 236–239.

Fondo del Sol Visual Arts Center. *Cuba–USA: The First Generation.* Washington, D.C.: Fondo del Sol Visual Arts Center, 1991, pp. 22–23.

Paul Sierra's Studio. An Official Web Site. Available online. URL: http://www.paulsierra.com. Downloaded on January 19, 2006.

Yorba, Jonathan. *Arte Latino: Treasures from the Smithsonian American Art Museum.* New York: Watson–Guptill Publications. 2001, pp. 86–87.

Smits, Jimmy
(1955–) *actor*

A dark, handsome leading man and an actor of great intelligence, Jimmy Smits has starred in three of the most successful dramatic television series of the past two decades. He was born in Brooklyn, New York, on July 9, 1955. His mother is Puerto Rican, and his father is from Suriname, a small country in South America. In high school, Smits excelled at football and acting. The drama-club's star, he went on to Brooklyn College where he majored in theater and received a bachelor of arts (B.A.) degree in 1980. He earned a master of fine arts (M.F.A.) from Cornell University in New York in 1982.

Smits soon found work as an actor in Off-Broadway plays in New York City. His stage successes led to roles in several films and some television work, including the two-hour pilot of the hit crime series *Miami Vice* in 1984. Two years later, he landed the role of attorney Victor Sifuentes on the hit drama *LA Law* (1986–94). Smits's character was the most idealistic and crusading of the firm's lawyers, and the part earned him four Emmy nominations for Outstanding Supporting Actor in a Drama Series. He finally won the award on the fourth try in 1990.

Soon after, he left the show to pursue a film career. He found some solid roles, especially as a committed general of the Mexican Revolution in *Old Gringo* (1989). The film was based on a novel by Carlos Fuentes about the last days of American writer Ambrose Bierce, who mysteriously disappeared in Mexico during the Mexican Revolution (1910–20). The film costarred Jane Fonda, who also was producer, and Gregory Peck as Bierce. Unfortunately, *Old Gringo* flopped at the box office despite some excellent reviews, and Smits's film career stalled.

He soon gravitated back to television, playing the title role in the cable movie *The Cisco Kid* (1994) with costar CHEECH MARIN. While on location in Morocco for another cable film, *Solomon and Sheba,* he received a message from *LA Law* producer Steven Bochco asking him to replace actor David Caruso in his new police series *NYPD Blue* (1993–2005). Ironically, Smits had been offered the role before Caruso and turned it down. Now, he was ready to accept it. He played Detective Bobby Simone and again earned an Emmy nomination each season he was on the show.

He found time from the demands of a weekly TV series to make *My Family, Mi Familia* (1995), an epic drama about the life of a Mexican-American family, directed by GREGORY NAVA. Smits left *NYPD Blue* in 1998, and his career was in limbo for a few years. Promised series never materialized, and he found few challenging film roles. Then he won the role of Senator Bail Organa in *Attack of the Clones* (2002), the first *Star Wars* prequel. He repeated the role in *Revenge of the Sith* (2005), gaining a whole new fan base of sci-fi enthusiasts.

In late 2003, Smits appeared on Broadway in the Pulitzer Prize–winning play *Anna of the Tropics.* The following year, he joined the cast of the award-winning political drama series *The West Wing* (1999–2006) as Texas Congressman Matthew Santos. In its last season, Santos campaigned to succeed Josiah Bartlett (MARTIN SHEEN) as president.

Smits is a founding member of the National Hispanic Foundation for the Arts, an organization dedicated to advancing the presence and quality of roles for Latinos in the entertainment industry. He owns the Conga Room Club in Los Angeles (LA) with partners JENNIFER LOPEZ and PAUL RODRIGUEZ. Smits has two daughters from his first marriage, which ended in divorce. He has been living with actress Wanda De Jesus since 1986.

"Celebrity hits like a bomb," Smits has said of his career. "So you have to find what makes you stable in the storm. Then, no matter what's happening around you, no matter what the hype or the publicity, you can still manage to make leaps in your work as an artist."

Further Reading

Cole, Melanie. *Jimmy Smits: A Real-Life Reader Biography.* Hockessin, Del.: Mitchell Lane Publishers, 1997.

Hispanic Heritage. "Jimmy Smits," Gale-Thomson Web Site. Available online. URL: http://www.gale.com/free_resources/chh/bio/smits_j.htm. Downloaded on March 24, 2006.

The Internet Movie Database. "Jimmy Smits," The Internet Movie Database Web Site. Available online. URL: http://www.imdb.com/name/nm0001751/. Downloaded on January 20, 2006.

Further Viewing

My Family, Mi Familia (1995). New Line Home Video, VHS/DVD, 1997/2004.

NYPD Blue—The Complete Third Season (2000). Fox Home Video, DVD box set, 2006.

Old Gringo (1989). Sony Pictures, VHS/DVD, 1994/2002.

T

Tacla, Jorge

(1958–) *painter, mixed-media artist*

An exceptionally cerebral artist, Jorge Tacla expresses the strange paradoxes and turns of modern life in his ambiguous architectural paintings and landscapes that are peopled with fragile sticklike figures. He was born in Santiago, Chile, on January 9, 1958. He was in his teens when General Augusto Pinochet seized power in Chile in 1973 and instituted a repressive regime. Tacla studied art at the Escuela de Bellas Artes, Universidad de Chile, in his hometown from 1976 to 1979. He immigrated to the United States in May 1981 and settled in New York City.

Tacla had his first exhibitions of paintings at galleries in Santiago and Lima, Peru, the following year. His first solo exhibitions in the United States took place in 1983. Originally, his architectural paintings seemed divorced from the real world, but by the early 1990s, his work was becoming more political, albeit in an oblique manner. *Project Transformation* depicts a mountainside with a pattern of tormented stick figures. In *Inverse Operations,* a diptych (a pair of related paintings on two panels), the stick figures dominate the canvas. "The emotional resonance of the postures of these figures—like agonized dancers—conveys Tacla's interest in the role of suffering in daily life," writes Joseph Ruzicka, "and the complex and uncertain relationships between victims and perpetrators."

Tacla's first public commission, *Memories of the Bronx,* a series of paintings, was completed in 1998 for the Bronx Housing Court and depicts the building of the courthouse on New York's Grand Concourse. The artist views the work as a way of connecting past memories with present realities.

Tacla's paintings have earned him an international audience, and his work has been exhibited in museums and galleries in Stockholm, Sweden; Valencia, Spain; and Caracas, Venezuela; among other places. In 2005, he had exhibits at the Center for Architecture, New York City; the Elaine L. Jacob Gallery, Wayne State University, Detroit, Michigan; and the Museo de Arte Del Banco de la República, Bogotá, Colombia. He is the recipient of a Guggenheim Foundation Fellowship (1988) and grants from the New York Foundation for the Arts (1987 and 1991). In 1992, he was the recipient of the Brazilian Eco Art Award. He is divorced and has a daughter.

"[The] ruined facades, abandoned interiors, and piles of detritus are among the images Tacla repeatedly returns to," wrote John Yau. "The world, his paintings suggest, is in a state of permanent decay. And yet, despite the recurrence of these images, the artist's intent is not didactic. . . . He is preoccupied with the imaginative space these decaying structures create in our mind, the way they both illuminate our past and our future."

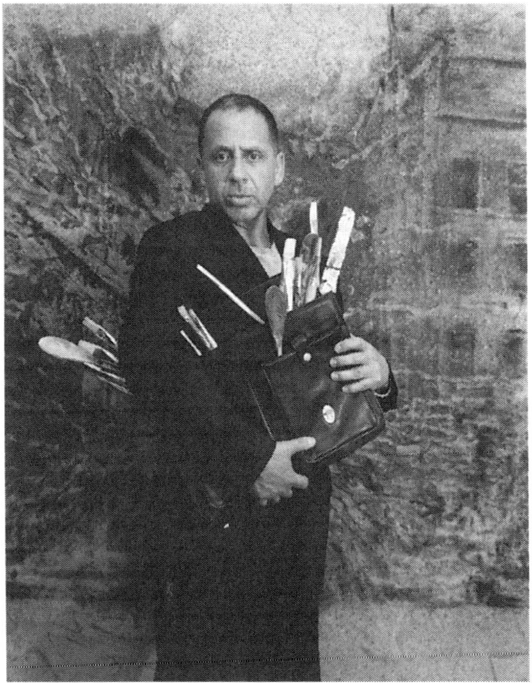

Chilean-born Jorge Tacla uses architectural drawings in his artwork to explore the decay of modern civilization. *(Kate Mathis)*

Further Reading

Przybilla, Carrie. *Art at the Edge: Jorge Tacla.* Atlanta, Ga.: High Museum of Art, 1991.

Ruzicka, Joseph. "Jorge Tacla at Nohra Haime—New York, New York—Review of Exhibitions." *Art in America,* June 1994, p. 102.

Tacla, Jorge. *Internal Biology.* New York: Garza Garcia, Galeria Ramis Basquet, 1994.

———. *Jorge Tacla: Shanty Town October–November 1991.* Galeria Ramis Basquet, 1998.

Tapia, Luis
(Luis Eligio Tapia)
(1950–) santero, *sculptor*

A self-taught artist, Luis Tapia has almost single-handedly revolutionized the centuries-old tradition of carved religious figures, *santos,* bringing it into the contemporary world. He was born Luis Eligio Tapia in Santa Fe, New Mexico, on July 6, 1950. His ancestors were among the first Spanish settlers of New Mexico. His father was a firefighter who died when he was a child. His mother worked as a counselor at the New Mexico School for the Deaf.

Although he showed early promise as an artist, Tapia's talent was discouraged at the Catholic high school that he attended. After graduating, he studied for a year at New Mexico State University in Las Cruces; he then got a job in a retail business. By age 20, he was becoming more and more interested in the traditional arts of his people, as were many young Southwestern artists. Tapia closely studied the *santos* in the storage rooms of the Museum of International Folk Art in Santa Fe. With no formal training as an artist but with the encouragement of his wife, he began to carve nudes out of wood. Soon after, he was creating *santos.*

In 1972, Tapia began to exhibit his artwork at numerous regional fiestas. The reaction from collectors and the public in general was not positive. While traditional *santeros* painted their figures with artificially aged colors to match those of the old *santos,* Tapia used bright, primary colors to make his figures fresh and innovative. The reaction to his work was so negative that he was urged to stop exhibiting at the annual Spanish Market in Santa Fe, the primary market for *santos.*

Undaunted, Tapia continued to make his unique *santos.* To support his family, he began to restore and build furniture, including religious altarpieces and other religious pieces for churches. He also joined six other Mexican-American artists to found La Cofradia de Artes y Artesanos Hispanicos (Brotherhood of Hispanic Arts and Artists) to advance traditional Latino arts and crafts in bold contemporary terms. The group has played a primary role in the revival of Southwest arts and crafts.

Tapia's work began to express more and more his own times and current Latino life and culture. This often meant taking traditional religious images and giving them a contemporary twist. His Saint Anthony, for example, in *The Temptation of St. Anthony* (1991), is not only tempted by the Devil with sexual immorality but also with over-indulgence in alcohol. His *Pieta* (1999) updates the traditional image of Mary, Mother of Jesus, holding the broken corpse of her son. In Tapia's version, a Latino woman holds the lifeless body of her tattooed son who has died from a bullet through his chest. The figures are in the shadow of a cross-shaped street lamp.

His work is not without its touches of humor. In *Death Cart* (1986), Tapia's angel of death takes the traditional form of a woman's skeleton, but her liveliness bears his own creative stamp. The skeleton sticks out her tongue from her bony mouth and stares with mica eyes. Red hair extends down her back in a ponytail.

After more than a decade, Tapia finally had his first one-person show at the Owings–Dewey Fine Arts Gallery in Santa Fe in 1991. Since then, the gallery has become a major outlet for the sale of his work. His most recent exhibition there, *Ay, Que Vida!,* took place in summer 2002. Tapia has won widespread critical praise for his work and is today one of the most admired folk artists in the United States. Since 1979, he has appeared as a guest lecturer at colleges in his native New Mexico and Arizona. His son Sergio Tapia (1972–) is also a well-known contemporary *santero.* "By combining an innovative use of media, bold color, and an occasional dose of good humor, I am able to use my art as an effective means of social commentary," Luis Tapia has said.

Further Reading

Beardsley, John, and Jane Livingston. *Hispanic Art in the United States: Thirty Contemporary Painters & Sculptors.* New York: Abbeville Press, 1987, pp. 244–245.

Connors, Andrew L. *Luis Tapia: Ay Que Vida!* Santa Fe, N.Mex.: Owings–Dewey Fine Art, 2003.

Riggs, Thomas, ed. *St. James Guide to Hispanic Artists.* Detroit, Mich.: St. James Press, 2002, pp. 585–587.

Torres, Liz (Elizabeth Torres)

(1947–) *actor, comedian, singer*

A big woman physically, with a talent to match, Liz Torres has been one of the most pervasive Latina faces on television for more than three decades. She was born Elizabeth Torres in the Bronx, New York, on January 1, 1947. Of Puerto Rican heritage, she started out as a stand-up comic and a singer in small clubs around New York City. After honing her stage act, she appeared on *The Tonight Show* with host Johnny Carson. The national exposure soon led to appearances on several top television variety shows; in 1969, Torres made her film debut as a prostitute in the comedy *Utterly without Redeeming Social Value.*

Her next big break came about through another actress's tragedy. Barbara Colby had completed only three episodes of the television sitcom *Phyllis* (1975–77), starring Cloris Leachman, when she was murdered in Venice, California. Torres was brought in to replace her in the supporting role. The following year, she landed a recurring role for a season on the popular sitcom *All in the Family* (1971–78). From there, Torres played starring roles in several short-lived sitcoms—*Checking In* (1981); *The New Odd Couple* (1982), based on the hit Neil Simon play; and *City* (1990). She finally got the hit show that her talents deserved, playing Mahalia Sanchez on *The John Larroquette Show* (1993–96), which depicted life in a big-city bus station. The role earned her several Emmy and Golden Globe nominations. Torres had previously won an Emmy for her guest appearance on the series *The Famous Teddy Z* (1989–90).

Torres has found far less success in movies where she has usually been relegated to small supporting

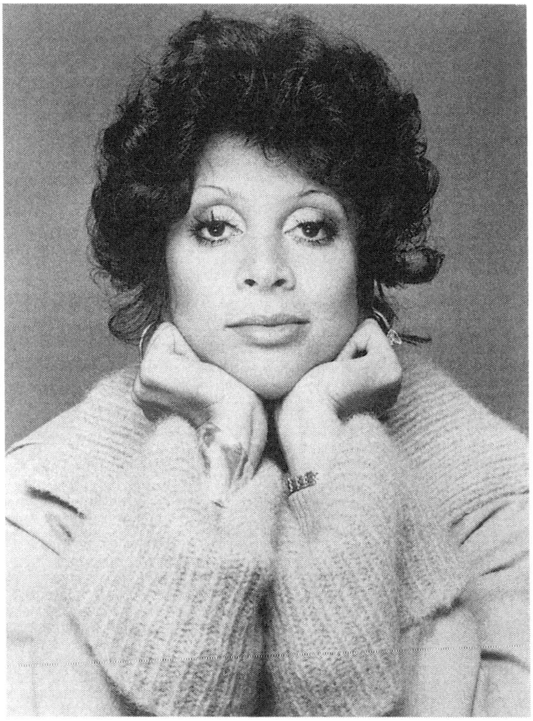

A veteran of no fewer than eight television series, Liz Torres has been seen most recently as dance teacher Miss Patty on *Gilmore Girls*. *(Photofest)*

roles; however, she has fared better in the theater. She replaced RITA MORENO on Broadway in the role of Googie Gomez, a crazy Latina entertainer in the hit comedy *The Ritz*. She was equally effective as the dizzy wife of a would-be songwriter in the dark comedy *House of Blue Leaves*.

Most recently, Torres has found perhaps her greatest exposure playing Miss Patty, a dance teacher, on the hit comedy/drama *Gilmore Girls* (2000–), a show about a single mother and her teenage daughter. She also appeared in director GREGORY NAVA's groundbreaking television-drama series about a Latino family, *American Family* (2001), on the Public Broadcasting System (PBS). Torres is the recipient of two American Comedy Awards and appeared at the White House in 1978 for the first National Hispanic Week Celebration at the invitation of President Jimmy Carter.

Liz Torres is active in several causes, most prominently the fight against acquired immunity deficiency syndrome (AIDS) and funding for public television. She lives in Los Angeles (LA), California.

Further Reading

The Internet Movie Database. "Liz Torres," The Internet Movie Database. Available online. URL: http://www.imdb.com/name/nm0005500/. Downloaded on February 6, 2006.

Nava, Yolanda. *It's All in the Frijoles: 100 Famous Latinos Share Real-Life Stories, Time-Tested Dichos, Favorite Folktales, and Inspiring Words of Wisdom.* New York: Fireside Books, 2000, pp. 264–265.

Reyes of Comedy Night. "Liz Torres," Congressional Hispanic Caucus Institute Web Site. Available online. URL: http://www.chci.org/events/2002/reyes/gentertain.htm. Downloaded on March 30, 2006.

Further Viewing

Gilmore Girls: Season 1. Warner Home Video, CD box set, 2004.

Torres, Raquel
(Wilhelmina von Osterman, Paula Marie Osterman, Hilda Torres)
(1908–1987) *actress*

The leading lady of the first truly "sound" movie, Raquel Torres had a brief but memorable career as one of Hollywood's top Latina stars. Paula Marie Osterman (some sources say her birth name was Wilhelmina von Osterman) was born in Hermosillo, Mexico, on November 11, 1908. Her father was a German mining engineer working in Mexico when he met and married her Mexican (possibly Spanish) mother. Paula attended a Mexican convent school where she learned German and Spanish. Her mother died when she was still a child, and her father moved the family to California. She finished her schooling at a convent school in Los Angeles (LA).

Her exotic beauty and acting ability soon won Osterman a contract with Metro Goldwyn–Mayer (MGM) studios. The studio wanted her to change her name to something more Latin sounding that would match her dark looks. She took her mother's maiden name of Torres and changed her first name to Hilda and then Raquel. At age 19, Torres made an auspicious film debut in the romance *White Shadows in the South Seas* (1928), an early sound film in which she played a South Sea island girl who falls in love with a white man. W. S. Van Dyke directed the film in an unusual semidocumentary style. According to many film historians, *White Shadows* was the first film to be fully synchronized for music, dialogue, and sound effects. It won an Academy Award for Best Cinematography.

The film made Torres a star, and during the next six years she appeared in about a dozen more films, usually playing an exotic Latina. Among the most interesting of these was *The Bridge of San Luis Rey* (1929), the first of three film adaptations of Thornton Wilder's famous novel about the destruction of a bridge in Peru and the people who died on it.

She also played the vamp Vera Marcal who tries to seduce Groucho Marx in the Marx Brothers' comedy classic *Duck Soup* (1933). It was to her that Groucho delivered his famous line, "I could dance with you until the cows came home. On second thought, I'd rather dance with the cows until you came home."

Torres made two more films and then retired from acting to marry wealthy businessman Stephen Ames in 1935. He died in 1955, and she married actor Jon Hall four years later. They later divorced.

Raquel Torres died from the aftereffects of a stroke at age 78 in Malibu, California, on August 10, 1987. (Some sources give her death date as August 13 or August 19.)

Further Reading

The Internet Movie Database. "Raquel Torres," The Internet Movie Database. Available online. URL: http://www.imdb.com/name/nm0868799/. Downloaded on February 8, 2006.

Rodriguez, Clara E. *Heroes, Lovers, and Others: The Story of Latinos in Hollywood.* Washington, D.C.: Smithsonian Books, 2004, pp. 15–17.

Silents are Golden. "'White Shadows in the South Seas' Reviews." Silentsaregolden.com. Available online. URL: http://www.silentsaregolden.com/whiteshadowsreview.html. Downloaded on March 26, 2006.

Further Viewing

Duck Soup (1933). MCA Home Video/Image Entertainment, VHS/DVD, 1992/1998.

Treviño, Jesse

(1946–) *painter, muralist*

The first Mexican-American artist to be exhibited at the Smithsonian Institute in Washington, D.C., Jesse Treviño is best known for his towering mosaic murals and his huge photorealistic portraits. He was born in Monterrey, Mexico, on December 24, 1946. When he was two, his family moved to the United States, settling in San Antonio, Texas. A budding artist from an early age, Treviño won his first art contest in elementary school. His father, a milkman, died when he was 11. After high school, Treviño enrolled in the Art Students League in New York City. He was developing as an artist and made plans to go to Paris, France, to study art when he received his draft notice at the height of the Vietnam War.

He was inducted into the army and was sent to Southeast Asia. Only three months after his arrival there, Treviño lost his right hand when a booby trap exploded near him. For an artist, it was the worst nightmare to be imagined—the loss of his painting hand. He remained hospitalized for the next two years. Determined to return to his art, Treviño doggedly worked on drawing, and later painting, with his left hand. When he was released from the hospital, he went back to school. He earned an Associate of Arts (A.A.) degree from San Antonio Junior College and then attended Our Lady of the Lake University also in San Antonio, earning a bachelor of arts (B.A.) degree in art. Later, he earned a master of fine arts (M.F.A.) degree in painting from the University of Texas–San Antonio.

Now skilled at painting with his left hand, Treviño began to paint the people and places he most loved in his old neighborhood on the West Side of San Antonio. His paintings were colorful and meticulously detailed in a style that is so close to reality that it is called photorealism. Some of these early paintings, such as *Mis Hermones* (My Brothers, 1976), virtually look like a posed photograph but capture the personalities of each of his six brothers in a way that a simple snapshot never could. In 1987, Jesse Treviño received the National Hispanic Heritage Award as Artist of the Year.

In more recent years, Treviño has concentrated on murals, which he conceives and executes on a grand style. His *Spirit of Healing,* a tile mosaic mural on the wall of the Santa Rosa Children's Hospital, is one of the largest murals in North America and a San Antonio landmark. The nine-story-high mural is composed of more than 150,000 pieces of German ceramic tile in 70 different colors. It depicts a guardian angel who is posed above a young boy. It was a labor of love for Treviño, whose own struggles have made him keenly sensitive to the pain of disease and injury in others.

More recently, he has been working on a 40-foot-tall three-dimensional *veladora,* or traditional religious candleholder, that he dedicates to the victims of the terrorist attacks of September 11, 2001.

Further Reading

The Artchive. "Jesse Treviño," Artchive.com. Available online. URL: http://www.artchive.com/artchive/T/trevino.html. Downloaded on February 14, 2006.

McDonnell, Sharon. "Treviño Creates a Vision of Hope," Hispanic Magazine.com. Available online. URL: http://www.hispaniconline.com/magazine/2003/dec/Cultura/index.html. Downloaded on March 15, 2006.

"Mural Masterpiece Is San Antonio Treasure—El Arte de Jesse Treviño," *Hispanic Times Magazine,* August–September 1998; LookSmart. Available online. URL: http://www.findarticles.com/p/articles/mi_mOFWK/is_n4-v19/ai_21260652. Downloaded on September 21, 2006.

Treviño, Jesús Salvador

(1946–) *filmmaker, screenwriter, television director, documentary filmmaker*

Starting out as a hard-hitting activist documentary filmmaker, Jesús Salvador Treviño is today perhaps the most successful Latino American director of television drama. He was born in El Paso, Texas, on March 26, 1946, into a poor Mexican-American family. "I remember waiting until Friday, when my dad got his payment, so that we could have some meat," he recalls about his childhood. "That was a big deal."

A good student, Treviño was awarded a scholarship in high school to attend Occidental College in Los Angeles (LA), California. While in college, he met Chicano farmworkers' labor leader Cesar Chavez. Chavez's example had a tremendous effect on Treviño's decision to become a filmmaker, documenting the injustices and struggles of Chicanos (Mexican Americans). His first film as a director was the documentary *Yo soy chicano* (I Am Chicano, 1972), which was funded and aired by the Public Broadcasting System (PBS). Other documentaries for PBS followed, all of them focusing on Chicano culture and politics.

In 1977, Treviño wrote and directed his first feature fictional film, *Raíces de sangre* (Roots of Blood). It is the story of a group of workers in a factory along the U.S. and Mexican border who attempt to organize their fellow workers to fight for better conditions. While the film was largely ignored in the United States, it was well received in Latin America and Spain, where it was named one of the top 50 Latin American films of all time at the Valladolid Film Festival.

In 1982, Treviño directed and wrote *Seguin,* an *American Playhouse* television movie about the siege of the Alamo in Texas, told from a Mexican perspective. It starred EDWARD JAMES OLMOS as Mexican general Santa Anna. As the decade progressed, Treviño worked more and more in television, directing the PBS educational series *Mathnet* (1987). In 1990, he made the move to commercial television, filming an episode of the dramatic series *Gabriel's Fire,* starring James Earl Jones as an ex-con. Soon, Treviño was directing for many of the decade's top dramatic series, including the medical dramas *ER* and *Chicago Hope.* But he found his deepest niche in directing science-fiction series, most notably *Star Trek: Deep Space Nine, Star Trek: Voyager,* and *Babylon 5.* One of his few theatrical features was *Thirdspace* (1998), a film based on *Babylon 5.* More recently, Treviño has worked on such popular series as *Crossing Jordan* and *The O.C.*

Treviño has not, however, abandoned his roots as a documentary filmmaker. The video *In Search of Aztlan* (2003) is an odd blend of comedy and documentary. It follows the Chicano comedy trio Culture Clash as they scour the Southwest in a 1952 Chevy in search of Aztlan, ancient home of the Aztec people of Mexico.

Treviño is also the author of *The Fabulous Sinkhole and Other Stories* (1995), a collection of short stories about life in a Texas barrio (a Latino inner city neighborhood). "You have to approach directing with a degree of perfectionism," he has said. "You have to set high standards and goals, and ask your actors, and your camera crew, and everyone working on the set to come along for the ride to see if we can really make this thing look terrific."

Further Reading

The Internet Movie Database. "Jesús Salvador Treviño," The Internet Movie Database. Available online. URL: http://www.imdb.com/name/nm0872442/. Downloaded on February 14, 2006.

Nava, Yolanda. *It's All in the Frijoles: 100 Famous Latinos Share Real-Life Stories, Time-Tested Dichos, Favorite Folktales, and Inspiring Words of Wisdom.* New York: Fireside Books, 2000, pp. 45–46.

Treviño, Jesús Salvador. *The Fabulous Sinkhole and Other Stories.* Houston, Tex.: Arte Publico Press, 1995.

Further Viewing

Thirdspace (1998). Warner Home Video, VHS, 1999.

Trujillo, Irvin L. (Lawrence Trujillo)
(1954–) *weaver*

A seventh-generation New Mexican weaver, Irvin L. Trujillo brings a personal perspective to his work that turns a time-honored craft into dazzling contemporary art. He was born in Chimayo, New Mexico, on December 17, 1954. His father, Jacobo Trujillo, was a master of the Chimayo style of weaving. This style is just one of a number of different styles that evolved in different regions of the Southwest among Native Americans beginning as early as 800 B.C. The Pueblo Indians were the first weavers, and they passed it on to other peoples, including the Navajo. After the Spanish came to the New World, they adapted the Indian style of weaving.

The Chimayo style emerged in the early 20th century and is a combination of the two stripes of the Rio Grande style and the center design of the

Saltillo technique. It has a uniform texture and is made on a commercial wool warp or lengthwise running threads. When Irvin was 11, his father began to teach him his craft. He wove on summer vacations, and by the time he graduated from high school in 1972, his father had built him a loom of his own for large-scale work. Trujillo owns and uses this same loom today.

While continuing his study of the craft of weaving, he attended the University of New Mexico–Los Alamos, where he studied civil engineering. While there, he met Lisa Rockwood, a marketing major; the couple married a week after graduation in 1984. Trujillo decided to forsake an engineering career to continue his career as a weaver and carry on a long family tradition with the assistance of his wife, who became his pupil.

The Trujillos, who have two children, have studied every kind of style of weaving and weave design. They have experimented with tools and technology, producing works of sublime beauty.

The Hook and the Spider (1995) is a large wool woven piece that is part of the permanent collection of the Smithsonian American Art Museum (SAAM) in Washington, D.C. In it, Trujillo combines Southwest elements with African ones, including the yellow-and-blue spider design and the repeated hook motif that give the piece its unusual name.

The Trujillos own and operate the Centenila Traditional Arts, a weavers' collective at a ranch in Chimayo, New Mexico, where they also raise goats and sheep. Sixteen weavers work and experiment with 11 different styles to make unique handwoven rugs and blanket-weight weavings as well as jackets, coats, pillows, purses, and scarves. "I try to capture the spirit of the old pieces while also expressing my own experience in the contemporary world," Trujillo has said.

Further Reading

Chimayo Weavers. "Irvin Trujillo," Chimayoweavers.com. Available online. URL: http://chimayoweavers.com/Merchant2/merchant.mv?Screen=CTGY&Category_Code =IT. Downloaded on February 9, 2006.

McKay, Mary Terence, and Lisa Trujillo. *The Centinela Weavers of Chimayo Unfolding Tradition: A Brief History of Weaving in New Mexico's Rio Grande Valley. . . .* Chimayo, N.Mex.: Treasure Chest Books, 1999.

Yorba, Jonathan. *Arte Latino: Treasures from the Smithsonian American Art Museum.* New York: Watson–Guptill Publications. 2001, pp. 94–95.

U

Underwood, Consuelo Jiménez
(1949–) *weaver, fiber artist, educator, museum curator*

A pioneering artist who has pushed the boundaries of her genre, Consuelo Jiménez Underwood has elevated the traditional craft of Southwestern weaving to an art form. She was born into a family of migrant agricultural workers in Sacramento, California, on April 29, 1949. Her father is of Huichol Indian descent, and her mother is Mexican American. "Throughout my high school years, we lived on both sides of the border simultaneously," she recalls. "After school, I would walk across the border to Mexicali, a small Mexican city, and walk to our adobe home, which came from my Mom's family. In the late evening, we would drive across the border to Calexico, California, to my Dad's wooden house in the United States." A good student in secondary school, Underwood attended Palamor College in San Marcos, California, and graduated with an Associate of Arts (A.A.) degree in religious studies in 1979. She continued her education at San Diego State University, where she earned a bachelor of arts (B.A.) degree in art in 1981. Four years later, she earned a master of arts (M.A.) degree from the school and then received a master of fine arts (M.F.A.) degree from San Jose State University in 1987.

Underwood's interest in weaving, primarily a decorative craft, soon became a means for expressing her feelings and attitudes toward culture and politics. One of her best-known works, *Virgen de los Caminos* (Virgin of the Roads, 1994), she calls "a memorial quilt to the children who perished while crossing the *frontera,* or border." She intended the quilt for her new granddaughter, but once she added the Virgin, the patron saint of those who make the dangerous journey across the U.S. border to find a better life, she changed her mind. "The quilt no longer belonged to my granddaughter, but to all daughters, especially the ones being pulled along by this crazy world."

The decorative floral border is interrupted by lines of barbed wire that symbolize the struggle and hardship that awaits these illegal immigrants. A picture of a fleeing family taken from warning road signs in southern California is made in white thread so as to be almost invisible against the white cotton fabric. Underwood's point is that these people *are* often invisible to North Americans who take the "good life" for granted.

While the barbed wire in *Virgen de los Caminos* is a woven depiction, Underwood has used real barbed wire as well as other unusual materials in other weavings. In *Frontera Rebozo's Dia/Noche,* she hooked hundreds of swatches of fabric with more than 10,000 safety pins. On each swatch is the border-sign image of the fleeing family, a grim motif to the work. "The work reflects the notion that once the indigenous woman crossed to *el*

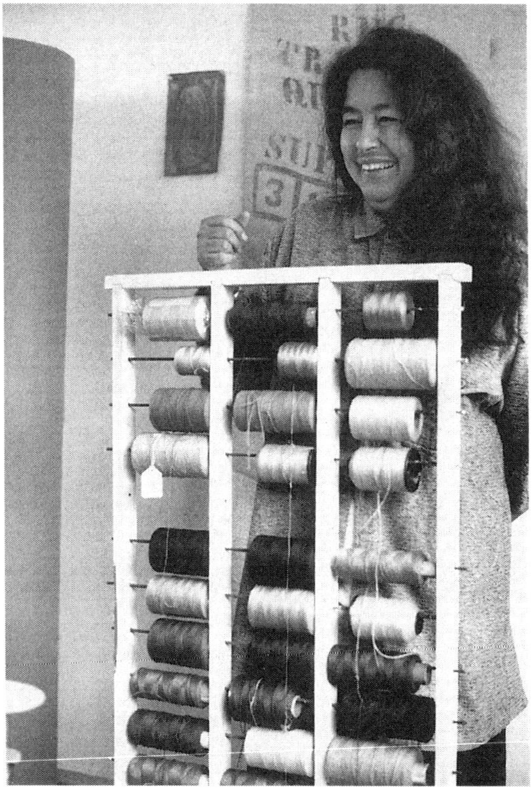

Consuelo Jiménez Underwood has transformed the decorative art of southwestern weaving into an art form of the deepest personal expression. *(Consuelo Jiménez Underwood)*

norte, there was no longer a cultural space to sew, let alone weave," she explains. "Even I use tape or even a stapler to mend my clothing on the run."

Underwood has had solo shows of her work at the Gorman Museum at the University of California–Davis; the Movimiento de Arte y Cultura Latino Americano (MACLA) in San Jose; the Museo de San Carmen in Mexico; and the Centro Cultural de Joan Miro in Madrid, Spain. Her work is in the permanent collections of the Smithsonian American Art Museum (SAAM) in Washington, D.C.; the Museum of Arts & Design in New York City; the Mexican Museum in San Francisco; and the Oakland Museum of Art in California.

She has taught art at San Jose State University's School of Art and Design since 1989 and became a full professor of art in 1995. Underwood has also lectured widely and is a member of the board of directors for Penland School of Arts and Crafts in Penland, North Carolina, and the San Jose Museum of Quilts and Textiles.

"With beauty, grace, and traditional form, my work expresses the quiet rage that has permeated indigenous peoples of the Americas for over 500 years," she has said.

Further Reading

Artist "Media Archive." Meet Consuelo Jiménez Underwood," Luce Foundation Center for American Art. Available online. URL: http://americanart.si.edu/luce/media.cfm?Key=372&type=Archive&subkey=471. Downloaded on September 21, 2006.

FiberScene. "Consuelo Jiménez Underwood," FiberScene.com. Available online. URL: http://www.fiberscene.com/artists/c_underwood.html. Downloaded on February 8, 2006.

Spark. "Consuelo Jiménez Underwood," KQED/Public TV Web Site. Available online. URL: http://www.kqed.org/artists-orgs/consuelooji.jsp. Downloaded on February 8, 2006.

Yorba, Jonathan. *Arte Latino: Treasures from the Smithsonian American Art Museum.* New York: Watson–Guptill Publications. 2001, pp. 96–97.

V

Valadez, John
(1951–) *painter, muralist*

The creator of the greatest landmark work of the Chicano (Mexican-American) mural movement in Southern California, John Valadez has fashioned an urban wonderland on canvas and wall that is celebratory and at times terrifying. He was born in East Los Angeles (East LA), California, in 1951. His parents later separated, and John and his younger brother went to live with their mother, who worked as a secretary and receptionist to support them. John enjoyed drawing as a child and after high school studied at East LA Junior College. It was the turbulent late 1960s, and Chicanos were joining African Americans and women in demonstrating against the discrimination that was entrenched in American society and speaking out for their rights.

While in college, Valadez joined The Mexican American Center for Creative Art (MACCA) under the direction of Emilio Delgado. The center supported a theater group that Valadez joined and for which he helped mount productions of social and political plays in community centers and prisons by such Chicano writers as LUIS VALDEZ. The theater with its drama and passion soon infused itself in Valadez's art.

During this time, he studied at California State University–Long Beach, where he earned a bachelor of fine arts (B.F.A.) degree in 1976. Soon after, he joined with fellow artists CARLOS ALMARAZ, FRANK ROMERO, and Richard Duarto to found the Public Art Center in Highland Park. The center provided space for young Chicano artists and supported the creation of cooperative murals. Valadez and Almaraz worked together on the Los Angeles production of Valdez's play *Zoot Suit* which tells of the unjust imprisonment of a group of young Chicano men for a gang murder in 1940s Los Angeles. Valadez painted a mural for the production on the wall of the Mark Taper Forum, where the play premiered in 1978.

In his brightly hued paintings and murals of this period, Valadez sought to capture the sights of the streets of Latino neighborhoods. The people in his murals were ordinary people, not the legendary characters that populated the murals of other Chicano and Mexican artists. But for all the gritty realism of his portraits, he endowed his subjects with a remarkable strength, dignity, and determination. There is also a dark undercurrent in his work that borders on the surreal. A prime example is *Beto's Vacation* (1985), where the sight of people swimming and boating is offset by a vision of sharks leaping from the water nearby. The unexplained threat is chilling and real.

In 1980, the owner of the Victor Clothing Co. on East LA's primary boulevard, Broadway, saw

Valadez's work in a group exhibition and invited him to propose portraits to be displayed in his store. The results was *The Broadway Mural* (1981), a grand vision of Latino peoples going about their business on the busy thoroughfare. The six-foot-tall and 80-foot-long mural remains Valadez's best-known work and the one on which his reputation rests. While it has since been sold to a private collector who had it moved, other Valadez murals are still in the public eye. These include murals at the federal courthouse in Santa Ana, California; the Yuselta Border Station in El Paso, Texas; and the Junipero Serra State Office Building's auditorium in downtown LA.

In 1987, Valadez was selected as the first American artist to receive an artist-in-residency fellowship at the Fondation d'Art de La Napoule, in France. In 2001, he was awarded a fellowship with the Joan Mitchell Foundation in New York City. Among his recent exhibitions are *John Valadez: La Frontera/The Border* at the Carnegie Art Museum in Oxnard, California, and the traveling show *Arte Latino: Treasures from the Smithsonian American Art Museum* (both 2001). John Valadez is married and has a daughter.

Further Reading

Beardsley, John, and Jane Livingston. *Hispanic Art in the United States: Thirty Contemporary Painters & Sculptors.* New York: Abbeville Press, 1987, pp. 246–248.

Nieto, Margarita, and Bill Lasarow. "John Valadez," Artscenecal.com. Available online. URL: http://artscenecal.com/ArticlesFile/Archive/Articles2004/Articles0904/JoValadezA.html. Downloaded on March 31, 2006.

Riggs, Thomas, ed. *St. James Guide to Hispanic Artists.* Detroit, Mich.: St. James Press, 2002, pp. 610–611.

Valadez, John, and David Baze. *Symbolic Realizites.* Dominguez Hills: California State University, 1985.

Valdez, Horacio

(1929–1992) santero

A late bloomer who only became a *santero,* a carver of religious figures, when he was in his mid-forties, Horacio Valdez created impressive artworks, full of life and spirit. He was a direct influence on such leading contemporary *santeros* as Luis Tapia and Charles M. Carrillo.

He was born in Dixon, New Mexico, just north of Santa Fe, on July 13, 1929. The family moved to Del Norte Colorado, when Horacio was a small child. His mother died when he was 13 and his father was drafted into the army a year later and killed in action during World War II (1939–1945). Horacio returned to Dixon, where he was raised by his grandmother and uncles. He attended high school and later moved to the nearby village of Apodaca, where he worked for many years as a carpenter.

One day, in November 1974, he suffered an accident on a construction site, and his right hand was seriously injured. Unable to work, Valdez whiled away the time making woodcarvings with his pocketknife. A devout Catholic, he eventually began to carve *santos,* religious figures in the time-honored southwestern tradition. His very first santos so impressed the Penitente brotherhood, a secret religious organization in northern New Mexico to which his father and grandfather had belonged, that they initiated him as a member.

However devout, Valdez was not a traditionalist when it came to his art. Traditional *Santeros* rarely painted their carvings, but Valdez did, in bright colors. He was one of the first *santeros* to display and sell painted work at Santa Fe's famed Spanish Market. His religious figures were often unconventional by traditional standards. His *Neustra Señora la Reina del Cielo* (Our Lady, Queen of Heaven, 1991) depicts Mary, mother of Jesus, holding a palm frond with a crown of silver posed above her head.

Although his career as an artist only spanned about 18 years, Valdez turned out an astonishing amount of work. He created more than 250 crucifixes alone. Each of his 14 Stations of the Cross at the Holy Family Church in Chimayo, New Mexico, consist of a scene from Jesus Christ's crucifixion and death painted on a large, hand-carved piece of sugar pine. He is probably best known, however, for his death carts, traditional Mexican reminders of mortality. During Holy Week at Easter time in the Southwest, *Penitentes* drag the carts through the streets in religious processions. Valdez's *Carreta de Muerte* (Death Cart, 1978) is a full-scale cart made of painted cottonwood, with a skeletal figure of death on the seat armed with a bow and arrow to strike down future victims. Both this piece and *Our Lady* are part of the permanent collection of the Smithsonian Museum of American Art (SAAM) in Washington, D.C.

Horacio Valdez died in Apodaca, New Mexico at age 63 on August 16, 1992. He always saw the accident that ended his career as a carpenter as heaven sent. "Nothing bad ever happens without resulting in some good," he often said.

Further Reading

Sagel, Jim. *Horacio Valdez: Master Santero.* Santa Fe: New Mexico Magazine, 1986, pp. 36–41.

Selected Artist Biographies. "Saint Makers: A Living Tradition in Folk Art," Available online. URL: http://www.tfaoi.com/aa/6aa/6aa72b.htm. Downloaded on March 31, 2006.

Yorba, Jonathan. *Arte Latino: Treasures from the Smithsonian American Art Museum.* New York: Watson–Guptill Publications. 2001, pp. 104–105.

Valdez, Luis

(1940–) filmmaker, playwright, stage director, screenwriter

The founder of contemporary Chicano (Mexican-American) theater and a pioneering Latino playwright and filmmaker, Luis Valdez has given voice to the poor and forgotten of American society. He was born in Delano, California, on June 26, 1940. His Mexican-American parents were migrant farmworkers, and he worked alongside them in the agricultural fields as a boy. When not engaged in the work that barely supported them, the Valdez family lived in San Jose, California, where Luis attended school. After high school, he attended San Jose State University on a scholarship as an English major. It was there where his first play, *The Shrunken Head of Pancho Villa,* was staged in 1963. After graduation in 1964, Valdez joined the San Francisco Mime Troupe for a year as an actor, learning theater techniques that he would later put to good use in his own plays.

In 1965, he joined the United Farm Workers (UFW) which was organized by labor leader Cesar Chavez to help the plight of poorly treated Chicano farm laborers. Valdez put his creative abilities to work to help the cause and founded a theatrical company, El Teatro Campesino (Farmworkers Theater). The pioneering company brought theater to people who had never seen it before—the poor Chicanos in the small towns of California. The troupe drove around the countryside in a flatbed truck, performing skits in Spanish that expressed the virtues of the union and that invited residents to become union members. It was political theater at its most basic, and it succeeded. El Teatro Campesino, under Valdez's guidance, not only helped spread the UFW's message and brought in new members, but it also became recognized for its innovative work in the national press and media. It inspired a generation of Chicano and Latino actors, directors, and writers.

"The Chicano Movement gave me a means to exist, a place where I could breathe," Valdez said in a 2000 interview. "I decided to be an explainer of my people to my own people first. It [the teatro] was the heart of what I wanted to do—use the theater to create social change and keep the integrity."

By 1967, Valdez was writing and directing full-length plays for the group that went beyond their first propagandic efforts. During the next decade, he wrote and directed such thought-provoking plays as *Los Vendidas* (The sell-outs, 1967), *Dark Root of a Scream* (1971), and *El Fin del Mundo* (The end of the world, 1976). He also directed his first film, the short *Yo soy Joaquín* (I am Joaquín, 1969), written by Chicano activist Corky Gonzalez.

Valdez's next work, *Zoot Suit* (1978), proved to be his breakthrough play. The fact-based drama with music told about the unjust arrest, conviction, and imprisonment in 1940 Los Angeles of a group of male Chicano youths that were feared and resented for their elaborate and outlandish clothing, known as zoot suits. The play was mounted by the Mark Taper Forum in Los Angeles and was a great success. The leading roles were played by Valdez's brother Daniel, who also wrote the musical numbers, and the then-unknown EDWARD JAMES OLMOS. The play was so successful that the production was moved to New York's Broadway in spring 1979 where it ran for about a month. Valdez directed a film adaptation in 1983 that was shot in the theater where the play ran. The movie, although not a great success, earned a Golden Globe nomination for best musical picture and boosted Olmos to stardom.

Valdez's next movie project would be both a critical and a commercial success. He turned back again in time to the 1950s and depicted the meteoric rise of RITCHIE VALENS, the first Latino rock star. *La Bamba* (1987) starred LOU DIAMOND PHILLIPS as Valens and ESAI MORALES as his troubled half-brother. The film was a hit with both Anglo and Latino audiences and was the first Hollywood film in a Spanish-language version to be successful with audiences in the United States.

Fresh from *La Bamba*'s success, Valdez went to work on a film adaptation of Mexican author Carlos Fuentes's novel *The Old Gringo* about American author Ambrose Bierce's involvement in the Mexican Revolution. However, Valdez had artistic differences with producer and star Jane Fonda and left the film. Since then, he has only directed two films, both for television—*La Pastorela* (The shepherd's tale, 1991) and *The Cisco Kid* (1994), which starred JIMMY SMITS as the legendary "Robin Hood of the West."

Valdez has managed to keep busy with other creative projects. He was playwright-in-residence at the San Diego Repertory Theater (SDRT) from 1998 to 2000, writing his first new play in 14 years, *Mummified Deer* (2000). The play, about the trials and tribulations of a family that descended from Mexico's Yanqui Indians, was produced by the SDRT in 2000 and was a resounding success. The same year, *Zoot Suit* was revived to great acclaim at Chicago's Goodman Theater. "To call Valdez a 'legendary' playwright is not merely to refer to his stature in contemporary Chicano theater," wrote Victor Payan in a review of *Mummified Deer,* "but also to note that he has always worked with the stuff of legend in his work."

Further Reading

Elam, Harry Justin. *Taking It to the Streets: The Social Protest Theater of Luis Valdez and Amiri Baraka.* Ann Arbor: University of Michigan Press, 2001 [reprint].

Mendaza, Sylvia. "Luis Valdez: A Trailblazer," *Cultura,* October 2000.

Sinnott, Susan. *Extraordinary Hispanic Americans.* Chicago: Children's Press, 1991, pp. 211–212.

Valdez, Luis. *Mummified Deer and Other Plays.* Houston, Tex.: Arte Publico Press, 2005.

———. *Zoot Suit and Other Plays.* Houston, Tex.: Arte Publico Press, 1992.

Further Viewing

La Bamba (1987). Sony Home Video, VHS/DVD, 1999.

Zoot Suit (1982). MCA Home Video, VHS/DVD, 1998/2003.

Valdez, Patssi

(1951–) *painter, muralist, conceptual artist, installation artist, performance artist, collagist, photographer, art director, set designer*

A celebrated contemporary Chicana (Mexican-American) artist, Patssi Valdez has charted the spiritual and social progress of her people and herself in a great variety of styles and media. She was born in East Los Angeles (East LA), California, on December 31, 1951. Her troubled family life would later become a major theme of her art. She attended Garfield High School, where she became politically active in the Chicano Movement that was just beginning to surface. In the early 1970s, after graduating from high school, she founded a conceptual performance group ASCO (Spanish for nausea) with fellow artists HARRY GAMBOA, JR., WILLIE HERRÓN, and GRONK.

The group was devoted to artistic experimentalism and street theater. While attacking the American society that they felt repressed Chicanos and other minorities, they did not spare their own Latino culture. *Walking Mural* (1972), a performance piece that they staged one memorable Christmas Eve in 1972, satirized both Latino mural art and Catholicism. Valdez, dressed in black as the Virgin Mary, accompanied Jesus Christ (Herrón) and a Christmas tree (Gronk) down East LA's busy Whittier Boulevard.

In 1980, Valdez left ASCO to return to school and earned a Bachelor of Fine Arts (B.F.A.) degree from Otis/Parsons School of Art and Design in 1981. Returning to her early love of photography, she produced *Downtown Los Angeles* (1983), a masterful photo-collage that celebrated both family and urban life.

Valdez turned to painting in 1988. At the same time, she shifted her focus from the political and the social to the personal. In her most famous works, paintings of domestic interiors, she explored her inner life and feelings. These depictions of homes were anything but tranquil refuges from the outside world. Although no human figures appeared in them, the inanimate objects—furniture, beds, and kitchen craft—had an almost malevolent life of their own. They left an impression of family violence and discord, which were undoubtedly drawn from her own early life.

In the 1990s, Valdez's search for her identity as an artist and a woman took her to a more peaceful place, reflected in such harmonious installations as *Living Room,* part of the exhibition *Patssi Valdez: A Room of One's Own* at the San Jose Museum of Art in California in 1995. Her interior paintings from this period reflect the calm and tranquility of her vacation home by the sea in Playas de Tijuana, Mexico.

In 1999, a retrospective of her work, *Patssi Valdez: A Precarious Comfort,* opened at the Mexican Museum in San Francisco. The same year, she was awarded a $25,000 Durfee Artist Fellowship. Her work was included in the touring show *Chicano Visions: American Painters on the Verge* (2001–06).

A multitalented artist, Valdez has served as a visual and cultural consultant on the Latino film *My Family, Mi Familia* (1995) and the Public Broadcasting System (PBS) series *American Family* (2002–04), both directed by GREGORY NAVA. "The beauty of an archetypal working class Chicano home with a proud presentation of ceramics, lace tablecloths, plastic furniture covers and family photos is what makes *La Familia . . .* so radiant," writes Rita Gonzalez about Valdez's set design for the film. In 2005, Valdez was commissioned by the Santa Fe Opera in New Mexico to make five paintings of their current opera season. "I just paint what I'm feeling and what I'm thinking and what I care about at that particular time in my life," she has said.

Further Reading

Gonzalez, Rita. "Patssi Valdez: Off the Wall and Out of the Box," Current Trends, San Diego Latino Film Festival Web Site. Available online. URL: http://

www.sdlatinofilm.com/trends20.html. Downloaded on March 16, 2006.

Riggs, Thomas, ed. *St. James Guide to Hispanic Artists.* Detroit, Mich.: St. James Press, 2002, pp. 612–614.

Smithsonian Oral History Interviews Collection. "Interview with Patssi Valdez," Smithsonian Archives of American Artists. Available online. URL: http://www.aaa.si.edu/collections/oral histories/transcripts/valdez99.htm. Downloaded on February 26, 2006.

Romo, Tere. *Patssi Valdez: A Precarious Comfort Una Comodidad Precaria.* San Francisco, Calif.: The Mexican Museum, 1999.

Yorba, Jonathan. *Arte Latino: Treasures from the Smithsonian American Art Museum.* New York: Watson-Guptill Publications. 2001, pp. 106–107.

Valens, Ritchie (Richard Steve Valenzuela)

(1941–1959) *rock singer, guitarist, songwriter*

The first Latino-American rock star, Ritchie Valens died tragically before he could realize the full potential of his musical talent. Richard Steve Valenzuela was born in Los Angeles, California, on May 13, 1941. His Mexican-American parents separated when he was three, and he spent much of his childhood living with his father in Pacoima in the San Fernando Valley. Valenzuela was barely a teenager when rock-and-roll music was born. He loved its energy and drive and was particularly drawn to rockabilly artists like the early Elvis Presley and the frenetic rhythm-and-blues (R&B) music of black singer Little Richard. Valenzuela taught himself the guitar and by junior high school was playing and singing for the other students at lunchtime.

At age 17, he auditioned for Bob Keane, president and founder of Del-Fi Records in Hollywood. Keane immediately recognized Valenzuela's talent and signed him to a recording contract. He convinced the singer to shorten his name to *Valens,* fearing that white teens would not buy records that were made by a Latino rocker. Valens's first release, the self-penned rocker "Come On, Let's Go," became a national hit and just missed the top-40 charts in early 1958.

At the time, Valens was in love with a girl named Donna, whose father would not allow her to date a Mexican American. Out of his yearning, he wrote a love ballad to her. "Donna" became his second and biggest hit, soaring to #2 on the pop charts. But it was the flip side of the record on which Valens's main legacy rests today. "La Bamba" was a Mexican folksong that Valens adapted into a rousing rock anthem in the original Spanish. Because he was not fluent in Spanish, he learned the lyrics phonetically. Although it was only a middling hit at the time, "La Bamba" has become a rock classic, recorded by numerous artists, including the Chicano rock group, Los Lobos, who were heavily influenced by Valens and his music.

By late 1958, Ritchie Valens was a rising star on the music scene. He appeared in the rock film *Go Johnny Go* (1958), performed on Dick Clark's *American Bandstand* television program, and toured the country with such top acts as Jackie Wilson and Eddie Cochran.

In early 1959, he signed on for the "Winter Dance Party" tour with Buddy Holly and The Big Bopper, a former deejay named J. P. Richardson who had a huge hit with the novelty song "Chantilly Lace." After a concert in Clear Lake, Iowa, on February 3, Holly charted a three-passenger plane to take him to the next gig in Fargo, North Dakota. Richardson, who had a severe cold, did not want to ride in the chilly, cramped tour bus and convinced Holly's bass player, Waylon Jennings, to give him his seat on the plane. Valens, who also had a cold, had never ridden in a small plane before. He persuaded Holly's guitarist Jerry Allsup to flip a coin for the third seat. Valens won the toss.

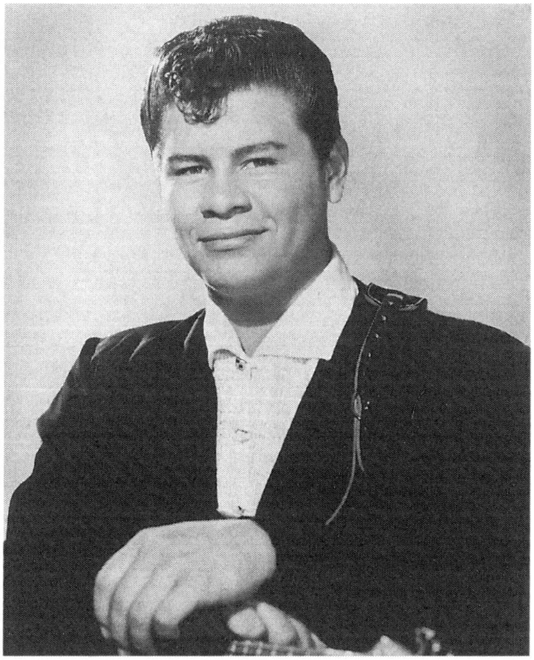

In his short career, Ritchie Valens brought a Latino sensibility to rock and roll in his classic recording "La Bamba." *(Photofest)*

The small plane took off in a gathering snowstorm, against the pilot's best judgment. Only moments later, it crashed in a cornfield, killing everyone aboard. The three stars' deaths were seen by many as the end of an innocent era in rock music. While Holly was a major artist at the time of his death, Valens was just getting started, and how far he would have risen in his career is impossible to say.

Most Americans had largely forgotten him when the biographical film *La Bamba* was released in 1987. Directed by LUIS VALDEZ and featuring an energetic performance by LOU DIAMOND PHILLIPS as Valens, it was a huge hit, as was the soundtrack, which featured Los Lobos and CARLOS SANTANA playing Valens's music. Valens and his reputation as a pioneer of rock were restored. He was inducted into the Rock-and-Roll Hall of Fame in 2001.

Further Reading

Lehmer, Larry. *The Day the Music Died: The Last Tour of Buddy Holly, the Big Bopper, and Ritchie Valens.* New York: Schirmer Books, 2004.

Mendheim, Beverly. *Ritchie Valens: The 1st Latino Rocker.* Tempe, Ariz.: Bilingual Review Press, 1987.

The Official Ritchie Valens Web Site. Available online. URL: http://www.ritchievalens.com. Downloaded on February 17, 2006.

Sinnott, Susan. *Extraordinary Hispanic Americans.* Chicago: Children's Press, 1991, pp. 232–233.

Further Listening

The Ritchie Valens Story. Rhino Records, CD, 2004.

Further Viewing

Go Johnny Go (1958). Anchor Bay Entertainment, VHS, 1989.

La Bamba (1987). Sony Pictures Home Entertainment, VHS/DVD, 2000/1999.

Vargas, Alberto
(Joaquin Alberto Vargas y Chavez, "Varga")
(1896–1982) *illustrator, painter*

One of the great American illustrators, Alberto Vargas's drawings and paintings of beautiful, young women were a cherished fantasy of male-magazine readers for more than five decades. Joaquin Alberto Vargas y Chavez was born in Arequipa, Peru, on February 9, 1896. His father was a successful photographer who taught Alberto the art of retouching portrait photographs. In 1911, Vargas traveled to Paris, France, with his father and brother. There, he fell under the spell of the Austrian artist and illustrator Raphael Kirchner, a pioneer of the "pin-up" girl, whom he created for popular postcards. The two sons continued to Switzerland where they attended school. Alberto was apprenticed to work at an English photography company in 1916, but World War I (1914–1918) was still raging across

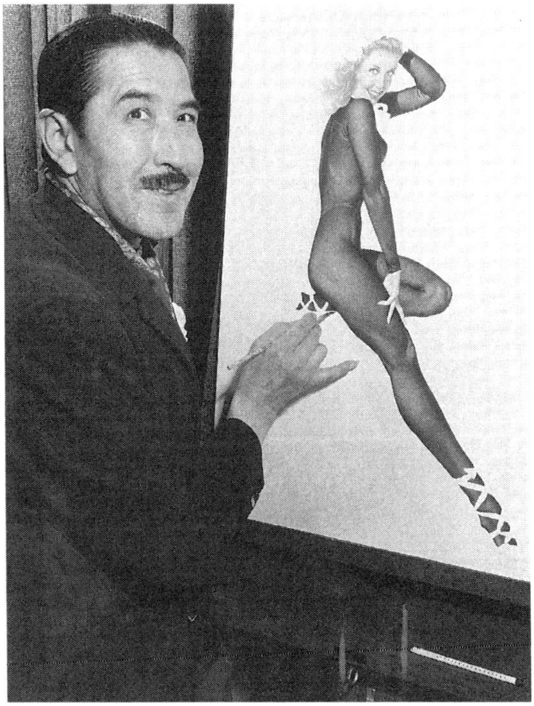

Alberto Vargas created an ideal of feminine beauty in his remarkable paintings and illustrations for the magazines *Esquire* and *Playboy*. *(Photofest)*

Europe, and Vargas was compelled to return home. He planned to reach Peru via the United States.

He arrived in New York City and was so impressed by the great metropolis and its career opportunities that he stayed there and never returned to live in Peru. He made a living by retouching photographs and painting. One day, in 1919, he was painting in a window-display promotion when the theatrical producer Florenz Ziegfeld happened by and saw him at work. He immediately hired Vargas to paint commercial portraits of the stars of his yearly Broadway musical extravaganza, the Follies. Vargas worked for Ziegfeld for 12 years, creating a sensation with his sensuous and stylish portraits of female performers. He married Ziegfeld dancer Anna Mae Clift in 1930. She would be the great love of his life and the inspiration for his art. A poor businessman who never learned how to handle money, Vargas had to borrow money to pay for their marriage license.

Unemployed in 1931, Vargas found little opportunity for work amid the Great Depression. He soon found himself churning out movie posters at low pay for Hollywood studios and became a naturalized U.S. citizen in 1939.

That same year, *Equire,* a popular men's magazine, hired Vargas to replace its house artist George Petty. Vargas copied Petty's style in his "Petty Girls" at first, but gradually the "Varga Girls" took on a distinctive, delicate style of their own. The magazine shortened the artist's last name by one letter to make it more exotic. Vargas's women were idealized beauties, sexy but never crudely so. They exhibited an independent spirit and exuberance that was typically American. The "Varga Girls" became extremely popular pin-ups for the American soldiers who were stationed abroad during World War II.

Esquire made Vargas famous but treated him poorly. For the first three years that he worked for the magazine, he received $75 a month and had to give *Esquire* half of any monies that he earned from selling his paintings. They even retained the rights to the name *Varga.* He eventually left the magazine in 1946, and a bitter lawsuit followed. The 1950s were another difficult era for the artist, during which he was reduced to licensing his art to appear on such products as playing cards. But his greatest period was yet to come.

In 1960, Hugh Hefner, publisher of *Playboy* magazine and a great fan of Vargas's work, hired him to paint foldout nudes for the men's magazine. For the next 16 years, the "Vargas girl" (full spelling of his name restored) was one of the most popular features in *Playboy.* Vargas finally received financial rewards and respect. He created more than 160 paintings for *Playboy* and was so loyal to the magazine that he rarely worked for anyone else.

Vargas retired from *Playboy* in 1976, two years after the death of his wife. He published his autobiography two years later. Alberto Vargas died of a stroke in Los Angeles, California, on December 30, 1982. Much of his original artwork resides with the Spencer Museum of Art at the University of Kansas in Lawrence. In September 2001, the museum sponsored an exhibit of his work entitled *Alberto Vargas: The Esquire Pinups.*

Further Reading

Illustrators. "Alberto Vargas," Illustrators Web Site. Available online. URL: http://www.bpib.com/illustras2/vargas.htm. Downloaded on February 19, 2006.

Martignette, Charles G., and Louis K. Meisel. *The Great American Pin-Up.* Los Angeles: Taschen, 2002.

Robottham, Tom. *Varga.* Bethany, Mo.: JG Press, 2003.

Vargas, Alberto. *Vargas.* New York: Random House, 1988 [reprint].

Vargas, Kathy

(1950–) photographer, mixed-media and installation artist, printmaker, arts director, educator

In her often ghostlike photographs, Mexican-American photographer Kathy Vargas attempts to capture the fragility of life, the mysteries of identity, and the ever presence of death. She was born in San Antonio, Texas, on June 23, 1950. Her Mexican-American family has a long and colorful heritage. Her great-great-grandfather fought with Mexican general Santa Ana against the U.S. Army in the battle for Texas. Her grandmother and father were accomplished storytellers. Her uncle was a commercial photographer who introduced her to the craft of taking pictures. As a youth, she hand-colored his photographs.

In 1971, she began work in special effects for a film production company. Two years later, Vargas became a professional photographer of rock-and-roll artists. During this time, she met painters MEL CASAS and Cesar Martinez, who were part of Con Safo, a San Antonio Chicano artist collective. They encouraged her to pursue art photography. Having already earned a bachelor of arts (B.A.) degree from the University of Texas–San Antonio, Vargas returned there to earn a master of fine arts (M.F.A.) degree in 1984. The following year, she became the director of the visual-arts program at the Guadeloupe Cultural Arts Center, a position she held until 2000.

Vargas is best known for her manipulated photographs that are often double-exposed or hand-tinted to express the elusiveness of personal identity and the power of death over life. Her series based on the Mexican Day of the Dead (1990) documents this unusual religious holiday when families visit the graves of their loved ones. She dedicated the series to two friends who died of acquired immune deficiency syndrome (AIDS). Vargas was one of four contributing photographers whose work appears in the book *Hospice: A Photographic Inquiry* (1996) about dying patients in hospice care. "I love life," Vargas has said, "but we really have to see the end to love the middle."

Another series, *My Alamo* (1995), offers an outsider's response to that historical landmark of Texan independence from Mexico. Putting her own family members into her portraits of the Alamo, Vargas is challenging that legacy and legend by offering a different perspective on the events.

Kathy Vargas was the recipient of a National Endowment for the Arts (NEA) grant in 1991. She was named Artist of the Year by the San Antonio Art League Museum in 1998. The first major retrospective of her work opened in December 2000 at the Marion Koogler McNay Art Museum in San Antonio. Vargas has taught photography at her alma mater and the Healy–Murphy Learning Center. Since 2000, she has been the chair of art music and assistant professor of art at the University of the Incarnate Word in San Antonio.

Further Reading

Congdon, Kristin G., and Kara Kelley Hallmark, *Artists from Latin American Cultures: A Biographical Dictionary.* Westport, Conn.: Greenwood Press, 2002, pp. 286–289.

Lippard, Lucy R., Malin Wilson-Powell, and Marion Koogler McNay Art Museum. *Kathy Vargas: Photographs, 1971–2000.* Austin: University of Texas Press, 2001.

Riggs, Thomas, ed. *St. James Guide to Hispanic Artists.* Detroit, Mich.: St. James Press, 2002, pp. 617–620.

Vargas, Kathy. *Print Series and Oracion, Valentine's Day/Day of the Dead Series.* Miami, Fla.: Frances Wolfson Art Gallery, 1990.

Vater, Regina

(1943–) *photographer, video artist, installation artist, painter, mixed-media artist, performance artist, computer graphics artist*

One of the first Latino American artists to use video to express herself, Regina Vater's installations, videos, and photographs explore contemporary humans' tenuous relationship with the natural world. She was born in Rio de Janeiro, Brazil, on May 11, 1943. Vater received a bachelor of arts (B.A.) degree in architecture from the Universidade Federal do Rio de Janeiro. She quickly established herself as a leading artist with both a social conscience and a sense of humor. In one staged happening, she created a sensation running ropes across a busy street, stopping traffic in the financial district of São Paulo. She moved to the United States at age 30 in 1973 after receiving a Guggenheim Fellowship. Vater studied video at the Downtown Video Community Center in New York City. Five years later, she moved to Austin, Texas, where she lives and works today. In Austin, Vater delved deeper into experimental video, using facilities at ACTV–Austin. She also studied photography at the University of Texas–Austin.

In much of her work, whatever the medium, Vater has investigated how modern humankind relates to the natural world. In *Electronic Nature* (1988), she used color photographs of wild animals from nature programs on television to point out how dislocated these creatures have become in our modern world. "For some today," she wrote about the exhibition, "the only contact wanted with natural realms is through the electronic screen. . . . That is, perhaps, our technological reward for choosing the fruits of knowledge over the fruits of life."

In *Cosmologies,* an exhibit of work at ArtSpace in San Antonio in summer 1999, she viewed this relationship from a number of vantage points, using such materials from indigenous Brazilian peoples' religious rites as popcorn and incense. No piece in the exhibit better demonstrated her thoughts on nature and the modern world than *El Teatro de la Lune or ARTiMIS a No US.* The viewer entered a roomlike space that is surrounded by a black curtain and then approached a large boulder with a small pool of water in its central crevice. Looking into the pool, the viewer could glimpse the moon's reflection, emanating from a video monitor mounted in the ceiling.

Vater has had numerous solo exhibitions at the Women and Their Work Gallery, Austin (1997); the Center for the Arts, San Francisco (1994); the Southeast Museum of Photography, Daytona Beach, Florida (1993); and the Galeria Paulo Figueiredo, São Paulo (1992). More recently, she has brought her art to the Web. A collection of 72 photographs she took during a train ride from the west coast to the east coast of the United States in 1981 were arranged for a Web site by Regina Celia Pinta in 2005.

Further Reading

Modern and Contemporary Art. "Regina Vater, B. 1943," The San Antonio Museum Web Site. Available online. URL: http://www.sa-museum.org/laac/laac_cd/MODERN/OBJECTS/6d9.HTM. Downloaded on February 28, 2005.

Riggs, Thomas, ed. *St. James Guide to Hispanic Artists.* Detroit, Mich.: St. James Press, 2002, pp. 622–624.

Vater, Regina. *Regina Vater 99.2 (New Work).* San Antonio, Tex.: International Artist-in-Residence Program, 1999.

The World's Women On-Line. "Regina Vater," The World's Women On-Line Web Site. Available online. URL: http://wwol.inre.asu.edu/vater.html. Downloaded on March 22, 2006.

Vélez, Lupe
(María Guadalupe Villalobos, Vélez)
(1908–1944) *actress, dancer, singer*

One of the first Latinos to find stardom in Hollywood, Lupe Vélez's personal life was as tumultuous as any of the many hot-tempered Latinas whom she portrayed on the silver screen. María Guadalupe Villalobos Vélez was born on July 18, 1908, in San Luis Potosi, a suburb of Mexico City, Mexico. Her father was an officer in the Mexican army who was killed during a military fight. Her mother, a former opera singer, sent María to a convent school in San Antonio, Texas, when she was 13.

A vivacious, petite beauty with little interest in school, María returned home a few years later and worked as a salesgirl in a department store to help her family financially. She took dance lessons and, in 1924, launched a successful career as a dancer and actress in nightclubs and on the stage. She moved to Hollywood in 1926, adapting the name Lupe Vélez, and performed in Los Angeles (LA) in a theatrical revue that was produced by Hollywood mogul Hal Roach. Roach was so impressed with her talents that he cast Vélez as the female lead opposite the comedy team of Laurel and Hardy in the silent short *Sailors, Beware* (1927). Later that year, silent star Douglas Fairbanks chose her to play opposite him in the feature-length film, *The Gaucho.* Her movie career established, Vélez appeared in a string of silent films, usually as a stereotypical hot-blooded Latin temptress.

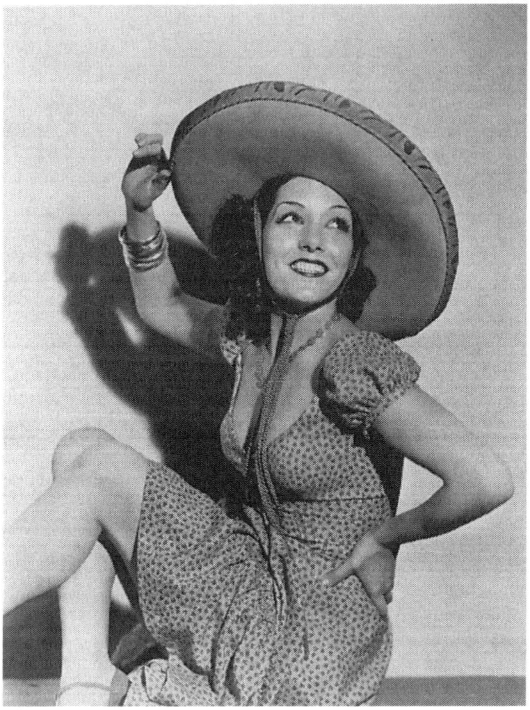

Lupe Vélez, who starred as the Mexican Spitfire in a series of 1940s films, was just as tempestuous in her personal life. *(Photofest)*

She made a successful transition to sound films in the early 1930s and was dramatically impressive in director Cecil B. DeMille's Western *The Squaw Man* (1931). Her off-screen romances, however, made bigger headlines than her acting. She had a torrid affair with actor Gary Cooper, which was broken up by his parents and studio bosses. In 1933, Vélez married screen Tarzan Johnny Weissmuller. Their frequent public quarrels were grist for the Hollywood gossip mill, and the marriage ended in 1939.

The following year, Vélez was cast as a tempestuous Mexican nightclub entertainer, Carmelita Fuentes, known as the Mexican Spitfire, in a B film, *The Girl from Mexico.* The modest film showcased

Vélez's considerable talent for comedy and was quickly followed by a sequel, *The Mexican Spitfire* (1940). Through 1943, she costarred with comic actor Leon Errol in six more Spitfire films with such titles as *The Mexican Spitfire Out West* (1940) and *Mexican Spitfire's Elephant* (1942). Although the character was stereotyped, she was an attractive, spunky, and successful young woman, a rare role for any Latina actress, especially in a film series.

When the Mexican Spitfire series ended, Vélez returned to Mexico to play the leading role in a film adaptation of the French novel *Nana* (1944). It would be her last film. She was pregnant by her latest lover, Viennese-born actor Harold Maresch (aka Harold Ramond), who refused to marry her. Despondent and fearful of having a child out of wedlock, Vélez retired to her bedroom in her Beverly Hills home on December 13, 1944, and died of an overdose of sleeping pills. She was 36 years old. Maresch, to whom she addressed one of two suicide notes, was partly blamed for her death, and his screen career was all but ruined.

Further Reading

The Internet Movie Database. "Lupe Vélez," The Internet Movie Database Web Site. Available online. URL: http://www.imdb.com/name/nm0892473/bio. Downloaded on December 5, 2004.

Katz, Ephraim, Fred Klein, and Ronald Dean Nolen. *The Film Encyclopedia,* 4th edition. New York: HarperResource, 2001, p. 1,413.

Rodriguez, Clara E. *Heroes, Lovers, and Others: The Story of Latinos in Hollywood.* Washington, D.C.: Smithsonian Books, 2004, pp. 65–73, 94–95.

Further Viewing

The Gaucho (1927). Kino Video, VHS/DVD, 1996/2001.

Mexican Spitfire (1940) and *The Smartest Girl in Town* (1936). Warner Home Video, VHS, 2002.

W

Welch, Raquel
(Jo Raquel Tejada)
(1940–) *actress, singer, dancer*

The biggest sex symbol in Hollywood movies in the 1960s, Raquel Welch has since proved that she can act and has embraced her Latino heritage, which was little known by the public for decades. Jo Raquel Tejada was born in Chicago, Illinois, on September 5, 1940. Her father was a Bolivian-born aerospace engineer, and her mother was Irish American. When she was still young, the family moved to southern California, where she attended La Jolla High School and took ballet and acting lessons. Her curvaceous figure and good looks won her numerous beauty contests in her teens, including such titles as Miss Photogenic, Miss Contour, and Miss Fairest of the Fair. She graduated from high school in 1957 and the following year married James Welch, her high-school sweetheart. They had two children but separated in 1961 and divorced three years later.

Seeking an acting career, Welch attended drama classes at San Diego State College and won parts in local theater productions. She later moved to Dallas, Texas, where she made a precarious living as a model and cocktail waitress. She returned to California in 1963 and played bit parts in several films, including the Elvis Presley vehicle *Roustabout* (1964).

About this time, she met former child actor and agent Patrick Curtis, who became her mentor. Together, they formed Curtwell Enterprises and set about marketing Welch as a sex symbol. Curtis eventually got Welch a contract with Twentieth Century Fox studios. Fox convinced her to use the last name Welch rather than her family name Tejada to avoid typecasting as a Latino. However, she refused to change her name from Raquel. Although her ethnicity was never noted in her films at the time, she claims today that she never deliberately hid her Latino roots.

Fox immediately cast its new starlet in two cult classics. In *Fantastic Voyage* (1966), she played a member of a medical team that is miniaturized to enter the body of an injured diplomat and save his life. In *One Million B.C.* (1966), she played a prehistoric cave woman. Although she had only three lines in the film, her luscious figure in a fur bikini made her a star and the dream girl of millions of young moviegoers. She married Patrick Curtis the following year; they divorced in 1972.

While generally cast for her sexiness and not her acting ability, Welch managed to appear in a number of interesting and offbeat films through the sixties. They included the Faustian comedy *Bedazzled* (1968), in which she appropriately played the role of Lillian Lust; the Frank Sinatra cop thriller *Lady in Cement* (1968); the western *100 Rifles* (1969), which paired her romantically

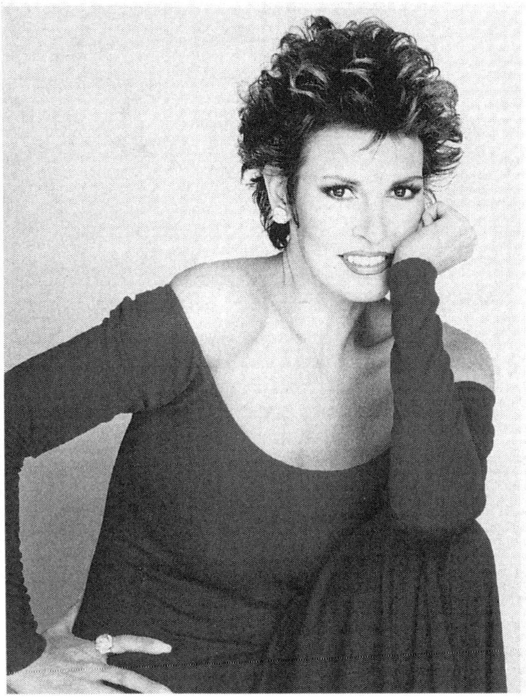

Raquel Welch refused to stay pigeonholed as a sex symbol and triumphed on stage and screen as a musical star and serious actor. *(Photofest)*

with former football star Jim Brown; and the all-star zany comedy *The Magic Christian* (1970).

Unsatisfied with sexpot roles, Welch began to develop her own film projects. In the most successful of these, *Kansas City Bomber* (1972), she played a struggling single mother who becomes a roller-derby star. She revealed a surprising flair for comedy in two *Musketeers* movies (1974–75) directed by Richard Lester. Her role as the clumsy maid Constance earned her a Golden Globe Award for Best Supporting Actress.

Welch proved that she could hold her own on stage when she replaced actress Lauren Bacall in the Broadway musical *Woman of the Year* in 1981. She later developed a successful touring cabaret act. Through the 1980s, she found her most challenging roles in television movies. She was an American Indian in *The Legend of Walks Far Woman* (1982) and a woman dying of Lou Gehrig's disease in *Right to Die* (1987), a harrowing performance that earned her another Golden Globe nomination as Best Actress in a Series or Movie Drama.

Although her film appearances have become less frequent in recent years, she has scored high in several movies, most notably as a voracious Mexican-American widow who sets her sight on retired restaurateur HECTOR ELIZONDO in the comedy/drama *Tortilla Soup* (2001). In real life, Welch married André Weinfeld in 1980; they divorced in 1990. Then she married restaurateur Richard Palmer in 1999; the couple has since divorced. Welch's son Damon and daughter Tahnee are both film actors.

"Americans have always had sex symbols," she has said. "It's a time-honored tradition and I'm flattered to have been one. But it's hard to have a long, fruitful career once you've been stereotyped that way. That's why I'm proud to say I've endured."

Further Reading

Haining, Peter. *Raquel Welch: Sex Symbol to Superstar.* New York: St. Martin's Press, 1985.

The Internet Movie Database. "Raquel Welch," The Internet Movie Database. Available online. URL: http://www.imdb.com/name/nm0000079/. Downloaded on March 3, 2005.

Latham, Caroline. *Raquel Welch: Brains and Beauty.* New York: Putnam Publishing Group, 1986.

Rodriguez, Clara E. *Heroes, Lovers, and Others: The Story of Latinos in Hollywood.* Washington, D.C.: Smithsonian Books, 2004, pp. 137–140.

Further Viewing

The Complete Musketeers (1975). Anchor Bay, DVD, 2003.

Fantastic Voyage (1966) / *Voyage to the Bottom of the Sea* (1961). Fox Home Video, DVD, 2000.

Kansas City Bomber (1972). Warner Home Video, DVD, 2005.

Tortilla Soup (2001). Sony Home Video, VHS/DVD, 2002.

Z

Zermeño, Andrew

(1935–) *illustrator, cartoonist, graphic designer, commercial artist*

The artist that brought Cesar Chavez's crusade for Chicano (Mexican-American) farmworkers graphically to life, Andrew Zermeño went on to have a successful career as a commercial artist, a graphic designer, and an advocate for solar energy. He was born in Salinas, California, at the mouth of the fertile Salinas Valley on December 10, 1935. At the time, his was one of the few Mexican-American families in this agricultural community. In 1954, Zermeño graduated from high school and attended the California College of Arts and Crafts in Oakland on a scholarship. On weekends, he worked at the local television station as a production artist and set designer.

Zermeño's brother Alex was a member of the Community Service Organization (CSO), a community activist group that promoted voter registration for Chicanos and that worked against discrimination. He invited Andrew to CSO meetings, and soon, the young artist designed a logo for the organization.

In 1958, Zermeño entered the Art Center School of Design in Los Angeles (LA) where he studied painting and drawing. He graduated with a Bachelor of Professional Arts (B.P.A.) degree in 1961. The following year, Cesar Chavez, general director of CSO, resigned his position and began a new organization, the National Farm Workers Association (NFWA), later to be renamed the United Farm Workers (UFW). Under Chavez's leadership, the UFW led a crusade to empower California's Chicano migrant workers who were poorly treated by employers such as the California grape growers. Knowing Zermeño's previous work for the CSO, Chavez sent him a rough sketch of an eagle to refine for the logo of the UFW. The resulting graphic was the black eagle that has been a symbol for the UFW ever since. Soon, Zermeño was creating a whole array of promotional material for the UFW, from inspiring posters to a humorous but pointed comic strip, *La Dolce Vida,* a collaboration with playwright and director Luis Valdez. Zermeño even lived with his family for a year in UFW headquarters at La Paz in Keen, California. While working for this important cause was rewarding in many ways, it could not support Zermeño financially.

He moved back home to LA and worked as a freelance commercial illustrator for an art studio. The work was demanding, and Zermeño eventually took a position of a cultural-enrichment program coordinator and instructor for the California Employment Training Program (CETP). In 1978, he went to work for the Hughes Aerospace Company as an assembly planner and illustrator. He eventually became a project engineer for a robotic engineering team.

Zermeño's interest in solar energy led him to leave Hughes in 1990 and start his own business, Solar Concepts. The business failed two years

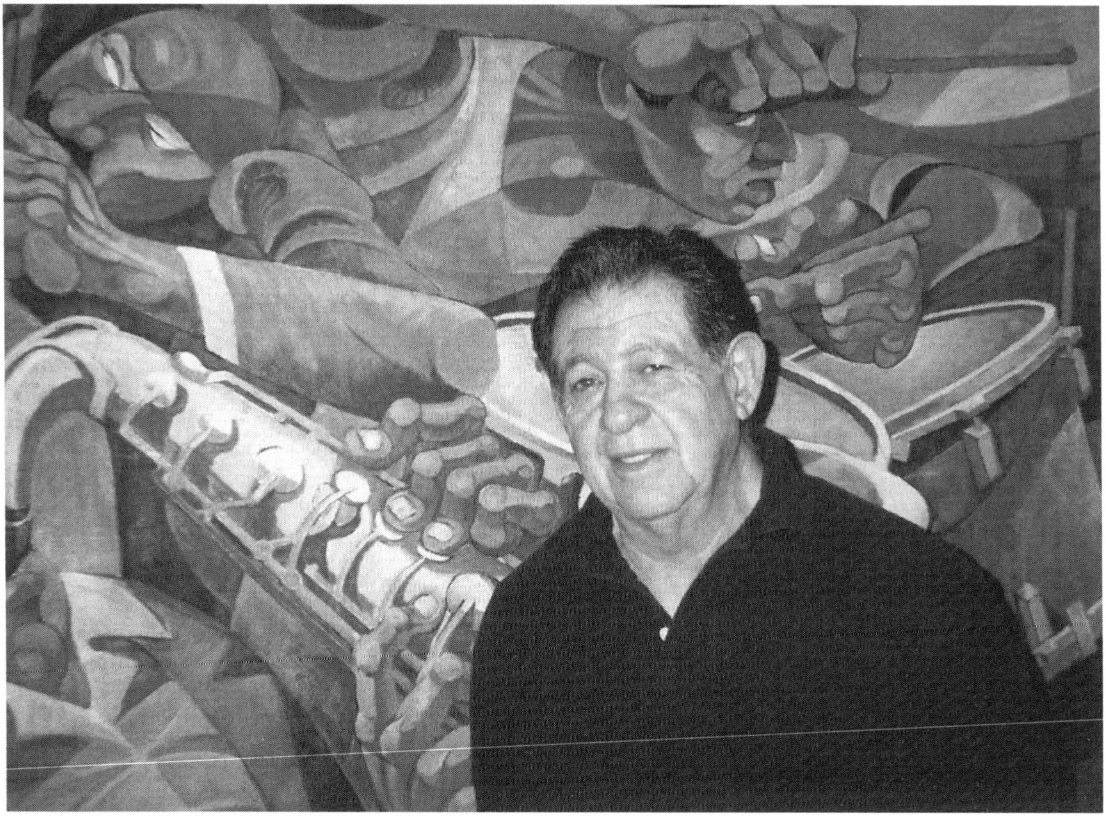

Andrew Zermeño rose to fame in the 1960s and 1970s as the staff artist of Cesar Chavez's United Farm Workers. Today, a retired commercial artist, he continues to paint fine art. *(Andrew Zermeño)*

later, and he returned to freelance illustration and graphic design. He retired in 1998 to devote himself to "exploring different design concepts, drawing, painting and writing." Zermeño's artwork for the Chicano Movement was part of a touring exhibition, *Chicano Art: Resistance and Affirmation* (1990–93).

"I will always be grateful to the United Farmworkers for providing me with the opportunity to contribute artwork and for the experience of working with a very special group of organizers and volunteers," says Zermeño.

Further Reading

"Background and History to the Chicano Art Movement," The Chicano Civil Rights Movement Through Art. Available online. URL: http://movies2.nytimes.com/gst/movies/filmography.html?p_id=62873. Downloaded on March 30, 2006.

Jones, Jessica. "Battle Emblems," Pop + Politics Web Site. Available online. URL: http://www.popandpolitics.com/articles_detail.cfm?articleID=1751. Downloaded on March 30, 2006.

Zermeño, Andrew. "Artistic Statement," unpublished.

Bibliography and Recommended Sources

Books

Beardsley, John, and Jane Livingston. *Hispanic Art in the United States: Thirty Contemporary Painters and Sculptors.* New York: Abbeville Press, 1987.

Cancel, Luis R., et al. *The Latin American Spirit: Art and Artists in the United States, 1920–1970.* New York: The Bronx Museum of the Arts and Harry N. Abrams, 1988.

Cockcroft, James D., assisted by Jane Canning. *Latino Visions: Contemporary Chicano, Puerto Rican, and Cuban American Artists.* New York: Franklin Watts, 2000.

Congdon, Kristin G., and Kara Kelley Hallmark. *Artists from Latin American Cultures: A Biographical Dictionary.* Westport, Conn.: Greenwood Press, 2002.

Erlewine, Michael, Valdimir Bogdanov, and Chris Woodstra, eds. *All Music Guide to Rock.* San Francisco: Miller Freeman Books, 1995.

Kanellos, Nicolas, ed. *The Hispanic Almanac: A Reference Work on Hispanics in the United States.* Detroit, Mich.: Gale Research, 1997.

———. *Hispanic First: Five Hundred Years of Extraordinary Achievement.* Detroit, Mich.: Gale Research, 1997.

Katz, Ephraim, Fred Klein, and Ronald Dean Nolen. *The Film Encyclopedia.* 4th edition, New York: HarperResource, 2001.

Marvis, Barbara. *Famous People of Hispanic History: Giselle Fernandez, Jon Secada, Desi Arnaz, Joan Baez.* Hockessin, Del.: Mitchell Lane Publishers, 1995.

Morey, Janet, and Wendy Dunn. *Famous Hispanic Americans.* New York: Dutton, 1996.

Nava, Yolanda. *It's All in the Frijoles: 100 Famous Latinos Share Real-Life Stories, Time-Tested Dishes, Favorite Folktales, and Inspiring Words of Wisdom.* New York: Fireside Books, 2000.

Nunn, Tey Marianna. *Sin Nombre: Hispanic and Hispano Artists of the New Deal Era.* Albuquerque: University of New Mexico Press, 2001.

Quirarte, Jacinto. *Mexican American Artists.* Austin: University of Texas Press, 1973.

Riggs, Thomas, ed. *St. James Guide to Hispanic Artists.* Detroit, Mich.: St. James Press, 2002.

Rodríguez, Clara E. *Heroes, Lovers and Others: The Story of Latinos in Hollywood.* Washington, D.C.: Smithsonian Books, 2004.

Schipper, Henry. *Broken Record: The Inside Story of the Grammy Awards.* New York: Birch Lane Press, 1992.

Sinnott, Susan. *Extraordinary Hispanic Americans.* Chicago: Children's Press, 1991.

Stambler, Irwin. *The Encyclopedia of Pop, Rock and Soul.* New York: St. Martin's Press, 1989.

Whitburn, Joel. *Top Pop Singles 1955–1996.* Menomonee Falls, Wisc.: Record Research, 1997.

Yorba, Jonathan. *Arte Latino: Treasures from the Smithsonian American Art Museum.* New York: Watson–Guptill Publications, 2001.

Zuver, Marc, curator. *Cuba–USA: The First Generation—In Search of Freedom.* Washington, D.C.: Fondo del Sol Visual Arts Center, 1991.

Web Sites

Cheech Martin Presents the Chicano Collection. URL: http://www. the chicanocollection.net/artists/html.

El Museo del Barrio. URL: http://www.elmuseo.org/.

Hispanic Heritage Biographies. Thomson Gale. URL: http://www.galegroup. com/free_resources/chh/bio/index.htm.

Smithsonian Archives of American Art. Oral History Interviews. URL: http://archivesofamericanart.si.edu/collections/oralhistories/.

ENTRIES BY AREA OF ACTIVITY

Stage Director

Stage Producer

Television Actor and Performer

Television Actress and Performer

Television Director

Television Producer

Video Artist

Weaver

ENTRIES BY YEAR OF BIRTH

1740–1879
Fresquís, Pedro Antonio

1880–1889
Carrillo, Leo
Moreno, Antonio

1890–1899
Gonzalez, Myrtle
Hernandez, Juano
Martínez, Agueda
Novarro, Ramón
Vargas, Alberto

1900–1909
Barela, Patrociño
Cugat, Xavier
del Rio, Dolores
Gomez, Thomas
Limón, José
López, George T.
Miranda, Carmen
Norton, Barry
Renaldo, Duncan
Roland, Gilbert
Romero, César
Torres, Raquel
Vélez, Lupe

1910–1919
Archuleta, Felipe
Arnaz, Desi
Arriola, Gus
Ferrer, José
Ferrer, Mel
Guerrero, Lalo
Hayworth, Rita
Lamas, Fernando
Page, Anita
Quinn, Anthony

1920–1929
Barretto, Ray
Casas, Mel
Cruz, Celia
Gonzalez-Gonzalez, Pedro
Jurado, Katy
Montalbán, Ricardo
Montez, Maria
Pelli, César
Puente, Tito
Quintero, José
San Juan, Olga
Santamaria, Mongo
Valdez, Horacio

1930–1939
Almendros, Néstor
Arreguín, Alfredo
Camnitzer, Luis
Elizondo, Hector
Fender, Freddy
Ferrer, Rafael
Gormé, Eydie
Jiménez, Flaco
Lopez, Trini
Marisol
Moreno, Rita
Rivera, Chita
Roman, Phil
Schifrin, Lalo
Zermeño, Andrew

1940–1944
Almaraz, Carlos
Azaceta, Luis Cruz
Baez, Joan
Bernal, Louis Carlos
Carr, Vikki
Charo
Garcia, Jerry
Garcia, Rupert
Hernandez, Ester
Jiménez, Luis
Juliá, Raúl
León, Tania
Mesa-Bains, Amalia
Montez, Chris
Portillo, Lourdes
Romero, Frank
Sheen, Martin
Sierra, Paul
Valdez, Luis
Valens, Ritchie
Vater, Regina
Welch, Raquel

1945–1949
Baca, Judy
Blades, Rubén
Bojórquez, Charles
Brito, María
Emilia, María
Esparza, Moctesuma
Feliciano, José
Fernández, Rudy
Garza, Carmen Lomas
Ichaso, Leon
Marin, Cheech
Mendieta, Ana
Morell, Aberlardo
Nava, Gregory
Ochoa, Victor
Olmos, Edward James
Ronstadt, Linda
Santana, Carlos
Torres, Liz
Treviño, Jesse
Treviño, Jesús Salvador
Underwood, Consuelo Jiménez

1950–1954
Alfonzo, Carlos
Carter, Lynda
Colón, Willie
Gamboa, Harry, Jr.
Gil de Montes, Roberto
Gronk
Herron, Willie
Legorreta, Robert
López, Ramón José
Lucero, Michael
Molina, Alfred
Moroles, Jesús
Prinze, Freddie
Rodriguez, Johnny
Rodriguez, Santiago
Serrano, Andres
Tapia, Luis
Trujillo, Irvin L.
Valadez, John
Valdez, Patssi
Vargas, Kathy

1955–1959
Carrillo, Charles M.
Cisneros, Evelyn
Climent, Elena
Diaz, Al
Diaz, David
Estefan, Gloria
Ferrer, Miguel
Garcia, Andy
Gómez-Peña, Guillermo
Guevara, Susan
Guzmán, Luis
Lamas, Lorenzo
Lopez, Lourdes
Osorio, Pepón
Rodríguez–Díaz, Angel
Rodriguez, Paul
Smits, Jimmy
Tacla, Jorge

1960–1964
Alcaraz, Lalo
Banderas, Antonio
Bratt, Benjamin
Castellanos, Carlos
Del Toro, Guillermo
Estevez, Emilio
Leguizamo, John
Lopez, Alma
Lopez, George
Martínez-Cañas, María
Morales, Esai
Muniz, Vik
Peña, Elizabeth
Perez, Rosie
Phillips, Lou Diamond
Quesada, Joe
Secada, Jon

1965–1969
Anthony, Marc
Aranda, Iris Nelia
Del Toro, Benicio
Fernández, Teresita
Hayek, Salma
Huerta, Salómon
Lopez, Jennifer
Rodriguez, Robert
Sheen, Charlie

1970–1979
Carey, Mariah
Cruz, Penelope
Dawson, Rosario
Diaz, Cameron
Martin, Ricky
Prinze, Freddie, Jr.
Rodriguez, Adam
Rodriguez, Michelle
Selena
Shakira

1980–1989
Aguilera, Christina

Entries by Ethnicity or Country of Origin

Garza, Carmen Lomas
Garcia, Rupert
Gil de Montes, Roberto
Gómez-Peña, Guillermo
Gonzales, Myrtle
Gonzalez-Gonzalez, Pedro
Gronk
Guerrero, Lalo
Guevara, Susan
Hayek, Salma
Hernandez, Ester
Herron, Willie
Huerta, Salomón
Jiménez, Flaco
Jiménez, Luis
Jurado, Katy
Legorreta, Robert
Limón, José
Lopez, Alma
Lopez, George
López, George T.
López, Ramón José
Lopez, Trini
Marin, Cheech
Martínez, Agueda
Mesa-Bains, Amalia
Montalbán, Ricardo
Montez, Chris
Moroles, Jesús
Nava, Gregory
Novarro, Ramón
Ochoa, Victor
Olmos, Edward James
Portillo, Lourdes
Quinn, Anthony
Rodriguez, Johnny
Rodriguez, Paul
Rodriguez, Robert
Roland, Gilbert
Roman, Phil
Romero, Frank
Ronstadt, Linda
Santana, Carlos
Selena
Tapia, Luis
Torres, Raquel
Terviño, Jesse
Treviño, Jesús Salvador
Trujillo, Irvin L.
Underwood, Conseulo Jiménez
Valadez, John
Valdez, Horacio
Valdez, Luis
Valdez, Patssi
Valens, Ritchie
Vargas, Kathy
Vélez, Lupe
Zermeño, Andrew

Panama
Aranda, Iris Nelia
Blades, Rubén
Quintero, José

Peru
Bratt, Benjamin
Vargas, Alberto

Puerto Rico
Anthony, Marc
Barretto, Ray
Colón, Willie
Dawson, Rosario
Del Toro, Benicio
Elizondo, Hector
Feliciano, José
Ferrer, José
Ferrer, Miguel
Ferrer, Rafael
Guzmán, Luis
Hernandez, Juano
Juliá, Raúl
Lopez, Jennifer
Martin, Ricky
Morales, Esai
Moreno, Rita
Osorio, Pepón
Perez, Rosie
Prinze, Freddie
Prinze, Freddie, Jr.
Puente, Tito
Rivera, Chita
Rodriguez, Adam
Rodriguez, Michelle
Rodríguez-Díaz, Angel
San Juan, Olga
Smits, Jimmy
Torres, Liz

Spain
Almendros, Néstor
Banderas, Antonio
Charo
Cruz, Penélope
Cugat, Xavier
Diaz, David
Elizondo, Hector
Estevez, Emilio
Garcia, Jerry
Gomez, Thomas
Gormé, Eydie
Hayworth, Rita
León, Tania
Lucero, Michael
Molina, Alfred
Montalbán, Ricardo
Montez, Maria
Moreno, Antonio
Phillips, Lou Diamond
Quintero, José
Renaldo, Duncan
Roland, Gilbert
Romero, Frank
Sheen, Charlie
Sheen, Martin

Suriname
Smits, Jimmy

Uruguay
Camnitzer, Luis

Venezuela
Carey, Mariah
Marisol

INDEX

Boldface locators indicate main entries. *Italic* locators indicate photographs.

W

X

Y

Z